Genealogical Guide

Master Index
of
Genealogy
in the
Daughters of the American Revolution Magazine

Volumes 1–84
1892–1950

with

Supplement
Volumes 85–89
1950–1955

Combined Edition

With a New Introduction by
Eric G. Grundset
Library Director, NSDAR

CLEARFIELD

Reprinted for
Clearfield Company, Inc. by
Genealogical Publishing Co., Inc.
Baltimore, Maryland
2005

Originally published: Washington, D.C., 1951, 1956
By the *Daughters of the American Revolution Magazine*
Copyright © new matter, 1994
By Genealogical Publishing Co., Inc.
All Rights Reserved
Reprinted by Genealogical Publishing Co., Inc. with the permission of the
Daughters of the American Revolution Magazine
and the Elizabeth Benton Chapter, N.S.D.A.R., Kansas City, Mo.
Library of Congress Catalogue Card Number 93-80321
International Standard Book Number 0-8063-1399-4
Made in the United States of America

Genealogical Guide

❖

MASTER INDEX

OF

GENEALOGY

IN THE

Daughters of the American Revolution Magazine

VOLUMES 1—84
1892-1950

❖

Compiled By

ELIZABETH BENTON CHAPTER, N. S. D. A. R.
Kansas City, Missouri
MRS. FRANK S. FORMAN, *Regent*
MRS. OMIE P. MACFARLANE, *General Chairman*

❖

Published By

DAUGHTERS OF THE AMERICAN REVOLUTION MAGAZINE
Gertrude S. Carraway, Editor
1776 D Street, N. W.
Washington 6, D. C.

1951

DEDICATED
To
Our Pioneer Ancestors
Whose
Foresight and Indomitable Courage
Gave Us
OUR AMERICA

—MURIEL LOVELAND (Mrs. Omie P.) MACFARLANE
General Chairman

Introduction

ince 1892, the *DAR Magazine*, under its several titles, has been the official publication of the National Society Daughters of the American Revolution. Besides containing much information on the National Society's internal business, projects and development, the *DAR Magazine* has published innumerable genealogical queries and many record abstracts and Bible transcriptions. Although annual indexes have provided researchers access to this information, a cumulative index always reveals in a much easier manner the contents of a periodical published over many decades.

In 1951 the *DAR Magazine* published *Genealogical Guide: Master Index of Genealogy in the Daughters of the American Revolution Magazine, Volumes 1–84 (1892–1950)*. As is true with many DAR projects, dedicated members of the National Society performed the detailed work of preparing this publication. In this instance more than forty members of the Elizabeth Benton Chapter, of Kansas City, Missouri, worked for months on the *Guide* under the direction of Mrs. Muriel L. MacFarlane. In all nearly 39,000 references evolved into an index of fifty-nine years of the *DAR Magazine*. Five years later, the same workers produced *Supplement to Genealogical Guide: Master Index of Genealogy in the Daughters of the American Revolution Magazine, Volumes 85–89 (1951–1955)* and the *DAR Magazine* published it.

The *DAR Magazine* itself can be found in genealogical libraries across the United States. It has had several titles since its inception in 1892: *American Monthly Magazine*, volume 1 (July 1892) to volume 42 (June 1913); *Daughters of the American Revolution Magazine*, volume 43 (July 1913) to volume 72 (December 1938); *National Historical Magazine*, volume 73 (1939) to volume 79 (1945); and, again, *Daughters of the American Revolution Magazine*, volume 80 (1946) to the present. Until volume 51 (July–December 1917) a volume comprised half of a year or six issues.

The *Genealogical Guide* and the *Supplement* are reproduced in their entirety in this new volume. Each contains three main parts in two sections. Section 1 is "Queries and Answers". Section 2 is "Bible and Family Records" and "Federal and State Records". The first section constitutes the greater portion of the two publications. Researchers must be aware of the uses and limitations of queries which are decades old.

- The DAR does not have any supporting correspondence behind the queries and answers. What is printed is the extent of each record.

- From the beginning of the "Genealogical Notes and Queries" column in volume 17:1 (July 1900) to volume 56:4 (April 1922), queries are accompanied only by the initials of the inquirer. The DAR does not have any records to identify these initials.

- Beginning with volume 56:5 (May 1922), the queries do contain the name and address of the inquirer.

- The queries and answers vary considerably in content and detail. They are based on the existing knowledge at that time of the person submitting them or responding to them. The value of this material is that a listing from many years ago, even a query which never received a reply, could contain a fragment of information once offered as a clue or a guess which could fill in a gap or lead to additional information even today. While there is little likelihood of contacting anyone placing a query during the period covered by these publications, genealogists should consider checking here for names of interest. Every clue is significant in genealogical research, even negative ones.

While queries comprise the major portion of the *Guide* and *Supplement*, additional material of genealogical value has peppered the pages of the *DAR Magazine* and appears in the indexes. Records of Bibles, cemeteries, courthouses, military units, and vital records offices are included and are accessible through these indexes. The contents of the *DAR Magazine* reflect in many ways the types of materials which comprise a major portion of the collections of the NSDAR's National

Headquarters in Washington, D.C. Researchers who use the *Guide* and *Supplement* are just scratching the surface of the vast holdings of the research offices, including the NSDAR Library. A visit to the NSDAR will likely yield genealogical information and clues not available elsewhere. The NSDAR welcomes researchers to tap the rich sources available there.

Eric G. Grundset
Library Director, NSDAR
Washington, D.C.
1 September 1993

GENEALOGICAL GUIDE

MASTER INDEX OF ALL GENEALOGY

D. A. R. MAGAZINE

Volumes 1 through 84—1892-1950

ALDRIDGE....Vol 52: 686—Vol 60: 366—Vol
64: 390
ALESON................Vol 66: 363
ALEXANDER....Vol 19: 207—Vol 22: 269--
Vol 23: 324, 326—Vol 24: 56, 456—Vol 25:
717, 718, 964—Vol 26: 55, 559, 561—Vol 27:
805—Vol 28: 61—Vol 31: 53, 748—Vol 32:
161, 164—Vol 33: 956—Vol 35: 1266—Vol
36: 351—Vol 37: 488—Vol 38: 328—Vol 39:
224—Vol 41: 213, 214—Vol 42: 14, 80, 186,
189—Vol 43: 544—Vol 44: 26, 84, 310—Vol
45: 104— Vol 46: 241, 387, 389—Vol 47: 32,
264, 341, 392—Vol 48: 446—Vol 50: 64, 67,
352—Vol 51: 355—Vol 52: 484, 684—Vol 54:
350, 351, 710—Vol 55: 285—Vol 56: 373, 624
—Vol 57: 680—Vol 59: 111, 112, 173, 525—
Vol 60: 115, 366—Vol 61: 64, 787—Vol 62:
306—Vol 67: 292—Vol 69: 119, 160, 246,
567—Vol 70: 876—Vol 71: 460—Vol 72:
(4-82)—Vol 73: (11-68)—Vol 75: 5, 43, 44,
46—Vol 76: 309, 710—Vol 77: 51—Vol 79:
161, 283—Vol 80: 557—Vol 81: 71—Vol 82:
501, 574, 796, 863, 936—Vol 83: 441
ALFORD....Vol 27: 809—Vol 28: 259—Vol 29:
290—Vol 33: 475—Vol 35: 57—Vol 53: 241
—Vol 60: 418
ALGER................Vol 36: 214—Vol 45: 195
ALGOOD................Vol 49: 191
ALISON................Vol 38: 36—Vol 81: 131
ALLAN................Vol 78: 107
ALLASON................Vol 30: 258—Vol 66: 599
ALLBECK................Vol 64: 388
ALLBEE................Vol 36: 578
ALLBRIGHT................Vol 81: 569
ALLEE................Vol 83: 173
ALLEGRE................Vol 28: 61
ALLEN....Vol 9: 57—Vol 18: 181—Vol 20: 163
—Vol 22: 145, 998—Vol 23: 326, 471—Vol
24: 149, 544—Vol 25: 797, 888—Vol 26: 54—
Vol 27: 44, 738—Vol 28: 365—Vol 29: 286,
511, 714, 716—Vol 30: 149, 339, 438, 439,
539, 541—Vol 31: 53, 412, 669, 861—Vol 32:
164, 718—Vol 33: 474, 956, 959—Vol 34:
659—Vol 35: 1100—Vol 36: 355, 356—Vol
37: 153, 353, 396—Vol 38: 332, 333—Vol 39:
22, 23, 324, 327—Vol 40: 75—Vol 41: 32, 71
—Vol 42: 190, 268—Vol 43: 422, 424, 482,
490, 494, 540—Vol 44: 26—Vol 45: 108, 109,
117, 119, 125, 192, 326—Vol 46: 241, 242, 244,
384, 389—Vol 47: 29, 393—Vol 48: 61, 445—
Vol 49: 130, 280—Vol 50: 70, 192, 280, 343,
348, 356—Vol 52: 229, 321, 557, 560, 561,
687, 732, 733—Vol 53: 118, 248, 331, 379,
572, 573, 691—Vol 54: 222, 421, 422, 537,
538, 647, 651, 710—Vol 55: 46, 339, 396, 653
—Vol 56: 110, 319, 373, 561, 564, 744—Vol
57: 175, 312, 352, 630—Vol 58: 331, 372, 586,
649, 650, 761—Vol 59: 48, 238, 440, 523, 588
—Vol 60: 114, 507, 747—Vol 61: 699, 708—
Vol 62: 122, 456, 460, 503—Vol 63: 247, 427,
507—Vol 64: 258, 523, 714—Vol 66: 461—
Vol 67: 43, 385, 514, 576—Vol 68: 241, 490,
491, 626—Vol 69: 244, 363—Vol 70: 352—
Vol 71: 164, 461, 678, 956—Vol 73: (11-68)
—Vol 74: (2-40)—Vol 75: (10-65), (10-67)
—Vol 76: 218, 653—Vol 77: 241, 663, 725—
Vol 78: 107, 650—Vol 79: 194—Vol 80: 84,
190, 277, 336, 432, 588—Vol 81: 131—Vol
82: 139, 500, 653, 934—Vol 83: 336, 442,
718, 873—Vol 84: 157, 244, 445, 447, 522, 966

ALLENDER................Vol 69: 119
ALLENWORTH................Vol 67: 647
ALLERTON................Vol 40: 225, 228
ALLEY................Vol 22: 998—Vol 41: 121, 126
ALLGOOD................Vol 49: 191
ALLIBODY................Vol 38: 36
ALLIN................Vol 26: 57
ALLING....Vol 20: 1064—Vol 21: 336—Vol 25:
384—Vol 28: 159, 160—Vol 34: 658—Vol 45:
127—Vol 80: 84
ALLIS................Vol 28: 61
ALLISON....Vol 42: 76—Vol 43: 481—Vol 44:
314—Vol 54: 54, 351, 537—Vol 56: 314—Vol
62: 390, 715—Vol 63: 58, 106—Vol 64: 307
—Vol 65: 160—Vol 67: 386—Vol 72: (10-
95), (12-68)—Vol 76: 581, 860—Vol 77: 52,
538—Vol 83: 627, 874
ALLYN....Vol 29: 800—Vol 44: 316—Vol 45:
189—Vol 55: 601
ALMIE................Vol 50: 349
ALMOND....Vol 34: 200, 421—Vol 58: 51—Vol
82: 726
ALMY................Vol 66: 824
ALPIN................Vol 48: 447
ALRED................Vol 75: (6-39)
ALSTON....Vol 26: 336—Vol 38: 219—Vol 39:
23, 272—Vol 43: 604—Vol 44: 81—Vol 45:
101—Vol 46: 386—Vol 47: 86—Vol 50: 191,
347—Vol 54: 55—Vol 61: 911—Vol 62: 648
—Vol 64: 257—Vol 83: 872
ALTER................Vol 65: 246
ALTON................Vol 18: 299—Vol 19: 70
ALVERSON................Vol 39: 274
ALVEY................Vol 66: 306
ALVORD................Vol 46: 24, 237
ALWARD................Vol 50: 357—Vol 51: 304
ALWORTH................Vol 64: 156
ALYER................Vol 59: 439
AMBLER................Vol 66: 252
AMBROSE................Vol 32: 720—Vol 81: 315
AMERMAN................Vol 31: 752
AMERY................Vol 67: 146
AMES....Vol 22: 375—Vol 26: 243—Vol 38:
274—Vol 43: 605—Vol 44: 151—Vol 49:
282—Vol 52: 687—Vol 69: 432—Vol 76: 654
—Vol 77: 239—Vol 82: 314—Vol 83: 873
AMICK................Vol 66: 600
AMIS................Vol 45: 28—Vol 58: 53
AMMERMAN....Vol 55: 46—Vol 58: 54, 171,
382—Vol 59: 47, 588—Vol 70: 360
AMMON................Vol 82: 933
AMORY................Vol 45: 23
AMOS................Vol 37: 65—Vol 48: 445
AMRINE................Vol 84: 703
AMSDEN................Vol 15: 350
ANCHORS................Vol 61: 157
ANDECKER................Vol 56: 690
ANDERSON....Vol 19: 307—Vol 26: 561—Vol
30: 441, 542—Vol 31: 412—Vol 34: 66—Vol
35: 58—Vol 36: 578—Vol 38: 219—Vol 39:
102, 275—Vol 40: 230—Vol 41: 164—Vol 42:
9, 193, 194, 342—Vol 43: 420, 427, 490, 492,
542, 547, 599—Vol 44: 23, 28, 236, 310—Vol
45: 17, 115, 184—Vol 46: 29, 99, 153, 391,
393—Vol 47: 27, 272—Vol 48: 58, 440—Vol
49: 133, 136, 189, 352—Vol 50: 68, 186, 280,
350—Vol 51: 354—Vol 52: 322, 561—Vol 53:
181, 243, 330, 378—Vol 54: 172, 225—Vol 56:
47, 115, 177, 479—Vol 57: 173—Vol 58: 369,
451—Vol 59: 114, 589—Vol 60: 49, 50, 156,

588—Vol 60: 633—Vol 64: 761—Vol 66: 252, 535, 733, 734, 827—Vol 67: 514, 645—Vol 68: 486—Vol 69: 632—Vol 70: 1265—Vol 74: (9-50)—Vol 75: (5-44), (5-47)—Vol 77: 243—Vol 80: 142, 192—Vol 84: 702
BAILLIE .... Vol 61: 62—Vol 67: 384
BAIN .... Vol 25: 718, 964
BAINBRIDGE .... Vol 26: 57
BAIR .... Vol 70: 573
BAIRD...Vol 24: 149—Vol 41: 210—Vol 46: 104, 243, 330—Vol 47: 24, 194—Vol 48: 62 —Vol 49: 355—Vol 53: 628—Vol 66: 537— Vol 72: (4-84)—Vol 76: 711—Vol 77: 118— Vol 78: 601—Vol 79: 35
BAITES .... Vol 48: 61
BAKEMAN .... Vol 42: 74
BAKER...Vol 14: 272—Vol 15: 347—Vol 22: 51—Vol 23: 64, 471—Vol 24: 149—Vol 26: 54, 558—Vol 27: 44, 735, 739—Vol 30: 260, 438—Vol 31: 669—Vol 32: 720—Vol 33: 958 —Vol 34: 201, 658—Vol 37: 152, 397—Vol 38: 331—Vol 40: 76—Vol 41: 121, 125, 126, 163—Vol 42: 269, 342—Vol 43: 492, 497, 543, 547—Vol 44: 25, 83, 84, 148—Vol 45: 104, 113, 195, 328—Vol 46: 99—Vol 47: 196, 270—Vol 48: 442—Vol 49: 192, 355—Vol 50: 188, 351, 415—Vol 51: 234, 354—Vol 52: 172, 686—Vol 53: 377, 627—Vol 54: 311, 467, 537—Vol 55: 108, 446, 521, 713—Vol 56: 174, 224, 482, 690—Vol 57: 175, 352, 566, 688, 691—Vol 58: 111, 112, 370, 372—Vol 59: 48, 440—Vol 60: 747—Vol 61: 66, 705—Vol 62: 52, 53, 307—Vol 63: 572, 633, 742, 749—Vol 64: 520—Vol 65: 300, 759, 761—Vol 66: 123, 161, 307, 365, 603, 670—Vol 67: 46, 48, 291, 293, 646, 750—Vol 68: 57, 120, 492, 552, 732 —Vol 69: 241, 363—Vol 70: 203—Vol 71: 676, 959, 1109—Vol 72: (7-75)—Vol 75: (2-60), (2-61), (10-65)—Vol 76: 60, 309— Vol 77: 118—Vol 79: 36—Vol 80: 511—Vol 81: 570, 571, 629—Vol 82: 503, 653, 793, 795, 935—Vol 83: 93, 173, 945—Vol 84: 245
BAKUS .... Vol 82: 397
BALAY .... Vol 63: 244
BALCH...Vol 30: 149—Vol 68: 488—Vol 82: 935
BALDING .... Vol 63: 59
BALDOCK .... Vol 41: 122
BALDRIDGE .... Vol 76: 400
BALDWIN...Vol 23: 399—Vol 26: 340—Vol 30: 338—Vol 31: 586—Vol 42: 191—Vol 43: 420, 491, 542—Vol 44: 312—Vol 45: 105, 192—Vol 46: 98, 335, 385—Vol 49: 130— Vol 52: 52, 485, 684—Vol 53: 628, 692—Vol 56: 743—Vol 58: 457—Vol 59: 176, 314— Vol 61: 705—Vol 63: 741—Vol 65: 763—Vol 68: 284—Vol 69: 362—Vol 70: 131—Vol 71: 463—Vol 73: (8-83), (9-65)—Vol 75: (10-64)—Vol 77: 242, 539—Vol 79: 160, 284— Vol 83: 91, 170, 440, 524—Vol 84: 703
BALE .... Vol 68: 58
BALES...Vol 47: 30—Vol 68: 733—Vol 84: 635
BALIS .... Vol 41: 214
BALL...Vol 19: 307—Vol 26: 559—Vol 27: 737, 738, 806, 809—Vol 28: 159—Vol 30: 64 —Vol 31: 861—Vol 33: 708—Vol 34: 67, 659—Vol 35: 439—Vol 39: 223—Vol 41: 213 —Vol 43: 494—Vol 44: 80—Vol 45: 25, 194, 198, 328—Vol 46: 153—Vol 47: 31—Vol 50:

67—Vol 52: 561, 564—Vol 53: 56, 627—Vol 55: 711—Vol 56: 690—Vol 60: 699—Vol 61: 276, 472—Vol 62: 248, 305, 587—Vol 63: 58 —Vol 64: 444—Vol 65: 58, 123—Vol 66: 251, 461—Vol 67: 243, 646, 648—Vol 68: 56, 239, 684—Vol 70: 455—Vol 71: 761—Vol 73: (10-76)—Vol 77: 389—Vol 78: 53—Vol 79: 331—Vol 80: 45, 85—Vol 82: 935—Vol 83: 93—Vol 84: 68
BALLANER .... Vol 67: 714
BALLANFANT .... Vol 49: 46
BALLARD...Vol 19: 432—Vol 26: 561—Vol 39: 103—Vol 40: 227—Vol 43: 493, 604—Vol 50: 352—Vol 52: 626—Vol 53: 248—Vol 58: 369—Vol 64: 716—Vol 75: (9-37), (9-41)— Vol 79: 35—Vol 80: 44—Vol 82: 314—Vol 83: 717
BALLER .... Vol 41: 31
BALLINGER .... Vol 63: 243—Vol 81: 264
BALLOU...Vol 15: 347—Vol 27: 670—Vol 43: 724—Vol 56: 480—Vol 64: 389—Vol 79: 112
BALSAM .... Vol 28: 548
BALSLEY .... Vol 42: 139
BALTZELL .... Vol 84: 634
BANCROFT...Vol 31: 53—Vol 40: 76—Vol 41: 214—Vol 52: 360—Vol 53: 247—Vol 65: 438—Vol 67: 646
BANDY .... Vol 79: 113
BANE...Vol 41: 33, 68—Vol 43: 427—Vol 47: 189—Vol 66: 162
BANGS .... Vol 49: 734—Vol 68: 491
BANKS...Vol 43: 545—Vol 45: 125—Vol 53: 55, 249—Vol 58: 764—Vol 75: (5-45)
BANKHEAD .... Vol 45: 183
BANNING .... Vol 82: 313
BANNISTER...Vol 75: (6-38), (10-65)—Vol 77: 663—Vol 84: 893
BANNON .... Vol 54: 229
BANTA .... Vol 31: 860
BANTZ .... Vol 70: 205, 453—Vol 79: 195
BAR .... Vol 58: 241—Vol 59: 441
BARBAR .... Vol 32: 163
BARBEE .... Vol 63: 507—Vol 80: 427
BARBER...Vol 21: 497—Vol 22: 53, 270, 374 —Vol 23: 399—Vol 34: 658—Vol 35: 1266— Vol 39: 276—Vol 41: 68, 72, 213—Vol 42: 14, 78, 268—Vol 45: 115, 242—Vol 48: 442— Vol 49: 283—Vol 55: 286—Vol 57: 175—Vol 65: 438—Vol 66: 366—Vol 70: 354, 355— Vol 81: 569
BARBERIE .... Vol 67: 383
BARBIE .... Vol 55: 47
BARBOUR...Vol 26: 56—Vol 37: 68—Vol 39: 276—Vol 46: 103, 245—Vol 48: 53—Vol 68: 490
BARCALOW .... Vol 59: 112
BARCE .... Vol 62: 502
BARCLAY...Vol 39: 143—Vol 40: 172—Vol 54: 308—Vol 64: 716—Vol 80: 44—Vol 81: 518
BARCUS .... Vol 66: 537—Vol 67: 241
BARD...Vol 45: 103, 323—Vol 47: 393—Vol 48: 121, 200—Vol 55: 520
BARDENET .... Vol 74: (3-45)
BARDIN .... Vol 81: 316—Vol 84: 702
BARDSLEY .... Vol 65: 635
BARE...Vol 58: 241—Vol 59: 441—Vol 69: 565—Vol 81: 569
BAREMA .... Vol 82: 860
BARFIELD ...... Vol 24: 542—Vol 64: 57, 121

BARGSTRESSER............................Vol 67: 148
BARK..Vol 27: 44
BARKER....Vol 2: 44—Vol 19: 308, 431—Vol
26: 143—Vol 29: 43, 652—Vol 30: 337—Vol
41: 210—Vol 48: 204—Vol 50: 61—Vol 53:
243—Vol 56: 43, 739—Vol 64: 446—Vol 72:
(4-83)—Vol 79: 561
BARKETT.....................................Vol 30: 258
BARKHURST.............................Vol 39: 274
BARKLEY....Vol 44: 236—Vol 46: 155—Vol
49: 186, 188—Vol 59: 113—Vol 61: 867—Vol
84: 67
BARKSDALE....Vol 73: (11-68)—Vol 75: (9-
52)—Vol 82: 861
BARLEY......................................Vol 82: 398
BARLOW....Vol 17: 383, 389—Vol 19: 206—
Vol 21: 62—Vol 30: 441—Vol 37: 73—Vol
39: 326—Vol 41: 122—Vol 45: 119—Vol 46:
160—Vol 47: 397—Vol 48: 201, 205—Vol 50:
194—Vol 54: 55, 590
BARMENTER...............................Vol 52: 485
BARMORE...................................Vol 60: 507
BARNABY...................................Vol 48: 370
BARNARD....Vol 28: 548—Vol 32: 59—Vol
46: 332, 336—Vol 47: 263—Vol 58: 650—
Vol 59: 679—Vol 62: 52—Vol 82: 933—Vol
83: 259
BARNER....................................Vol 71: 462, 675
BARNES....Vol 10: 298—Vol 19: 207—Vol 24:
262, 544—Vol 26: 241—Vol 28: 548—Vol
29: 717—Vol 30: 339, 438—Vol 31: 750—
Vol 33: 709—Vol 39: 223—Vol 40: 172—Vol
43: 421, 605—Vol 46: 23—Vol 47: 273—Vol
52: 319—Vol 54: 589—Vol 55: 445, 523, 600
—Vol 56: 43—Vol 57: 176, 691—Vol 59: 176
—Vol 60: 698—Vol 61: 154, 868—Vol 62:
459—Vol 63: 245, 425—Vol 64: 446, 588,
715—Vol 65: 635—Vol 68: 154—Vol 70: 876
—Vol 72: (4-83)—Vol 75: (6-39)—Vol 76:
309—Vol 80: 336—Vol 81: 316, 369, 630—
Vol 82: 725, 935—Vol 83: 627—Vol 84: 245,
523
BARNET....................................Vol 31: 749
BARNETT....Vol 25: 716—Vol 28: 366—Vol
34: 539—Vol 39: 227—Vol 45: 22—Vol 46:
335—Vol 47: 193—Vol 48: 369—Vol 50: 69
—Vol 56: 45—Vol 62: 160—Vol 63: 244—
Vol 70: 358—Vol 73: (9-63)—Vol 74: (11-
60)—Vol 75: (1-54)—Vol 84: 244, 519
BARNETTE................................Vol 30: 259
BARNEY....Vol 18: 300—Vol 43: 601—Vol 51:
301—Vol 55: 598—Vol 58: 170
BARNHAM.................................Vol 66: 306
BARNHARDT............................Vol 83: 259
BARNHILL..............Vol 49: 186—Vol 56: 109
BARNS..............Vol 46: 152, 392—Vol 59: 49
BARNUM....Vol 26: 242—Vol 30: 441—Vol
37: 158—Vol 40: 227
BARNWELL..............................Vol 58: 763
BARR....Vol 22: 998—Vol 23: 398—Vol 24:
242—Vol 44: 387—Vol 45: 236, 241—Vol 46:
153—Vol: 54: 54, 352, 419—Vol 59: 441, 680,
763—Vol 61: 913—Vol 68: 686—Vol 76: 62
—Vol 79: 194—Vol 80: 45—Vol 83: 261, 718
BARRET....Vol 37: 66—Vol 42: 335—Vol 44:
234—Vol 48: 442
BARRETT....Vol 23: 64—Vol 33: 41—Vol 34:
660—Vol 35: 435, 1038—Vol 42: 269—Vol
45: 28, 237, 323—Vol 48: 58—Vol 57: 480,
691—Vol 58: 501—Vol 60: 635—Vol 62: 649

—Vol 63: 428—Vol 67: 576—Vol 71: 761—
Vol 75: (9-37)—Vol 80: 383—Vol 84: 244
BARRIKLOW..............Vol 50: 348—Vol 52: 54
BARRINGER..............Vol 23: 64—Vol 60: 250
BARRINGTON.........Vol 41: 127—Vol 50: 353
BARRON....Vol 24: 543—Vol 26: 143—Vol 67:
387—Vol 74: (5-43)—Vol 79: 369
BARROT......................................Vol 63: 244
BARROW..........Vol 27: 672—Vol 30: 538, 540
BARROWS....Vol 30: 149—Vol 32: 718—Vol
43: 481—Vol 84: 522
BARRY....Vol 22: 272—Vol 38: 330—Vol 41:
28, 215—Vol 46: 151—Vol 61: 704, 785—Vol
74: (2-42)—Vol 76: 144—Vol 80: 192, 335—
Vol 82: 654
BARSTOW....Vol 20: 607—Vol 27: 737—Vol
28: 261
BARTEAU...............................Vol 72: (2-63)
BARTGES...................................Vol 64: 521
BARTHOLOMEW....Vol 34: 537—Vol 56: 481
—Vol 58: 108
BARTLET............Vol 31: 750—Vol 46: 242
BARTLETT....Vol 23: 243—Vol 24: 260—Vol
29: 45—Vol 33: 955—Vol 36: 761—Vol 37:
487, 488—Vol 38: 275, 328, 329—Vol 39: 222
—Vol 41: 128, 163—Vol 42: 74, 81—Vol 43:
421, 422, 427, 484, 541, 597—Vol 44: 79, 231,
388—Vol 45: 105, 189, 242, 329—Vol 46:
154—Vol 47: 30, 199, 389, 393—Vol 49: 186,
188—Vol 50: 69, 187—Vol 52: 359, 437, 626,
687—Vol 55: 446, 709—Vol 57: 481—Vol
58: 587—Vol 63: 572—Vol 64: 651—Vol 65:
367, 442, 635, 668—Vol 66: 824—Vol 68: 155
—Vol 70: 207—Vol 71: 163—Vol 72: (9-92)
—Vol 76: 61—Vol 82: 796—Vol 83: 91, 872
—Vol 84: 70
BARTLEY....................................Vol 67: 241
BARTLOW.................................. Vol 64: 649
BARTON....Vol 26: 53, 54—Vol 29: 513—Vol
31: 54—Vol 36: 214—Vol 38: 329—Vol 41:
120, 123—Vol 42: 11, 268, 269—Vol 43: 604
—Vol 45: 121—Vol 46: 239—Vol 47: 23—
Vol 53: 746—Vol 54: 354, 418, 591—Vol 59:
388—Vol 65: 570—Vol 67: 711, 751—Vol
73: (1-63)—Vol 80: 656—Vol 83: 521, 524
BARTRIAM...............................Vol 43: 486
BARWIN.....................................Vol 82: 794
BASCOM....Vol 26: 139, 241—Vol 27: 738—
Vol 29: 286
BASH..Vol 76: 710
BASKIN....................Vol 57: 176, 431
BASKINE...................................Vol 61: 65
BASS....Vol 43: 427, 481—Vol 44: 387—Vol
45: 116, 236—Vol 52: 322—Vol 54: 53—Vol
57: 174, 480—Vol 58: 52—Vol 61: 868—Vol
62: 651—Vol 64: 124—Vol 80: 45—Vol 81:
518—Vol 82: 140—Vol 84: 444
BASSET........................... Vol 50: 190
BASSETT....Vol 24: 149, 242—Vol 25: 719,
968—Vol 27: 737, 738—Vol 28: 159—Vol 29:
45, 717—Vol 39: 143, 325—Vol 42: 139—
Vol 43: 422—Vol 45: 19—Vol 47: 269—Vol
48: 365—Vol 53: 329, 746—Vol 58: 501—
Vol 60: 115, 364, 366—Vol 63: 60—Vol 66:
309—Vol 72: (3-70)—Vol 73: (8-82)—Vol
84: 159
BASTABLE..................................Vol 49: 49
BASTARD.................................Vol 46: 156
BASYE.......................................Vol 65: 440
BATCHELDER....Vol 26: 143—Vol 40: 24—

BECHTEL............Vol 63: 700—Vol 64: 123
BECK....Vol 44: 314—Vol 45: 187—Vol 61:
608—Vol 64: 56—Vol 74: (6-37)—Vol 75:
(6-38)
BECKER....Vol 25: 798, 964—Vol 46: 389—
Vol 55: 166, 443—Vol 74: (7-53), (8-53)
BECKETT....Vol 65: 758—Vol 76: 654—Vol
82: 503
BECKHAM....Vol 17: 383, 389—Vol 19: 67—
Vol 62: 648—Vol 84: 633
BECKLEY..........................Vol 61: 232
BECKMAN............................Vol 27: 44
BECKWITH....Vol 22: 51—Vol 28: 162—Vol
30: 542—Vol 41: 165—Vol 45: 189—Vol 49:
393
BEDELL....Vol 26: 143, 338, 339—Vol 27: 892
—Vol 28: 162—Vol 53: 242—Vol 70: 1170
BEDFORD.........................Vol 82: 796
BEDINGER......................Vol 12: 62, 63
BEDLE........................Vol 53: 377, 748
BEEBE....Vol 26: 54, 337—Vol 42: 191—Vol
43: 546, 599—Vol 45: 189—Vol 49: 134—
Vol 56: 225—Vol 64: 588—Vol 69: 245—
Vol 70: 1019, 1167
BEECHER....Vol 25: 799—Vol 27: 738—Vol
28: 159, 363—Vol 58: 370, 585
BEECKER..........................Vol 27: 806
BEECRAFT..........................Vol 66: 252
BEEDE..............................Vol 84: 247
BEEDLE....Vol 24: 151—Vol 28: 478—Vol 41:
31—Vol 44: 231, 232, 383—Vol 45: 101, 193
—Vol 70: 1170
BEEKMAN....Vol 3: 682—Vol 19: 532—Vol
28: 479—Vol 30: 62—Vol 43 493, 543. 598
—Vol 66: 827
BEEKS..............................Vol 56: 176
BEELER....Vol 45: 322—Vol 46: 28—Vol 66:
162—Vol 67: 385—Vol 68: 491—Vol 69: 159
—Vol 82: 794
BEELS.............................Vol 39: 274
BEEM..............Vol 63: 570—Vol 65: 123
BEEMAN....Vol 38: 34, 217—Vol 39: 20—Vol
43: 486—Vol 46: 99—Vol 50: 188—Vol 56:
689
BEEN..............................Vol 57: 176
BEENSON..........................Vol 27: 807
BEERS....Vol 22: 272—Vol 29: 289, 511—Vol
32: 284—Vol 43: 424—Vol 65: 634
BEERY............................Vol 29: 803
BEESLAY.........................Vol 67: 647
BEESON....Vol 25: 967—Vol 26: 241, 559—
Vol 28: 59—Vol 63: 247—Vol 70: 455, 877,
1089—Vol 77: 538—Vol 82: 931
BEETLE...........................Vol 58: 330
BEGGS............................Vol 62: 389
BEGHTOL.........................Vol 76: 860
BEGUN............................Vol 48: 449
BEHETHLAND............Vol 53: 177, 632
BEID.........................Vol 72: (4-82)
BEIDERFISCH......................Vol 47: 83
BEIGHLEY.........................Vol 61: 469
BEIGHT...........................Vol 63: 247
BEISTEL..........................Vol 84: 447
BEKMAN...........................Vol 44: 150
BELASH...........................Vol 43: 423
BELDEN....Vol 9: 166—Vol 27: 667, 668—Vol
28: 548—Vol 29: 651—Vol 41: 32—Vol 55:
600—Vol 64: 520—Vol 68: 121
BELDING....Vol 27: 808—Vol 38: 330—Vol

43: 604—Vol 44: 81—Vol 57: 691—Vol 58:
449
BELK..............Vol 77: 539—Vol 79: 283
BELKNAP..........................Vol 82: 499
BELL—Vol 27: 383—Vol 29: 290, 714, 716—
Vol 33: 956, 960, 1033—Vol 34: 67—Vol 36:
217—Vol 40: 77—Vol 41: 125—Vol 42: 339
—Vol 43: 489, 540, 597, 598, 602—Vol 44:
78, 235—Vol 45: 103, 106, 112—Vol 47: 33,
190—Vol 48: 64—Vol 49: 189—Vol 51: 234
Vol 52: 562—Vol 53: 492—Vol 54: 464—
Vol 56: 171, 172, 173—Vol 57: 176, 352, 435,
479, 529—Vol 58: 110, 111, 112, 171, 241—
Vol 61: 152—Vol 62: 649—Vol 63: 636—
Vol 65: 248—Vol 67: 575—Vol 68: 285, 490
—Vol 69: 240, 247—Vol 71: 88, 1108—Vol
73: (1-62)—Vol 76: 581, 653—Vol 77: 240,
481—Vol 80: 191, 557, 658—Vol 81: 315,
518—Vol 82: 502—Vol 83: 172, 946—Vol
84: 632
BELLA............................Vol 44: 154
BELLAMY........................Vol 75: (6-38)
BELLINGER.......................Vol 80: 192
BELLIS...........................Vol 45: 21
BELLOW.........................Vol 75: (4-54)
BELLOWS....Vol 42: 340—Vol 50: 191, 347—
Vol 56: 372—Vol 84: 704
BELMAN..........................Vol 79: 283
BELT.............................Vol 30: 259
BELTZ............................Vol 57: 174
BELVEAL....Vol 44: 314—Vol 64: 758
BELVILLE.........................Vol 64: 758
BEMENT............Vol 29: 801—Vol 31: 751
BEMIS....Vol 22: 373, 374—Vol 30: 542—Vol
32: 59—Vol 33: 475, 707—Vol 67: 118, 240,
513
BENBOW..........................Vol 45: 127
BENDER............Vol 77: 241—Vol 82: 396
BENEDICT....Vol 33: 1168—Vol 38: 35—Vol
40: 274—Vol 41: 119—Vol 46: 332—Vol 64:
761—Vol 65: 123—Vol 68: 57—Vol 74: (5-
39)
BENFIELD........................Vol 48: 449
BENGE...........................Vol 65: 298
BENHAM....Vol 31: 750—Vol 54: 466—Vol
58: 112—Vol 84: 705
BENJAMIN—Vol 22: 272—Vol 29: 89—Vol
32: 284—Vol 61: 228—Vol 63: 168—Vol 64:
649—Vol 67: 577—Vol 70: 576—Vol 72:
(4-84)—Vol 76: 581—Vol 78: 696—Vol 82:
863
BENN............................Vol 81: 216
BENNET....Vol 39: 224—Vol 40: 77, 78—Vol
41: 31—Vol 42: 16, 79, 138—Vol 43: 485—
Vol 45: 24, 197—Vol 54: 464, 537
BENNETT....Vol 18: 298—Vol 19: 432—Vol
20: 608—Vol 21: 253—Vol 22: 50—Vol 23:
325—Vol 24: 459—Vol 26: 139—Vol 27: 380
—Vol 29: 47—Vol 32: 159, 160, 284—Vol 35:
652—Vol 36: 575—Vol 39: 277—Vol 43: 596
—Vol 44: 313—Vol 45: 26, 119, 322—Vol
46: 242, 391—Vol 47: 396—Vol 48: 119, 303,
369—Vol 49: 133, 188, 189, 191, 287—Vol
50: 188, 190, 191—Vol 53: 692—Vol 54:
464, 466, 537—Vol 55: 165—Vol 56: 226,
560—Vol 57: 116, 480, 691—Vol 58: 370,
371, 702, 764—Vol 59: 441—Vol 60: 634—
Vol 61: 700—Vol 62: 390, 460, 649—Vol 64:
521—Vol 65: 248—Vol 66: 730—Vol 68:
373—Vol 70: 207, 1170—Vol 72: (1-64)—

Vol 75: (9-37)—Vol 76: 859—Vol 77: 242, 479, 725—Vol 78: 696—Vol 79: 332—Vol 80: 44, 193, 276—Vol 82: 796—Vol 83: 1014—Vol 84: 328

BENNINGTON............Vol 79: 613

BENSON....Vol 31: 669—Vol 38: 219—Vol 39: 275—Vol 47: 392—Vol 49: 285—Vol 50: 192—Vol 54: 709

BENT....Vol 24: 458—Vol 43: 482—Vol 45: 26, 104

BENTHAL............Vol 49: 188

BENTLEY....Vol 22: 998—Vol 26: 560—Vol 31: 54—Vol 50: 189, 356—Vol 53: 181, 634 —Vol 54: 224—Vol 57: 218—Vol 63: 427, 739—Vol 65: 761—Vol 75: (4-54)—Vol 80: 432

BENTLY............Vol 51: 166

BENTON....Vol 22: 155—Vol 30: 539—Vol 35: 1264—Vol 46: 101—Vol 48: 372—Vol 59: 589—Vol 60: 419, 745—Vol 62: 649—Vol 75: (4-53)

BEOUGHER............Vol 72: (7-75)

BERANS............Vol 36: 76

BEREMAN............Vol 71: 1024

BERG............Vol 83: 441

BERGAN............Vol 48: 449

BERGER............Vol 48: 62—Vol 76: 783

BERKELEY............Vol 44: 228

BERKLEY............Vol 84: 68

BERKSHIRE............Vol 77: 240

BERKSTRASER............Vol 67: 148

BERLIN............Vol 43: 496—Vol 67: 115, 711

BERNARD....Vol 47: 195—Vol 53: 632—Vol 77: 242—Vol 79: 560—Vol 81: 430

BERRIE............Vol 58: 328

BERRIEN............Vol 1: 604

BERRITT............Vol 61: 158

BERRY....Vol 26: 244, 561—Vol 27: 807—Vol 39: 23—Vol 43: 416—Vol 46: 153, 393—Vol 47: 393—Vol 50: 350—Vol 52: 560—Vol 53: 492, 570, 693—Vol 55: 339—Vol 56: 481, 627—Vol 57: 310, 434—Vol 58: 172, 371, 450, 500, 587—Vol 59: 763—Vol 60: 50, 634, 696 —Vol 68: 553—Vol 74: (1-51), (2-42)—Vol 75: (6-39)—Vol 76: 710—Vol 77: 240—Vol 78: 294—Vol 79: 160—Vol 81: 631—Vol 83: 261

BERRYHILL............Vol 66: 160

BERRYMAN....Vol 53: 177, 632—Vol 66: 734 —Vol 67: 148—Vol 71: 1024—Vol 84: 68

BERTHOLF............Vol 61: 157

BERTINE............Vol 37: 150

BERTOLF............Vol 61: 157

BESS............Vol 23: 398

BESSE............Vol 37: 157, 268

BEST....Vol 26: 340—Vol 53: 52—Vol 61: 788 —Vol 83: 794

BESTOR............Vol 64: 520

BETHAY............Vol 54: 54

BETS............Vol 59: 314

BETTIS............Vol 50: 352—Vol 57: 689

BETTLEYONE............Vol 40: 228

BETTS....Vol 19: 433—Vol 30: 337—Vol 32: 61—Vol 37: 396, 488—Vol 44, 231

BETTY............Vol 19: 432—Vol 74: (5-42)

BETZ............Vol 57: 174

BEUGE............Vol 78: 155

BEVANS............Vol 29: 45, 801—Vol 39: 104

BEVENS............Vol 19: 207—Vol 56: 319

BEVERLEY....Vol 41: 165—Vol 42: 73—Vol 43: 539

BEVIER............Vol 17: 383, 389—Vol 81: 130

BEVILLE............Vol 54: 535

BEVINGS............Vol 30: 542

BEVINS....Vol 30: 335—Vol 37: 156—Vol 44: 28—Vol 69: 501

BIBB....Vol 44: 388—Vol 45: 109, 128—Vol 46: 23—Vol 57: 115, 433—Vol 61: 865

BIBBINS............Vol 30: 542—Vol 71: 1109

BIBBS............Vol 43: 600, 603

BICKERSTAFF............Vol 59: 681

BICKERSTETH............Vol 38: 332

BICKERTON....Vol 43: 495—Vol 44: 24—Vol 66: 308—Vol 68: 122—Vol 69: 681

BICKHAM............Vol 48: 60

BICKLEY............Vol 58: 451—Vol 84: 706

BICKMAN............Vol 49: 130

BICKNELL............Vol 25: 798

BIDDICK............Vol 30: 543

BIDDLE....Vol 17: 383, 389—Vol 24: 458—Vol 27: 380—Vol 53: 116, 379, 575—Vol 70: 1170—Vol 83: 336

BIDWELL............Vol 45: 189

BIEBER............Vol 43: 486, 604

BIEDERFISCH............Vol 45: 128

BIEHLER............Vol 43: 493

BIERCE............Vol 62: 502

BIERLY....Vol 45: 114—Vol 46: 243—Vol 56: 481—Vol 66: 55—Vol 70: 456

BIEVELHEIMER............Vol 48: 205

BIGELOW....Vol 4: 31—Vol 21: 61—Vol 22: 375—Vol 27: 736, 889—Vol 38: 87, 275—Vol 43: 546, 599—Vol 46: 385—Vol 65: 440

BIGGER............Vol 46: 28—Vol 48: 60

BIGGERSTAFF............Vol 69: 630—Vol 70: 54

BIGGES............Vol 57: 113

BIGGS....Vol 38: 218—Vol 48: 446—Vol 56: 628—Vol 57: 113—Vol 59: 315, 762—Vol 63: 569—Vol 67: 386—Vol 79: 518—Vol 80: 510

BIGHAM....Vol 41: 32—Vol 48: 121, 444—Vol 55: 652

BIGLER............Vol 58: 52

BIGLY............Vol 57: 480

BIGSRAFF............Vol 38: 332

BILL....Vol 28: 482—Vol 48: 308—Vol 57: 689 —Vol 74: (1-51), (12-53)

BILLINGS....Vol 32: 508—Vol 33: 473—Vol 34: 661—Vol 35: 651—Vol 42: 343—Vol 43: 483—Vol 54: 464—Vol 56: 372—Vol 58: 370 —Vol 61: 610—Vol 65: 768—Vol 67: 386—Vol 68: 241—Vol 83: 173

BILLINGSLEY....Vol 40: 26—Vol 64: 522—Vol 81: 518

BILLINGTON............Vol 41: 33, 68

BILLS............Vol 45: 21—Vol 79: 331

BILLUPS............Vol 37: 149

BING............Vol 29: 717

BINGHAM....Vol 23: 325—Vol 24: 56—Vol 32: 507—Vol 33: 1031—Vol 47: 27—Vol 54: 466—Vol 66: 536

BINKLEY............Vol 58: 586

BINNEY............Vol 45: 21—Vol 47: 22

BINOM............Vol 66: 160

BINON............Vol 41: 164

BIRCH............Vol 41: 70—Vol 43: 493

BIRCHARD............Vol 79: 284

BIRD....Vol 26: 561—Vol 34: 539—Vol 40: 274—Vol 41: 65—Vol 43: 419—Vol 45: 103 —Vol 46: 240—Vol 53: 746—Vol 54: 53—

Vol 55: 282—Vol 57: 743—Vol 68: 373—Vol 71: 959—Vol 72: (4-82)—Vol 75: (8-43)—Vol 82: 396
BIRDSALL....Vol 29: 45—Vol 41: 72, 122—Vol 42: 72—Vol 48: 307—Vol 55: 445—Vol 64: 387—Vol 81: 264
BIRDSONG................Vol 71: 845—Vol 76: 60
BIRELY................................Vol 65: 160
BIRGE..Vol 26: 339
BIRKHEAD............................Vol 43: 422
BISBEE....Vol 21: 498—Vol 38: 87—Vol 80: 588
BISBEY................................Vol 66: 308
BISCOE................................Vol 42: 81
BISHOP....Vol 13: 611—Vol 24: 58—Vol 28: 162, 548—Vol 30: 539—Vol 31: 50, 862—Vol 33: 43—Vol 36: 216—Vol 45: 238—Vol 51: 302—Vol 53: 245, 627—Vol 54: 114—Vol 55: 286—Vol 60: 572—Vol 61: 65, 278—Vol 63: 568—Vol 70: 55, 455—Vol 73: (10-75)—Vol 82: 314, 501
BISSEL..Vol 41: 71
BISSELL....Vol 26: 55, 242—Vol 31: 588—Vol 42: 10, 14, 15—Vol 49: 46—Vol 67: 114—Vol 80: 383
BITLEY..Vol 76: 63
BITTINGER..............Vol 81: 630—Vol 82: 397
BITTNER................................Vol 32: 507
BIVENS....Vol 36: 76—Vol 57: 311—Vol 69: 501
BIVINS....Vol 38: 84—Vol 39: 104—Vol 42: 341—Vol 72: (6-78)
BIXLER............................Vol 83: 874—Vol 84: 328
BIZZELL....Vol 62: 388, 648—Vol 64: 56, 121
BLACHLEY................................Vol 84: 964
BLACK....Vol 26: 56, 57—Vol 35: 1101—Vol 36: 216—Vol 38: 34, 327—Vol 39: 224—Vol 41: 31, 34, 67, 68—Vol 43: 486, 495, 541—Vol 44: 23, 83—Vol 45: 115—Vol 46: 236, 389, 391—Vol 47: 33—Vol 48: 59, 121—Vol 50: 60—Vol 53: 241, 692—Vol 55: 714—Vol 60: 418—Vol 62: 712—Vol 63: 374—Vol 67: 46, 750, 753—Vol 70: 132—Vol 76: 311 —Vol 77: 183—Vol 83: 945—Vol 84: 68, 521, 633
BLACKBURN....Vol 33: 957—Vol 34: 66—Vol 39: 326—Vol 46: 27—Vol 47: 197—Vol 52: 283, 483—Vol 53: 180, 448—Vol 54: 51, 422 —Vol 58: 587—Vol 68: 486, 625—Vol 84: 632
BLACKETER................................Vol 84: 635
BLACKFORD....Vol 43: 491—Vol 71: 464—Vol 75: (5-44)
BLACKMAN....Vol 30: 63—Vol 38: 87, 273—Vol 40: 24, 26, 108—Vol 50: 60—Vol 53: 692—Vol 54: 652
BLACKMAR................................Vol 57: 310
BLACKMER................................Vol 29: 512
BLACKMORE....Vol 45: 125—Vol 67: 645—Vol 68: 731, 733
BLACKSHEAR................Vol 41: 122, 209
BLACKSTONE....Vol 44: 230, 231, 383—Vol 45: 101
BLACKWELDER..........................Vol 77: 118
BLACKWELL....Vol 35: 654—Vol 46: 159, 244—Vol 47: 397—Vol 48: 302, 369—Vol 53: 376—Vol 54: 223—Vol 71: 162
BLACKY................................Vol 59: 238
BLAIR....Vol 22: 271—Vol 26: 54—Vol 30: 64 —Vol 38: 34, 114, 217—Vol 39: 20—Vol 41:

70—Vol 42: 138, 267, 334—Vol 45: 238—Vol 46: 103, 386—Vol 47: 28, 29—Vol 48: 370—Vol 49: 42, 132, 395—Vol 50: 68, 349—Vol 52: 228—Vol 53: 626—Vol 55: 165, 166, 284, 433, 655, 714—Vol 56: 45, 109, 369, 477—Vol 59: 47—Vol 61: 278—Vol 66: 600—Vol 69: 565—Vol 74: (7-52), (8-52), (11-56), (11-57)—Vol 83: 260, 946
BLAISDELL................................Vol 56: 318
BLAKE....Vol 27: 45—Vol 41: 127—Vol 42: 340—Vol 43: 420, 495—Vol 45: 22, 124—Vol 46: 246—Vol 50: 64—Vol 51: 303—Vol 56: 564—Vol 57: 352—Vol 60: 507—Vol 63: 373 —Vol 65: 508—Vol 66: 309--Vol 80: 44
BLAKELEY................................Vol 76: 654
BLAKELY....Vol 29: 289—Vol 44: 310—Vol 63: 569
BLAKEMAN....Vol 18: 298—Vol 22: 154—Vol 60: 116
BLAKEMORE................................Vol 47: 83
BLAKESLEE....Vol 29: 800—Vol 39: 23—Vol 64: 260—Vol 66: 826—Vol 76: 784
BLAKESLEY................................Vol 66: 826
BLAKEY..................Vol 71: 87—Vol 76: 709
BLALOCK................................Vol 27: 807
BLANCHARD....Vol 21: 62—Vol 47: 33—Vol 48: 372—Vol 52: 321—Vol 60: 113—Vol 67: 41, 576—Vol 74: (12-53)—Vol 84: 68
BLAND....Vol 42: 73, 79—Vol 49: 286—Vol 52: 51—Vol 63: 165—Vol 65: 248—Vol 66: 161—Vol 70: 880—Vol 71: 559
BLANKENBAKER....Vol 37: 396—Vol 45: 199, 329—Vol 52: 734—Vol 53: 55—Vol 54: 111, 468
BLANKENSHIP....Vol 48: 58—Vol 49: 40—Vol 61: 913
BLANKS................................Vol 43: 422
BLANTON....Vol 34: 323—Vol 49: 396—Vol 58: 588—Vol 59: 174, 389, 442, 761
BLARE................................Vol 41: 70
BLASER................................Vol 31: 590
BLATCHLEY........................Vol 22: 52, 272
BLAUVELT..........Vol 64: 712—Vol 72: (1-70)
BLAYLOCK................................Vol 29: 44
BLAZE................................Vol 53: 53
BLAZOR................................Vol 53: 52
BLEAKNEY....Vol 49: 49, 136—Vol 50: 183—Vol 53: 571
BLEDSOE....Vol 1: 450—Vol 43: 545—Vol 44: 228—Vol 47: 195—Vol 64: 256, 761—Vol 66: 732—Vol 70: 709, 877—Vol 73: (5-89), (11-65)—Vol 75: (6-36)
BLEECKER................................Vol 50: 354
BLETHEN................................Vol 45: 118
BLEVINS..............Vol 48: 203—Vol 82: 500
BLEWEOS................................Vol 53: 245
BLEWER................................Vol 54: 422
BLIID................................Vol 67: 646
BLIN................................Vol 52: 686
BLINCO................................Vol 46: 387
BLISS....Vol 1: 342—Vol 5: 58—Vol 27: 806—Vol 28: 59, 159
BLIZARD..............Vol 62: 503—Vol 65: 366
BLODGETT....Vol 31: 862—Vol 46: 243—Vol 54: 109—Vol 59: 763—Vol 68: 491
BLOEN................................Vol 65: 635
BLOKER................................Vol 56: 746
BLOOD....Vol 23: 399—Vol 24: 56, 542—Vol 26: 241—Vol 30: 541—Vol 40: 229—Vol 49: 135—Vol 50: 64—Vol 55: 445

BORLAND............Vol 36: 761
BORMER............Vol 58: 328, 701
BORRADAILE............Vol 72: (1-65)
BORROUM............Vol 40: 228
BORST............Vol 35: 56—Vol 43: 601
BOSARE............Vol 41: 67
BOSART............Vol 41: 32
BOSKET............Vol 45: 241
BOSLEY............Vol 54: 52
BOSTON............Vol 61: 157
BOSTWICK....Vol 22: 679—Vol 29: 513—Vol
34: 67, 321, 323—Vol 40: 229—Vol 43: 491
—Vol 44: 79, 150—Vol 49: 46—Vol 61: 60
BOSWELL....Vol 36: 352—Vol 38: 272, 329—
Vol 39: 224—Vol 41: 210, 213—Vol 45: 193
—Vol 48: 57—Vol 49: 48, 284—Vol 50: 191
—Vol 51: 356—Vol 52: 320—Vol 61: 854—
Vol 65: 298—Vol 70: 1168—Vol 79: 194
Vol 84: 703
BOSWORTH....Vol 41: 70—Vol 49: 134—Vol
60: 572—Vol 82: 727
BOTHWELL............Vol 71: 1025
BOTKIN............Vol 62: 500, 775
BOTKINS............Vol 58: 54—Vol 59: 521
BOTSFORD....Vol 28: 162—Vol 31: 585—Vol
36: 216, 762—Vol 47: 192—Vol 57: 566—
Vol 58: 751
BOTTS....Vol 48: 449—Vol 57: 218, 687—Vol
69: 120—Vol 84: 523, 703
BOTTUM............Vol 32: 160
BOUCHER............Vol 53: 746—Vol 82: 499
BOUCK............Vol 68: 733—Vol 69: 431
BOUGHNER............Vol 55: 600
BOUGHTON............Vol 45: 200
BOUKER............Vol 48: 442
BOULDEN............Vol 43: 482
BOULDIN............Vol 42: 270
BOULWARD............Vol 46: 157
BOULWARE....Vol 61: 546, 547—Vol 76: 783
BOUN............Vol 78: 53
BOUND............Vol 57: 174
BOUNDURANT............Vol 83: 336
BOURBON............Vol 46: 243
BOURLAND............Vol 46: 102—Vol 69: 246
BOURNE............Vol 60: 248—Vol 70: 204
BOUTON....Vol 39: 276—Vol 40: 273—Vol 48:
56—Vol 67: 384—Vol 75: (2-57)
BOUTWELL............Vol 42: 270—Vol 76: 653
BOVEE............Vol 48: 444—Vol 71: 675
BOW............Vol 39: 142—Vol 58: 501
BOWDEN............Vol 84: 894
BOWDISH............Vol 48: 61, 366
BOWDRE............Vol 83: 872
BOWEN....Vol 26: 561—Vol 28: 549—Vol 30:
65—Vol 37: 265, 488—Vol 40: 229—Vol 43:
425, 597—Vol 44: 21—Vol 45, 326—Vol 46:
243, 391, 393—Vol 47: 26, 30, 33, 272—Vol
48: 121, 366—Vol 49: 48, 189—Vol 50: 191,
193, 349—Vol 51: 357—Vol 52: 485—Vol 54:
51, 419—Vol 56: 564—Vol 58: 112, 240, 372,
652—Vol 59: 525—Vol 60: 419—Vol 61: 473,
546, 609—Vol 62: 650—Vol 63: 508—Vol 64:
650—Vol 71: 57—Vol 73: (10-77)—Vol 77:
52—Vol 81: 19—Vol 82: 653
BOWER....Vol 32: 160—Vol 42: 76—Vol 43:
544—Vol 44: 80—Vol 49: 133—Vol 66: 827
—Vol 83: 1013
BOWERS....Vol 32: 160—Vol 40: 227—Vol 41:
126, 213—Vol 44: 84—Vol 48: 306—Vol 49:

133—Vol 50: 351—Vol 65: 441—Vol 69: 684
—Vol 70: 206
BOWIE............Vol 82: 933
BOWLER............Vol 44: 26, 382
BOWLES....Vol 21: 496—Vol 42: 268—Vol 53:
53, 179—Vol 54: 422—Vol 57: 218—Vol 58:
241, 701—Vol 70: 1021—Vol 75: (1-54)—
Vol 76: 654—Vol 79: 160—Vol 80: 382
BOWLING............Vol 70: 574—Vol 80: 510
BOWMAN....Vol 26: 242—Vol 29: 45—Vol 30:
543—Vol 31: 749—Vol 32: 632—Vol 40: 274
—Vol 45: 190—Vol 48: 449—Vol 54: 421—
Vol 57: 310—Vol 60: 248—Vol 65: 366—Vol
67: 43, 385, 512, 513, 516—Vol 70: 1171—
Vol 71: 673—Vol 84: 893
BOWNE....Vol 29: 510—Vol 36: 756—Vol 46:
155—Vol 57: 313—Vol 63: 572, 697
BOWYER............Vol 58: 53, 450
BOWYERS............Vol 46: 99
BOWZER............Vol 65: 56
BOX............Vol 82: 141—Vol 83: 1014
BOYCE....Vol 33: 959—Vol 47: 193, 392—Vol
48: 62—Vol 52: 51—Vol 56: 624—Vol 57:
214—Vol 59: 682— Vol 60: 417—Vol 70: 135
Vol 83: 521—Vol 84: 704
BOYD....Vol 17: 383, 389—Vol 26: 340—Vol
28: 61, 478—Vol 36: 757—Vol 37: 266—Vol
39: 102—Vol 42: 340—Vol 43: 420, 425—Vol
44: 225—Vol 45: 103, 197—Vol 46: 160, 241
—Vol 49: 287, 347—Vol 51: 301—Vol 52:
52, 173, 562—Vol 57: 435—Vol 58: 52, 110—
Vol 61: 912—Vol 62: 502—Vol 65: 297—Vol
67: 146—Vol 71: 676, 761—Vol 73: (9-67)—
Vol 76: 655, 859—Vol 77: 52, 183, 331—Vol
81: 71—Vol 82: 499, 933, —Vol 83: 718—Vol
84: 704
BOYDSTON............Vol 62: 247
BOYDSTUN....Vol 37: 152—Vol 39: 143—Vol
42: 264
BOYER....Vol 56: 749—Vol 57: 564, 630, 687—
Vol 58: 450, 586—Vol 71: 675—Vol 78: 53,
457, 600—Vol 81: 629—Vol 82: 796—Vol 84:
519
BOYERS............Vol 56: 173
BOYES............Vol 27: 738—Vol 38: 272
BOYETT............Vol 43: 423
BOYKIN....Vol 63: 165, 166—Vol 64: 56—Vol
82: 396, 498
BOYLAN............Vol 42: 270
BOYLE....Vol 37: 488—Vol 46: 241—Vol 48:
121—Vol 63: 428—Vol 79: 614
BOYLES............Vol 56: 744
BOYNTON....Vol 31: 53, 667, 749—Vol 32: 59,
717—Vol 40: 274—Vol 42: 72—Vol 46: 103
—Vol 55: 46—Vol 60: 573—Vol 65: 248
BOYS............Vol 68: 243
BOZART............Vol 41: 67
BOZARTH............Vol 45: 109
BOZEMAN............Vol 59: 113
BOZERT............Vol 36: 758—Vol 37: 266
BRABHAM............Vol 52: 562
BRABSTON............Vol 32: 794
BRACE....Vol 19: 626—Vol 21: 404—Vol 38:
88—Vol 42: 343—Vol 43: 421—Vol 57: 309
—Vol 59: 237, 441—Vol 60: 48, 416—Vol
71: 461
BRACEE............Vol 60: 48, 416
BRACEY....Vol 29: 288—Vol 43: 421—Vol 60:
48, 416
DRACKEN............Vol 1: 450—Vol 68: 242

BRACKENS................Vol 73: (9-63)
BRACKETT........Vol 30: 336, 540—Vol 49: 394
BRACKNEY....................Vol 67: 577
BRACY....Vol 41: 34, 161—Vol 42: 338, 343—
Vol 43: 482
BRADDOCK—Vol 20: 277—Vol 21: 169, 400
—Vol 47: 31—Vol 57: 176—Vol 59: 524—
Vol 67: 45, 515
BRADEN................Vol 34: 201
BRADFIELD........Vol 57: 312—Vol 65: 246
BRADFORD—Vol 25: 799, 887—Vol 26: 561
—Vol 27: 380, 382—Vol 30: 148—Vol 35:
656—Vol 36: 73, 215—Vol 42: 270, 335—Vol
43: 494, 723—Vol 44: 27, 152—Vol 45: 28,
116, 117, 197, 327—Vol 46: 29—Vol 49: 134
—Vol 53: 242, 694—Vol 54: 422—Vol 55:
339, 444—Vol 58: 51, 650—Vol 60: 419, 507,
634, 745—Vol 64: 445—Vol 65: 763—Vol 66:
460—Vol 68: 550, 624, 686—Vol 69: 116, 158
—Vol 70: 1166—Vol 72: (1-65)—Vol 74:
(5-41)—Vol 75: (10-67)
BRADING................Vol 61: 156
BRADLEE................Vol 81: 493
BRADLEY....Vol 8: 879—Vol 16: 191—Vol 23:
398—Vol 24: 151—Vol 25: 798—Vol 26: 53
339—Vol 29: 288—Vol 33: 476—Vol 36: 356,
761—Vol 39: 22, 226—Vol 40: 25—Vol 41:
71—Vol 44: 85—Vol 45: 26, 27, 115—Vol
46: 101—Vol 47: 33—Vol 49: 44, 48, 133—
Vol 50: 63, 275—Vol 53: 627—Vol 55: 165,
444—Vol 56: 44, 174—Vol 61: 707—Vol 65:
365—Vol 66: 461—Vol 67: 444—Vol 74:
(3-44)—Vol 79: 561—Vol 80: 589—Vol 83:
92, 793—Vol 84: 244
BRADSHAW....Vol 30: 258—Vol 32: 634—
Vol 56: 560—Vol 58: 174—Vol 61: 66—Vol
66: 305—Vol 67: 239, 515—Vol 71: 959—
Vol 75: (5-47)
BRADSTREET....Vol 31: 53—Vol 40: 25—Vol
67: 145
BRADT—Vol 21: 167—Vol 40: 227, 272—Vol
60: 505—Vol 68: 492
BRADWAY................Vol 30: 335
BRADY....Vol 21: 335—Vol: 70: 572—Vol 72:
(3-71)
BRAET................Vol 19: 626
BRAFORD................Vol 67: 715
BRAGDON................Vol 65: 246
BRAGG....Vol 39: 275—Vol 41: 71, 162—Vol
59: 763—Vol 79: 613
BRAGGS................Vol 68: 243
BRAILEY................Vol 66: 669
BRAINARD........Vol 22: 271—Vol 45: 191
BRAINERD........Vol 45: 27—Vol 71: 956
BRAISTED................Vol 50: 61
BRAKE....Vol 48: 445—Vol 53: 328—Vol 75:
(2-61)—Vol 84: 67
BRALEY................Vol 55: 397
BRAMBLE................Vol 69: 362
BRAME................Vol 40: 272—Vol 41: 29
BRAMHALL................Vol 72: (9-87)
BRAMLET................Vol 72: (11-59)
BRAMLETTE................Vol 46: 391
BRANCH....Vol 55: 338—Vol 56: 689—Vol 70:
359—Vol 71: 673—Vol 74: (11-60)—Vol 76:
309—Vol 78: 502—Vol 84: 632
BRAND................Vol 59: 525—Vol 60: 113, 417
BRANDEGEE........Vol 22: 997—Vol 23: 167
BRANDEN................Vol 40: 227

BRANDENBURG....Vol 55: 602—Vol 77: 331,
480—Vol 84: 635
BRANDON....Vol 39: 224—Vol 59: 175—Vol
62: 246—Vol 79: 561—Vol 83: 336
BRANDT....Vol 45: 110, 325—Vol 54: 588—
Vol 55: 108
BRANHAM....Vol 42: 340—Vol 45: 20—Vol
46: 329—Vol 49: 48, 185—Vol 69: 243
BRANNAMAN................Vol 74: (2-41)
BRANNON................Vol 81: 517
BRANSCOMBE................Vol 84: 324
BRANSON........Vol 47: 194—Vol 56: 691
BRANT................Vol 77: 725
BRANTLEY........Vol 40: 75, 108—Vol 49: 188
BRAS................Vol 54: 590
BRASEWELL................Vol 45: 117
BRASFIELD................Vol 84: 522
BRASHEARS....Vol 46: 104—Vol 54: 110,
352— Vol 57: 481—Vol 80: 153—Vol 84:
519
BRASTOW................Vol 67: 147
BRASY................Vol 41: 34
BRATE................Vol 43: 422
BRATT................Vol 68: 492
BRATTEN................Vol 77: 538
BRATTLE................Vol 54: 174
BRATTON....Vol 39: 103—Vol 41: 126—Vol
53: 493—Vol 54: 227—Vol 70: 708—Vol 72:
(5-68)—Vol 82: 795
BRAWNER................Vol 61: 785
BRAXTON................Vol 29: 651—Vol 43: 495
BRAY................Vol 81: 316
BRAYTON....Vol 29: 650—Vol 52: 359—Vol
54: 172—Vol 74: (2-43)
BRAZELTON................Vol 79: 562
BRECK................Vol 61: 470
BRECKENRIDGE....Vol 43: 488—Vol 80: 46
BREECE................Vol 70: 574
BREED....Vol 41: 33, 161—Vol 46: 245—Vol
48: 371—Vol 49: 191, 350—Vol 57: 40—Vol
70: 452
BREEDING................Vol 39: 225
BREEDLORE................Vol 38: 33
BREEDLOVE....Vol 55: 46—Vol 57: 480—Vol
82: 499
BREEDWELL........Vol 45: 111—Vol 46: 334
BREESE....Vol 42: 76, 136, 265—Vol 43: 494
—Vol 44: 24—Vol 64: 158
BREESLAU................Vol 61: 451
BREINER................Vol 47: 268
BRENEISER................Vol 69: 57
BRENEMAN................Vol 57: 566
BRENN................Vol 66: 306
BRENNEMAN................Vol 80: 336
BRENNER................Vol 66: 461
BRERETON................Vol 29: 650
BRESIE................Vol 74: (11-61)
BRESSLER................Vol 82: 796
BRESSLEY................Vol 78: 600
BRETT................Vol 42: 341—Vol 43: 420, 540
BREVARD....Vol 37: 153—Vol 48: 80, 441—
Vol 72: (1-64)—Vol 82: 396
BREVOORT....Vol 40: 275—Vol 41: 29, 122—
Vol 45: 18, 189
BREWER....Vol 32: 61—Vol 51: 353—Vol 53:
180—Vol 57: 312—Vol 58: 329—Vol 62:
773—Vol 66: 825—Vol 67: 113, 242, 576, 751
—Vol 68: 284—Vol 69: 57—Vol 70: 207—
Vol 71: 1109—Vol 72: (6-78), (7-74)—Vol

79: 35—Vol 82: 141—Vol 83: 793—Vol 84: 158
BREWSTER....Vol 22: 373—Vol 26: 56, 241—Vol 27: 739, 892—Vol 30: 339—Vol 31: 750 —Vol 32: 631—Vol 39: 227—Vol 40: 73—Vol 42: 268—Vol 44: 147—Vol 49: 134, 352, 355—Vol 63: 635—Vol 66: 307—Vol 68: 554 —Vol 72: (7-74), (9-88), (11-60)—Vol 75: (9-37—Vol 78: 295—Vol 82: 313—Vol 84: 894
BREWTON................Vol 19: 432
BRIAN...............   ....Vol 49: 136
BRIANT............ ....Vol 23: 242—Vol 61: 611
BRICE....Vol 45: 126—Vol 54: 709—Vol 58: 652—Vol 61: 606—Vol 64: 758—Vol 68: 120 —Vol 69: 244—Vol 72: (4-84)—Vol 75: (2-60)
BRICELAN.......Vol 46: 332, 335—Vol 84: 703
BRICELAND..............Vol 53: 692
BRICELIN...............Vol 53: 692
BRICK.................Vol 30: 335
BRICKELL..........Vol 56: 743—Vol 66: 731
BRICKET.............Vol 83: 944—Vol 84: 70
BRICKEY.................Vol 42: 193
BRIDE........... .. ..Vol 67: 118
BRIDGE....Vol 23: 326—Vol 44: 28—Vol 67: 577—Vol 84: 703
BRIDGEFORTH...............Vol 83: 794
BRIDGER....... ....Vol 44: 25, 147
BRIDGES....Vol 26: 340, 560—Vol 41: 125—Vol 42: 77—Vol 44: 227—Vol 45: 128, 329—Vol 66: 534—Vol 70: 707—Vol 71: 239—Vol 79: 284—Vol 80: 192—Vol 82: 142
BRIDWELL...............Vol 73: (10-77)
BRIEN. ....Vol 47: 269
BRIGGS....Vol 28: 549—Vol 31: 749—Vol 38: 219—Vol 39: 23—Vol 45: 19, 321—Vol 47: 266, 392—Vol 48: 120, 448—Vol 49: 192—Vol 53: 492—Vol 54: 52, 223, 229, 308, 353—Vol 56: 561—Vol 57: 567, 690—Vol 59: 388 —Vol 60: 115—Vol 70: 357, 707—Vol 80: 336, 383, 556—Vol 84: 965
BRIGHAM....Vol 60: 250, 417, 569—Vol 71: 464—Vol 77: 241
BRIGHT—Vol 31: 750—Vol 49: 134, 353—Vol 50: 58, 65—Vol 63: 165—Vol 65: 299—Vol 78: 695—Vol 81: 216
BRIGHTMAN...............Vol 28: 58
BRIMHALL...............Vol 34: 203
BRINDLEY...............Vol 67: 145, 645
BRINK....Vol 43: 601—Vol 44: 81—Vol 84: 158
BRINKER.................Vol 38: 87
BRINKERHOFF...............Vol 52: 687
BRINKLEY............Vol 42: 16—Vol 66: 537
BRINTON...............Vol 33: 1032—Vol 49: 46
BRISACK...............Vol 39: 276
BRISBIN...............Vol 43: 602
BRISCOE....Vol 30: 338—Vol 49: 187, 390—Vol 50: 69—Vol 58: 54—Vol 69: 683—Vol 70: 135—Vol 73: (5-89)—Vol 82: 798
BRISTOL....Vol 22: 998—Vol 28: 58—Vol 29: 289—Vol 31: 53, 670, 750—Vol 33: 960—Vol 37: 395—Vol 44: 315—Vol 46: 29—Vol 64: 716—Vol 82: 725
BRISTOW...............Vol 55: 285—Vol 56: 739
BRISWOLD...............Vol 46: 332
BRITT....Vol 42: 341—Vol 43: 420, 540—Vol 45: 114—Vol 53: 177, 631
BRITTAIN...............Vol 40: 77

BRITTEN...............Vol 58: 174
BRITTIN...............Vol 50: 194
BRITTINGHAM...............Vol 53: 55
BRITTON....Vol 27: 740—Vol 31: 669—Vol 34: 423—Vol 42: 138—Vol 46: 29—Vol 50: 70—Vol 55: 599—Vol 56: 627—Vol 58: 331 —Vol 62: 460—Vol 74: (11-57)—Vol 77: 664—Vol 83: 794
BRIUTT...............Vol 39: 143
BRIX...............Vol 46: 27
BROACH...............Vol 81: 264
BROADUS...............Vol 82: 140, 398
BROADDUS......Vol 75: (4-54)—Vol 79: 283
BROADNAX......Vol 80: 431—Vol 81: 20
BROADSTON...............Vol 81: 630
BROADSTREET...............Vol 77: 240
BROADWATER......Vol 60: 698—Vol 83: 260
BROADWELL......Vol 21: 168—Vol 82: 725
BROCK....Vol 48: 305—Vol 63: 700—Vol 66: 250—Vol 68: 285—Vol 74: (11-58)—Vol 82: 654—Vol 84: 69
BROCKETT...............Vol 26: 57—Vol 79: 332
BROCKMAN...............Vol 45: 23
BROCKWAY....Vol 29: 652—Vol 30: 149—Vol 31: 51—Vol 39: 225—Vol 40: 73—Vol 44: 233, 311—Vol 45: 18—Vol 47: 266—Vol 56: 173—Vol 60: 417—Vol 71: 558—Vol 84: 67
BRODNAX....Vol 45: 237—Vol 47: 95—Vol 73: (9-64)—Vol 84: 67
BROKAW....Vol 41: 213—Vol 42: 134—Vol 66: 366
BROMLEY—Vol 24: 54—Vol 27: 890, 891—Vol 28: 481
BROMMELLY...............Vol 49: 190
BROMMERLEY...............Vol 49: 350
BRONAUGH............Vol 63: 507—Vol 81: 264
BRONSON....Vol 26: 54—Vol 30: 438—Vol 33: 955—Vol 43: 488—Vol 54: 537—Vol 57: 176, 565—Vol 63: 572—Vol 64: 161—Vol 70: 1171—Vol 74: (6-38)—Vol 75: (6-39)
BROOCKS...............Vol 56: 225
BROOKBANK...............Vol 48: 120
BROOKE....Vol 41: 209—Vol 42: 337—Vol 43: 425, 488, 495, 598—Vol 54: 352—Vol 55: 520—Vol 57: 630—Vol 58: 174, 764—Vol 59: 765—Vol 63: 633—Vol 71: 162—Vol 73: (5-88)—Vol 84: 158
BROOKENS...............Vol 83: 260
BROOKES............Vol 21: 169—Vol 67: 243
BROOKFIELD......Vol 61: 782—Vol 68: 284
BROOKIN...............Vol 47: 269
BROOKING....Vol 45: 26, 237—Vol 47: 95, 199 —Vol 58: 172—Vol 73: (9-64), (9-65)—Vol 84: 67
BROOKINGS...............Vol 23: 399
BROOKINS......Vol 43: 417—Vol 68: 553
BROOKS....Vol 11: 616—Vol 21: 169, 497—Vol 22: 50, 154, 269, 272, 998—Vol 27: 671—Vol 29: 289, 800—Vol 31: 53—Vol 36: 352, 759—Vol 37: 154, 158—Vol 38: 329, 331—Vol 40: 25, 108—Vol 41: 31, 126—Vol 42: 77, 78—Vol 43: 423, 425, 487, 488, 492, 541, 598—Vol 44: 83, 312, 382, 387—Vol 45: 27, 101, 189—Vol 46: 100, 154, 330, 335, 392—Vol 47: 191—Vol 50: 60, 190—Vol 52: 485, 559, 686 —Vol 53: 329, 377—Vol 54: 173, 540—Vol 55: 711—Vol 57: 214, 689—Vol 58: 174, 327, 371, 764—Vol 59: 441, 682—Vol 60: 248, 572—Vol 62: 309—Vol 64: 648—Vol 68: 242—Vol 69: 630—Vol 71: 840—Vol 74:

(1-50), (4-58), (11-60)—Vol 75: (6-38)—
Vol 76: 654—Vol 81: 19—Vol 82: 726, 933—
Vol 83: 172
BROOM..Vol 70: 207
BROSSMAN..Vol 67: 713
BROTHERS..Vol 37: 270
BROTHERTON......................................Vol 50: 353
BROUGH..Vol 60: 572
BROUGHTON....Vol 19: 205, 307, 308—Vol 48:
372—Vol 65: 367—Vol 69: 627
BROUWER..Vol 65: 758
BROWER....Vol 30: 440, 441—Vol 45: 188, 195
Vol 50: 66—Vol 58: 701—Vol 70: 357, 1019
—Vol 75: (4-53)—Vol 78: 156
BROWN....Vol 3: 383—Vol 11: 438—Vol 19:
307, 626—Vol 21: 61, 62, 169, 497—Vol 22:
269, 272, 375—Vol 23: 168, 243—Vol 25: 39,
966—Vol 26: 242, 559, 562—Vol 27: 45, 46,
670, 740—Vol 28: 60, 61—Vol 29: 47, 290,
513, 650, 715, 717—Vol 30: 64, 149, 257, 438,
439, 440, 541, 542—Vol 31: 51, 413, 749, 750,
862, 863—Vol 32: 59, 159, 163, 282, 283, 634
—Vol 33: 41, 475, 709, 1032—Vol 34: 538—
Vol 36: 573, 577, 756, 759—Vol 37: 68, 71,
394, 488—Vol 39: 223—Vol 40: 78, 172, 226,
273—Vol 41: 33, 71, 119, 121, 125, 126, 162,
164, 209—Vol 42: 15, 80, 137, 343—Vol 43:
483, 488, 546, 601—Vol 44: 27, 151—Vol 45:
24, 27, 104, 105, 110, 120, 124, 126, 198—Vol
46: 22, 23, 100, 101, 240, 241, 330, 332, 335—
Vol 47: 22, 33, 394—Vol 48: 55, 59, 302, 448
—Vol 49: 46, 49, 128, 130, 189, 191, 284, 285,
396—Vol 50: 61, 66, 70, 192, 193, 353, 355—
Vol 51: 166, 303—Vol 52: 51, 173, 319, 357,
360—Vol 53: 378, 572, 573—Vol 54: 225—
Vol 55: 339—Vol 56: 225, 372, 564, 627—Vol
57: 39, 214, 216, 349, 435, 480, 629—Vol 58:
50, 52, 172, 329, 452, 453, 502, 587, 702—Vol
59: 111, 312, 441, 523—Vol 60: 634—Vol 61:
158, 232—Vol 62: 587—Vol 63: 246, 293, 373
—Vol 64: 57, 259—Vol 65: 296, 633, 636, 761
—Vol 66: 122, 252, 462, 669, 825—Vol 67:
443, 444, 647, 751, 752—Vol 68: 154, 488,
625, 735—Vol 69: 243, 247, 363, 567, 631—
Vol 70: 205, 277, 452, 454, 708, 1167, 1265—
Vol 71: 460, 759, 762, 481, 957—Vol 73: (1-
63)—Vol 74: (2-42),)5-39)—Vol 75: (8-
43), (9-41)—Vol 76: 62, 400, 401, 582—Vol
77: 244, 333, 389, 664—Vol 79: 160, 194, 284,
331—Vol 80: 46, 432, 510—Vol 81: 316, 630
Vol 82. 140, 313, 314, 668, 933—Vol 83: 92,
93, 94, 521, 524, 871, 945, 946—Vol 84: 69,
246, 326, 327, 444, 519, 632, 702, 706, 946, 966
BROWNALOR......................................Vol 66: 161
BROWNE....Vol 43: 546—Vol 44: 235—Vol
49: 355—Vol 66: 366—Vol 70: 351—Vol 82:
502—Vol 84: 445
BROWNELL....Vol 37: 396—Vol 38: 272—Vol
44: 85—Vol 46: 337—Vol 58: 372—Vol 65:
248—Vol 70: 1169—Vol 74: (9-49)
BROWNELLER....................................Vol 66: 161
BROWNING....Vol 22: 270—Vol 37: 488—Vol
53: 245—Vol 54: 228, 539—Vol 56: 372, 558
—Vol 69: 246—Vol 71: 829—Vol 77: 238,
239—Vol 78: 696—Vol 81: 629—Vol 84: 636
BROWNLEE....Vol 42: 77, 136—Vol 66: 119—
Vol 76: 653—Vol 79: 35
BROWNLEY..Vol 58: 173
BROWNSON....Vol 57: 627—Vol 64: 161, 585
BROXTON..Vol 69: 565
BROYLES............................Vol 55: 209, 655

BRUCE....Vol 24: 542—Vol 43: 545—Vol 44:
83—Vol 45: 124—Vol 56: 627—Vol 60: 48—
Vol 63: 635—Vol 65: 366, 437—Vol 73: (1-
63), (8-84)—Vol 76: 656—Vol 78: 108—Vol
82: 398—Vol 83: 91—Vol 84: 894
BRUCH..Vol 60: 572
BRUIN....................Vol 53: 446—Vol 78: 695
BRUINGTON..Vol 49: 283
BRUITT..Vol 37: 152
BRUMFIELD....................Vol 69: 56, 242
BRUMMITT..Vol 60: 50
BRUMNETT..Vol 55: 712
BRUN..Vol 54: 228
BRUNDAGE..Vol 55: 166
BRUNER....Vol 65: 571—Vol 66: 365—Vol 67:
716—Vol 75: (2-58)
BRUNNER......................................Vol 43: 599
BRUNSON....Vol 33: 955—Vol 43: 492—Vol
61: 65—Vol 64: 161
BRUSH....Vol 55: 109—Vol 59: 49—Vol 61:
65, 66, 232—Vol 63: 572, 697
BRUSIE..Vol 41: 32
BRUSTER..Vol 84: 894
BRUTON..Vol 62: 501
BRUYN..Vol 32: 163
BRYAM....................Vol 19: 308—Vol 20: 276
BRYAN....Vol 17: 283—Vol 29: 44—Vol 34:
539, 540—Vol 38: 86—Vol 39: 103—Vol 41:
122, 125, 209—Vol 42: 11, 15, 16—Vol 44:
315—Vol 45: 187—Vol 46: 103, 335—Vol
48: 199, 444—Vol 49: 352—Vol 50: 139, 344,
352—Vol 52: 318, 558—Vol 53: 52, 249, 574
—Vol 56: 743, 745—Vol 57: 174, 434, 481,
688, 742—Vol 62: 53, 120, 247, 458—Vol 63:
57—Vol 64: 757—Vol 68: 283—Vol 70: 358
—Vol 74: (1-50)—Vol 75: (2-61)—Vol 82:
398, 499, 793, 794—Vol 83: 259, 337, 873—
Vol 84: 327, 446
BRYANT... Vol 21: 498—Vol 23: 168—Vol 24:
456—Vol 25: 796, 799, 887—Vol 27: 382—
Vol 29: 512—Vol 39: 328—Vol 41: 214—Vol
43: 489—Vol 45: 322—Vol 48: 64—Vol 61:
611—Vol 64: 56, 121, 122, 257, 384—Vol 67:
440—Vol 75: (2-61)—Vol 82: 653, 862
BRYCE..Vol 39: 224
BRYMBERRY....................................Vol 83: 1013
BRYSON....................Vol 66: 536—Vol 84: 634
BUCHANAN....Vol 18: 181—Vol 26: 54—Vol
30: 63, 338, 439, 441, 541—Vol 31: 52—Vol
37: 352—Vol 38: 327—Vol 39: 328—Vol 44:
82, 388—Vol 46: 30—Vol 49: 131, 353—Vol
52: 173, 687—Vol 53: 379—Vol 55: 165—
Vol 56: 742—Vol 58: 111, 240—Vol 60: 114
—Vol 61: 785—Vol 62: 308, 714—Vol 65:
633, 635—Vol 66: 366—Vol 67: 444, 648, 751
—Vol 68: 58, 687—Vol 69: 58, 158, 241, 565
—Vol 70: 357—Vol 71: 958—Vol 72: (2-62)
—Vol 74: (2-39)—Vol 75: (4-53), (5-44)—
Vol 81: 571—Vol 82: 863
BUCHANON......Vol 29: 513—Vol 50: 276, 413
BUCHER..Vol 64: 443
BUCHNAN................................ Vol 80: 84
BUCK....Vol 27: 381, 670—Vol 31: 668—Vol
37: 70, 349—Vol 40: 273—Vol 41: 34, 65,
120—Vol 44: 316—Vol 46: 337—Vol 48: 124,
367—Vol 49: 46—Vol 58: 111—Vol 61: 546,
869—Vol 64: 388—Vol 68: 735—Vol 69:
121—Vol 74: (5-43)—Vol 77: 243—Vol 84:
520, 706
BUCKALOW......................................Vol 59: 47
BUCKARD..Vol 33: 710

BUCKBEE_____Vol 30: 259
BUCKHALTER_____Vol 43: 546—Vol 45: 327
BUCKINGHAM__Vol 29: 649—Vol 53: 379—
Vol 55: 339—Vol 56: 476—Vol 64: 756—Vol
78: 600—Vol 84: 246
BUCKLAND_____Vol 26: 558
BUCKLES_____Vol 57: 174—Vol 68: 623
BUCKLEY__Vol 22: 997—Vol 26: 561—Vol
27: 382—Vol 61: 65—Vol 64: 715—Vol 80:
383—Vol 82: 795
BUCKLIN_____Vol 60: 506
BUCKMAN_____ Vol 67: 715
BUCKMASTER_____Vol 47: 33
BUCKMINSTER_____Vol 56: 46
BUCKNER__Vol 37: 269—Vol 42: 78, 136—
Vol 45: 183—Vol 49: 132—Vol 53: 243—Vol
66: 54
BUCKSHORT_____Vol 66: 161
BUCKWAR_____Vol 55: 521
BUDD_____Vol 48: 306
BUECHLER_____Vol 50: 281
BUEL_____Vol 59: 588
BUELL__Vol 22: 374—Vol 39: 223—Vol 55:
711
BUFORD__Vol 30: 542—Vol 57: 175, 349—
Vol 66: 121, 160
BUFFINGTON__Vol 45: 120—Vol 47: 190—
Vol 54: 111
BUFFUM_____Vol 76: 582
BUGBEE_____Vol 42: 80, 266—Vol 75: (5-47)
BUGG_____Vol 79: 561
BUIE_____Vol 46: 240
BULKELEY_____Vol 40: 77—Vol 64: 260
BULKLEY_____Vol 47: 192—Vol 48: 54
BULL__Vol 7: 271—Vol 19: 206, 531—Vol 28:
260—Vol 30: 256—Vol 32: 720—Vol 33: 473
—Vol 48: 306—Vol 49: 188—Vol 50: 66,
186—Vol 52: 360, 686—Vol 53: 573—Vol
54: 308, 589—Vol 56: 371—Vol 60: 49—Vol
66: 121, 307, 828—Vol 68: 57—Vol 83: 173
—Vol 84: 246
BULLARD__Vol 31: 751—Vol 36: 356—Vol
52: 173, 562—Vol 66: 160, 309—Vol 69:
160, 245
BULLEFANT_____Vol 4: 65
BULLEJAUT_____Vol 40: 171, 172—Vol 42: 9
BULLEN__Vol 28: 364—Vol 32: 632—Vol 45:
191—Vol 82: 794
BULLER_____Vol 57: 435, 565
BULLINGTON_____Vol 41: 33, 68
BULLIS_____Vol 64: 650—Vol 66: 460
BULLOCK__Vol 25: 719—Vol 38: 328—Vol
39: 275—Vol 46: 241—Vol 48: 307, 372—
Vol 54: 590—Vol 59: 175—Vol 61: 65, 152
—Vol 62: 309, 648, 649—Vol 67: 384, 645—
Vol 80: 192, 335—Vol 81: 518—Vol 83: 717
BUMGARDNER_____Vol 46: 99
BUMPAS_____Vol 67: 291
BUNCE__Vol 26: 56—Vol 28: 549—Vol 45:
28—Vol 71: 760
BUND_____Vol 39: 22
BUNDY_____Vol 66: 121
BUNKER_____Vol 59: 763
BUNN__Vol 11: 318—Vol 30: 540—Vol 56:
563
BUNNELL__Vol 31: 586, 751—Vol 33: 476—
Vol 42: 74, 81, 138, 266—Vol 44: 233, 383—
Vol 45: 186—Vol 48: 203—Vol 49: 133—
Vol 57: 628—Vol 58: 449—Vol 65: 441, 633
Vol 66: 56—Vol 73: (12-63)
BUNTAIN_____Vol 46: 246—Vol 49: 133

BUNTAIRS_____Vol 43: 486
BUNTEN_____Vol 55: 521
BUNTERS_____Vol 43: 486
BUNTON_____Vol 37: 74, 394—Vol 58: 501
BURBANK__Vol 44: 231—Vol 46: 388—Vol
50: 350—Vol 55: 338—Vol 56: 560—Vol 69:
57
BURBECK_____Vol 54: 351
BURCH__Vol 18: 299—Vol 45: 184—Vol 46:
386—Vol 47: 95, 199, 266—Vol 50: 189—Vol
51: 239—Vol 54: 351—Vol 61: 470—Vol 63:
425—Vol 64: 258—Vol 84: 444
BURCHAN_____Vol 61: 471—Vol 72: (1-66)
BURCHARD__Vol 25: 798—Vol 54: 54—Vol
58: 652—Vol 59: 315—Vol 77: 244
BURD_____Vol 69: 121
BURDEN_____Vol 19: 532
BURDETT_____Vol 45: 322—Vol 57: 691
BURDICK__Vol 28: 261—Vol 31: 751—Vol
41: 215—Vol 47: 263—Vol 58: 111—Vol 59:
238, 587—Vol 62: 207
BURDINE_____Vol 33: 958
BURFORD_____Vol 41: 124
BURGAN_____Vol 57: 215
BURGE__Vol 38: 274—Vol 56: 174—Vol 62:
306
BURGER_____Vol 24: 58, 457—Vol 63: 373
BURGES_____Vol 43: 723
BURGESS__Vol 22: 270—Vol 23: 168, 169—
Vol 25: 718, 964—Vol 48: 443—Vol 54: 54,
419—Vol 55: 166—Vol 56: 370—Vol 57:
687—Vol 59: 113, 681—Vol 64: 158—Vol
66: 827—Vol 70: 707—Vol 75: (6-38)—Vol
77: 240
BURGETT_____Vol 67: 715—Vol 68: 58
BURGIN__Vol 43: 596—Vol 78: 600—Vol 84:
704
BURK_____Vol 31: 589—Vol 63: 293
BURKE__Vol 43: 604—Vol 44: 26—Vol 61:
788—Vol 84: 936
BURKES_____Vol 63: 293
BURKETT_____Vol 55: 601—Vol 78: 246
BURKHALTER_____Vol 56: 148
BURKHARDT__Vol 59: 49—Vol 68: 58—Vol
80: 192, 657
BURKS__Vol 34: 14—Vol 63: 426—Vol 84:
446, 704
BURLEIGH__Vol 26: 243—Vol 43: 419—Vol
62: 307
BURLEN_____Vol 60: 572
BURLESON_____Vol 48: 307
BURLEY__Vol 30: 65—Vol 62: 307
BURLINGAME__Vol 24: 54—Vol 31: 54, 860
—Vol 33: 38—Vol 57: 175, 690—Vol 58:
173, 598—Vol 64: 522
BURLINGHAM_____Vol 35: 437—Vol 36: 73
BURLINGHAME_____Vol 19: 432
BURLINGTON_____Vol 38: 219
BURLISON_____Vol 27: 739
BURN__Vol 42: 138, 267—Vol 54: 592
BURNAM_____Vol 56: 225
BURNAP_____Vol 58: 648
BURNELL_____Vol 40: 75—Vol 66: 734
BURNET_____Vol 34: 540—Vol 83: 522
BURNETT__Vol 35: 489—Vol 56: 625—Vol
57: 219—Vol 60: 419—Vol 64: 760—Vol 67:
514—Vol 80: 335—Vol 82: 861, 862
BURNHAM__Vol 29: 653—Vol 39: 224—Vol
45: 107, 242—Vol 47: 28—Vol 50: 351—Vol
54: 308—Vol 57: 565—Vol 60: 249, 699—
Vol 72: (11-59)—Vol 73: (11-67)—Vol 74:

(5-41), (7-53), (8-53)—Vol 77: 725—Vol
83: 523
BURNS—Vol 42: 341—Vol 45: 104, 119—Vol
53: 242—Vol 54: 52, 224—Vol 55: 714—Vol
56: 173, 746—Vol 59: 112—Vol 63: 294—
Vol 66: 160—Vol 67: 517—Vol 69: 58—Vol
75: (5-47), (9-41)—Vol 78: 108—Vol 81:
216, 430
BURNSIDE—Vol 37: 396—Vol 41: 72—Vol
54: 173—Vol 58: 501
BURNSIDES—Vol 75: (10-66)—Vol 76: 710
BURRELL—Vol 45: 114—Vol 80: 588—Vol
83: 522
BURRES..Vol 56: 745
BURRESS..Vol 84: 703
BURRIDGE..Vol 23: 169
BURRIS..Vol 84: 447
BURRITT—Vol 17: 480—Vol 18: 298—Vol
49: 129—Vol 56: 689, 746—Vol 61: 787
BURSON..Vol 82: 63
BURT—Vol 58: 651—Vol 67: 442—Vol 75:
(9-37)
BURR—Vol 21: 498—Vol 22: 272, 995—Vol
27: 44—Vol 32: 632—Vol 35: 1104—Vol 42:
190—Vol 47: 266—Vol 50: 193, 279, 347—
Vol 52: 54—Vol 57: 173—Vol 63: 742—Vol
68: 490, 732—Vol 69: 117—Vol 70: 351—Vol
84: 704
BURROUGHS—Vol 19: 532—Vol 21: 253—
Vol 42: 78—Vol 43: 427—Vol 44: 148—Vol
45: 113—Vol 49: 134—Vol 68: 735—Vol 83:
336
BURROWS—Vol 45: 191—Vol 47: 269—Vol
48: 365—Vol 56: 746—Vol 59: 114—Vol 61:
704—Vol 65: 442—Vol 83: 717
BURRUS..Vol 38: 332—Vol 39: 142
BURSON..Vol 76: 400—Vol 83: 262, 945
BURT—Vol 15: 350—Vol 22: 156—Vol 26:
562—Vol 27: 808—Vol 39: 327
BURTIS..Vol 45: 191—Vol 68: 734
BURTNETT..Vol 70: 1019
BURTON—Vol 15: 348—Vol 22: 998—Vol 27:
44, 736—Vol 32: 284—Vol 38: 330—Vol 41:
72, 120, 125—Vol 42: 76, 79—Vol 43: 488,
497—Vol 44: 23—Vol 45: 122, 240, 329—
Vol 46: 22, 159, 238—Vol 48: 449—Vol 51:
689—Vol 52: 485—Vol 55: 47—Vol 62: 584
—Vol 72: (3-74)—Vol 73: (12-63)—Vol 74:
(11-57)—Vol 75: (8-42)—Vol 76: 582—Vol
78: 108
BURWELL—Vol 37: 480—Vol 38: 87, 217,
328—Vol 41: 214—Vol 43: 421—Vol 44: 228
—Vol 46: 153—Vol 50: 116—Vol 56: 628—
Vol 57: 565, 743—Vol 67: 45—Vol 82: 396
BUSBY—Vol 54: 536—Vol 64: 716—Vol 72:
(4-82)—Vol 76: 928—Vol 78: 53—Vol 79:
112, 283
BUSCH..Vol 77: 603
BUSH—Vol 27: 808—Vol 30: 441—Vol 39:
276—Vol 44: 23—Vol 52: 172, 563—Vol 56:
562—Vol 58: 502—Vol 62: 123—Vol 64: 59
—Vol 66: 250—Vol 67: 443—Vol 77: 603
BUSHBY..Vol 61: 784
BUSHNELL—Vol 22: 679—Vol 27: 45, 383—
Vol 49: 45—Vol 55: 602—Vol 56: 173, 316,
368, 478—Vol 65: 57, 365—Vol 66: 732—Vol
73: (1-62)—Vol 83: 259
BUSHROD..Vol 57: 689
BUSIC..Vol 48: 441
BUSS..Vol 70: 135—Vol 81: 631
BUSSEY—Vol 43: 544—Vol 49: 284—Vol 71:

463—Vol 74: (6-38)
BUSTER—Vol 50: 188, 275, 415—Vol 62: 307,
649
BUTCHER—Vol 53: 746—Vol 62: 246—Vol
75: (11-70)—Vol 81: 569
BUTLER—Vol 21: 61—Vol 33: 1033—Vol 40:
172—Vol 41: 128—Vol 42: 75, 188, 193—Vol
43: 547, 603, 604—Vol 44: 152, 230—Vol 45:
123, 193, 327—Vol 46: 21, 152, 153, 154—Vol
47: 32—Vol 48: 61, 63, 64, 204, 305—Vol 49:
393—Vol 50: 70, 188, 275, 281, 415—Vol 52:
625—Vol 53: 242—Vol 54: 652—Vol 55: 446
—Vol 57: 481—Vol 58: 52, 701, 702—Vol
60: 634—Vol 63: 373, 571—Vol 65: 572—Vol
66: 160—Vol 67: 444—Vol 68: 58—Vol 70:
129—Vol 75: (6-39)—Vol 77: 117—Vol 78:
294—Vol 80: 43, 276, 557—Vol 84: 245, 247,
634
BUTMAN..Vol 67: 712
BUTTER..Vol 57: 690
BUTTERFIELD—Vol 36: 218—Vol 38: 35—
Vol 58: 241—Vol 66: 300—Vol 70: 1265—
Vol 81: 71
BUTTERICK..Vol 60: 506, 696, 745
BUTTMAN..Vol 38: 88
BUTTOLPH..Vol 46: 153—Vol 71: 558
BUTTON—Vol 41: 70—Vol 43: 547, 599—Vol
44: 81, 150, 381—Vol 45: 116, 184—Vol 49:
135, 393—Vol 54: 537—Vol 58: 652—Vol
62: 503—Vol 63: 247—Vol 69: 631—Vol 83:
872
BUTTRICK—Vol 49: 351, 352—Vol 50: 114—
Vol 67: 242
BUTTS—Vol 43: 547, 599—Vol 44: 81, 150,
381—Vol 45: 184—Vol 48: 59—Vol 49: 136
—Vol 54: 709
BUXTON—Vol 42: 140—Vol 45: 124—Vol
76: 710
BUYCK..Vol 39: 21
BUYSS..Vol 48: 446
BYERLY—Vol 45: 124—Vol 46: 152—Vol 48:
306—Vol 67: 48
BYERS—Vol 41: 120, 124—Vol 43: 489—Vol
44: 84—Vol 46: 99—Vol 47: 190—Vol 60:
506—Vol 63: 374
BYINGTON..Vol 25: 38
BYNUM..Vol 38: 328—Vol 66: 160
BYRAM..Vol 67: 45
BYRD—Vol 41: 65—Vol 53: 628—Vol 58: 702
—Vol 62: 309—Vol 65: 365, 441, 507—Vol
68: 373, 687—Vol 71: 950—Vol 75: (8-43)
BYRDS..Vol 64: 384
BYRNE..Vol 62: 120
BYRNES..Vol 67: 517
BYRNSIDE..Vol 70: 58
BYRON..Vol 53: 446
BYRUM..Vol 46: 100
BYSER..Vol 43: 603
BYUS..Vol 61: 606

C

CABANIS..Vol 43: 424
CABANISS..Vol 65: 635
CABEEN—Vol 45: 104—Vol 47: 192
CABELL..Vol 27: 668, 669
CABINESS..Vol 42: 342
CABLE—Vol 19: 627—Vol 56: 624
CABOT..Vol 44: 243
CADDALL..Vol 48: 305
CADMAN..Vol 70: 1169
CADOGAN..Vol 58: 369—Vol 67: 242

CHAPLIN............Vol 82: 795
CHAPMAN....Vol 25: 384, 888—Vol 26: 243
—Vol 29: 718—Vol 30: 441—Vol 31: 862—
Vol 34: 659—Vol 37: 149—Vol 39: 227, 274
—Vol 40: 228—Vol 41: 29, 33, 123, 164—Vol
42: 13, 340—Vol 43: 596, 599—Vol 44: 316
—Vol 45: 18, 189—Vol 46: 384—Vol 50: 356
—Vol 54: 225, 540—Vol 55: 714—Vol 56:
176, 690—Vol 57: 114, 217, 690—Vol 59:
762—Vol 60: 505—Vol 63: 427—Vol 67: 292
—Vol 68: 284—Vol 70: 877—Vol 71: 1109—
Vol 73: (2-64)—Vol 74: (2-41)—Vol 76:
401—Vol 82: 798—Vol 84: 636
CHAPPELL....Vol 31: 413—Vol 38: 327—Vol
42: 342—Vol 45: 195—Vol 67: 291—Vol
68: 552
CHARCOTE.......................Vol 66: 305
CHARISSON...................Vol 34: 539
CHARITON....................Vol 69: 630
CHARLES.......................Vol 84: 158
CHARLOCK...................Vol 59: 681
CHARLTON....Vol 49: 355—Vol 68: 625—Vol
82: 933—Vol 83: 521—Vol 84: 247
CHASE...Vol 28: 59—Vol 29: 290—Vol 30:
338, 339—Vol 31: 50—Vol 35: 1263—Vol
36: 348, 579—Vol 37: 487—Vol 39: 103, 325
—Vol 46: 198, 242—Vol 47: 196—Vol 48:
45, 283, 353—Vol 50: 58—Vol 53: 180—Vol
54: 222—Vol 55: 165, 597—Vol 59: 588—
Vol 61: 278, 912—Vol 62: 716—Vol 63: 246,
295, 427—Vol 64: 58—Vol 65: 245, 441—Vol
68: 490, 687—Vol 69: 245—Vol 73: (9-63)
—Vol 75: (5-44), (9-41)—Vol 76: 582—Vol
78: 155—Vol 81: 570—Vol 82: 313, 398—
Vol 84: 328, 446, 894, 966
CHASTAIN.........Vol 46: 335—Vol 75: (9-40)
CHATFIELD....Vol 28: 159—Vol 39: 227—
Vol 43: 605—Vol 46: 246
CHATTERTON....Vol 46: 103—Vol 48: 53—
Vol 56: 174
CHATTLE.........................Vol 31: 55
CHATWIN........................Vol 68: 686
CHAUDEY...........Vol 68: 552—Vol 74: (3-45)
CHAUNCY......................Vol 62: 651
CHEADLE.......................Vol 26: 141
CHEATHAM....Vol 38: 33—Vol 39: 103—Vol
44: 234—Vol 57: 690—Vol 66: 460—Vol 69:
362—Vol 74: (4-52)
CHEATWOOD....Vol 29: 512—Vol 37: 354—
Vol 42: 80—Vol 43: 418, 603—Vol 48: 121
CHEVINGTON..................Vol 68: 289
CHEESEBOROUGH....................Vol 35: 55
CHEETHAM.............Vol 30: 67, 258
CHEEZEN........................Vol 39: 226
CHEGOW...........................Vol 58: 53
CHENAULT...........Vol 57: 353—Vol 70: 455
CHENEWITH.....................Vol 33: 957
CHENEY....Vol 38: 327—Vol 39: 272—Vol 57:
567
CHENOWETH..........Vol 3: 524—Vol 57: 744
CHENOWITH....Vol 31: 52—Vol 32: 634—Vol
44: 232—Vol 58: 109—Vol 64: 308
CHERAWS........................ Vol 32: 717
CHEREVOY...........Vol 45: 239—Vol 70: 876
CHESEBROUGH....Vol 46: 331—Vol 48: 58—
Vol 49: 40—Vol 50: 112
CHESIRE........................Vol 63: 373
CHESLEY......................Vol 70: 877
CHESNEY......................Vol 76: 709
CHESTER......................Vol 79: 560

CHESTNUT............Vol 59: 589—Vol 61: 707
CHETWOOD......................Vol 48: 121
CHEVALIER....Vol 36: 75—Vol 66: 827—Vol
67: 575
CHEVAULT......................Vol 62: 583
CHEVIS.........................Vol 49: 46
CHEW...Vol 30: 147, 336—Vol 53: 572—Vol
54: 230—Vol 61: 382—Vol 79: 113—Vol 81:
316
CHEWNING......................Vol 70: 134
CHEYNEY.......................Vol 71: 557
CHICK..............Vol 27: 380—Vol 49: 286
CHIDESTER........Vol 74: (6-37)—Vol 75: (9-
37)
CHILCOAT......................Vol 84: 327
CHILCUTT......................Vol 74: (5-40)
CHILD....Vol 27: 807—Vol 30: 147, 542—Vol
47: 394—Vol 69: 245
CHILDERS....Vol 72: (8-89)—Vol 73: (4-83)
CHILDRESS....Vol 37: 151, 159—Vol 57: 116,
433, 434, 565—Vol 58: 586—Vol 67: 48
CHILDS....Vol 27: 373—Vol 42: 140—Vol 50:
189—Vol 67: 713—Vol 68: 283—Vol 76: 710
CHILES....Vol 37: 159—Vol 45: 197, 328—Vol
46: 237—Vol 55: 110, 209—Vol 63: 571—Vol
71: 759
CHILSON....Vol 26: 57—Vol 53: 55—Vol 56:
175, 560
CHILTON............Vol 81: 216—Vol 83: 91
CHIPMAN......................Vol 32: 282
CHIPP.........................Vol 73: (9-64)
CHIPS.........................Vol 73: (9-64)
CHISEM........................Vol 58: 174
CHISHOLM....Vol 27: 44—Vol 41: 123—Vol
57: 629—Vol 58: 174—Vol 59: 680—Vol 65:
759—Vol 67: 751
CHISMAN....Vol 44: 149—Vol 56: 43—Vol 57:
744—Vol 69: 244
CHISUM............Vol 65: 759—Vol 67: 751
CHITTENDEN....Vol 24: 459—Vol 42: 334—
Vol 45: 184—Vol 46: 23
CHITWOOD......................Vol 48: 121
CHIVERS.......................Vol 82: 397
CHLOE.........................Vol 82: 501
CHOAT.........................Vol 30: 543
CHOATE....Vol 22: 272—Vol 38: 330—Vol 44:
234, 384—Vol 49: 135
CHOBARD......................Vol 74: (3-45)
COCHRAN.............Vol 59: 761—Vol 84: 706
CHODRICK......................Vol 47: 270
CHRISFIELD....................Vol 64: 714
CHRISLER.............Vol 45: 199, 329
CHRISTESON...................Vol 70: 1265
CHRISTIAN....Vol 37: 149—Vol 41: 31, 209—
Vol 43: 496, 543, 603—Vol 44: 21—Vol 53:
330—Vol 60: 249—Vol 76: 709—Vol 83: 92
CHRISTIE....Vol 28: 546—Vol 35: 1103—Vol
75: (3-41)
CHRISTISON...................Vol 70: 1265
CHRISTMAN....Vol 46: 30—Vol 64: 388
CHRISTMAS...................Vol 26: 336
CHRISTY....Vol 40: 77—Vol 41: 127—Vol 45:
121—Vol 84: 69, 706
CHRYSLER.....................Vol 69: 630
CHRYSTIE......................Vol 5: 571
CHUBB.........................Vol 70: 356
CHUBBUCK......................Vol 48: 60
CHUMLEY......................Vol 57: 176
CHUNN.........................Vol 55: 47
CHURCH....Vol 20: 607—Vol 26: 142—Vol 27:

CLICKENER............Vol 66: 733—Vol 81: 629
CLICKENGER......................Vol 66: 733
CLIFF...Vol 77: 117
CLIFFORD....Vol 46: 388—Vol 55: 338—Vol
56: 318—Vol 60: 699—Vol 68: 487—Vol 82:
314, 936
CLIFTON....Vol 45: 119—Vol 46: 152—Vol
48: 205—Vol 77: 603
CLIMER.................................Vol 71: 1025
CLINE...Vol 47: 196—Vol 57: 353—Vol 58:
501—Vol 80: 154—Vol 84: 702
CLINKENBEARD.........................Vol 34: 540
CLINTON....Vol 9: 501—Vol 25: 968—Vol 26:
140, 141—Vol 27: 44, 808—Vol 28: 161, 363
—Vol 31: 413—Vol 46: 152—Vol 56: 625—
Vol 57: 478—Vol 59: 173—Vol 60: 366, 503,
504—Vol 75: (9-41)
CLOCK....................Vol 45: 28—Vol 48: 306
CLOGSTON............................Vol 27: 670
CLOPTON.................Vol 32: 163—Vol 65: 440
CLORE............................Vol 68: 686
CLOSE...Vol 30: 146—Vol 45: 199—Vol 65:
570—Vol 75: (6-39)
CLOSSON............................... Vol 21: 497
CLOTHIER....Vol 22: 155—Vol 31: 52—Vol
39: 223—Vol 41: 119
CLOUGH....Vol 24: 58—Vol 30: 441—Vol 32:
632—Vol 36: 579—Vol 41: 214—Vol 49: 46
—Vol 76: 400
CLOUTMAN.............................Vol 64: 522
CLOVER.................................Vol 39: 102
CLOWNEY................................Vol 42: 191
CLUGGAGE.............................Vol 30: 440
CLUTCH................................Vol 82: 795
CLUTE....................Vol 46: 335—Vol 57: 566
CLYDE ....Vol 68: 488
CLYMER....Vol 26: 340—Vol 43: 421, 422—
Vol 71: 1025
COAD..................................Vol 53: 244
COALTER.... ....Vol 38: 328
COARD.................................Vol 45: 125
COATE.................................Vol 46: 244
COATES...Vol 38: 35—Vol 39: 20, 101—Vol
40: 78—Vol 48: 306—Vol 53: 181—Vol 56:
372, 482—Vol 57: 689
COATS................Vol 38: 35—Vol 81: 569
COBB....Vol 26: 55—Vol 37: 154, 395—Vol 40:
26—Vol 43: 424, 497, 545, 600—Vol 45: 28—
Vol 46: 22—Vol 47: 392—Vol 49: 285, 356,
391 Vol 55: 443—Vol 57: 214, 311, 434, 687
—Vol 61: 869—Vol 67: 388, 517—Vol 71:
1026, 1027—Vol 74: (7-53), (8-53)—Vol 75:
(2-56)—Vol 81: 216—Vol 82: 935—Vol 83:
943—Vol 84: 632
COBBS..................Vol 67: 117—Vol 74: (1-51)
COBURN .. Vol 36: 352—Vol 60: 506—Vol 67:
713—Vol 70: 55—Vol 83: 522, 523—Vol 84:
247
COCHRAN....Vol 19: 432—Vol 39: 275—Vol
45: 323—Vol 46: 99, 243—Vol 50: 354—Vol
52: 111—Vol 54: 51, 222, 419—Vol 55: 108—
Vol 63: 295—Vol 64: 259—Vol 70: 358—Vol
71: 677, 759—Vol 72: (8-86), (10-95)—Vol
77: 480—Vol 79: 194—Vol 80: 382, 383, 588
—Vol 81: 569—Vol 82: 125—Vol 83: 795—
Vol 84: 69
COCHRANE...Vol 22: 52—Vol 48: 441—Vol
56: 47, 478—Vol 67: 115
COCHRUN............................Vol 84: 706
COCK.. ... . Vol 83: 718

COCKBURN...............................Vol 19: 627
COCKE.... ....Vol 65: 441—Vol 83: 872
COCKERHAM...........................Vol 84: 706
COCKEY..................................Vol 54: 648
COCKINS.......................Vol 62: 54, 389
COCKLEY.................................Vol 48: 65
COCKRELL ....Vol 68: 283
CODDING..............Vol 39: 327—Vol 44: 235
CODDINGTON....Vol 56: 174—Vol 75: (2-58),
(2-60)
CODLING................................Vol 82: 863
CODWIN..............................Vol 48: 450
CODY...................................Vol 59: 388
COE ...Vol 18: 182—Vol 19: 308—Vol 44: 153
—Vol 57: 480, 744, 746—Vol 60: 573, 699—
Vol 61: 63—Vol 64: 159—Vol 65: 571—Vol
66: 365—Vol 67: 716
COENS...................................Vol 71: 163
COES..Vol 38: 218
COEYMANS..............................Vol 27: 891
COFFEE ....Vol 75: (4-54)
COFFEEN................................Vol 63: 699
COFFEY....Vol 34: 659—Vol 36: 574—Vol 38:
275—Vol 45: 197—Vol 46: 237—Vol 58:
702—Vol 59: 312—Vol 62: 308—Vol 63:
635—Vol 75: (4-54)
COFFIN....Vol 15: 347—Vol 43: 427—Vol 45:
23—Vol 52: 435, 685—Vol 56: 371—Vol 63:
699—Vol 64: 385—Vol 68: 554—Vol 82: 653
—Vol 84: 445
COFFINBERRY........Vol 65: 442—Vol 66: 459
COFFMAN........Vol 65: 438—Vol 68: 492—Vol
77: 479
COGER...................................Vol 57: 177
COGGESHALL....Vol 8: 80, 238—Vol 57: 353
COGGSWELL.............................Vol 79: 614
COGHILL.................................Vol 57: 567
COGSWELL ...Vol 22: 375, 679—Vol 48: 450
—Vol 49: 128—Vol 50: 357—Vol 56: 371—
Vol 69: 361
COGSWILL..............................Vol 70: 454
COHOON.................................Vol 60: 366
COINER....Vol 56: 171, 176, 317—Vol 57: 116,
477, 686
COIT....................................Vol 20: 279
COKER..................Vol 54: 421—Vol 64: 713
COLBERT.................................. Vol 64: 259
COLBURN...Vol 42: 169—Vol 44: 152—Vol
75: (10-67)—Vol 76: 61
COLBY....Vol 33: 955—Vol 44: 23—Vol 46: 27
—Vol 48: 446—Vol 54: 710—Vol 65: 763—
Vol 80: 383
COLDWELL...........Vol 31: 414—Vol 83: 717
COLE...Vol 21: 497—Vol 26: 338—Vol 27:
382, 671, 739, 808—Vol 28: 482—Vol 29: 46,
648—Vol 30: 63, 257—Vol 34: 660—Vol 36:
578—Vol 37: 156—Vol 40: 25, 272—Vol 41:
210—Vol 43: 603—Vol 45: 22, 105, 128—
Vol 46: 392—Vol 47: 27—Vol 49: 132—Vol
50: 356—Vol 52: 230—Vol 55: 286, 600, 655,
712, 714—Vol 56: 226, 480, 629—Vol 58:
329, 652—Vol 60: 634—Vol 61: 154—Vol
63: 699—Vol 64: 159—Vol 65: 439, 759—
Vol 66: 56, 121—Vol 67: 515—Vol 70: 133,
207, 1166—Vol 72: (4-83)—Vol 73: (9-64)
—Vol 76: 711—Vol 77: 240, 479
COLEMAN...Vol 22: 375—Vol 27: 737—Vol
29: 512—Vol 33: 1033—Vol 34: 659—Vol
39: 273—Vol 40: 271—Vol 42: 78, 343—Vol
44: 236, 384—Vol 45: 20, 115, 238—Vol 47:

27, 269, 341—Vol 52: 51—Vol 53: 181—Vol
55: 338, 603, 652—Vol 56: 373—Vol 57: 113,
174, 567—Vol 58: 650—Vol 59: 237, 440—
Vol 63: 372—Vol 64: 521—Vol 65: 58, 440—
Vol 67: 647—Vol 69: 362—Vol 70: 207, 577,
1170—Vol 74: (11-56)—Vol 76: 859—Vol
80: 512—Vol 81: 315, 517, 570, 631—Vol 83:
171—Vol 84: 245
COLES...Vol 40: 172
COLGATE.................Vol 37: 353—Vol 38: 113
COLGLAZIER.............................Vol 66: 55
COLGLAZURE.............................Vol 66: 55
COLGROVE.................................Vol 31: 414
COLLARD...Vol 46: 392—Vol 58: 501—Vol
70: 133
COLLIER...Vol 33: 475—Vol 39: 104—Vol
42: 268—Vol 43: 421—Vol 44: 313—Vol 45:
121—Vol 46: 337—Vol 47: 23—Vol 48: 122,
367—Vol 53: 117—Vol 57: 689—Vol 66: 826
—Vol 71: 958—Vol 72: (2-63)—Vol 75:
(2-57), (2-61)—Vol 80: 45—Vol 81: 569—
Vol 84: 444
COLLINGS.................Vol 31: 441—Vol 58: 370
COLLINS...Vol 19: 308—Vol 20: 278—Vol
22: 155—Vol 27: 806—Vol 28: 479—Vol 32:
282—Vol 39: 104, 327—Vol 41: 214—Vol
42: 267—Vol 43: 424, 492, 597—Vol 45:
110, 241—Vol 46: 243, 245—Vol 47: 267,
390—Vol 48: 53, 205—Vol 49: 46, 354—Vol
53: 571—Vol 56: 690—Vol 57: 175, 312—
Vol 60: 116—Vol 63: 635, 742—Vol 64: 389,
650, 715—Vol 68: 551—Vol 69: 58, 245—
Vol 74: (5-43), (12-53)—Vol 75: (10-65)—
Vol 76: 62, 654, 859—Vol 78: 398—Vol 81:
570—Vol 82: 500, 793, 795, 798—Vol 83: 337
—Vol 84: 326
COLLIS...Vol 52: 321
COLLISTER.................................Vol 57: 313
COLLOM...Vol 45: 18
COLLYER.............................Vol 42: 269, 335
COLMAN.......................................Vol 45: 326
COLTER...Vol 36: 758
COLTON...Vol 22: 157—Vol 26: 142—Vol 38:
35—Vol 49: 186—Vol 50: 348
COLVER...Vol 37: 67—Vol 67: 383—Vol 84:
704
COLVERT.......................................Vol 83: 718
COLVILLE.............................Vol 42: 138, 339
COLVIN...Vol 39: 23—Vol 41: 214—Vol 52:
564—Vol 53: 379—Vol 55: 522—Vol 70: 573
—Vol 75: (9-37)
COLWELL...Vol 41: 72—Vol 42: 135, 188—
Vol 64: 157—Vol 84: 702
COLYAR...Vol 48: 122
COLYER...Vol 45: 122, 327—Vol 48: 122—Vol
84: 444
COMBS...Vol 24: 542—Vol 26: 53—Vol 47:
394—Vol 49: 48—Vol 53: 180—Vol 56: 571
—Vol 58: 650—Vol 74. (3-45)—Vol 76: 653
—Vol 83: 522
COMER...Vol 55: 46
COMEGGS...Vol 67: 15, 86, 712—Vol 68: 443,
623
COMFORT...Vol 33: 474—Vol 42: 77—Vol
50: 349, 415—Vol 51: 165, 357—Vol 55: 712
COMINS.......................Vol 33: 959—Vol 66: 121
COMPTESSE.................................Vol 43: 482
COMPTON...Vol 36: 755—Vol 41: 169—Vol
45: 197, 328—Vol 47: 28—Vol 64: 716—Vol
65: 365—Vol 83: 258

COMSTOCK....Vol 29: 45, 800—Vol 30: 539,
543—Vol 36: 353—Vol 38: 113—Vol 41: 67,
72—Vol 45: 18, 189, 198, 329—Vol 46: 153,
330—Vol 50: 355—Vol 67: 712—Vol 69: 360
CONANT....Vol 34: 657—Vol 37: 157, 268—
Vol 45: 21, 116—Vol 47: 22—Vol 82: 499
CONAWAY.................Vol 65: 366—Vol 69: 247
CONDE.........Vol 36: 350, 355—Vol 38: 34, 86
CONDIT.....................Vol 19: 628—Vol 81: 316
CONDUIT.....................................Vol 43: 491
CONE...Vol 26: 339
CONEN...Vol 34: 199
CONER...............................Vol 77: 479, 602
CONERLY...Vol 84: 68
CONEY...Vol 30: 149
CONGDON...Vol 40: 26—Vol 57: 219—Vol
60: 417
CONGER....Vol 36: 756, 760—Vol 37: 265, 266
—Vol 44: 84—Vol 60: 572—Vol 65: 572—
Vol 67: 444—Vol 82: 139
CONGERS.......................................Vol 68: 488
CONINE...Vol 83: 439
CONKEP...Vol 59: 387
CONKEY...Vol 82: 314
CONKLIN...Vol 23: 400—Vol 24: 148—Vol
37: 151—Vol 53: 745—Vol 66: 366—Vol 67:
517, 715—Vol 70: 573, 1017—Vol 77: 538—
Vol 80: 45—Vol 81: 316
CONKLING—Vol 39: 223—Vol 75: (2-60)—
Vol 77: 538
CONLEY.................Vol 42: 342—Vol 74: (1-49)
CONN...................Vol 75: (5-43)—Vol 79: 283
CONNABLE.................Vol 48: 306—Vol 49: 41
CONNARD.......................................Vol 58: 502
CONNELL...Vol 39: 102—Vol 44: 225—Vol
59: 176, 389, 522—Vol 60: 416—Vol 74:
(3-45)—Vol 82: 141—Vol 83: 1014
CONNELLY...Vol 25: 39—Vol 42: 342—Vol
43: 425, 496—Vol 45: 241—Vol 50: 192—
Vol 55: 108
CONNER...Vol 40: 227—Vol 49: 133—Vol 56:
743—Vol 62: 651—Vol 65: 441—Vol 70: 133
—Vol 71: 840—Vol 82: 794, 798
CONNOR....Vol 48: 441—Vol 56: 742—Vol 58:
502—Vol 63: 107—Vol 64: 761—Vol 67:
576—Vol 82: 313
CONOVER....Vol 53: 242—Vol 57: 567—Vol
59: 765—Vol 66: 366—Vol 71: 957
CONOWAY.......................................Vol 25: 39
CONRAD...Vol 24: 58—Vol 38: 330—Vol 44:
312—Vol 54: 591—Vol 61: 522—Vol 64: 758
—Vol 67: 716—Vol 77: 239
CONRO...Vol 70: 1169
CONSILYEA.................................Vol 54: 536
CONSTABLE.................Vol 30: 147, 336
CONSTANT....Vol 34: 540—Vol 68: 283—Vol
69: 56—Vol 82: 797
CONSTIBLE.................................Vol 46: 245
CONTEE................Vol 45: 195—Vol 46: 101
CONTER...Vol 43: 601
CONVER................Vol 54: 591—Vol 55: 108
CONVERSE...Vol 21: 404—Vol 22: 373, 678
—Vol 24: 542—Vol 26: 52, 53, 338—Vol 27:
671—Vol 30: 148—Vol 41: 73—Vol 44: 79—
Vol 52: 321
CONWAY...Vol 26: 559—Vol 27: 737—Vol
41: 29, 32—Vol 50: 194—Vol 53: 447—Vol
61: 382—Vol 67: 713—Vol 68: 373—Vol 76:
581
CONWELL....Vol 25: 799—Vol 45: 119—Vol

46: 159, 392—Vol 66: 599—Vol 68: 488—
Vol 69: 159—Vol 74: (7-52), (8-52)—Vol
82: 797—Vol 84: 247
CONYERS....Vol 44: 316—Vol 45: 236—Vol
46: 99—Vol 69: 158
COOGER............Vol 57: 177
COOK....Vol 19: 433—Vol 23: 399—Vol 25:
383—Vol 27: 380—Vol 28: 479—Vol 29:
45, 286—Vol 31: 414—Vol 32: 162, 718—Vol
33: 41—Vol 41: 126, 127, 210—Vol 42: 192,
268—Vol 43: 546, 598, 599—Vol 44: 24, 312
—Vol 45: 122, 189, 194, 241—Vol 46: 28,
153—Vol 49: 123, 131, 134, 136, 355—Vol 50:
190—Vol 53: 176, 631—Vol 55: 47, 714—
Vol 56: 177, 371, 373, 628—Vol 58: 587—
Vol 59: 588, 680—Vol 61: 707—Vol 64: 713
—Vol 66: 730, 733—Vol 68: 491—Vol 69:
120—Vol 70: 454—Vol 72: (9-88)—Vol 73:
(1-63)—Vol 74: (4-50)—Vol 77: 480—Vol
79: 113—Vol 80: 84—Vol 82: 727—Vol 83:
872—Vol 84: 702, 894, 964
COOKE....Vol 22: 270—Vol 26: 241, 561—
Vol 27: 737—Vol 30: 538—Vol 43: 423—
Vol 48: 64—Vol 53: 747—Vol 54: 648—Vol
57: 219, 745—Vol 59: 175, 441—Vol 61: 452,
868—Vol 66: 538—Vol 67: 148, 751—Vol
68: 683—Vol 69: 363—Vol 79: 467—Vol
80: 46—Vol 83: 91
COOKER............Vol 70: 1169
COOKSON............Vol 27: 670
COOLBAUGH............Vol 42: 77
COOLEY....Vol 39: 223—Vol 41: 164—Vol 42:
134—Vol 48: 372—Vol 52: 485—Vol 58: 500
—Vol 60: 572—Vol 65: 365—Vol 71: 86
COOLIDGE....Vol 56: 688—Vol 82: 501—Vol
84: 158
COOLING............Vol 43: 491
COOMBES............Vol 27: 738
COOMBS....Vol 27: 382—Vol 75: (11-68), (11-
69)
COOMES............Vol 53: 493
COON....Vol 22: 271—Vol 41: 215—Vol 42:
139—Vol 45: 322—Vol 48: 450—Vol 56: 227
—Vol 65: 437—Vol 69: 629—Vol 71: 87,
164, 357, 461—Vol 73: (11-65)—Vol 74:
(5-38), (11-57)—Vol 81: 315, 517
COONRADT............Vol 45: 113
COONTZ............Vol 65: 758
COOPER....Vol 20: 62—Vol 26: 143, 338—Vol
27: 46, 669—Vol 28: 164—Vol 29: 512—Vol
30: 256—Vol 32: 719—Vol 33: 957—Vol 34:
65—Vol 35: 654—Vol 37: 156—Vol 38: 35,
87—Vol 39: 102, 327—Vol 42: 16—Vol 43:
422—Vol 44: 154, 311—Vol 45: 112—Vol
46: 335—Vol 47: 194, 197, 388—Vol 48: 59,
369, 370—Vol 49: 394—Vol 52: 173—Vol
53: 744—Vol 54: 224, 225, 465, 649—Vol 55:
285, 445—Vol 56: 480—Vol 58: 451—Vol
59: 588—Vol 60: 51, 115—Vol 62: 648—Vol
63: 105—Vol 65: 762—Vol 66: 121, 249, 308
—Vol 67: 44, 146, 147, 385—Vol 68: 492—
Vol 69: 58—Vol 70: 1171—Vol 71: 672, 761,
1111—Vol 73: (9-68)—Vol 74: (1-51)—Vol
76: 144—Vol 83: 439—Vol 84: 68
COOPWOOD............Vol 38: 274
COOR............Vol 46: 154
COOTES............Vol 58: 763
COPAS............Vol 76: 860
COPE............Vol 78: 650—Vol 79: 112, 613
COPELAND....Vol 22: 156—Vol 42: 336—Vol

56: 561—Vol 57: 176, 565—Vol 70: 877—
Vol 77: 539—Vol 80: 85—Vol 82: 398
COPEMAN............Vol 62: 501
COPENGERM............Vol 67: 387
COPHER............Vol 47: 193
COPLEY............Vol 39: 274—Vol 82: 931
COPP....Vol 39: 225—Vol 40: 23—Vol 45: 116
COPPAGE............Vol 68: 243
COPPEDGE............Vol 37: 68
COPPENROLL............Vol 38: 221
COPPOCK............Vol 78: 600
CORAS............Vol 84: 325
CORBET............Vol 39: 102
CORBIN....Vol 19: 432—Vol 43: 423—Vol 61:
611—Vol 77: 52—Vol 84: 966
CORBIT............Vol 55: 521
CORBITT....Vol 54: 709—Vol 55: 47—Vol 82:
396
CORBYN............Vol 45: 101
CORDELL....Vol 49: 355, 393—Vol 54: 310—
Vol 68: 686
CORDNER............Vol 58: 111
COREY............Vol 33: 957
CORLESS............Vol 29: 647—Vol 34: 658
CORLISS....Vol 24: 458—Vol 32: 61—Vol 44:
79—Vol 59: 49
CORMICK............Vol 47: 394
CORN............Vol 54: 352—Vol 74: (2-40)
CORNEL............Vol 81: 20
CORNELISON............Vol 43: 491
CORNELIUS....Vol 40: 25—Vol 43: 481—Vol
76: 219—Vol 77: 479—Vol 83: 335, 1014
CORNELL....Vol 25: 38—Vol 29: 287—Vol 32:
718—Vol 39: 143, 224—Vol 45: 128—Vol
63: 427—Vol 84: 704
CORNICK............Vol 48: 201
CORNING............Vol 22: 268
CORNISH............Vol 50: 65, 115—Vol 55: 519
CORNS............Vol 84: 706
CORNWALL....Vol 22: 50—Vol 41: 31—Vol
54: 464—Vol 58: 370—Vol 65: 122—Vol 66:
251
CORNWALLIS............Vol 75: (2-59)
CORNWELL....Vol 28: 60, 260—Vol 46: 242—
Vol 49: 396—Vol 64: 757, 758—Vol 69: 160
—Vol 71: 240—Vol 76: 861—Vol 82: 933
CORPE............Vol 71: 161
CORRELL............Vol 45: 18
CORSE............Vol 52: 356—Vol 74: (2-41)
CORSNITZ............Vol 74: (5-40)
CORSON....Vol 29: 44—Vol 65: 124—Vol 75:
(6-37)
CORTELYOU............Vol 68: 443
CORTRIGHT....Vol 73: (11-66), (11-69)—Vol
74: (3-44)
CORWIN............Vol 82: 726—Vol 83: 335
CORY....Vol 47: 266—Vol 50: 191—Vol 73:
(7-70)
CORYELL............Vol 33: 708
COSART....Vol 22: 54, 271—Vol 24: 55—Vol
31: 860
COSBY....Vol 27: 672—Vol 64: 761—Vol 65:
159—Vol 68: 626—Vol 70: 55
COSS............Vol 58: 650
COSSART............Vol 31: 860—Vol 66: 307, 602
COSSEN............Vol 53: 241
COST............Vol 67: 711
COSTON....Vol 54: 308—Vol 75: (10-66)
COTERALL............Vol 42: 81
COTES............Vol 53: 634

CRUTCHER....Vol 43: 427—Vol 44: 232—Vol 45: 185
CRUTCHFIELD............Vol 43: 603—Vol 74: (4-50)
CRUTE............Vol 56: 47
CRUTHERS............Vol 84: 324
CRUZEN....Vol 43: 423, 483—Vol 44: 148—Vol 45: 242—Vol 46: 21
CRYDER............Vol 40: 228
CRYER............Vol 45: 104—Vol 67: 45
CRYMES............Vol 76: 710
CUBBERLY............Vol 59: 48—Vol 64: 713
CUDDEBACK............Vol 83: 522
CUDWORTH............Vol 23: 399
CULBER............Vol 67: 145
CULBERTSON............Vol 36: 216, 349
CULBREATH............Vol 39: 23
CULLUM............Vol 75: (10-64)
CULP............Vol 45: 196, 328—Vol 51: 355
CULPEPER............Vol 36: 355—Vol 53: 448
CULPEPPER....Vol 35: 1100—Vol 56: 176—Vol 80: 507
CULVER....Vol 22: 680—Vol 31: 586—Vol 33: 476—Vol 37: 67—Vol 49: 134—Vol 61: 66—Vol 67: 48—Vol 76: 709—Vol 77: 539—Vol 79: 332
CUMMING............Vol 54: 228
CUMMINGS....Vol 22: 372—Vol 30: 257—Vol 36: 356—Vol 37: 154—Vol 40: 275—Vol 41: 66, 119—Vol 43: 602—Vol 44: 79—Vol 46: 100, 102—Vol 50: 63, 349—Vol 53: 246—Vol 54: 589—Vol 55: 285—Vol 56: 562—Vol 59: 237—Vol 63: 507—Vol 66: 121—Vol 71: 957—Vol 79: 368—Vol 80: 45
CUMMINS....Vol 21: 403—Vol 40: 25—Vol 47: 395—Vol 60: 115—Vol 73: (7-70)—Vol 80: 511
CUNNARD............Vol 59: 238
CUNNING............Vol 63: 508
CUNNINGHAM....Vol 28: 548—Vol 32: 633—Vol 39: 223—Vol 43: 602—Vol 44: 81—Vol 47: 341—Vol 48: 203, 444—Vol 49: 131—Vol 53: 447—Vol 56: 174, 628—Vol 57: 214, 746—Vol 59: 763—Vol 60: 248—Vol 62: 307—Vol 63: 246, 428—Vol 64: 308—Vol 65: 442—Vol 83: 262
CUPP............Vol 56: 482, 744
CURL....Vol 41: 164—Vol 56: 177—Vol 66: 461, 731
CURRIE............Vol 36: 215
CURRIER....Vol 28: 262, 364—Vol 34: 322—Vol 82: 312
CURRY....Vol 1: 450—Vol 45: 119—Vol 56: 46—Vol 57: 481—Vol 58: 172, 648—Vol 59: 764—Vol 84: 634
CURTICE............Vol 65: 635, 760
CURTIN............Vol 32: 163
CURTIS....Vol 25: 384—Vol 26: 562—Vol 28: 261—Vol 33: 476—Vol 36: 216, 579, 762—Vol 38: 35—Vol 41: 70, 128—Vol 42: 191—Vol 43: 493, 496—Vol 44: 314—Vol 46: 239, 332—Vol 49: 187, 190—Vol 50: 60—Vol 53: 330, 692—Vol 55: 600—Vol 56: 626, 745—Vol 59: 173—Vol 60: 248—Vol 64: 758—Vol 65: 366, 760—Vol 67: 574, 715—Vol 68: 627—Vol 71: 86—Vol 73: (9-63), (11-68), (11-69)—Vol 75: (10-65)—Vol 79: 613—Vol 80: 557—Vol 82: 314
CURTISS....Vol 31: 860—Vol 38: 86—Vol 48:

308—Vol 56: 560, 740—Vol 57: 311—Vol 63: 295
CURTIX............Vol 70: 1266, 1267
CUSHING....Vol 32: 284—Vol 44: 79, 151—Vol 52: 626—Vol 82: 727
CUSHMAN—Vol 27: 383—Vol 33: 709—Vol 36: 254—Vol 37: 74, 350—Vol 45: 327—Vol 47: 395—Vol 48: 201—Vol 57: 567—Vol 70: 710
CUSTER....Vol 25: 799—Vol 54: 420—Vol 56: 318—Vol 59: 237, 522—Vol 67: 576—Vol 79: 332—Vol 83: 93
CUTHBERT............Vol 82: 797—Vol 83: 628
CUSTIS............Vol 49: 350
CUTLER............Vol 61: 698—Vol 84: 632
CUTTER....Vol 22: 54, 155, 271—Vol 24: 55—Vol 37: 70—Vol 46: 159
CUTTING....Vol 41: 125—Vol 44: 28—Vol 46: 239, 240—Vol 57: 566
CUTTS....Vol 27: 738—Vol 29: 286—Vol 37: 269, 271
CYPRET............Vol 58: 699

                                       D

DABNEY....Vol 30: 540—Vol 32: 507—Vol 33: 473—Vol 43: 596, 602—Vol 44: 81—Vol 45: 235—Vol 58: 453—Vol 60: 245, 744, 745—Vol 66: 159—Vol 67: 292—Vol 75: (2-61)—Vol 78: 246—Vol 79: 194
DABY............Vol 56: 479
DACARAY............Vol 33: 956
DACUS............Vol 33: 957
DADE....Vol 20: 278—Vol 53: 632—Vol 62: 388—Vol 68: 243
DAFFELL............Vol 21: 250
DAGGART............Vol 81: 571
DAGGETT....Vol 38: 221—Vol 63: 373—Vol 70: 1265
DAGUE............Vol 82: 141
DAILEY....Vol 26: 560—Vol 60: 419—Vol 71: 676—Vol 76: 310
DAILY............Vol 39: 103—Vol 54: 109
DAKIN....Vol 68: 491—Vol 69: 432—Vol 81: 264
DALE....Vol 32: 59—Vol 44: 230—Vol 45: 115—Vol 47: 95—Vol 57: 216—Vol 58: 112—Vol 64: 714—Vol 65: 517—Vol 67: 443—Vol 68: 626, 735—Vol 71: 356—Vol 73: (12-63)—Vol 75: (9-41)—Vol 79: 518—Vol 81: 431
DALLAS............Vol 45: 28—Vol 58: 451
DALLING............Vol 43: 599
DALLY............Vol 61: 787
DALRYMPLE....Vol 39: 273—Vol 47: 27—Vol 65: 297
DALTON....Vol 32: 633—Vol 42: 77—Vol 43: 596—Vol 44: 25, 310—Vol 70: 1169—Vol 77: 241
DALYRMPLE............Vol 45: 104
DAMERON....Vol 73: (10-76)—Vol 84: 521
DAMON....Vol 42: 266—Vol 46: 23—Vol 47: 87, 197, 265—Vol 52: 434—Vol 53: 690—Vol 54: 308—Vol 55: 446, 602—Vol 70: 708
DANA............Vol 71: 842
DANALAY............Vol 58: 328
DANCE....Vol 43: 603—Vol 44: 316—Vol 45: 195, 236, 328
DANDLEY............Vol 58: 328
DANDRIDGE....Vol 42: 192—Vol 43: 495, 544—Vol 49: 35, 190—Vol 56: 626—Vol 62: 502—Vol 76: 144

DANELS_____Vol 82: 575
DANFORTH____Vol 2: 189, 527—Vol 31: 586—
Vol 43: 424, 540, 597—Vol 44: 148—Vol 48:
371—Vol 57: 628—Vol 74: (2-43)
DANGERFIELD__Vol 38: 331—Vol 83: 717
Vol 84: 70
DANIEL__Vol 28: 163, 548—Vol 39: 223—
Vol 42: 270—Vol 43: 422, 546, 603—Vol 45:
120, 198, 323—Vol 48: 449—Vol 49: 130,
191—Vol 56: 45—Vol 61: 781—Vol 62:
159, 648, 774—Vol 63: 293—Vol 71: 466
DANIELL_____Vol 63: 107
DANIELLE_____Vol 63: 293
DANIELS__Vol 38: 276—Vol 44: 85, 235—
Vol 54: 286—Vol 57: 174, 371—Vol 59: 48—
Vol 61: 707—Vol 63: 508—Vol 71: 760
DANISON_____Vol 55: 339
DANLEY_____Vol 58: 328
DANLY_____Vol 58: 328
DANN_____Vol 59: 652
DANNER_____Vol 71: 1028
DANNITTE_____Vol 43: 494
DARBIE_____Vol 65: 440
DARBY__Vol 43: 423, 483—Vol 46: 153—Vol
54: 54—Vol 63: 633—Vol 64: 156, 587—
Vol 83: 1014
DARBYSHIRE_____Vol 36: 76
DARDEN_____Vol 56: 175
DARLEY_____Vol 43: 546
DARLING__Vol 34: 322—Vol 43: 491, 542—
Vol 54: 591—Vol 56: 479
DARLINGTON__Vol 46: 386—Vol 49: 129,
146
d'ARMAND_____Vol 70: 577
DARNALL__Vol 60: 698—Vol 67: 386—Vol
81: 569
DARNE _____Vol 65: 759
DARNELL_____Vol 55: 519—Vol 67: 386
DARNER_____Vol 57: 745
DARNLEY_____Vol 58: 328
DARR_____Vol 54: 225—Vol 76: 62, 581
DARRAH__Vol 44: 28—Vol 56: 629—Vol 72:
(7-75)
DARROW__Vol 18: 299—Vol 21: 59—Vol 26:
141, 337, 560—Vol 40: 225, 228—Vol 68:
285—Vol 69: 57—Vol 72: (7-75)
DART__Vol 26: 241—Vol 38: 220—Vol 43:
601
DARWIN_____Vol 22: 997—Vol 35: 1265
DASHER_____Vol 36: 578
DASKAM_____Vol 65: 441
DATON_____Vol 64: 258
D' AUBIN_____Vol 56: 319
DAUBIN_____Vol 56: 319
DAUGERRE_____Vol 50: 62, 277
DAUGHERTY__Vol 37: 74—Vol 39: 274—
Vol 43: 602—Vol 67: 293—Vol 68: 242—
Vol 69: 564—Vol 70: 56—Vol 71: 1025
DAVENPORT__Vol 21: 252, 497—Vol 22:
374—Vol 29: 650—Vol 30: 257—Vol 43:
603—Vol 44: 231, 316, 383—Vol 45: 119—
Vol 46: 152—Vol 48: 61—Vol 54: 174—
Vol 55: 599, 711—Vol 56: 412, 687—Vol
57: 219—Vol 58: 174—Vol 63: 699—Vol 64:
588—Vol 65: 298, 763—Vol 66: 733—Vol
67: 44, 46, 750—Vol 68: 156—Vol 73: (9-66)
—Vol 76: 580—Vol 78: 696—Vol 81: 71—
Vol 83: 1014
DAVEY_____Vol 75: (6-40)
DAVID__Vol 32: 505—Vol 38: 33—Vol 43:

427, 484—Vol 62: 307, 503—Vol 63: 106,
742—Vol 70: 206, 706, 879—Vol 73: (4-83)
—-Vol 84: 68
DAVIDS_____Vol 47: 267
DAVIDSON__Vol 38: 273—Vol 39: 103—Vol
40: 271, 275—Vol 41: 29—Vol 44: 82, 227—
Vol 45: 125, 242—Vol 46: 242, 387—Vol 50:
561—Vol 52: 561—Vol 53: 630—Vol 54: 536
—Vol 55: 107, 522, 597—Vol 56: 111, 372—
Vol 59: 765—Vol 60: 419—Vol 61: 382, 470
—Vol 71: 673—Vol 73: (2-64)—Vol 74:
(2-41)—Vol 75: (2-57)—Vol 76: 219—Vol
82: 314, 499, 500, 574
DAVIES__Vol 26: 561—Vol 66: 54, 160, 461—
Vol 84: 965
DAVIS__Vol 10: 184—Vol 19: 434—Vol 20:
608, 1063, 1064—Vol 21: 250—Vol 22: 54,
375—Vol 23: 62, 169, 401—Vol 24: 262, 543
—Vol 25: 382, 717—Vol 26: 55—Vol 27:
671, 737—Vol 28: 159—Vol 29: 512, 647—
Vol 30: 66—Vol 31: 55, 414, 586, 862—Vol
32: 283, 718—Vol 34: 659, 660—Vol 35: 58,
1264—Vol 36: 217, 218—Vol 37: 269—Vol
38: 330—Vol 39: 102, 226—Vol 40: 75, 227
—Vol 41: 72, 122, 124—Vol 42: 76, 191, 192,
193, 265, 340—Vol 43: 420, 423, 489, 490,
494, 497, 543, 600, 603—Vol 44: 24, 149, 312,
313, 388—Vol 45: 18, 23, 100, 107, 110, 119,
129, 190, 240, 327, 329—Vol 46: 99, 246, 330,
334, 385, 392—Vol 47: 32, 84, 196, 268, 271
—Vol 48: 61, 119, 123, 448—Vol 49:
136, 188, 279, 281—Vol 50: 62, 66, 192, 185—
Vol 52: 52, 360—Vol 53: 53, 177, 179, 329,
746—Vol 54: 354, 535, 648, 709—Vol 55:
444, 445, 598—Vol 56: 176, 626, 629, 688,
689, 745, 746—Vol 57: 217, 311, 351, 352,
691, 744—Vol 58: 51, 328, 450, 453, 587, 761
—Vol 59: 237, 238, 764, 765—Vol 61: 471,
552, 869—Vol 62: 308, 459, 587—Vol 63:
245, 293, 373, 424, 508—Vol 64: 307, 389,
520, 587, 712, 757, 761—Vol 65: 245, 298,
438, 759—Vol 67: 118, 712, 714, 756—Vol
68: 122, 155, 488, 489, 551, 733—Vol 69: 57,
121, 630—Vol 70: 1169—Vol 71: 86, 357,
460, 1026—Vol 72: (4-83), (6-79)—Vol 73:
(2-65), (2-66), (7-70), (8-82), (9-64), (9-
66), (9-68), (11-69)—Vol 74: (4-49)—Vol
75: (6-39), (6-40), (10-65)—Vol 76: 400,
653, 654, 709, 859—Vol 77: 241, 242, 332,
480—Vol 78: 53, 295, 600, 650—Vol 79: 194,
613—Vol 80: 84, 511, 587, 656—Vol 81: 71—
Vol 82: 797, 500—Vol 83: 93, 172, 336, 440,
521, 524—Vol 84: 632, 965
DAVISON__Vol 24: 54—Vol 44: 81—Vol 46:
386—Vol 67: 48—Vol 79: 332
DAVISSON__Vol 33: 708—Vol 41: 164—Vol
61: 158, 277
DAWES—Vol 11: 317—Vol 31: 749—Vol 36:
579
DAWKINS_____Vol 67: 576
DAWSON__Vol 33: 1031—Vol 37: 66—Vol
41: 35, 127—Vol 43: 496, 543, 603, 723—Vol
44: 235—Vol 45: 22, 189—Vol 46: 246—Vol
47: 27, 95—Vol 49: 354—Vol 50: 63, 185,
345, 348—Vol 52: 52, 173, 357—Vol 57: 309,
351—Vol 59: 653—Vol 60: 417, 572—Vol
63: 427—Vol 64: 159, 760—Vol 65: 246—
Vol 66: 54—Vol 67: 45—Vol 68: 735—Vol
73: (3-86), (12-63)—Vol 74: (11-59)—Vol

75: (5-46)—Vol 76: 480—Vol 80: 44—Vol 84: 326

DAY...Vol 3: 686—Vol 6: 599—Vol 20: 279— Vol 21: 61—Vol 30: 334—Vol 34: 660—Vol 36: 579—Vol 40: 227, 228—Vol 43: 600, 605 Vol '45: 199—Vol 49: 136—Vol 57: 480— Vol 58: 53—Vol 59: 388, 442, 764—Vol 62: 503—Vol 64: 258, 446—Vol 66: 160—Vol 68: 488—Vol 69: 564—Vol 70: 1018, 1165 —Vol 72: (9-88)—Vol 77: 768—Vol 78: 650 —Vol 80: 84—Vol 82: 654

DAYFOOT_____Vol 40: 171, 251
DAYTON...Vol 56: 177—Vol 64: 258—Vol 75: (5-45)—Vol 80: 657
DEADERICK_____Vol 56: 743
DEAKE_____ Vol 25: 968—Vol 57: 690
DEAKINS...Vol 38: 221—Vol 61: 231, 606— Vol 80: 45
DEAL...Vol 47: 32—Vol 56: 227—Vol 60: 116, 506—Vol 84: 247
DEALE_____Vol 60: 116, 506
DEAMER_____Vol 50: 62
DEAN...Vol 22: 272—Vol 25: 718—Vol 26: 53—Vol 27: 671—Vol 35: 1038—Vol 36: 214—Vol 42: 192—Vol 45: 114—Vol 46: 389—Vol 50: 64—Vol 51: 301, 303, 433— Vol 57: 113, 561, 566—Vol 60: 572—Vol 63: 427, 699—Vol 67: 751—Vol 68: 552— Vol 69: 361—Vol 70: 877, 1266—Vol 82: 501—Vol 83: 261, 522—Vol 84: 324
DEANE_____Vol 52: 358—Vol 65: 299
DEARBORN...Vol 28: 364—Vol 44: 315—Vol 45: 114
DEARDORFF_____Vol 48: 61
DEARING_____ _____Vol 28: 161—Vol 83: 171
DE ARMOND_____ ____Vol 70: 577
DEARTH_____Vol 48: 446
DEAVER_____Vol 46: 392
DEBARD_____Vol 71: 239
DE BAUM_____Vol 30: 540
DE BELL_____Vol 68: 625
DE BERNIERE _____Vol 46: 332
DE BERRY_____Vol 41: 122
DEBERVOORT_____Vol 34: 538
DE BOLT_____Vol 75: (10-65)
DE BREVOORT_____Vol 45: 25
DEBUSK_____Vol 81: 570
DE CAMP...Vol 18: 181—Vol 37: 153—Vol 38: 329
DECHERT_____Vol 65: 758
DECKER...Vol 19: 433—Vol 26: 340—Vol 43: 423—Vol 45: 189, 196—Vol 49: 191—Vol 54: 590—Vol 58: 327—Vol 73: (11-69)— Vol 74: (2-41)—Vol 80: 191, 277, 382—Vol 81: 570—Vol 83: 258
DE COSTA_____ ____Vol 80: 656—Vol 84: 68
DECOSTER_____Vol 80: 656
DE COSTON_____Vol 54: 173, 468
DE COURCEY_____Vol 78: 457
DE DUZETTE_____Vol 57: 313
DEEDS_____Vol 64: 444
DEEM_____Vol 82: 314
DEENIS_____Vol 65: 571—Vol 67: 716
DEENMARKEN_____Vol 69: 435
DEERING_____Vol 82: 396
DEETZ_____Vol 59: 441
DEFENPOORT_____Vol 68: 156
DEFFENBAUGH_____Vol 55: 599
DE FOE_____Vol 65: 367
DE FONVILLE_____Vol 31: 752

DE FOOR_____Vol 65: 247
DE FORD_____Vol 60: 697
DE FOREST_____Vol 79: 113
DEFORREST_____Vol 47: 273
DE FRANCE_____Vol 67: 752
DE GRAFF...Vol 13: 612—Vol 45: 110—Vol 46: 236
DE GRAFFENREID...Vol 41: 121, 127—Vol 56: 482
DEGRAW_____Vol 27: 808
DE GROOT_____Vol 67: 148—Vol 70: 55
DE HAAS_____Vol 58: 369
DE HAES_____Vol 58: 369
DE HART_____Vol 57: 311—Vol 82: 501
DE HAVEN...Vol 39: 143—Vol 40: 24. 25, 108 —Vol 41: 69, 72—Vol 71: 1110
DE HOFFEN_____Vol 39: 143
DE HOOGEN_____Vol 84: 69
DEIGHTON_____Vol 64: 258
DEITZ_____Vol 56: 315
DEKLE _____Vol 81: 518
DE LA HUNTE_____Vol 30: 260—Vol 49: 43
DELAMAR_____Vol 63: 293
DE LA MATER_____ Vol 45: 329—Vol 47: 281
DE LANCY_____Vol 60: 50
DELANEY...Vol 45: 237—Vol 48: 63—Vol 75: (2-60)
DE LANNOY_____Vol 30: 538
DELANO...Vol 30: 538—Vol 45: 104, 238— Vol 56: 372, 559, 691—Vol 57: 37, 432—Vol 58: 368, 647—Vol 61: 552—Vol 62: 309— Vol 63: 168
DE LANOY_____Vol 44: 150
DE LA NOYE_____Vol 30: 538
DELAPLAINE_____ Vol 59: 682—Vol 84: 326
DE LA VERNE_____Vol 69: 630
DELBAUGH_____Vol 44: 383
DE LIVE_____Vol 71: 675
DELL_____Vol 52: 359—Vol 61: 869
DELLENOY_____Vol 56: 176
DELLINGER_____Vol 48: 444
DE LOACH_____Vol 83: 947
DE LONG...Vol 34: 538—Vol 37: 148—Vol 49: 188, 354—Vol 59: 440
DELONG_____Vol 59: 314
DE MARLL_____Vol 66: 120
DEMAREE_____Vol 66: 120—Vol 84: 704
DEMAREST...Vol 39: 143—Vol 46: 391—Vol 47: 87—Vol 53: 572—Vol 66: 120
DE MASTERS_____Vol 81: 429
DEMENT_____Vol 46: 101
DE MILT_____Vol 43: 602
DEMING...Vol 22: 154, 268—Vol 28: 482— Vol 66: 536—Vol 74: (6-37)—Vol 82: 575
DEMMING_____Vol 29: 44
DEMMON_____Vol 66: 537
DEMON_____Vol 47: 197
DEMOOILE_____Vol 48: 123
DE MOSS_____Vol 82: 501
DE MOTT_____Vol 81: 517
DEMOTT_____Vol 82: 63
DEMPCY_____Vol 45: 128
DEMPEY_____Vol 46: 101
DEMPSEY_____Vol 71: 88—Vol 80: 46
DEMPSIE_____Vol 61: 704
DENBO_____ ____Vol 68: 733
DENBY_____Vol 79: 518
DENHAM...Vol 30: 146—Vol 45: 194, 328— Vol 50: 193
DENIG_____ ____Vol 53: 571

DENIER_____Vol 63: 102
DENIO___Vol 43: 418—Vol 47: 391—Vol 81: 518
DENISON___Vol 29: 649—Vol 37: 396—Vol 54: 53—Vol 63: 167—Vol 67: 145—Vol 68: 734
DENISTOWN_____Vol 80: 45
DENMAN___Vol 45: 196—Vol 50: 62—Vol 77: 242
DENMARK_____Vol 53: 447
DENNIE_____Vol 5: 576
DENNING_____Vol 13: 605
DENNIS___Vol 27: 383—Vol 30: 339—Vol 31: 749—Vol 32: 161—Vol 43: 603—Vol 49: 395—Vol 66: 365—Vol 75: (2-61)—Vol 76: 653—Vol 77: 117, 333—Vol 78: 295, 554—Vol 79: 283—Vol 80: 277
DENNISON___Vol 31: 51—Vol 33: 41—Vol 48: 122—Vol 53: 745—Vol 54: 52—Vol 55: 712—Vol 62: 715—Vol 68: 734
DENNISTON___Vol 26: 141—Vol 27: 808—Vol 28: 363—Vol 39: 326
DENNY_____Vol 24: 457—Vol 49: 43, 44
DENSLOW___Vol 23: 325—Vol 25: 381—Vol 40: 78
DENT___Vol 41: 32—Vol 42: 79—Vol 48: 122 —Vol 54: 588—Vol 64: 523, 713—Vol 65: 367, 758—Vol 66: 252—Vol 73: (11-66)— Vol 74: (11-56)—Vol 84: 68
DENTON___Vol 33: 43, 706—Vol 49: 190— Vol 50: 349—Vol 51: 303—Vol 53: 180— Vol 58: 702
DEPEW___Vol 25: 798—Vol 32: 284—Vol 45: 106
DePEYSTER_____Vol 3: 683
DEPOY_____Vol 61: 865—Vol 69: 361
DEPRESS_____Vol 67: 577
DE PRIEST_____Vol 67: 577
DE PUE_____Vol 71: 164
DE PUY_____Vol 42: 16, 264
DERBY_____Vol 23: 64—Vol 67: 45
DE REMER_____Vol 40: 76
DERINGER_____Vol 68: 492
DERMOTT_____Vol 61: 470
DEROCHBRUNE_____Vol 61: 470
DE ROCHE_____Vol 37: 69
DERR_____Vol 83: 628
DERRIN_____Vol 73: (11-68)
DERRY_____Vol 61: 784
DERWENT_____Vol 58: 701
DE SALSMAN_____Vol 33: 476
DE SALTZMAN_____Vol 33: 476
DE SAUSSURE_____Vol 48: 205—Vol 49: 280
DESHA_____Vol 1: 450
DESHAW_____Vol 36: 578
DE SHAY_____Vol 82: 501
DE SHAZO_____Vol 72: (1-66)
DESHLER_____Vol 50: 355
DE SILLE_____Vol 26: 559
DE SILVER_____Vol 36: 353
DE TAR_____Vol 79: 518
DE TAU_____Vol 63: 507
DE TAY_____Vol 63: 507
DETRICH_____Vol 83: 874
DETRICK_____Vol 64: 158
DETTOR_____Vol 47: 195
DEUEL_____Vol 70: 1169
DEUYSE_____Vol 26: 244
DEVANE_____Vol 64: 385
DEVANEY_____Vol 66: 827

DE VAUCNE_____Vol 59: 239
DEVAULT_____Vol 76: 61
DEVEAU_____Vol 29: 287
DE VEAUX_____Vol 61: 152—Vol 67: 384
DEVER_____Vol 83: 872, 946
DE VERE_____Vol 65: 572
DEVEREAUX_____Vol 71: 674
DE VINNE_____Vol 54: 464
DEVINS_____Vol 56: 318
DEVIT_____Vol 32: 163
De VLAMING_____Vol 79: 369
DE VOE___Vol 29: 652, 800—Vol 30: 438
DEVOL_____Vol 42: 79—Vol 72: (4-83)
DEVORE___Vol 59: 237—Vol 70: 1267—Vol 83: 946
DE VOTIE_____Vol 19: 70
DEVOTION_____Vol 29: 649
DEVOUR_____Vol 70: 1267
DEW___Vol 66: 55, 828—Vol 67: 444—Vol 77: 389—Vol 79: 193
DEWEES_____Vol 39: 142—Vol 46: 153
DEWEL_____Vol 43: 486
DEWESE_____Vol 64: 388
DEWEY___Vol 21: 403—Vol 29: 289—Vol 37: 150—Vol 44: 236—Vol 45: 101—Vol 49: 41, 287, 393—Vol 58: 649—Vol 65: 299—Vol 69: 119
DE WISNER_____Vol 53: 492
DEWIT_____Vol 58: 451
DEWITT_____Vol 31: 413
DE WITT___Vol 50: 348—Vol 60: 572—Vol 64: 387
DE WOLF___Vol 43: 599—Vol 74: (11-61)— Vol 77: 481
DEXTER___Vol 29: 800—Vol 45: 22, 23—Vol 46: 389—Vol 58: 588—Vol 71: 161—Vol 75: (1-54)
DEY_____Vol 75: (6-40)
DEYERLE_____Vol 34: 659
DEYGERT_____Vol 46: 335—Vol 53: 329
DEYO___Vol 56: 628—Vol 57: 351—Vol 83: 439
DEZARN_____Vol 82: 500
DIAH_____Vol 56: 690
DIAL_____Vol 58: 173
DIAMONT_____Vol 49: 44
DIBBLE___Vol 25: 717—Vol 41: 32—Vol 44: 233—Vol 64: 587—Vol 66: 824
DICE_____Vol 58: 331—Vol 63: 59
DICH_____Vol 30: 64, 65
DICK_____Vol 58: 331—Vol 61: 65, 470
DICKENS_____Vol 43: 605—Vol 57: 566
DICKENSON___Vol 27: 668—Vol 34: 657— Vol 38: 330—Vol 46: 244—Vol 50: 189
DICKERMAN___Vol 29: 514—Vol 36: 761— Vol 39: 273
DICKER_____Vol 60: 250
DICKERHOOF_____Vol 71: 88
DICKERSON___Vol 48: 64—Vol 58: 53—Vol 59: 48, 314—Vol 61: 232—Vol 64: 756— Vol 67: 115—Vol 78: 295—Vol 82: 313
DICKEY___Vol 19: 531, 532—Vol 28: 366— Vol 36: 758—Vol 37: 147, 159—Vol 48: 205 —Vol 54: 422—Vol 58: 450—Vol 64: 587— Vol 67: 293—Vol 71: 959—Vol 75: (2-59)— Vol 81: 569—Vol 83: 717—Vol 84: 158
DICKINSON___Vol 32: 283—Vol 38: 332— Vol 39: 142, 223, 275—Vol 40: 25, 229—Vol 42: 15—Vol 44: 233, 310, 316—Vol 45: 125 —Vol 49: 283—Vol 52: 559, 731—Vol 57:

177, 349, 352, 565, 630, 687—Vol 62: 309—
Vol 63: 60—Vol 70: 56—Vol 76: 62—Vol
78: 457—Vol 81: 20—Vol 82: 725
DICKISON..Vol 62: 651
DICKS........................Vol 64: 651—Vol 81: 130
DICKSON....Vol 27: 740—Vol 28: 479—Vol
48: 121—Vol 50: 64—Vol 59: 441, 524—Vol
60: 570—Vol 62: 161, 498, 499—Vol 66: 249
—Vol 70: 357—Vol 71: 759—Vol 72: (1-64)
—Vol 74: (5-40)
DICTER..Vol 21: 252
DIEHL................Vol 37: 396, 487—Vol 43: 493
DIEHM..Vol 82: 314
DIERDURFF..................................Vol 48: 61
DIETRICH....Vol 35: 655—Vol 41: 121, 162—
Vol 42: 185—Vol 46: 335—Vol 59: 338—
Vol 60: 250—Vol 64: 158
DIETZ................Vol 55: 598—Vol 56: 373
DIEVENBACH........................Vol 55: 599
DIGBY..Vol 55: 603
DIGGES....Vol 37: 269—Vol 67: 617—Vol 71:
674, 839—Vol 83: 92
DIGGINS..Vol 21: 62
DIGGS........................Vol 64: 120—Vol 68: 735
DIGHT..Vol 67: 714
DIKE........................Vol 45: 109—Vol 48: 307
DILAHUNTY........................Vol 30: 260
DILCHER..Vol 70: 206
DILDANE..Vol 43: 418
DILDAY..Vol 76: 653
DILDINE..Vol 42: 138
DILL........................Vol 65: 246—Vol 71: 759
DILLA..Vol 43: 417
DILLARD....Vol 17: 283, 389—Vol 39: 102—
Vol 43: 545—Vol 44: 80—Vol 48: 60—Vol
57: 630—Vol 70: 206—Vol 76: 861—Vol 84:
324, 966
DILLEY..Vol 57: 434
DILLIE..Vol 56: 625
DILLIN..Vol 76: 710
DILLINGHAM....Vol 65: 440, 548—Vol 66:
362—Vol 77: 664
DILLON....Vol 34: 659—Vol 45: 21—Vol 59:
46, 588—Vol 74: (11-55)—Vol 75: (2-58)—
Vol 76: 710
DILWORTH..Vol 43: 493
DIMMICK....Vol 35: 1264—Vol 41: 32, 67—
Vol 45: 113—Vol 58: 329
DIMMITT..Vol 66: 159
DIMMOCK..Vol 46: 235
DIMOCK..Vol 42: 13
DIMON........................Vol 39: 223—Vol 49: 44
DINGEE..Vol 54: 422
DINGS..Vol 58: 652
DINKINS....Vol 30: 338—Vol 49: 43, 131, 353
DINKLES..Vol 58: 453
DINMAN..Vol 70: 207
DINMORE........................Vol 61: 471, 704
DINNEY..Vol 25: 800
DINSMORE....Vol 32: 281—Vol 42: 75, 188,
265—Vol 46: 239—Vol 54: 650—Vol 55: 163,
284, 710—Vol 56: 108, 315, 626—Vol 61:
610
DINWIDDIE........................Vol 54: 709—Vol 84: 324
DIRON..Vol 45: 28
DISBROW....Vol 53: 378—Vol 64: 159—Vol
83: 873
DISCOLL..Vol 50: 281
DISEKER..Vol 50: 70
DISHMAN..Vol 34: 422

DISKILL..Vol 50: 281
DISMUKES....Vol 47: 198—Vol 82: 726—Vol
84: 247
DISON..Vol 58: 174
DISSOWAY..Vol 22: 54
DITZLER..Vol 44: 150
DIVELBISS..Vol 54: 222
DIVER..Vol 76: 654
DIX....Vol 29: 651—Vol 30: 64—Vol 45: 108,
238—Vol 46: 22—Vol 56: 564—Vol 57: 39—
Vol 64: 651
DIXON....Vol 20: 278—Vol 25: 798—Vol 28:
479—Vol 37: 270—Vol 48: 121, 122—Vol
63: 293—Vol 66: 825—Vol 68: 733—Vol 72:
(4-83), (12-67)—Vol 73: (2-66)—Vol 74:
(5-40)—Vol 80: 84
DIXSON..Vol 74: (5-40)
DOAK....Vol 39: 227—Vol 40: 73, 223—Vol 42:
185—Vol 43: 495—Vol 44: 152, 230
DOAN..Vol 38: 218
DOANE....Vol 30: 257—Vol 31: 669—Vol 49:
396
DOBBIN....Vol 36: 760—Vol 41: 126—Vol 69:
629
DOBBINS....Vol 44: 236—Vol 49: 136—Vol
69: 121—Vol 74: (11-58)—Vol 77: 242—Vol
79: 35
DOBBS..Vol 60: 635
DOBNEY..Vol 60: 248
DOBSON....Vol 63: 39—Vol 67: 714—Vol 78:
697
DOBY..Vol 61: 473, 787
DOBYN..Vol 41: 126
DOBYNS....Vol 31: 412—Vol 41: 211—Vol 42:
13—Vol 59: 49—Vol 63: 428
DOCKINS..Vol 67: 576
DOD..Vol 70: 1165
DODD....Vol 45: 125—Vol 69: 625, 630—Vol
79: 518
DODDS....Vol 43: 542—Vol 58: 702—Vol 61:
473, 786—Vol 70: 1165
DODGE....Vol 23: 398—Vol 24: 56—Vol 25:
967—Vol 28: 161—Vol 42: 140—Vol 47: 268
—Vol 50: 353—Vol 57: 310—Vol 59: 314—
Vol 73: (8-82), (11-69)—Vol 76: 859—Vol
81: 131—Vol 82: 140—Vol 83: 945
DODS..Vol 70: 1165
DODSON....Vol 48: 122—Vol 63: 295—Vol 68:
372
DOERINGER..Vol 68: 492
DOGGETT................Vol 64: 760—Vol 66: 122
DOGHERTY..Vol 36: 757
DOHERTY..Vol 63: 568
DOLAN..Vol 76: 580
DOLBEE..Vol 30: 147
DOLLAR..Vol 50: 65
DOLLARD..Vol 64: 714
DOLLEY..Vol 66: 366
DOLSON..Vol 62: 309
DOMINICK..Vol 21: 62
DONAHUR..Vol 39: 328
DONALDSON....Vol 29: 652, 801—Vol 33: 42
—Vol 38: 329—Vol 39: 21—Vol 44: 25, 236
—Vol 57: 173, 219, 566—Vol 63: 428, 697,
739—Vol 64: 650—Vol 66: 361—Vol 69: 333
DONELSON..Vol 6: 58
DONEY..Vol 55: 520
DONLEY..Vol 63: 699
DONNELL................Vol 54: 350—Vol 55: 108
DONOHOO..Vol 50: 61

DONYNS_____Vol 30: 440
DOODY_____Vol 59: 314
DOOLEY_____Vol 42: 140—Vol 43: 481
DOOLITTLE___Vol 22: 50, 997—Vol 27: 383—
 Vol 39: 101, 103—Vol 55: 112, 224—Vol 56:
 521, 710—Vol 58: 587—Vol 59: 650
DOORES_____Vol 41: 124
DORA_____Vol 78: 246
DORAN_____Vol 41: 68, 71—Vol 57: 630
DORCHESTER_____Vol 22: 997
DORE_____Vol 28: 481
DOREMUS_____Vol 41: 122—Vol 45: 25
DORLAND_____Vol 27: 892
DORMAN___Vol 27: 738—Vol 28: 159—Vol
 39: 276—Vol 45: 19—Vol 46: 235
DORN_____Vol 36: 575
DORR_____Vol 52: 52
DORRAL_____Vol 53: 629
DORRANCE_____Vol 81: 430
DORRIS_____Vol 57: 352
DORSET_____Vol 55: 601—Vol 82: 501
DORSEY___Vol 27: 671—Vol 29: 715—Vol 30:
 147—Vol 34: 321, 658—Vol 35: 655—Vol
 39: 142, 325—Vol 45: 106, 191—Vol 46: 386
 —Vol 50: 355—Vol 54: 420, 648—Vol 56:
 225, 743—Vol 57: 312—Vol 60: 571—Vol
 61: 157, 231—Vol 63: 698—Vol 65: 365,
 568, 750—Vol 66: 361—Vol 68: 239—Vol
 71: 958—Vol 74: (1-49)
DORTCH_____Vol 46: 328—Vol 52: 322
DOSS_____Vol 52: 357
DOTSON_____Vol 43: 485
DOTY___Vol 28: 158—Vol 34: 658—Vol 46:
 159—Vol 59: 524, 764—Vol 67: 145
DOUBLEDAY_____Vol 28: 159
DOUD_____Vol 45: 199
DOUDLE_____Vol 56: 47
DOUDS_____Vol 63: 427—Vol 70: 357
DOUGH_____Vol 37: 73
DOUGHERTY_____Vol 31: 414
DOUGHTY___Vol 28: 479—Vol 72: (6-78)—
 Vol 79: 368—Vol 80: 383
DOUGLAS___Vol 19: 628—Vol 20: 165—Vol
 27: 891—Vol 33: 474—Vol 36: 754, 762—
 Vol 37: 267—Vol 38: 221—Vol 41: 34—Vol
 44: 310—Vol 46: 104, 158—Vol 47: 82—Vol
 49: 126—Vol 53: 492—Vol 54: 464—Vol
 56: 562—Vol 57: 174—Vol 59: 388—Vol
 60: 418—Vol 63: 632—Vol 64: 649—Vol 68:
 492—Vol 71: 1024—Vol 72: (10-77)—Vol
 75: (2-58), (5-47)—Vol 76: 582—Vol 79:
 332—Vol 82: 935—Vol 84: 324
DOUGLASS___Vol 45: 124—Vol 47: 83—Vol
 48: 442—Vol 54: 229—Vol 62: 584—Vol 67:
 243—Vol 73: (10-77)
DOUSE_____Vol 81: 20
DOUTHITT_____Vol 73: (4-83)
DOYING_____Vol 54: 54
DOW___Vol 29: 290—Vol 30: 64—Vol 31: 53,
 667, 749—Vol 34: 658—Vol 37: 161—Vol
 41: 32—Vol 43: 427, 540—Vol 57: 351
DOWD___Vol 23: 244—Vol 46: 385—Vol 48:
 54
DOWDEN_____Vol 49: 352
DOWDLE_____Vol 82: 396
DOWELL_____Vol 80: 191
DOWEY_____Vol 34: 68
DOWNER___Vol 43: 416—Vol 47: 30, 264—
 Vol 76: 860—Vol 80: 85, 511

DOWNES___Vol 32: 162—Vol 41: 122—Vol
 64: 444
DOWNEY_____Vol 53: 55
DOWNIE_____Vol 43: 602
DOWNING___Vol 27: 891—Vol 35: 1101, 1263
 —Vol 38: 221, 330—Vol 42: 266—Vol 43:
 418—Vol 52: 359—Vol 61: 868—Vol 67:
 752—Vol 69: 118, 563—Vol 70: 708—Vol
 79: 332, 613
DOWNINGS_____Vol 68: 685
DOWNMAN_____Vol 80: 556
DOWNS___Vol 22: 680—Vol 25: 716—Vol 39:
 23—Vol 42: 137—Vol 45: 235—Vol 46: 245
 —Vol 57: 312—Vol 60: 506—Vol 68: 373
DOWS_____Vol 81: 20
DOWSE_____Vol 81: 20
DOXIE_____Vol 36: 758—Vol 37: 266
DOXSIE_____Vol 36: 758
DOYLE_____Vol 47: 341
DOYNE_____Vol 61: 153
DOZIER___Vol 43: 494—Vol 44: 80, 309—Vol
 49: 285—Vol 64: 713
DRAGOO___Vol 50: 350—Vol 53: 57—Vol 72:
 (9-89)—Vol 77: 239
DRAKE___Vol 20: 1064—Vol 23: 168—Vol 28:
 259, 260, 479—Vol 29: 289, 512—Vol 30:
 337—Vol 40: 76—Vol 41: 72, 127, 162—Vol
 42: 78, 191—Vol 43: 494, 604—Vol 45: 198—
 Vol 48: 445—Vol 52: 323—Vol 53: 117—
 Vol 54: 464, 465—Vol 55: 209, 285, 654—
 Vol 56: 688—Vol 57: 348—Vol 59: 173—
 Vol 61: 65, 551, 785—Vol 67: 752—Vol 68:
 735—Vol 69: 116—Vol 72: (3-71)—Vol 76:
 62—Vol 77: 238—Vol 82: 503
DRANE___Vol 42: 15—Vol 45: 120—Vol 46:
 337
DRAPER___Vol 32: 59—Vol 34: 202—Vol 38:
 220—Vol 42: 263—Vol 43: 601—Vol 48: 57,
 63, 205, 303, 305, 368, 437—Vol 66: 305—Vol
 67: 45
DRAUGHN_____Vol 42: 336
DRAYTON_____Vol 30: 62—Vol 33: 1031
DREKES_____Vol 57: 353
DRENMAN_____Vol 48: 448
DRENNAN___Vol 47: 87, 197, 265—Vol 50: 70
 —Vol 70: 1267
DRESCHER_____Vol 82: 860
DRESSER_____Vol 45: 111
DREUNAN_____Vol 52: 53
DREW___Vol 21: 403—Vol 39: 103—Vol 83:
 944
DRIGGS_____Vol 68: 487
DRINKER_____Vol 46: 333
DRINKWATER_____Vol 38: 331
DRISCOLL_____Vol 39: 224—Vol 50: 281
DROREBACK_____Vol 67: 241
DROUGHT_____Vol 74: (4-51)
DROWN_____Vol 42: 79
DRUMMOND___Vol 45: 20—Vol 57: 746—Vol
 67: 146
DRURY___Vol 30: 146—Vol 53: 177, 628—Vol
 54: 311—Vol 55: 160—Vol 57: 566, 689—
 Vol 69: 631—Vol 70: 54—Vol 75: (11-701)
 —Vol 79: 35
DUBOIS___Vol 43: 486—Vol 44: 23—Vol 46:
 158—Vol 47: 198—Vol 77: 118, 479
DU BOSE_____Vol 74: (11-59)
DUCKWORTH_____Vol 43: 601
DUCOLM_____Vol 27: 808
DUDGEON_____Vol 67: 147—Vol 74: (2-40)

DUDLEY___Vol 17: 480—Vol 18: 179—Vol 25: 800, 966—Vol 26: 56—Vol 27: 383—Vol 42: 79, 336, 342—Vol 43: 492, 496—Vol 45: 235 —Vol 46: 239—Vol 49: 394—Vol 58: 762— Vol 61: 868—Vol 64: 389—Vol 71: 163— Vol 76: 710—Vol 77: 117, 603, 725—Vol 82: 862, 935
DUDROW_____Vol 36: 352
DUELL___Vol 42: 139, 267—Vol 43: 418, 494
DUFF___Vol 32: 284—Vol 50: 354—Vol 57: 691
DUFFERIN_____Vol 43: 495
DUFFEY_____Vol 80: 431
DUFFIE_____Vol 69: 246
DUFFIELD_____Vol 59: 238
DUFFIL_____Vol 48: 124
DUFFY_____Vol 83: 871
DUGAL_____Vol 52: 322
DUGAN_____Vol 67: 753
DUGAR_____Vol 48: 441
DUGGER_____Vol 82: 142
DUKE___Vol 34: 199—Vol 48: 63—Vol 49: 353—Vol 53: 628—Vol 55: 286—Vol 61: 706—Vol 69: 684—Vol 74: (11-60)—Vol 80: 511, 556
DULANEY___Vol 39: 22—Vol 43: 485, 487— Vol 45: 106—Vol 75: (4-54)—Vol 81: 569— Vol 82: 314
DULANY_____Vol 61: 153, 470
DULIN_____Vol 57: 745—Vol 80: 335
DULL___Vol 56: 482—Vol 58: 110—Vol 81: 431
DULMAGE_____Vol 82: 933
DUMM_____Vol 83: 335
DUMMER_____Vol 28: 159
DUN_____Vol 84: 523
DUNAGAN_____Vol 67: 443—Vol 68: 154
DUNBAR___Vol 24: 342—Vol 25: 963—Vol 40: 227—Vol 41: 70—Vol 44: 387—Vol 45: 106 —Vol 48: 446—Vol 49: 127—Vol 50: 356— Vol 54: 588—Vol 55: 396—Vol 67: 387— Vol 68: 122, 155, 489
DUNCAN___Vol 23: 63—Vol 25: 383—Vol 27: 739—Vol 37: 72—Vol 39: 142—Vol 42: 79, 189—Vol 45: 123, 327—Vol 46: 159, 241, 341— Vol 48: 58, 64, 300—Vol 49: 286, 392—Vol 55: 602—Vol 66: 366—Vol 67: 443—Vol 68: 443—Vol 71: 763—Vol 72: (10-94)—Vol 75: (6-40)—Vol 77: 238—Vol 82: 653—Vol 84: 706
DUNCANSON_____Vol 61: 382
DUNCOMBE_____Vol 69: 245
DUNGAN_____Vol 68: 154
DUNGINS_____Vol 68: 154
DUNHAM___Vol 23: 167—Vol 27: 382—Vol 30: 540—Vol 37: 352—Vol 43: 418—Vol 48: 59, 203, 450—Vol 49: 40, 128—Vol 52: 435— Vol 53: 690—Vol 54: 310, 647—Vol 56: 481 —Vol 61: 275, 473, 609—Vol 64: 287—Vol 65: 299—Vol 76: 218—Vol 79: 194, 561
DUNHANE_____Vol 54: 420
DUNKIN_____Vol 39: 142
DUNKLE_____Vol 50: 64, 277
DUNKLEE_____Vol 45: 27
DUNLAP___Vol 38: 276—Vol 41: 71, 162—Vol 45: 323—Vol 47: 273—Vol 58: 501—Vol 62: 773—Vol 64: 587—Vol 67: 714—Vol 68: 123—Vol 69: 630—Vol 77: 603—Vol 79: 561—Vol 80: 45—Vol 82: 654—Vol 83: 440
DUNLAVY_____Vol 62: 586

DUNMAN_____Vol 73: (8-84)
DUNMETT_____Vol 60: 506
DUNN___Vol 28: 60—Vol 34: 322, 324—Vol 39: 227—Vol 40: 73, 223—Vol 41: 34—Vol 42: 10, 185—Vol 43: 423, 546—Vol 44: 78, 80—Vol 45: 102—Vol 46: 99—Vol 58: 764— Vol 59: 47, 652—Vol 64: 390, 585—Vol 71: 674—Vol 73: (1-64)—Vol 75: (8-43)—Vol 76: 582—Vol 80: 556—Vol 83: 1013, 1014— Vol 84: 328
DUNNAHOO_____Vol 83: 871
DUNNE_____Vol 84: 446
DUNNING_____Vol 25: 798—Vol 38: 35
DUNNINGTON_____Vol 77: 480—Vol 82: 860
DUNNOCK_____Vol 46: 392
DUNNONG_____Vol 67: 292
DUNSMORE_____Vol 75: (5-47)
DUNSTER_____Vol 41: 126
DUNSTON_____Vol 33: 957—Vol 58: 112
DUNWELL_____Vol 45: 123
DUNWOODY_____Vol 59: 173
DUPRE___Vol 25: 800—Vol 42: 336—Vol 47: 195—Vol 52: 322—Vol 53: 693—Vol 61: 912
DURAND_____Vol 59: 112
DURANT___Vol 26: 561—Vol 27: 380—Vol 61: 383
DURBIN___Vol 45: 25—Vol 57: 310, 480—Vol 66: 601—Vol 71: 763
DUREN_____Vol 81: 629
DURETT_____Vol 32: 161
DURFEE___Vol 36: 218—Vol 39: 326—Vol 40: 224—Vol 49: 283
DURHAM___Vol 22: 997—Vol 43: 545—Vol 45: 24—Vol 54: 421—Vol 77: 118—Vol 82: 931—Vol 84: 894
DURHAN_____Vol 81: 571
DURIE_____Vol 31: 860
DURKEE___Vol 42: 79—Vol 56: 626—Vol 63: 293—Vol 79: 517
DURNELL_____Vol 59: 524
DURPHY_____Vol 42: 80
DURYEA_____Vol 78: 649—Vol 82: 653
DUSENBERRE_____Vol 67: 243—Vol 70: 129
DUSENBERRY___Vol 60: 699—Vol 67: 243— Vol 70: 129
DUSENBURY___Vol 25: 383—Vol 57: 351— Vol 60: 699—Vol 67: 243—Vol 70: 129—Vol 81: 516—Vol 84: 325
DUSTIN___Vol 47: 265—Vol 48: 365—Vol 63: 636—Vol 77: 603
DUTCHER___Vol 33: 960—Vol 38: 220, 327— Vol 41: 30—Vol 48: 450—Vol 53: 448, 690— Vol 54: 353, 648—Vol 55: 108, 653—Vol 59: 49, 312—Vol 60: 418, 635—Vol 63: 508, 634 —Vol 76: 62
DUTRO_____Vol 47: 270
DUTTON___Vol 43: 423—Vol 53: 446—Vol 54: 228—Vol 75: (6-38), (10-65)—Vol 76: 653 —Vol 80: 277, 335
DUTY_____Vol 41: 68
DUVAL_____Vol 42: 79
DUVALL___Vol 46: 153, 243—Vol 48: 121— Vol 57: 116, 481—Vol 59: 237—Vol 69: 565 —Vol 70: 356
DUVOL_____Vol 42: 79
DUYCHINCK_____Vol 30: 541
DWELLE_____Vol 74: (5-37)
DWELLY_____Vol 28: 162, 261
DWIGHT_____Vol 80: 335
DWIRE_____Vol 75: (4-55)

EGGLESTON—Vol 22: 375—Vol 30: 64—Vol 32: 719—Vol 34: 67—Vol 41: 31—Vol 46: 242—Vol 50: 70, 349—Vol 52: 228, 425—Vol 57: 113, 689—Vol 66: 307, 602—Vol 67: 387—Vol 68: 284
EGLESTON............................Vol 67: 113
EGMONT..............................Vol 43: 422
EGNOR................................Vol 84: 522
EIB.....................................Vol 77: 244
EICHELBERGER...Vol 47: 95—Vol 54: 710
EICHER...............................Vol 30: 147
EICK...............Vol 31: 863—Vol 67: 291, 712
EIGHUY..............................Vol 65: 123
EIGHWE.............................Vol 65: 123
EIKENBARY.......................Vol 67: 387
EIKENBERRY.....................Vol 39: 273
EILAND—Vol 25: 800—Vol 68: 122—Vol 75: (8-43), (11-70)—Vol 77: 768
EKENS.................................Vol 56: 172
EKINS..................................Vol 56: 172
ELAM—Vol 50: 350—Vol 57: 215—Vol 75: (8-43)—Vol 76: 582—Vol 80: 335—Vol 82: 140, 860
ELDER—Vol 29: 651—Vol 58: 371—Vol 71: 675—Vol 82: 862
ELDERKIN...............Vol 38: 86, 114, 273
ELDRED..........................Vol 75: (8-43)
ELDREDGE—Vol 32: 162—Vol 33: 473—Vol 34: 659—Vol 39: 102—Vol 54: 710—Vol 62: 714
ELDRIDGE—Vol 44: 232—Vol 53: 243—Vol 54: 224, 591—Vol 61: 65—Vol 76: 218, 310
ELEY...................................Vol 43: 604
ELGIN—Vol 25: 800—Vol 45: 197, 328—Vol 53: 446, 690—Vol 71: 675
ELIOT..................Vol 45: 237—Vol 57: 433
ELKIN.................................Vol 69: 241
ELKINS—Vol 31: 33—Vol 55: 285—Vol 56: 739—Vol 60: 699—Vol 64: 758—Vol 67: 711—Vol 68: 283—Vol 84: 324
ELLCOTT............................Vol 53: 626
ELLEBARGER....................Vol 40: 227
ELLENWOOD......................Vol 59: 113
ELLER...................Vol 46: 387—Vol 82: 862
ELLERSON....................Vol 52: 321, 557
ELLERY..............................Vol 56: 627
ELLESON............................Vol 40: 76
ELLET..................................Vol 65: 248
ELLINGTON—Vol 39: 104—Vol 41: 213—Vol 42: 14—Vol 62: 502—Vol 84: 894
ELLINGWOOD.......Vol 29: 803—Vol 59: 113
ELLIOT—Vol 57: 115, 744—Vol 58: 173, 652 —Vol 62: 712—Vol 65: 248
ELLIOTT—Vol 19: 432—Vol 32: 632—Vol 33: 955, 960—Vol 35: 439—Vol 40: 76—Vol 41: 32—Vol 43: 547, 599—Vol 45: 23, 24, 28, 107—Vol 46: 156, 237, 386, 391—Vol 47: 265—Vol 48: 440—Vol 49: 129—Vol 52: 565—Vol 53: 447, 745—Vol 54: 310—Vol 57: 115, 744—Vol 66: 120, 669—Vol 68: 57, 551—Vol 73: (11-68)—Vol 74: (5-37)—Vol 78: 52, 247—Vol 79: 161—Vol 80: 190—Vol 82: 142—Vol 84: 703
ELLIS—Vol 21: 802—Vol 27: 382—Vol 28: 258, 366, 481—Vol 32: 283—Vol 33: 706—Vol 34: 202—Vol 39: 224—Vol 41: 215—Vol 42: 16—Vol 43: 482, 488, 489, 492, 542 —Vol 45: 108, 124—Vol 47: 30—Vol 49: 353—Vol 52: 173, 357, 557—Vol 53: 247—Vol 55: 165—Vol 56: 46, 172, 369, 480, 625—

Vol 57: 689—Vol 58: 50—Vol 61: 707—Vol 62: 500, 583—Vol 64: 308, 388—Vol 65: 246 —Vol 67: 752—Vol 68: 491, 685—Vol 69: 118, 564—Vol 71: 959—Vol 72: (2-64)—Vol 75: (9-41)—Vol 76: 218—Vol 79: 284—Vol 81: 310—Vol 84: 69
ELLISON—Vol 39: 225—Vol 49: 355—Vol 83: 335—Vol 84: 964
ELLMAKER.........................Vol 71: 163
ELLSWORTH—Vol 24: 149—Vol 29: 290, 714 —Vol 39: 225—Vol 41: 126—Vol 46: 22, 244, 337—Vol 47: 391—Vol 48: 366—Vol 49: 39—Vol 50: 274—Vol 57: 690—Vol 58: 172—Vol 65: 160—Vol 82: 935
ELLZEY—Vol 21: 61—Vol 22: 51—Vol 27: 383—Vol 28: 163—Vol 42: 342—Vol 43: 483
ELMARE.............................Vol 65: 246
ELMORE—Vol 37: 156—Vol 77: 481—Vol 80: 192
ELMS.................................Vol 76: 582
ELROD.............................Vol 43: 603
ELSBREE..........................Vol 58: 370
ELSON..............................Vol 19: 531
ELTING............................Vol 34: 658
ELTINGE................Vol 36: 762—Vol 40: 74
ELTON...............Vol 52: 568—Vol 84: 158
ELWELL—Vol 54: 647—Vol 55: 598—Vol 84: 246
ELWOOD..........................Vol 73: (7-70)
ELY—Vol 6: 599—Vol 28: 162—Vol 29: 715—Vol 32: 58—Vol 40: 76—Vol 53: 241, 694—Vol 58: 500
ELYA................................Vol 70: 880
EMANUEL........................Vol 69: 363
EMBREE—Vol 25: 717—Vol 30: 65—Vol 59: 238
EMBREY—Vol 62: 387, 388—Vol 73: (10-77)
EMBRIE.............................Vol 45: 236
EMERICK...............Vol 45: 122—Vol 47: 83
EMERSON—Vol 24: 149—Vol 33: 41—Vol 36: 216, 353—Vol 37: 260, 271—Vol 38: 35, 221—Vol 40: 170, 229—Vol 41: 69—Vol 42: 268—Vol 43: 496—Vol 46: 158—Vol 48: 119—Vol 53: 241, 244—Vol 57: 743—Vol 63: 742—Vol 78: 246, 456—Vol 81: 630
EMERY—Vol 57: 745—Vol 58: 371—Vol 61: 469—Vol 82: 932
EWES................................Vol 36: 756
EMLEREE..........................Vol 44: 316
EMLOT..............................Vol 43: 427
EMLOTT............................Vol 43: 484
EMMES..............................Vol 82: 314
EMMETT............................Vol 50: 351
EMMONS—Vol 37: 154—Vol 43: 487—Vol 45: 27—Vol 52: 559—Vol 61: 473—Vol 64: 648—Vol 65: 439—Vol 78: 457
EMONS..............................Vol 65: 568
EMORY..............................Vol 25: 967
EMRICH.............................Vol 35: 439
ENDALY............................Vol 50: 63
ENDERS................Vol 35: 656—Vol 45: 116
ENDICOTT—Vol 57: 113—Vol 65: 160—Vol 71: 164—Vol 77: 52, 117
ENDSLEY...........................Vol 83: 259
ENGARD............................Vol 22: 375
ENGEL...............................Vol 71: 958
ENGLAND—Vol 35: 1104—Vol 36: 73—Vol 52: 436—Vol 53: 54, 629
ENGLE—Vol 40: 77, 171—Vol 48: 57, 63, 367 —Vol 49: 393—Vol 52: 231, 232—Vol 64:

FICKLING............................Vol 59: 588
FICKNOR..............................Vol 59: 681
FIDLER.................................Vol 67: 47
FIELD...Vol 20: 607—Vol 21: 62—Vol 22:
998—Vol 23: 242—Vol 29: 512, 715—Vol
42: 337—Vol 48: 443—Vol 50: 62—Vol 53:
246, 329, 748—Vol 58: 651—Vol 61: 869—
Vol 63: 572, 700—Vol 65: 572, 634—Vol 67:
444, 645—Vol 70: 1020—Vol 71: 161, 672—
Vol 74: (6-38)—Vol 82: 141
FIELDER.............................Vol 49: 188—Vol 50: 112
FIELDING...........................Vol 69: 119
FIELDS...Vol 43: 602—Vol 44: 149—Vol 45:
115, 240, 327—Vol 53: 53—Vol 58: 241—
Vol 59: 523—Vol 60: 115—Vol 64: 308—Vol
74: (11-58)—Vol 77: 602
FIFIELD..............................Vol 67: 575
FIKES.................................Vol 47: 271
FILER..................................Vol 71: 162
FILES.................................Vol 38: 33—Vol 76: 655
FILKINS.............................Vol 60: 50
FILLMORE....Vol 28: 482—Vol 43: 600, 601
—Vol 58: 764
FILLOON............................Vol 55: 520
FILMER..............................Vol 57: 690
FILSON...............................Vol 26: 141
FINCH...Vol 22: 679—Vol 26: 54—Vol 27:
737—Vol 32: 160—Vol 47: 192—Vol 48: 54,
308—Vol 58: 329—Vol 60: 506, 572—Vol 61:
62, 788—Vol 72: (3-70)—Vol 73: (9-65)—
Vol 76: 401—Vol 77: 239
FINDLAY............................Vol 71: 676
FINDLEY....Vol 54: 465—Vol 55: 522, 710—
Vol 56: 367, 474—Vol 59: 589, 680—Vol 60:
48, 114—Vol 61: 608—Vol 80: 46
FINE....................................Vol 81: 629—Vol 82: 220
FINEPOCH..........................Vol 34: 200
FINK..................................Vol 50: 65—Vol 82: 140, 397
FINLEY...Vol 22: 271—Vol 27: 740—Vol 43:
492—Vol 50: 63—Vol 52: 626—Vol 53: 244
—Vol 64: 588—Vol 70: 1167
FINNEY...Vol 34: 423—Vol 42: 341—Vol 44:
153—Vol 45: 185—Vol 53: 571—Vol 59: 387
—Vol 84: 158, 634
FINNIE...............................Vol 51: 355
FIREASH............................Vol 30: 543
FIRMAN.............................Vol 69: 565
FISH...Vol 26: 141—Vol 32: 718—Vol 36:
759—Vol 43: 494—Vol 49: 355—Vol 55: 46
—Vol 56: 480—Vol 68: 121—Vol 69: 120—
Vol 70: 1170 Vol 71: 838—Vol 75: (2-59)
—Vol 82: 860
FISHBACK...........................Vol 56: 372
FISHER...Vol 40: 75—Vol 44: 234, 311—Vol
47: 269—Vol 48: 120, 371—Vol 50: 188, 345
—Vol 52: 229, 563—Vol 53: 56—Vol 54: 589
—Vol 55: 519—Vol 56: 224—Vol 58: 54—
Vol 60: 51, 247—Vol 67: 716—Vol 68: 683—
Vol 73: (11-67)—Vol 77: 239—Vol 78: 554
—Vol 81: 71—Vol 84: 522
FISK...Vol 21: 253—Vol 26: 562—Vol 33: 38
—Vol 37: 488—Vol 38: 274—Vol 45: 18—
Vol 48: 443
FISKE...Vol 27: 734—Vol 45: 189—Vol 73:
(11-68)
FITCH...Vol 18: 182—Vol 19: 68—Vol 24:
459—Vol 27: 807—Vol 32: 508—Vol 33: 43
—Vol 38: 329—Vol 39: 222—Vol 42: 339—
Vol 43: 539, 603—Vol 44: 81, 84, 151—Vol
45: 20—Vol 50: 280—Vol 52: 230—Vol 54:

352—Vol 56: 373—Vol 74: (9-50)—Vol 76:
401—Vol 80: 277
FITHIAN.............................Vol 29: 514
FITZ...Vol 46: 388—Vol 48: 448—Vol 52: 485
FITZGERALD...Vol 54: 535—Vol 77: 769—
Vol 78: 457
FITZHERBERT....................Vol 83: 1014
FITZHUE...........................Vol 52: 320
FITZHUGH...Vol 26: 559—Vol 37: 269—Vol
43: 539—Vol 45: 123—Vol 46: 392—Vol 48:
122—Vol 50: 61—Vol 58: 452—Vol 60: 417
—Vol 64: 159, 761
FITZPATRICK...Vol 39: 223—Vol 45: 124—
Vol 82: 502, 863
FITZ RANDOLPH...Vol 56: 744—Vol 61:
855, 856—Vol 77: 480, 538—Vol 78: 53
FITZWATER...Vol 43: 421—Vol 69: 362—
Vol 78: 53—Vol 83: 1015
FLAGG...Vol 27: 380—Vol 45: 184—Vol 64:
307
FLAKE................................Vol 33: 474
FLANDERS....Vol 52: 109—Vol 82: 653, 863
FLECK................................Vol 49: 133—Vol 50: 351
FLEENOR...........................Vol 45: 123
FLEMING...Vol 22: 53—Vol 33: 1032—Vol
37: 66, 351—Vol 39: 274—Vol 46: 160—Vol
47: 396—Vol 49: 353—Vol 56: 689—Vol 57:
746—Vol 61: 784—Vol 62: 503—Vol 64:
761—Vol 65: 636—Vol 67: 441—Vol 68: 56
—Vol 69: 246—Vol 78: 600—Vol 84: 446
FLEMISTER.........................Vol 68: 240
FLEMMING.........................Vol 72: (12-68)
FLENNER...........................Vol 66: 669—Vol 67: 513
FLESHER............................Vol 83: 488
FLETCHER...Vol 26: 143—Vol 31: 53—Vol
32: 62—Vol 33: 39, 956—Vol 38: 87, 273—
Vol 41: 69—Vol 43: 486, 493, 496, 601—Vol
44: 227—Vol 45: 321—Vol 46: 329, 332—
Vol 48: 305, 445—Vol 49: 190—Vol 55: 47
—Vol 56: 171—Vol 59: 388—Vol 60: 573,
747—Vol 62: 716—Vol 63: 59—Vol 64: 307
—Vol 68: 285—Vol 69: 121—Vol 70: 1265—
Vol 71: 1027—Vol 72: (11-59)—Vol 75:
(10-66)—Vol 79: 284—Vol 80: 154—Vol 83:
438
FLEUNILLING....................Vol 56: 174
FLEWELLING.....................Vol 30: 337
FLEWELLYN.......................Vol 84: 157
FLEXOR.............................Vol 36: 74
FLICK...Vol 49: 133—Vol 57: 628—Vol 59:
109
FLING.................................Vol 71: 1025
FLINN................................Vol 61: 375—Vol 75: (12-63)
FLINT...Vol 26: 562—Vol 29: 717—Vol 45:
108—Vol 52: 686—Vol 65: 123, 367—Vol
79: 112—Vol 82: 574
FLIPPEN.............................Vol 82: 796
FLOCK...............................Vol 49: 133
FLOOD...Vol 43: 491—Vol 68: 156—Vol 82:
794, 795
FLORENCE.........................Vol 83: 522
FLOUGH.............................Vol 38: 35—Vol 43: 496
FLOURNOY...Vol 41: 121, 127—Vol 47: 193,
271, 390—Vol 49: 395—Vol 50: 190—Vol
61: 61—Vol 73: (10-75)—Vol 79: 369
FLOWER...Vol 19: 308—Vol 26: 561—Vol
30: 148, 336, 540—Vol 31: 411, 412—Vol 33:
959—Vol 37: 152—Vol 38: 276—Vol 39: 143
—Vol 53: 744—Vol 54: 354—Vol 58: 588—
Vol 59: 110

FOWNES...............Vol 61: 470
FOX...Vol 22: 51—Vol 28: 164—Vol 38: 87,
332—Vol 41: 128, 210—Vol 42: 269, 335,
338—Vol 43: 544—Vol 44: 84—Vol 45: 23—
Vol 46: 28, 391, 392—Vol 48: 446—Vol 49:
394—Vol 53: 54, 245—Vol 55: 286—Vol 57:
218—Vol 58: 111—Vol 66: 825—Vol 70:
203—Vol 71: 240, 960, 1024—Vol 72: (10-
95)—Vol 73: (8-83)—Vol 75: (6-38)—Vol
76: 401—Vol 77: 52—Vol 80: 277—Vol 82:
860
FOY................Vol 82: 142—Vol 83: 943, 1015
FOYE...............Vol 56: 742
FRAIM................Vol 52: 434—Vol 73: (4-83)
FRAIN................Vol 56: 412
FRAME...Vol 30: 148—Vol 46: 154—Vol 47:
83—Vol 54: 111—Vol 59: 524—Vol 64: 160,
386
FRANCES...............Vol 51: 303
FRANCIS...Vol 32: 632—Vol 33: 709—Vol
52: 626—Vol 53: 245—Vol 55: 337—Vol 61:
382—Vol 68: 284—Vol 70: 131, 354—Vol
71: 1109—Vol 72: (6-78)
FRANCISCO...............Vol 44: 152—Vol 54: 172
FRANCKS...............Vol 47: 190
FRANCUM...............Vol 70: 575
FRANK...Vol 45: 117, 118—Vol 66: 55, 162—
Vol 73: (4-83)
FRANKHAM...Vol 66: 669—Vol 67: 444—
Vol 70: 575
FRANKLIN...Vol 21: 61—Vol 29: 513—Vol
30: 257—Vol 35: 651, 1104—Vol 38: 221—
Vol 39: 326, 328—Vol 40: 273—Vol 47: 396,
397—Vol 48: 449—Vol 50: 63, 349—Vol 56:
746—Vol 59: 113—Vol 63: 508—Vol 66: 365
—Vol 67: 443, 574—Vol 68: 372—Vol 72:
(4-82)—Vol 82: 312, 654—Vol 83: 439, 627,
874
FRANKLINFIELD...............Vol 59: 441
FRANKS...Vol 34: 660—Vol 46: 240—Vol 60:
115—Vol 67: 291—Vol 83: 92
FRANKUM...............Vol 70: 575
FRANTZ...............Vol 59: 48
FRARY...............Vol 46: 237
FRASER...Vol 56: 628—Vol 65: 124, 248—
Vol 68: 487
FRASHER...............Vol 68: 487
FRATTS...............Vol 71: 463
FRAZEE...............Vol 64: 59—Vol 67: 515
FRAZER...Vol 21: 62—Vol 26: 55—Vol 48:
123—Vol 68: 487—Vol 71: 959
FRAZEY...............Vol 67: 574
FRAZIER...Vol 23: 324—Vol 29: 802—Vol
50: 191—Vol 53: 571—Vol 65: 124—Vol 68:
487—Vol 76: 582—Vol 83: 439—Vol 84: 324
FRED...............Vol 52: 485
FREDERICKS...............Vol 33: 474
FREEBORN...Vol 68: 687—Vol 69: 56—Vol
77: 664
FREEBOURNE...............Vol 68: 687—Vol 69: 56
FREELAND...............Vol 45: 25
FREEMAN...Vol 22: 53, 270—Vol 26: 56, 241
—Vol 27: 46, 892—Vol 33: 957—Vol 34: 540
—Vol 35: 652—Vol 36: 463—Vol 43: 424,
491, 598—Vol 45: 105, 324—Vol 46: 242, 384
—Vol 47: 24, 48, 134—Vol 55: 106, 598—
Vol 56: 745—Vol 58: 450, 651—Vol 60: 113,
633—Vol 61: 157—Vol 64: 258—Vol 65: 245,
635—Vol 67: 647—Vol 74: (5-41), (7-51),

(8-51)—Vol 75: (6-38)—Vol 77: 241, 480—
Vol 82: 139
FREENEY...............Vol 74: (11-58)
FREER...............Vol 39: 275
FREESE...............Vol 48: 308—Vol 49: 42
FREIBERGER...............Vol 37: 157
FREMONT...............Vol 46: 101
FRENCH...Vol 26: 56—Vol 28: 164, 478—Vol
29: 650—Vol 31: 861—Vol 32: 282—Vol 35:
654—Vol 37: 270, 271—Vol 38: 35—Vol 44:
312—Vol 45: 102—Vol 46: 98, 102, 238, 336
—Vol 47: 95—Vol 48: 121—Vol 49: 354—
Vol 54: 352—Vol 56: 225, 688—Vol 58: 173,
329—Vol 59: 587, 589, 680—Vol 61: 383—
Vol 63: 247—Vol 64: 446—Vol 65: 57, 508
—Vol 67: 444—Vol 68: 551—Vol 70: 134,
354—Vol 80: 44—Vol 82: 396, 499—Vol 83:
520
FRENEAU...............Vol 13: 384
FRESHOUR...............Vol 60: 365
FRETTS...............Vol 23: 244
FREW...............Vol 50: 193
FREY...Vol 45: 23—Vol 53: 492, 630—Vol 69:
624
FREYER...............Vol 23: 324
FRIDAY...............Vol 66: 734
FRIEDABAUGH...............Vol 43: 496
FRIEND...Vol 33: 956—Vol 39: 273—Vol 42:
193—Vol 44: 151, 229—Vol 46: 27, 336—
Vol 55: 522
FRIER...............Vol 43: 486
FRINK...Vol 27: 806—Vol 28: 160, 259—Vol
71: 461—Vol 72: (2-64), (10-95)
FRISBEE...............Vol 36: 217
FRISBIE...Vol 17: 61, 282—Vol 26: 56—Vol
37: 160—Vol 42: 193—Vol 78: 697
FRISBY...............Vol 26: 56
FRISTOE...............Vol 56: 739
FRITTS...............Vol 57: 480—Vol 66: 162
FRITZ...Vol 66: 162—Vol 82: 861—Vol 84:
704
FRIZEL...............Vol 56: 319
FRIZZELL...Vol 46: 154—Vol 47: 30—Vol
50: 69, 187—Vol 76: 63, 144
FRIZZLE...............Vol 50: 191
FROMAN...............Vol 62: 588—Vol 63: 58, 739
FROST...Vol 22: 997—Vol 36: 757—Vol 56:
415—Vol 67: 43, 240—Vol 76: 400—Vol 78:
52—Vol 84: 444
FRY...Vol 41: 65—Vol 52: 108, 355—Vol 54:
594—Vol 57: 691—Vol 59: 315—Vol 64: 389
—Vol 67: 575—Vol 75: (2-57)
FRYE...Vol 19: 432—Vol 27: 381—Vol 83:
440, 1014
FRYER...............Vol 43: 423—Vol 44: 23
FUGLER...............Vol 48: 60
FULCHER...............Vol 77: 664
FULK...............Vol 60: 157
FULKERSON...Vol 52: 173—Vol 63: 38
FULKS...............Vol 81: 517
FULLER—Vol 2: 45—Vol 17: 283—Vol 20:
62, 166, 352—Vol 22: 269—Vol 28: 162, 262
—Vol 30: 66—Vol 32: 60, 508—Vol 33: 38,
709, 960—Vol 34: 539, 656—Vol 38: 88—Vol
40: 272—Vol 41: 211—Vol 42: 13, 343—Vol
43: 422, 496, 604—Vol 44: 228, 314—Vol 45:
108, 184, 197—Vol 46: 235—Vol 48: 445—
Vol 49: 280, 285, 354—Vol 50: 64, 351—Vol
51: 303, 357—Vol 52: 229, 626—Vol 53: 116,
117, 378, 575—Vol 54: 112, 222—Vol 56:

481—Vol 59: 239, 314, 763—Vol 60: 48—Vol
62: 775—Vol 64: 521, 649—Vol 65: 245—
Vol 66: 365—Vol 67: 145, 241, 716—Vol 68:
550—Vol 69: 56—Vol 70: 877, 1170—Vol 71:
161, 839, 959—Vol 74: (2-40), (12-53)—Vol
75: (5-47), (10-67)—Vol 77: 241—Vol 82:
794—Vol 84: 247
FULLERTON............Vol 30: 439—Vol 79: 193
FULMER...Vol 37: 157
FULMORE.......................................Vol 63: 700
FULTON....Vol 11: 435—Vol 18: 58—Vol 19:
205, 434—Vol 29: 44, 289, 649—Vol 31: 751
—Vol 37: 161—Vol 45: 28—Vol 50: 353—
Vol 74: (7-52), (8-52), (12-53)
FULWOOD.....................................Vol 33: 1032
FUNDERBURG...............................Vol 83: 94
FUNK....Vol 49: 284—Vol 50: 65, 113—Vol
78: 601
FUNKHOUSE...................................Vol 40: 228
FUQUA....Vol 36: 353—Vol 43: 426, 494—Vol
45: 110—Vol 66: 122—Vol 84: 446
FURGUSON......................................Vol 33: 474
FURLONG...Vol 59: 652
FURMAN ....Vol 43: 424—Vol 69: 565
FURNESS..Vol 76: 654
FURR..Vol 46: 392
FURRER..Vol 46: 392
FURROW..Vol 46: 392
FURRY..................Vol 82: 501—Vol 84: 523
FUTCHIN..Vol 54: 172
FYFFE..Vol 74: (1-49)
FYLER..Vol 51: 302
FYLES..Vol 38: 33

G

GAAR....Vol 37: 396—Vol 45: 199, 237, 329—
Vol 83: 943
GABBARD...Vol 82: 141
GABBERT..Vol 55: 520
GABLE ....Vol 45: 189—Vol 73: (11-67)
GABRIEL...Vol 84: 324
GADDIS..................Vol 49: 189—Vol 54: 51
GAERTA..Vol 70: 354
GAFFNEY...Vol 50: 63
GAGE....Vol 24: 543—Vol 25: 716—Vol 44:
231—Vol 54: 466—Vol 55: 286—Vol 56:
46, 114, 223, 475—Vol 74: (3-44)
GAGEBY...Vol 46: 152
GAGER....Vol 26: 241—Vol 47: 396—Vol 48:
56
GAIL........................Vol 48: 204—Vol 55: 519
GAILEY...Vol 78: 696
GAILLARD...Vol 59: 46
GAINE..Vol 84: 328
GAINER........Vol 42: 15, 16—Vol 75: (4-53)
GAINES....Vol 27: 809—Vol 30: 257, 540—Vol
37: 488—Vol 39: 22—Vol 43: 423, 426, 483,
539—Vol 59: 46—Vol 61: 149, 609, 786—Vol
64: 521, 649—Vol 82: 140, 398, 726, 935—
Vol 83: 442
GAINS...Vol 59: 237
GAITHER....Vol 21: 251—Vol 58: 450—Vol
59: 48, 313—Vol 83: 92—Vol 84: 523
GAITNER...Vol 57: 312
GALAGHER...Vol 46: 334
GALBRAITH....Vol 41: 125—Vol 47: 189, 199,
265, 387—Vol 53: 693—Vol 54: 227—Vol 58:
112
GALBREATH............Vol 53: 52—Vol 77: 481
GALBREATHS..................................Vol 53: 379

GALE....Vol 28: 160—Vol 29: 287—Vol 41:
164—Vol 45: 28, 107, 199—Vol 47: 199, 269,
389—Vol 53: 177, 632—Vol 55: 446, 519—
Vol 57: 311—Vol 58: 328—Vol 60: 419—Vol
63: 572, 696—Vol 65: 634—Vol 82: 935
GALES..Vol 26: 241
GALLATIN..................Vol 28: 61—Vol 20: 287
GALLBRAITH....................................Vol 39: 324
GALLION................Vol 54: 466—Vol 67: 117
GALLOP...Vol 38: 218
GALLOWAY....Vol 31: 751—Vol 56: 745—Vol
59: 176—Vol 75: (2-58)—Vol 80: 432—Vol
82: 933—Vol 84: 705
GALLUP—Vol 28: 259—Vol 35: 439—Vol 43:
418, 496—Vol 49: 284, 390—Vol 75: (5-44)
GALLEY...Vol 32: 508
GALPIN....Vol 48: 372—Vol 53: 692—Vol 56:
474—Vol 60: 635
GALT...Vol 44: 28
GALUSHA....Vol 36: 757—Vol 37: 266, 348—
Vol 38: 276
GAMAGE..Vol 72: (4-84)
GAMBLE....Vol 26: 561—Vol 48: 444—Vol 53:
116, 575—Vol 60: 699—Vol 61: 64—Vol 79:
369
GAMBOL..................................Vol 53: 116, 575
GAMMON...Vol 45: 110
GANNAWAY................................Vol 56: 176, 739
GANNON................Vol 70: 576—Vol 82: 863
GANO..........................Vol 5: 61—Vol 77: 332
GANT..Vol 67: 648
GANTT...Vol 67: 648
GAPEN..Vol 31: 52
GANKINS...Vol 84: 68
GANNETT...Vol 84: 894
GAR...Vol 83: 943
GARD..................Vol 35: 439—Vol 60: 634
GARDENER....Vol 33: 954—Vol 41: 125, 210
—Vol 42: 134—Vol 43: 601—Vol 45: 27
GARDIN...Vol 60: 573
GARDINER....Vol 3: 684—Vol 33: 707—Vol
42: 343—Vol 44: 228—Vol 46: 97—Vol 55:
601—Vol 61: 698—Vol 65: 160—Vol 70:
577, 1170—Vol 73: ((11-67)—Vol 78: 156
GARDINIER..Vol 83: 873
GARDNER....Vol 3: 688—Vol 26: 54, 340—
Vol 27: 737, 738, 739—Vol 30: 146—Vol 32:
162, 507—Vol 34: 658—Vol 38: 332—Vol
47: 396—Vol 48: 59, 60, 302, 304, 371—Vol
49: 45, 134, 190—Vol 62: 308—Vol 66: 364—
Vol 67: 645—Vol 69: 362—Vol 70: 577,
1170—Vol 72: (7-75)—Vol 75: (6-39)—Vol
83: 260—Vol 84: 245, 706
GAREGUS...Vol 57: 216
GARES...Vol 56: 560
GAREY..................Vol 52: 625—Vol 53: 117
GARFIELD....Vol 43: 482, 547, 600—Vol 45:
200
GARGACINGER.................................Vol 32: 718
GARGER..Vol 28: 164
GARLACH..Vol 62: 714
GARLAND....Vol 22: 375—Vol 25: 887—Vol
34: 199—Vol 37: 148, 355, 487—Vol 38: 218
—Vol 41: 68, 71—Vol 44: 231—Vol 48: 370,
447—Vol 55: 109—Vol 57: 477—Vol 65:
249—Vol 74: (5-41)
GARLINGTON............Vol 65: 572—Vol 67: 444
GARLIS..Vol 56: 560
GARLOCK...Vol 62: 714
GARMEN...Vol 59: 442

GARNER....Vol 39: 226—Vol 40: 24—Vol 46: 335—Vol 59: 238—Vol 82: 313
GARNETT....Vol 33: 960—Vol 49: 286—Vol 51: 355—Vol 67: 117—Vol 68: 488—Vol 82: 862
GAROUTTE....Vol 31: 588, 589—Vol 32: 60, 631
GARR..............Vol 45: 17—Vol 83: 943
GARRABRANT........Vol 32: 160—Vol 33: 960
GARRARD....Vol 35: 1102—Vol 41: 125—Vol 45: 123—Vol 47: 83—Vol 49: 286—Vol 71: 240—Vol 80: 554
GARRETSON....Vol 33: 1033—Vol 45: 27—Vol 55: 110—Vol 58: 369, 762
GARRETT....Vol 32: 62, 719—Vol 35: 438—Vol 38: 219—Vol 39: 277—Vol 45: 102, 119 —Vol 48: 58, 202, 302—Vol 49: 48, 132—Vol 57: 630—Vol 68: 492—Vol 75: (10-66), (12-63)—Vol 82: 313, 860, 931—Vol 84: 445
GARRETTSON........Vol 65: 439—Vol 69: 680
GARRIGUES....................Vol 43: 425
GARRIGUS.......................Vol 57: 216
GARRISON....Vol 33: 1033—Vol 50: 66, 349—Vol 55: 110—Vol 56: 372—Vol 58: 50—Vol 60: 417—Vol 61: 869—Vol 62: 306—Vol 67: 443—Vol 68: 489—Vol 70: 136—Vol 71: 164—Vol 72: (7-75)—Vol 78: 554—Vol 84: 705
GARRITSON................Vol 55: 110—Vol 58: 50
GARTICK........................Vol 67: 291
GARVIN............Vol 61: 473, 706—Vol 62: 248
GARWOOD....Vol 52: 53, 228—Vol 53: 53, 329 —Vol 54: 539
GARY....Vol 42: 270, 335—Vol 47: 270—Vol 53: 379—Vol 59: 681—Vol 60: 698—Vol 61: 276—Vol 64: 650—Vol 65: 122, 571—Vol 66: 364—Vol 67: 115, 715—Vol 76: 62
GASCOYNE..........................Vol 82: 500
GASHKILL...........................Vol 61: 231
GASKELL............................Vol 42: 193
GASKILL............Vol 55: 47—Vol 63: 247
GASPER...............................Vol 59: 48
GASSAWAY............Vol 60: 506—Vol 61: 63
GASTON....Vol 21: 168—Vol 34: 202—Vol 43: 491—Vol 57: 478—Vol 74: (5-42)
GATES....Vol 18: 181—Vol 19: 69—Vol 22: 53, 269—Vol 27: 45, 671—Vol 28: 61—Vol 30: 337—Vol 31: 52, 666—Vol 32: 631—Vol 33: 41—Vol 39: 225—Vol 40: 73—Vol 41: 31, 70, 161 Vol 47: 24 Vol 50: 352—Vol 52: 319—Vol 58: 172—Vol 59: 763—Vol 60: 116, 507, 572, 699—Vol 61: 154—Vol 62: 503 —Vol 68: 122—Vol 69: 120, 161, 244—Vol 70: 880—Vol 71: 676—Vol 74: (5-38), (6-38)—Vol 80: 191
GATEWOOD....Vol 37: 396—Vol 38: 333—Vol 70: 1165—Vol 78: 502—Vol 81: 631—Vol 82: 220—Vol 83: 94
GATLIN....................Vol 28: 161—Vol 47: 395
GAULDEN...........................Vol 36: 574
GAULT..............................Vol 60: 419
GAUMER.........................Vol 75: (10-65)
GAUNT............Vol 61: 470—Vol 67: 146, 648
GAUSEY............................Vol 81: 315
GAUTIER............Vol 30: 147—Vol 45: 114
GAVET..............................Vol 24: 149
GAW................................Vol 71: 957
GAWDY.............................Vol 45: 324
GAY....Vol 40: 230—Vol 43: 546—Vol 44: 150

—Vol 46: 153—Vol 59: 48—Vol 60: 248—Vol 63: 508—Vol 71: 460
GAYER.............................Vol 3: 687
GAYLE............Vol 58: 53—Vol 82: 934
GAYLEY............................Vol 82: 139
GAYLOR............................Vol 66: 249
GAYLORD....Vol 22: 374—Vol 28: 263—Vol 29: 714—Vol 31: 588—Vol 35: 436—Vol 36: 72—Vol 40: 78—Vol 42: 136, 185—Vol 45: 106—Vol 46: 104, 238—Vol 47: 29, 83—Vol 66: 825—Vol 68: 57—Vol 83: 627
GAYMAN..........................Vol 69: 362
GEAR..............................Vol 24: 58
GEARY............................Vol 70: 577
GEBHARDT.........................Vol 54: 308
GEDDY.............................Vol 63: 59
GEDNEY...........................Vol 30: 337
GEE..............................Vol 56: 690
GEER....Vol 30: 66—Vol 44: 83—Vol 45: 128, 327—Vol 48: 119—Vol 49: 43
GEHR............Vol 43: 496—Vol 68: 154
GEIGER....Vol 17: 283, 389—Vol 36: 762—Vol 43: 426—Vol 44: 227—Vol 49: 44, 183—Vol 71: 356—Vol 73: (9-65)
GEIRICH...........................Vol 46: 30
GEISELMAN........................Vol 40: 172
GEIST............................Vol 37: 396
GELWICKS.........................Vol 65: 441
GENADO..........................Vol 73: (8-84)
GENET............Vol 26: 141—Vol 27: 44
GENISON..........................Vol 57: 311
GENTRY....Vol 35: 1104—Vol 37: 351, 354—Vol 43: 596—Vol 57: 434—Vol 83: 523
GEORGE....Vol 36: 215—Vol 38: 330—Vol 43: 723—Vol 48: 61, 63, 119, 203—Vol 50: 281, 348—Vol 55: 598—Vol 58: 370, 649—Vol 62: 457—Vol 65: 365, 507, 508—Vol 69: 245 —Vol 73: (5-88)—Vol 78: 52, 295—Vol 80: 556
GEORGES............Vol 53: 178—Vol 68: 241
GEORGIA..........................Vol 82: 860
GERALD...........................Vol 84: 69
GERARD....Vol 36: 35—Vol 47: 266—Vol 83: 944
GERARDS..........................Vol 22: 54
GERLACH..........................Vol 57: 628
GERMAIN..........................Vol 67: 516
GERMAN...........................Vol 67: 516
GERMANY..........................Vol 43: 485
GERMOND............Vol 62: 584—Vol 67: 516
GERRAND.................Vol 39: 104, 328
GERRARD....Vol 37: 396—Vol 47: 87, 265—Vol 67: 115—Vol 69: 117
GERRISH..........................Vol 34: 322
GERRY............................Vol 70: 577
GERST............................Vol 37: 396
GEST.............................Vol 67: 716
GETCHELL.........................Vol 68: 552
GETMAN...........................Vol 44: 153
GETS.............................Vol 79: 369
GETTYS....Vol 44: 152—Vol 52: 169—Vol 54: 650—Vol 66: 160—Vol 69: 119
GHOLSON............Vol 39: 326—Vol 65: 670
GHRIST............Vol 39: 223—Vol 79: 518
GIBBONEY....Vol 42: 342—Vol 43: 420, 602—Vol 44: 316
GIBBONS....Vol 15: 676—Vol 36: 762—Vol 54: 591—Vol 56: 626—Vol 57: 629—Vol 61: 704—Vol 64: 522—Vol 84: 522
GIBBONY..........................Vol 45: 111

GIBBS....Vol 25: 38—Vol 43: 421, 422, 492—
Vol 44: 26—Vol 45: 20, 21—Vol 46: 332,
392—Vol 56: 43, 368, 414, 477—Vol 60: 573
—Vol 61: 157, 912—Vol 63: 107—Vol 69:
564—Vol 70: 708—Vol 71: 1026—Vol 74:
(3-45), (7-53), (8-53)—Vol 79: 331
GIBSON....Vol 21: 404—Vol 26: 336—Vol 29:
514—Vol 30:'67—Vol 31: 413—Vol 35: 653
—Vol 36: 217—Vol 38: 88, 218—Vol 44: 25,
82—Vol 45: 127—Vol 46: 99, 152—Vol 48:
306—Vol 50: 188, 189, 193, 352—Vol 52:
483, 563—Vol 53: 632—Vol 54: 56, 111, 466,
536—Vol 58: 174, 450—Vol 59: 111, 764—
Vol 61: 472—Vol 63: 293—Vol 64: 258,
520—Vol 66: 825—Vol 67: 114—Vol 73:
(2-66)—Vol 76: 310, 927—Vol 81: 630—Vol
82: 139, 142—Vol 83: 172, 522—Vol 84: 70,
244, 893
GIDDEN...Vol 78: 53
GIDDING...............................Vol 73: (10-75)
GIDDINGS.......Vol 55: 108, 397—Vol 56: 175
GIDEON...Vol 56: 743
GIFFORD....Vol 20: 278—Vol 28: 164—Vol
30: 538—Vol 31: 860—Vol 32: 718—Vol 63:
246
GILBERT....Vol 18: 299—Vol 19: 431, 625—
Vol 20: 279—Vol 23: 324, 325, 400—Vol 25:
384—Vol 28: 159—Vol 31: 54—Vol 36: 759
—Vol 39: 224—Vol 43: 423—Vol 44: 23—
Vol 45: 242—Vol 46: 385—Vol 48: 123—
Vol 52: 109—Vol 53: 182, 492—Vol 57: 218
—Vol 59: 765—Vol 67: 712—Vol 75: (11-
70)—Vol 76: 860—Vol 80: 383—Vol 82:
860—Vol 83: 262
GILCHRIST..............................Vol 72: (7-75)
GILDERSLEEVE.............................Vol 77: 603
GILES....Vol 36: 354—Vol 41: 124—Vol 42:
16—Vol 45: 24, 237—Vol 49: 132—Vol 58:
331—Vol 65: 248—Vol 68: 243—Vol 73:
(9-67)—Vol 79: 284
GILHAM....Vol 38: 219—Vol 41: 28—Vol 58:
452
GILKEY....Vol 28: 163—Vol 35: 653—Vol 48:
55—Vol 56: 745—Vol 73: (10-76)—Vol 84:
705
GILL....Vol 29: 288—Vol 30: 63—Vol 31: 55—
Vol 32: 632—Vol 47: 27—Vol 48: 307—Vol
57: 176—Vol 61: 707—Vol 70: 1167—Vol
73: (12-63)—Vol 84: 244
GILLENTINE.............Vol 57: 743—Vol 58: 170
GILLENWATER.................................Vol 58: 54
GILLESPIE ....Vol 25: 39—Vol 35: 655—Vol
37: 353—Vol 41: 126, 163—Vol 43: 597—
Vol 44: 82, 388—Vol 46: 236—Vol 47: 193—
Vol 57: 115, 432—Vol 62: 161—Vol 63: 245,
425—Vol 64: 121—Vol 70: 1170—Vol 80:
512
GILLETT....Vol 38: 88—Vol 42: 268—Vol 56:
108, 316, 626—Vol 64: 389, 649—Vol 65:
246, 507
GILLETT....Vol 39: 327—Vol 41: 211—Vol
42: 339—Vol 46: 23, 155—Vol 48: 57, 302—
Vol 54: 53, 226, 351—Vol 61: 610, 911—Vol
68: 241—Vol 79: 34
GILLETTE....Vol 27: 380—Vol 51: 302—Vol
53: 245—Vol 56: 688—Vol 66: 827—Vol 67:
711—Vol 76: 219
GILLHAM.................................Vol 24: 459
GILLIAM....Vol 49: 355—Vol 50: 59, 69—Vol
55: 286, 655—Vol 62: 308—Vol 63: 427—

Vol 64: 757—Vol 67: 42—Vol 72: (2-62)—
Vol 75: (8-62)
GILLILAND.................................Vol 74: (6-37)
GILLIS.............Vol 45: 105—Vol 46: 100
GILLISPIE...Vol 48: 119
GILLMORE.............Vol 44: 387—Vol 45: 236
GILLOW.................................... Vol 49: 353
GILLSON.......................................Vol 73: (2-64)
GILLUM..Vol 65: 299
GILMAN....Vol 29: 46, 47, 651—Vol 30: 441—
Vol 31: 585, 586—Vol 36: 579—Vol 44: 313,
314—Vol 45: 121, 124, 321, 326—Vol 46: 330
—Vol 49: 46, 184, 186, 187, 349—Vol 50: 112
—Vol 52: 108—Vol 61: 157—Vol 64: 758—
Vol 71: 163—Vol 83: 171
GILMER....Vol 43: 600—Vol 52: 733—Vol 55:
521—Vol 58: 651—Vol 82: 794
GILMORE....Vol 38: 35, 275—Vol 44: 26, 228,
310—Vol 45: 184—Vol 48: 203—Vol 49: 134
—Vol 52: 434—Vol 54: 590—Vol 56: 691—
Vol 57: 316, 435—Vol 58: 371—Vol 62: 123
—Vol 65: 761...Vol 80: 191, 335, 336—Vol
81: 631—Vol 82: 794—Vol 84: 68
GILMOUR..Vol 59: 764
GILSON....Vol 32: 60—Vol 34: 201—Vol 44:
382—Vol 53: 377—Vol 71: 460—Vol 73:
(2-64)—Vol 82: 312
GILSTON....Vol 31: 587—Vol 32: 60—Vol 33:
38
GILTNER.............................Vol 83: 523, 524
GINDER...Vol 46: 337
GINN..............................Vol 67: 242, 576
GINTHER................................. Vol 45: 23
GIRARDEAU....Vol 62: 52, 54, 121—Vol 63:
426
GIRDNER...Vol 56: 318
GIRTMAN.......................................Vol 47: 267
GISHER..Vol 58: 502
GIST....Vol 25: 38—Vol 30: 543—Vol 37: 396
—Vol 46: 101—Vol 57: 176...Vol 70: 457,
458
GITTAN...Vol 44: 152
GITTS...Vol 61: 470
GIVEN.............................Vol 47: 198—Vol 50: 65
GIVENS....Vol 47: 199—Vol 75: (5-44)—Vol
78: 649
GIVINS....Vol 29: 649—Vol 45: 186—Vol 46:
393
GLADDEN.................Vol 39: 327—Vol 41: 211
GLADDING.....................................Vol 42: 336
GLADDIS..Vol 54: 419
GLADISH...Vol 55: 602
GLADMAN.......................................Vol 78: 600
GLANFELDER................................Vol 53: 54
GLASCOCK....Vol 47: 28—Vol 52: 436—Vol
79: 368—Vol 80: 191—Vol 82: 796
GLASGOW.............Vol 45: 328—Vol 52: 323
GLASO...Vol 63: 507
GLASS....Vol 31: 414, 750—Vol 39: 224—Vol
41: 70—Vol 43: 427—Vol 44: 81, 150—Vol
45: 184—Vol 46: 27—Vol 49: 191—Vol 53:
55—Vol 54: 350—Vol 58: 453—Vol 60: 699
—Vol 79: 332
GLAZEBROOK....Vol 46: 243—Vol 73: (12-
63)
GLAZIER....Vol 63: 102, 505—Vol 66: 538—
Vol 80: 81
GLEASON......................................Vol 30: 146
GLEN...Vol 69: 157
GLENN....Vol 25: 719—Vol 32: 506—Vol 43:

596—Vol 59: 441—Vol 64: 308—Vol 65: 296
—Vol 66: 461—Vol 74: (2-40)—Vol 75:
(10-66)—Vol 77: 183—Vol 81: 20—Vol 84:
445
GLESON..Vol 82: 583
GLESSON..Vol 75: (2-58)
GLICK................Vol 30: 335—Vol 43: 486, 604
GLIDDEN..Vol 32: 633
GLIDDONS..Vol 7: 51
GLISSON................Vol 63: 245, 425—Vol 71: 164
GLOCKNER..Vol 66: 827
GLOEFELLER..Vol 83: 91
GLORE..Vol 45: 23
GLOTFELDER..Vol 53: 54
GLOVER....Vol 24: 543—Vol 28: 548—Vol 36:
574—Vol 42: 75—Vol 44: 26—Vol 56: 562—
Vol 67: 442—Vol 79: 194—Vol 82: 397
GLOYD..Vol 49: 130
GOAR..Vol 73: (11-66)
GOBER.. Vol 41: 213
GOBLE..Vol 21: 251—Vol 58: 763
GODARD..Vol 49: 44
GODBY..Vol 65: 634
GODDARD....Vol 33: 474—Vol 37: 151—Vol
49: 44—Vol 61: 607—Vol 68: 491
GODFREY....Vol 45: 104—Vol 49: 49—Vol
67: 117—Vol 82: 500
GODFRY..Vol 58: 331
GODLOVER..Vol 50: 355
GODMAN..Vol 72: (2-62)
GODWIN..Vol 66: 121
GOE..Vol 33: 706
GOERTNER..Vol 56: 318
GOFF....Vol 51: 355—Vol 55: 601—Vol 56:
367—Vol 61: 704—Vol 64: 387—Vol 71: 86
GOGGIN..Vol 44: 153
GOLD....Vol 22: 272, 995—Vol 31: 860—Vol
43: 605—Vol 56: 627—Vol 60: 51—Vol 80:
84
GOLDEN........................Vol 50: 348, 415—Vol 52: 483
GOLDSBOROUGH....Vol 46: 332—Vol 47: 85
—Vol 50: 65—Vol 61: 704—Vol 64: 390, 713
GOLDSMITH....Vol 26: 244—Vol 32: 633—
Vol 69: 120
GOLIGHTLY..Vol 28: 366
GOLL..Vol 65: 763
GOLLADAY........................Vol 59: 651—Vol 60: 633
GOLLIDAY..Vol 58: 651
GOLLODAY..Vol 34: 659
GOLTRY..Vol 74: (11-61)
GOMER..Vol 76: 860
GONZALAS..Vol 58: 762
GOOCH....Vol 32: 61—Vol 34: 423—Vol 37:
159—Vol 41: 211—Vol 42: 14, 16—Vol 44:
152, 383—Vol 45: 112—Vol 46: 101, 155—
Vol 53: 377—Vol 82: 574
GOODALE....Vol 20: 164—Vol 48: 122—Vol
55: 712—Vol 80: 657—Vol 82: 932
GOODALL..Vol 53: 377
GOODDING..Vol 71: 460
GOODE....Vol 43: 491—Vol 44: 388—Vol 45:
20, 236—Vol 70: 1265
GOODELL....Vol 30: 148—Vol 32: 508—Vol
62: 586—Vol 82: 727—Vol 83: 93
GOODEN..Vol 65: 439
GOODENOUGH....Vol 22: 375—Vol 43: 605—
Vol 53: 180—Vol 59: 525
GOODING..Vol 65: 298
GOODLOE........................Vol 25: 718—Vol 62: 648
GOODLOVE..Vol 68: 284

GOODMAN........Vol 38: 218—Vol 75: (7-29),
(7-30)
GOODNIGHTS..Vol 50: 350
GOODNOW..Vol 24: 544
GOODRICH....Vol 32: 61—Vol 43: 488—Vol
44: 316—Vol 45: 121—Vol 46: 22, 244—Vol
55: 165, 338, 397, 654—Vol 57: 114—Vol 58:
371, 698—Vol 63: 428—Vol 65: 761—Vol
83: 258, 628
GOODRIDGE..Vol 59: 388
GOODRUM..Vol 80: 512
GOODSELL..Vol 41: 71
GOODSON..Vol 84: 245
GOODSPED..Vol 33: 476
GOODSPEED....Vol 34: 322—Vol 50: 190—
Vol 51: 356—Vol 55: 286—Vol 61: 158, 277
GOODWIN....Vol 21: 169—Vol 28: 60—Vol
30: 336—Vol 31: 411, 589—Vol 32: 284—
Vol 36: 574—Vol 37: 63, 265—Vol 43: 426—
Vol 44: 26, 310—Vol 56: 689—Vol 65: 439—
Vol 74: (11-59)
GOODWYN..Vol 82: 142
GOODYEAR....Vol 18: 299—Vol 22: 995—Vol
44: 85—Vol 45: 127
GOODYHOONTZ..Vol 78: 457
GOOLD........................Vol 45: 111, 192—Vol 70: 715
GOOLSBY..Vol 79: 194
GORDAN..Vol 63: 507
GORDEN..Vol 53: 494
GORDON....Vol 20: 279—Vol 21: 61—Vol 22:
157—Vol 23: 398—Vol 24: 151—Vol 26: 57,
140—Vol 39: 223—Vol 43: 497—Vol 45:
117, 239, 328—Vol 46: 157—Vol 47: 392—
Vol 48: 63, 124—Vol 49: 130—Vol 52: 108,
109—Vol 53: 329—Vol 54: 53, 54, 353—Vol
57: 174—Vol 58: 372, 587—Vol 59: 442—
Vol 61: 788, 913—Vol 65: 635—Vol 68: 121
—Vol 70: 1168, 1267—Vol 78: 649—Vol 79:
614—Vol 82: 501—Vol 83: 173—Vol 84:
247, 520, 523
GORE....Vol 18: 181—Vol 55: 601—Vol 56:
112, 624—Vol 66: 160—Vol 73: (1-63),
(11-66)
GORGON..Vol 21: 497
GORHAM....Vol 13: 74—Vol 28: 60, 364—Vol
29: 512, 715—Vol 45: 19—Vol 47: 197—
Vol 55: 710—Vol 58: 370—Vol 74: (4-51)—
Vol 82: 141
GORLEY..Vol 62: 586
GORMAN........................Vol 28: 159—Vol 59: 442
GORNER..Vol 55: 602
GORRELL........................Vol 82: 931—Vol 83: 336
GORSUCH..Vol 46: 101
GORTON....Vol 26: 54—Vol 41: 123—Vol 42:
11—Vol 46: 154—Vol 48: 61, 304, 366
GORYON..Vol 42: 341
GOSDEN..Vol 76: 928
GOSENG..Vol 38: 328
GOSNELL..Vol 70: 1166
GOSNOLD..Vol 67: 648
GOSS....Vol 47: 198, 272—Vol 51: 302—Vol
62: 546, 775—Vol 67: 711
GOSSAGE..Vol 39: 327
GOSSETT..Vol 60: 50
GOSTON..Vol 56: 625
GOTT....Vol 31: 861—Vol 64: 588—Vol 67:
289
GOTTCHALK..Vol 84: 703
GOTTER..Vol 39: 223
GOTTSCHALK..Vol 60: 249

GOUCH..Vol 49: 45
GOUGES......................................Vol 61: 784
GOUGH....................................Vol 72: (11-59)
GOULD....Vol 13: 615—Vol 22: 995—Vol 25:
968—Vol 30: 339—Vol 34: 537—Vol 35: 57
—Vol 44: 312—Vol 45: 116, 127, 192—Vol
46: 242—Vol 49: 45, 48—Vol 51: 302—Vol
52: 113—Vol 56: 627, 743—Vol 60: 51, 506,
696—Vol 67: 575, 577—Vol 69: 630—Vol
71: 1025—Vol 72: (8-86)—Vol 79: 518—
Vol 80: 193, 276—Vol 83: 873
GOURLEY............................Vol 60: 51, 290, 570
GOUVERNEUR.............................Vol 58: 241
GOVER...............Vol 47: 199—Vol 49: 396
GOWAN...Vol 47: 197
GOWEN...............Vol 37: 151—Vol 47: 192
GOWER...............Vol 46: 329—Vol 68: 154
GOYLE......................................Vol 43: 425
GRAAF..............Vol 55: 165, 283, 336, 652
GRACE.....................................Vol 67: 242
GRACEY...............................Vol 72: (1-64)
GRACIE....................................Vol 72: (1-64)
GRACY....................................Vol 72: (1-64)
GRADDY..............Vol 62: 121, 247, 628
GRADY...Vol 26: 561—Vol 52: 433—Vol 62:
121, 247, 648—Vol 63: 105, 165, 244, 425
GRAEF...........................Vol 52: 231, 232
GRAF...Vol 55: 283, 336, 652—Vol 62: 165,
649
GRAFF...Vol 52: 231—Vol 57: 113—Vol 62:
459—Vol 63: 107
GRAFTON...............Vol 55: 519—Vol 84: 324
GRAHAM...Vol 20: 608—Vol 22: 153—Vol
25: 38—Vol 28: 546—Vol 33: 476—Vol 34:
540—Vol 35: 1266—Vol 36: 349—Vol 37:
71, 155, 354—Vol 41: 212—Vol 42: 337—
Vol 44: 153, 154, 227, 236—Vol 45: 100, 127
—Vol 46: 156, 387—Vol 47: 96—Vol 48: 59
60, 122, 440, 448—Vol 49: 134—Vol 50: 357
—Vol 51: 302—Vol 52: 173, 432—Vol 53:
117—Vol 56: 171, 318—Vol 57: 567—Vol 59:
524—Vol 62: 306, 501, 587—Vol 63: 58, 247
—Vol 64: 160, 648—Vol 67: 239—Vol 68:
490—Vol 71: 761—Vol 72: (4-83)—Vol 75:
(6-38)—Vol 80: 272, 336, 588, 656—Vol 82:
499, 500, 798—Vol 83: 94—Vol 84: 521
GRAINGER..Vol 63: 741
GRAMBLIR...................................Vol 76: 653
GRANADE.............................Vol 75: (6-38)
GRANDIN......................................Vol 38: 329
GRANGER...Vol 6: 599—Vol 57: 115—Vol
75: (5-44)—Vol 83: 173
GRANNIS....................Vol 40: 75—Vol 45: 242
GRANT...Vol 8: 251, 888—Vol 23: 169—Vol
24: 543—Vol 25: 797—Vol 27: 46, 670—Vol
34: 202—Vol 35: 654—Vol 36: 214—Vol 38:
34, 217—Vol 43: 417, 604—Vol 44: 85, 225—
Vol 48: 441—Vol 50: 65—Vol 54: 222, 535—
Vol 55: 164—Vol 59: 113—Vol 60: 506—
Vol 61: 700—Vol 62: 309—Vol 67: 712—
Vol 68: 554—Vol 69: 118—Vol 70: 354—Vol
75: (5-44)—Vol 76: 783—Vol 80: 192, 277—
Vol 82: 796
GRANTHAM...Vol 41: 163, 165—Vol 42: 186
—Vol 75: (1-55)—Vol 83: 173
GRASTY......................................Vol 62: 389
GRATEHOUSE............Vol 36: 215—Vol 38: 32
GRAUDIN......................................Vol 36: 351
GRAUTLAND...............................Vol 56: 560
GRAVATT......................................Vol 49: 135

GRAVES...Vol 22: 680—Vol 29: 286—Vol 32:
60—Vol 33: 38, 40—Vol 40: 76, 172—Vol
41: 65, 68—Vol 42: 14, 15—Vol 43: 486—
Vol 46: 157—Vol 48: 64, 303—Vol 49: 132,
282—Vol 52: 687—Vol 55: 445—Vol 57:
115, 432, 691—Vol 60: 289—Vol 63: 244—
Vol 64: 713—Vol 65: 246, 761—Vol 67: 384
—Vol 69: 243—Vol 70: 709—Vol 73: (1-62)
—Vol 76: 783—Vol 80: 657—Vol 81: 71,
569—Vol 82: 314, 931—Vol 83: 794, 947
GRAW......................................Vol 56: 227
GRAY...Vol 21: 253, 404—Vol 24: 459—Vol
28: 363—Vol 34: 322—Vol 36: 761—Vol 38:
34—Vol 39: 276—Vol 40: 228, 274—Vol 41:
32, 34, 212, 213—Vol 42: 72, 266—Vol 44:
312—Vol 45: 125, 240—Vol 46: 100—Vol
47: 31, 396—Vol 48: 307, 445—Vol 49: 347—
Vol 52: 321—Vol 54: 225—Vol 55: 110, 166
—Vol 56: 691—Vol 57: 176, 431—Vol 58:
112, 587—Vol 61: 65—Vol 63: 635—Vol 65:
760—Vol 66: 461—Vol 67: 386—Vol 71: 462
—Vol 73: (8-83)—Vol 77: 769—Vol 83:
947—Vol 84: 523
GRAYSON.................................Vol 75: (10-67)
GRAYTON......................................Vol 29: 513
GREACEY...................................Vol 72: (1-64)
GREATHOUSE................................Vol 83: 439
GREATON......................................Vol 65: 366
GREAVES......................................Vol 31: 587
GREELEY................................Vol 75: (4-54)
GREEN...Vol 18: 58—Vol 19: 206—Vol 21:
253, 400—Vol 25: 797—Vol 26: 55, 57—Vol
27: 381, 807, 889—Vol 30: 260—Vol 31:
666, 861—Vol 33: 162—Vol 33: 708, 959,
1031—Vol 34: 203—Vol 38: 34, 273—Vol
39: 143—Vol 40: 77, 171, 227—Vol 41: 212—
Vol 42: 263, 342—Vol 43: 494—Vol 44: 80—
Vol 45: 101, 199—Vol 46: 100, 157, 241, 242
—Vol 47: 24, 33, 273—Vol 48: 61—Vol 49:
42, 44, 285, 287, 391, 394—Vol 50: 64, 113,
193—Vol 52: 109, 359—Vol 53: 117, 242,
626—Vol 54: 537, 709—Vol 55: 443, 445,
523—Vol 56: 173, 175, 371, 626—Vol 58:
111, 502, 652, 763—Vol 59: 388—Vol 60: 50,
157, 289, 363—Vol 61: 708, 788, 868—Vol
62: 248—Vol 63: 246, 742—Vol 64: 157, 259
—Vol 65: 248—Vol 66: 364, 826—Vol 67:
242, 291, 441, 715—Vol 68: 57—Vol 69: 362
—Vol 70: 572, 876—Vol 71: 241—Vol 74:
(2-43), (9-50)—Vol 75: (9-46), (10-65)—
Vol 76: 61—Vol 77: 51, 603—Vol 78: 155,
245—Vol 79: 194, 517—Vol 81: 316, 431,
571—Vol 82: 141, 220, 503, 654, 861, 935—
Vol 83: 172, 173, 258, 259—Vol 84: 246, 324,
444, 523, 703
GREENAWALT.................................Vol 71: 676
GREENE...Vol 20: 352—Vol 21: 61, 250, 251
—Vol 24: 459—Vol 25: 799—Vol 26: 53,
54, 336, 338—Vol 29: 716—Vol 30: 259, 339
—Vol 31: 55, 666—Vol 32: 284, 632—Vol
33: 708, 1030—Vol 36: 436, 437, 1103—Vol
39: 142, 143—Vol 40: 108, 228, 273—Vol 41:
123—Vol 42: 11, 342—Vol 44: 235—Vol 45:
108, 112, 118, 238—Vol 46: 242—Vol 49:
285—Vol 53: 243, 244, 627—Vol 54: 227,
228—Vol 55: 520—Vol 56: 108, 174—Vol
58: 52, 650, 652—Vol 59: 681—Vol 60: 50,
157, 289, 363, 507—Vol 64: 648, 651—Vol
65: 121—Vol 67: 387, 752—Vol 68: 121—
Vol 69: 362—Vol 70: 133, 207—Vol 71: 908

—Vol 76: 218, 859—Vol 77: 241—Vol 79:
160—Vol 82: 932
GREENFIELD........Vol 39: 275—Vol 42: 72
GREENLEAF...Vol 45: 326—Vol 46: 22, 240
GREENLEE............................Vol 56: 482
GREENMAN...Vol 43: 486—Vol 44: 23, 316—
Vol 45: 118, 128, 239, 327
GREENOUGH........Vol 39: 102—Vol 54: 432
GREENSLIT....................................Vol 64: 587
GREENUP................................Vol 63: 700
GREENWAY...............................Vol 24: 544
GREENWELL.................................Vol 78: 108
GREENWOOD...Vol 18: 58—Vol 42: 339—
Vol 46: 235—Vol 64: 445—Vol 68: 490
GREER...Vol 45: 18, 189—Vol 53: 176—Vol
64: 124—Vol 69: 764—Vol 81: 264—Vol 82:
653
GREG.............................Vol 43: 485, 488
GREGG...Vol 29: 803—Vol 31: 863—Vol 42:
338, 343—Vol 43: 421, 482—Vol 44: 233—
Vol 62: 460—Vol 66: 537—Vol 73: (11-67)
—Vol 74: (5-41)—Vol 79: 369
GREGORY...Vol 38: 331—Vol 39: 276—Vol
42: 76, 79, 189—Vol 43: 495—Vol 44: 154—
Vol 48: 57—Vol 50: 348—Vol 65: 636—Vol
67: 646—Vol 68: 56—Vol 71: 760—Vol 77:
243, 664
GREIDER...................................Vol 46: 30
GREINER...Vol 55: 209—Vol 58: 369—Vol
59: 49
GREMMER..................................Vol 43: 603
GRENELL................Vol 21: 167—Vol 29: 802
GRESHAM...Vol 26: 142—Vol 36: 351—Vol
40: 25—Vol 41: 122—Vol 45: 105, 195, 328
—Vol 50: 65—Vol 81: 571—Vol 83: 260—
Vol 84: 247
GRETZINGER...........................Vol 43: 493
GREY...Vol 28: 159—Vol 58: 174—Vol 67:
576
GRIDEN..................................Vol 40: 230
GRIDER...................................Vol 42: 80
GRIDLEY...Vol 27: 735—Vol 40: 273—Vol
45: 112—Vol 63: 247—Vol 75: (9-36)
GRIER...Vol 34: 424—Vol 69: 764—Vol 72:
(6-78)—Vol 83: 522
GRIESTE.................................Vol 57: 565
GRIESEMER..............................Vol 61: 375
GRIFFEN...Vol 33: 959—Vol 41: 213—Vol
46: 385—Vol 52: 433—Vol 61: 157—Vol
75: (1 51), (5-47)
GRIFFIN...Vol 41: 71, 128, 162—Vol 44: 388
—Vol 45: 105, 119—Vol 46: 104—Vol 50:
349—Vol 54: 422—Vol 55: 710—Vol 57:
689, 746—Vol 58: 174, 502—Vol 62: 459—
Vol 64: 650—Vol 65: 367, 634—Vol 66: 460
—Vol 68: 374—Vol 70: 133—Vol 74: (1-49)
—Vol 76: 710—Vol 79: 160—Vol 83: 260—
Vol 84: 67, 447, 965
GRIFFING...Vol 26: 337—Vol 33: 956—Vol
34: 536—Vol 55: 710
GRIFFITH...Vol 27: 807—Vol 30: 62—Vol
37: 396—Vol 46: 243—Vol 47: 29, 30—Vol
50: 354—Vol 52: 112—Vol 57: 744—Vol
59: 175—Vol 60: 506—Vol 63: 104—Vol 67:
43, 752—Vol 68: 58, 735—Vol 69: 631—Vol
72: (2-64), (3-70), (7-76)—Vol 73: (1-63),
(9-64)—Vol 75: (6-37)—Vol 80: 192—Vol
82: 502, 727, 794
GRIGG.................................Vol 76: 144
GRIGGS...Vol 34: 657—Vol 39: 223—Vol 42:

16, 188—Vol 45: 240—Vol 46: 335—Vol 49:
48, 281—Vol 56: 371—Vol 58: 700—Vol 65:
508
GRIGS...............................Vol 49: 48
GRIGSBY...Vol 45: 109, 119—Vol 46: 152,
244—Vol 47: 25—Vol 52: 358—Vol 58: 241
—Vol 66: 535—Vol 74: (5-42)—Vol 75:
(5-45)
GRIMES...Vol 22: 156—Vol 26: 244—Vol 39:
275—Vol 42: 72—Vol 46: 152, 241—Vol 63:
105—Vol 66: 250, 826—Vol 69: 247—Vol
71: 462—Vol 74: (2-40)—Vol 80: 588—Vol
81: 630—Vol 82: 220, 859
GRIMLEY...................................Vol 67: 47
GRIMMER...............................Vol 82: 932
GRIMSLEY.............Vol 43: 496—Vol 80: 45
GRINDER.................................Vol 48: 205
GRINELL.................................Vol 53: 633
GRINNELL...Vol 39: 276—Vol 40: 108—Vol
44: 234—Vol 53: 179—Vol 54: 55, 174, 224,
536, 540—Vol 63: 427
GRISHAM................................Vol 82: 930
GRISOM..................................Vol 72: (1-66)
GRIST..................Vol 39: 223—Vol 57: 565
GRISTE..................................Vol 57: 565
GRISWOLD...Vol 21: 235, 497—Vol 22: 154,
373—Vol 25: 967—Vol 26: 53, 240, 561—
Vol 29: 649—Vol 31: 670—Vol 36: 574—
Vol 38: 218, 274, 276—Vol 40: 274—Vol 41:
215—Vol 42: 72—Vol 47: 31, 85—Vol 50:
350—Vol 51: 303, 321, 565—Vol 53: 117, 448,
494—Vol 55: 339—Vol 56: 476—Vol 57:
744—Vol 58: 174—Vol 60: 571—Vol 62:
501, 502—Vol 63: 570—Vol 65: 635—Vol
70: 708—Vol 73: (3-86)—Vol 84: 326
GRIZZARD...............................Vol 39: 277
GROCE...................................Vol 31: 411
GROESBECK........................Vol 49: 47, 184
GROFF...Vol 52: 52—Vol 63: 57—Vol 67: 514
—Vol 69: 119, 631
GROGAN.................................Vol 71: 162
GROMARRIN............................Vol 47: 195
GROMMON...............................Vol 50: 65
GROOCH.............................Vol 39: 22, 275
GROOMES................................Vol 80: 190
GROOT................Vol 46: 236—Vol 56: 176
GROOVER................................Vol 41: 213
GROSCUP............Vol 29: 652—Vol 31: 411
GROSS...Vol 19: 307—Vol 21: 497—Vol 29:
652—Vol 31: 411—Vol 49: 287
GROSSCUP...........Vol 75: (2-57)—Vol 82: 861
GROSSKOLB..............................Vol 31: 411
GROSVENOR..............................Vol 66: 308
GROUT..................................Vol 44: 83
GROVE...Vol 56: 176, 628—Vol 60: 49, 417—
Vol 62: 459—Vol 64: 389, 586—Vol 65: 571,
757—Vol 66: 365—Vol 67: 716—Vol 69:
119, 631
GROVER...Vol 44: 316—Vol 47: 197—Vol 64:
757—Vol 66: 366—Vol 80: 511—Vol 82:
141, 313
GROVES...Vol 33: 709—Vol 47: 95, 199—Vol
63: 570
GROW......................................Vol 57: 175
GRUBB ....Vol 26: 241, 559—Vol 73: (5-88)
GRUBBS...Vol 51: 353—Vol 60: 115—Vol 68:
374—Vol 72: (7-74)
GRUBS................Vol 43: 596—Vol 52: 355
GRUENDIKE..............................Vol 56: 174
GRUMAN.......................................Vol 60: 365

HALL—Vol 17: 283—Vol 19: 532—Vol 20: 277—Vol 21: 336—Vol 22: 997—Vol 24: 58, 151, 262—Vol 25: 381, 383, 719—Vol 26: 56, 242, 335, 336—Vol 27: 382, 737—Vol 28: 60, 260, 261, 363, 545—Vol 29: 47, 652, 649—Vol 30: 66, 67, 149, 438, 541—Vol 31: 410, 411, 588, 667, 748, 752, 863—Vol 32: 60, 632, 719—Vol 34: 66, 538, 658—Vol 35: 434—Vol 36: 578—Vol 37: 73, 158—Vol 38: 221, 274, 330—Vol 39: 21, 141, 222—Vol 40: 23, 24, 25, 223—Vol 41: 33, 125, 211, 215—Vol 42: 11, 13, 75, 78, 79, 188, 189, 193, 264—Vol 43: 417, 427, 481, 494, 495, 497—Vol 44: 24, 80, 233, 383—Vol 45: 104, 108, 115, 119, 186, 193, 196, 240, 323—Vol 46: 29, 99, 158, 243, 245—Vol 47: 197—Vol 48: 61, 62, 301, 449—Vol 49: 132, 282, 286, 348, 395—Vol 50: 68, 184, 278—Vol 51: 165, 303—Vol 53: 54, 116, 178, 379, 575, 690—Vol 54: 354, 648—Vol 55: 46, 109, 165, 209, 286—Vol 56: 46, 47, 173, 225, 313, 316, 369, 374, 477, 626, 629, 743, 745—Vol 57: 37, 113, 116, 312, 313, 480, 481, 691, 742—Vol 58: 51, 111, 240, 369, 370, 702—Vol 59: 46, 111, 388, 653—Vol 60: 419, 507, 697—Vol 61: 157, 473, 788, 911—Vol 62: 160, 308—Vol 63: 508—Vol 64: 59, 120, 522—Vol 65: 298, 763—Vol 66: 824—Vol 70: 56, 574, 576—Vol 71: 357, 761, 956, 1026, 1027—Vol 72: (4-84)—Vol 73: (5-88)—Vol 74: (11-56)—Vol 75: (2-56)—Vol 76: 400, 655—Vol 79: 561—Vol 80: 432, 657—Vol 81: 20—Vol 82: 863—Vol 83: 262—Vol 84: 324, 634

HALLADAY................Vol 42: 139
HALLECK............Vol 42: 340—Vol 84: 447
HALLER....................Vol 83: 944
HALLET—Vol 33: 1033—Vol 43: 421, 422—Vol 54: 110—Vol 84: 632
HALLEY—Vol 57: 435—Vol 64: 257—Vol 65: 571—Vol 66: 365—Vol 67: 716
HALLOCK—Vol 36: 77—Vol 71: 88—Vol 73: (10-76).
HALLOMAN.............Vol 45: 19
HALLOWAY..............Vol 42: 343
HALLOWELL—Vol 22: 53—Vol 45: 108—Vol 74: (5-41)
HALSEY—Vol 2: 299—Vol 56: 175, 317—Vol 60: 698
HALSTEAD—Vol 21: 496—Vol 29: 801—Vol 36: 77—Vol 39: 274—Vol 42: 76—Vol 45: 189—Vol 54: 466—Vol 55: 522—Vol 63: 168—Vol 68: 241—Vol 69: 160
HALTON...........Vol 39: 143
HAM—Vol 30: 259—Vol 64: 258—Vol 77: 240
HAMBLIN..........Vol 53: 181—Vol 67: 44
HAMEL...................Vol 77: 603
HAMELE.................Vol 32: 164
HAMELL.................Vol 32: 164
HAMER..............Vol 54: 350, 465
HAMILIN.................Vol 43: 539
HAMILL.................Vol 32: 164
HAMILTON—Vol 6: 182—Vol 21: 336—Vol 22: 678—Vol 27: 736—Vol 30: 338—Vol 32: 161, 507—Vol 33: 41—Vol 34: 320—Vol 35: 1037—Vol 38: 87, 220—Vol 39: 20, 140—Vol 40: 275—Vol 41: 29—Vol 42: 75, 188, 193, 263, 265, 334—Vol 43: 489, 597—Vol 44: 78, 316—Vol 45: 120, 198, 239—Vol 46: 158—Vol 48: 448—Vol 49: 186, 190—Vol 50: 192, 351, 352—Vol 54: 54, 465—Vol 55: 166,

603—Vol 58: 54—Vol 60: 249, 697—Vol 61: 157, 912—Vol 63: 272—Vol 64: 761—Vol 65: 438, 632, 762—Vol 66: 162, 460, 535, 825—Vol 68: 626—Vol 70: 876, 1020, 1167—Vol 71: 241—Vol 73: (2-65), (11-67)—Vol 74: (4-50), (5-39), (12-53)—Vol 77: 117—Vol 80: 154—Vol 81: 518—Vol 82: 141, 314, 861—Vol 83: 443, 947—Vol 84: 893

HAMITAR.................Vol 58: 451
HAMLER..................Vol 66: 461
HAMLETT.................Vol 82: 796
HAMLIN—Vol 31: 586—Vol 39: 102—Vol 48: 372—Vol 53: 181—Vol 61: 707—Vol 62: 56—Vol 67: 239—Vol 79: 332—Vol 82: 935
HAMMEL.................Vol 32: 164
HAMMER—Vol 25: 716—Vol 37: 148—Vol 70: 359
HAMMETT................Vol 62: 502
HAMMOCK—Vol 45: 188—Vol 74: (11-56)—Vol 81: 431
HAMMOND—Vol 22: 269—Vol 27: 672—Vol 29: 45—Vol 34: 67, 657—Vol 35: 1262—Vol 36: 575—Vol 37: 63, 155—Vol 38: 32, 88, 328—Vol 39: 227—Vol 41: 70, 213—Vol 42: 339—Vol 49: 134, 349, 354—Vol 50: 61, 185, 276—Vol 65: 439—Vol 67: 752—Vol 70: 455, 707—Vol 80: 85—Vol 82: 653—Vol 84: 522
HAMMONDS..............Vol 79: 112
HAMNER—Vol 53: 176—Vol 56: 415—Vol 57: 477
HAMPSON................Vol 62: 459
HAMPTON—Vol 30: 541—Vol 33: 1031—Vol 34: 202, 320, 423—Vol 36: 574, 758—Vol 41: 28—Vol 44: 153—Vol 47: 396—Vol 48: 205, 370—Vol 49: 136, 282, 283—Vol 53: 244—Vol 59: 388—Vol 64: 650—Vol 67: 513—Vol 68: 241—Vol 73: (11-67)—Vol 80: 46—Vol 82: 653
HANCE....................Vol 68: 284
HANCHETT...............Vol 68: 626
HANCOCK—Vol 18: 181—Vol 25: 783—Vol 26: 55—Vol 44: 22—Vol 45: 105—Vol 46: 160—Vol 49: 353—Vol 52: 358—Vol 61: 552, 787—Vol 66: 307—Vol 67: 242—Vol 68: 492—Vol 73: (9-66)—Vol 81: 516, 630—Vol 83: 794, 947—Vol 84: 519
HAND—Vol 31: 585—Vol 39: 222, 274—Vol 43: 426, 483, 546—Vol 45: 239—Vol 46: 245, 337, 384, 391—Vol 47: 85—Vol 48: 440—Vol 50: 63
HANDCOCK...............Vol 84: 632
HANDLEY.............Vol 81: 216, 518
HANDY—Vol 45: 113—Vol 62: 459—Vol 66: 825
HANEY—Vol 46: 335—Vol 49: 193—Vol 55: 520
HANFORD................Vol 39: 327
HANGER.................Vol 38: 329
HANIE...................Vol 55: 520
HANKINS.......Vol 63: 294, 570—Vol 78: 295
HANKINSON—Vol 42: 138—Vol 43: 418—Vol 53: 631
HANKS—Vol 28: 161—Vol 45: 240—Vol 46: 24, 155—Vol 56: 624—Vol 77: 243—Vol 82: 139—Vol 84: 443
HANKSON................Vol 30: 339
HANLON.................Vol 55: 520
HANMORE................Vol 70: 359
HANNA—Vol 22: 678—Vol 32: 163...Vol 40:

Vol 58: 50, 110, 241—Vol 59: 175, 524, 682 —Vol 60: 113—Vol 61: 61, 62, 868, 905— Vol 62: 122—Vol 63: 572—Vol 64: 259— Vol 65: 121—Vol 66: 733—Vol 67: 292, 647 —Vol 68: 155, 373, 553—Vol 69: 242—Vol 70: 456—Vol 71: 467, 956—Vol 72: (3-70), (10-94)—Vol 73: (2-64), (10-75)—Vol 74: (5-43)—Vol 75: (7-36, (10-65)—Vol 78: 456—Vol 79: 368, 383—Vol 81: 264, 516— Vol 82: 396, 500—Vol 83: 628, 947—Vol 84: 327, 521

HARRISON...Vol 21: 251, 401—Vol 25: 718— Vol 26: 56—Vol 30: 147—Vol 34: 320, 322— Vol 36: 353—Vol 37: 155, 391, 395, 489— Vol 38: 86, 87—Vol 39: 20—Vol 40: 76— Vol 41: 33, 215—Vol 42: 338, 339—Vol 43: 419, 420, 421, 422, 424, 483, 490, 601, 602, 604—Vol 44: 26, 27, 81, 154, 227, 382, 387, 388—Vol 45: 184, 195—Vol 46: 101, 153— Vol 47: 195—Vol 48: 123—Vol 49: 47, 134, 190—Vol 50: 61, 188—Vol 52: 108, 561— Vol 53: 181, 446, 492, 634—Vol 54: 223, 537, 594, 647—Vol 55: 109—Vol 56: 416, 481, 482, 562, 629, 740, 742—Vol 57: 219, 352, 432, 566, 626—Vol 58: 53, 331, 451, 588, 651, 652, 762—Vol 60: 48, 114, 365—Vol 62: 122, 308, 389—Vol 63: 166, 571, 738—Vol 64: 122, 256, 758, 759—Vol 65: 122—Vol 66: 252, 365, 535, 732—Vol 68: 488, 490, 625— Vol 69: 360, 501—Vol 70: 358, 707, 876— Vol 71: 88, 161, 460, 673—Vol 72: (11-59)— Vol 73: (2-66)—Vol 74: (11-61)—Vol 75: (12-63)—Vol 79: 562—Vol 80: 382—Vol 82: 793, 933—Vol 83: 521, 523, 946—Vol 84: 247, 324, 521, 893

HARROD...Vol 50: 355—Vol 51: 234—Vol 56: 562—Vol 57: 219

HARROLD..Vol 59: 765
HARROUN............................Vol 57: 434, 688
HARRY..Vol 49: 134
HARSH..........................Vol 47: 273—Vol 49: 356
HARSHA....................................Vol 42: 193, 334
HARSHEY..Vol 67: 515
HART...Vol 27: 735—Vol 28: 158, 482—Vol 30: 257, 539—Vol 31: 54, 587—Vol 32: 718 —Vol 38: 329—Vol 39: 21, 22—Vol 40: 25 —Vol 41: 69, 121, 163, 166, 209—Vol 43: 496, 602, 604—Vol 44: 25, 313—Vol 45: 112, 126—Vol 46: 100, 101, 240, 329—Vol 47: 32—Vol 48. 124, 204, 205, 308, 309—Vol 49: 189—Vol 50: 116, 345, 414—Vol 52: 434— Vol 53: 179, 241, 245, 247, 690—Vol 54: 55, 110, 227, 354, 420, 537, 647, 651—Vol 55: 163, 712—Vol 56: 744—Vol 57: 215—Vol 58: 587—Vol 60: 249—Vol 62: 773—Vol 64: 121—Vol 65: 367—Vol 66: 734—Vol 67: 146 —Vol 69: 120, 243—Vol 73: (8-84), (9-64), (10-76)—Vol 74: (5-43), (12-53)—Vol 75: (3-40)—Vol 76: 401—Vol 77: 538—Vol 82: 141, 314, 861—Vol 83: 337

HARTER...Vol 22: 996—Vol 50: 352—Vol 60: 49—Vol 70: 204

HARTFORD.........Vol 45: 112—Vol 74: (3-44)
HARTGERS..Vol 33: 473
HARTLE..Vol 37: 157
HARTLEY...Vol 41: 68, 71—Vol 60: 157— Vol 65: 248—Vol 76: 653
HARTMAN...Vol 46: 30—Vol 55: 520—Vol 71: 956—Vol 75: (4-53)—Vol 77: 241

HARTRANFT............................Vol 52: 358
HARTRIDGE............................Vol 29: 802
HARTSHORN............................Vol 57: 353
HARTSOL............................Vol 36: 755
HARTUPEE............................Vol 62: 459
HARTWELL...Vol 39: 275—Vol 40: 275— Vol 41: 66, 112—Vol 77: 389
HARTZELL...Vol 25: 37—Vol 59: 111, 521, 524—Vol 76: 710
HARUM............................Vol 60: 634
HARVARD...Vol 40: 275—Vol 41: 29—Vol 61: 786—Vol 75: (2-59)
HARVEY...Vol 27: 44—Vol 34: 321—Vol 41: 70—Vol 42: 138—Vol 43: 418—Vol 46: 94, 388—Vol 52: 357—Vol 56: 629—Vol 57: 176, 215—Vol 60: 249—Vol 64: 651—Vol 66: 160—Vol 70: 1167—Vol 71: 163—Vol 73: (2-64)—Vol 75: (2-61)—Vol 78: 52— Vol 83: 441
HARVIE............................Vol 52: 110, 557
HARWOOD—Vol 26: 143—Vol 30: 259—Vol 69: 246—Vol 75: (10-66)—Vol 82: 796
HARYMAN............................Vol 71: 357
HASEY............................Vol 57: 116
HASKELL...Vol 22: 375—Vol 23: 326—Vol 39: 103—Vol 41: 164—Vol 43: 545—Vol 48: 371—Vol 55: 445—Vol 58: 501
HASKENS............................Vol 75: (5-45)
HASKILL............................Vol 82: 860
HASKING............................Vol 82: 313
HASKINS...Vol 22: 155—Vol 26: 242—Vol 41: 72—Vol 42: 76—Vol 44: 23—Vol 49: 191, 193—Vol 53: 693—Vol 56: 481—Vol 68: 489—Vol 72: (7-75)—Vol 81: 19—Vol 82: 575
HASSEL............................Vol 81: 71
HASSELL............................Vol 68: 243—Vol 75: (8-43)
HASSENBERGER............................Vol 55: 601
HASSINGER............................Vol 68: 121, 685
HASSLER............................Vol 68: 554
HASTAIN............................Vol 47: 394
HASTINGS...Vol 29: 287 - Vol 30: 539—Vol 48: 442—Vol 49: 126, 395—Vol 52: 173— Vol 54: 222—Vol 69: 243, 361—Vol 71: 87, 463—Vol 82: 796—Vol 83: 261—Vol 84: 327
HASWELL............................Vol 49. 283
HATCH...Vol 23: 325—Vol 29: 289—Vol 36: 76—Vol 37: 157—Vol 38: 330—Vol 42: 15, 75—Vol 45: 240—Vol 46: 242—Vol 50: 61, 188—Vol 55: 446—Vol 56: 476, 691—Vol 57: 172—Vol 58: 700—Vol 59: 682—Vol 61: 280—Vol 70: 352—Vol 83: 172
HATCHER...Vol 36: 576—Vol 47: 195—Vol 49: 394—Vol 67: 48—Vol 82: 313, 575
HATCHETT............................Vc' 81: 630
HATCHETTE............................Vol 43: 496
HATFIELD...Vol 31: 589—Vol 35: 1102— Vol 37: 396, 488—Vol 45: 119, 200—Vol 53: 54—Vol 58: 501
HATHAWAY...Vol 20: 166—Vol 39: 326— Vol 42: 78—Vol 45: 22—Vol 54: 53—Vol 61: 698—Vol 63: 294—Vol 65: 299, 439— Vol 68: 490—Vol 69: 56, 117, 245—Vol 82: 863
HATLER............................Vol 67: 752²—Vol 71: 1112
HAUBER............................Vol 75. (6-38)
HAUCK............................Vol 83: 171
HAUGH............................Vol 26: 141—Vol 46: 99
HAUSE............................Vol 83: 873

HEIMS ....Vol 80: 657
HEINECKE ....Vol 36: 754
HEISKELL ....Vol 38: 218—Vol 40: 228
HEISS ....Vol 37: 488
HEITER ....Vol 65: 247—Vol 83: 628
HEIZER ....Vol 58: 330
HELLER ....Vol 43: 422—Vol 71: 88
HELLEY ....Vol 57: 173
HELLINGS ....Vol 56: 373
HELLUMS ....Vol 82: 796
HELM....Vol 45: 188—Vol 58: 588, 699—Vol 79: 283
HELME ....Vol 77: 538
HELMES ....Vol 43: 423—Vol 46: 99
HELMS....Vol 34: 538—Vol 70: 134—Vol 81: 631—Vol 83: 93
HEMDRICKS ....Vol 55: 519
HEMENWAY ....Vol 50: 60—Vol 53: 692
HEMINGER ....Vol 79: 518
HEMINGERE ....Vol 42: 15
HEMINGWAY ....Vol 29: 290—Vol 30: 146
HEMMENWAY ....Vol 27: 736
HEMMINGWAY ....Vol 78: 600
HEMPHILL ....Vol 56: 687
HEMPSTEAD ....Vol 38: 330
HEMSTEAD ....Vol 39: 142
HENBY ....Vol 49: 132
HENCHER ....Vol 46: 154
HENDEE....Vol 23: 326—Vol 45: 28, 113—Vol 50: 412—Vol 52: 53
HENDERSHOT ....Vol 43: 604
HENDERSHOTT ....Vol 83: 93
HENDERSON....Vol 27: 740—Vol 29: 802—Vol 30: 65—Vol 32: 161—Vol 38: 275—Vol 39: 143, 277—Vol 41: 34, 120—Vol 43: 492 —Vol 44: 152, 313—Vol 50: 357—Vol 54: 351, 709—Vol 56: 369, 562, 690, 691—Vol 59: 49, 387, 442, 652, 765—Vol 60: 250—Vol 61: 274, 707—Vol 65: 763—Vol 66: 461— Vol 67: 242, 573, 646, 753—Vol 68: 122— Vol 72: (1-66)—Vol 77: 538—Vol 80: 85, 155, 192—Vol 82: 142, 500.
HENDRICKS....Vol 41: 120, 124—Vol 43: 426, 483—Vol 46: 384—Vol 55: 285, 520—Vol 56: 46—Vol 81: 629—Vol 83: 628—Vol 84: 244
HENDRICKSON....Vol 40: 274—Vol 47: 270 —Vol 56: 690—Vol 70: 352, 1168—Vol 80: 46
HENDRIX....Vol 40: 74—Vol 52. 51—Vol 81: 629
HENDRY ....Vol 47: 27
HENDRYX ....Vol 57: 313
HENEY ....Vol 55: 520
HENING ....Vol 58: 764
HENKLE ....Vol 58: 450
HENLEY....Vol 44: 309—Vol 60: 366—Vol 61: 382
HENLY ....Vol 44: 27
HENNAS ....Vol 80: 588
HENNON ....Vol 60: 418
HENRY....Vol 17: 480, 568—Vol 22: 155—Vol 26: 559—Vol 39: 274—Vol 46: 243, 388— Vol 47: 268—Vol 48: 305—Vol 49: 40—Vol 53: 242, 243, 379—Vol 54: 56, 591—Vol 56: 371—Vol 58: 763—Vol 59: 239—Vol 64: 756 —Vol 68: 242—Vol 69: 361, 567—Vol 71: 673—Vol 78: 155—Vol 82: 502—Vol 83: 439 —Vol 84: 326

HENSHAW....Vol 47: 32—Vol 72: (4-82)— Vol 78: 107—Vol 83: 173—Vol 84: 706
HENSLEE ....Vol 59: 682
HENSLEY....Vol 71: 464—Vol 78: 456—Vol 84: 633
HENSON ....Vol 76: 653
HENTHOM ....Vol 65: 296
HENTON....Vol 45: 21—Vol 61: 156—Vol 67: 387—Vol 77: 243
HEPNER ....Vol 82: 503
HERBERT....Vol 40: 274—Vol 56: 482, 629, 740—Vol 57: 479—Vol 64: 257—Vol 75: (10-66)—Vol 81: 316
HERBERTS ....Vol 71: 357
HERCULES ....Vol 77: 333
HEREFORD....Vol 56: 744—Vol 61: 704—Vol 68: 733—Vol 69: 363—Vol 75: (8-42)—Vol 82: 933
HERITAGE ....Vol 77: 603
HERKIMER....Vol 2: 694—Vol 8: 87, 244— Vol 45: 321
HERNDON....Vol 78: 398—Vol 80: 428—Vol 82: 798—Vol 83: 439
HEROD ....Vol 57: 219
HERREFORD ....Vol 69: 363
HERREN....Vol 30: 260—Vol 49: 193—Vol 54: 465
HERRICK....Vol 25: 798—Vol 41: 126—Vol 42: 12—Vol 45: 121—Vol 50: 64—Vol 53: 177—Vol 55: 338, 446, 521, 712—Vol 56: 112, 226—Vol 59: 650—Vol 67: 116, 514— Vol 84: 632
HERRIFORD ....Vol 68: 733—Vol 78: 53
HERRING....Vol 49: 43, 131, 133, 183, 193— Vol 57: 218—Vol 62: 498—Vol 63: 166— Vol 64: 121—Vol 66: 248—Vol 84: 634
HERRINGTON....Vol 57: 348—Vol 61: 473, 868—Vol 62: 390, 501—Vol 69: 563
HERRIOTT ....Vol 56: 173, 625
HERRON....Vol 54: 51—Vol 68: 733—Vol 69: 431, 567—Vol 81: 430
HERSEY ....Vol 65: 300
HERSHEY....Vol 40: 229—Vol 46: 30, 238— Vol 57: 115, 433—Vol 62: 585—Vol 70: 1266
HERTER ....Vol 2: 695
HERTZLER ....Vol 40: 230—Vol 46: 30
HERVEY ....Vol 54: 465
HERYFORD ....Vol 82: 931
HESKETT ....Vol 81: 264
HESS....Vol 33: 1032—Vol 34: 198—Vol 38: 274—Vol 43: 492—Vol 46: 30, 391—Vol 83: 523
HESSAR ....Vol 46: 156
HESSER ....Vol 42: 77—Vol 77: 183
HESSLER ....Vol 84: 522
HESTER....Vol 51: 354—Vol 56: 479—Vol 60: 116—Vol 70: 205
HESTON ....Vol 76: 654
HETFIELD........Vol 30: 62, 63—Vol 61: 906
HEUGH................Vol 37: 66—Vol 40: 170
HEUSTED ....Vol 37: 151
HEUSTIS ....Vol 21: 496
HEWES....Vol 22: 52—Vol 36: 350, 355—Vol 42: 341
HEWETT ....Vol 65: 248—Vol 76: 62
HEWITT....Vol 25: 383—Vol 27: 806—Vol 30: 336—Vol 32: 163—Vol 33: 473—Vol 45: 114, 239—Vol 57: 40—Vol 63: 246—Vol 64: 388—Vol 65: 248—Vol 66: 537—Vol 81: 570—Vol 82: 935

HEWLETT..................Vol 42: 140
HEXT..................Vol 63: 371
HEYL..................Vol 77: 768—Vol 78: 295
HEYWARD...Vol 17: 480, 569—Vol 18: 57—
Vol 19: 67
HEYWOOD...Vol 17: 181, 282—Vol 49: 189,
350—Vol 56: 176
HIAL..................Vol 44: 312
HIATT...Vol 41: 72—Vol 50: 353—Vol 51:
358—Vol 52: 358—Vol 56: 564—Vol 72:
(10-95)
HIBBARD...Vol 25: 717, 886—Vol 26: 57—
Vol 31: 861—Vol 44: 381—Vol 45: 199—
Vol 58: 173—Vol 67: 145—Vol 68: 490—
Vol 81: 570—Vol 84: 446
HIBBLER..................Vol 84: 771
HIBLER..................Vol 38: 276—Vol 70: 360
HICKBEE..................Vol 62: 585
HICKEY..................Vol 74: (4-52)
HICKLEN..................Vol 53: 180
HICKLIN..................Vol 53: 634
HICKMAN...Vol 33: 955, 958—Vol 34: 66—
Vol 50: 62—Vol 54: 350—Vol 56: 44—Vol
58: 329—Vol 60: 699—Vol 62: 502—Vol 64:
712—Vol 75: (2-58)—Vol 82: 932—Vol 84:
519, 704
HICKOK...Vol 54: 230—Vol 65: 247—Vol 67:
751
HICKOX...Vol 46: 238—Vol 52: 52—Vol 53:
572—Vol 54: 352, 536—Vol 55: 165—Vol
56: 416—Vol 64: 522—Vol 65: 247—Vol
71: 462
HICKS...Vol 18: 58—Vol 21: 498—Vol 42:
340—Vol 43: 420—Vol 51: 301—Vol 54: 350
—Vol 58: 172—Vol 62: 160, 161—Vol 63:
506, 700—Vol 64: 256, 714—Vol 66: 121,
249, 461—Vol 71: 675—Vol 76: 861—Vol
80: 45, 193—Vol 81: 517—Vol 82: 798—Vol
83: 440, 718, 946
HICKSON..................Vol 56: 624—Vol 58: 174
HIDGEN..................Vol 82: 796
HIERONYMUS..................Vol 47: 395—Vol 49: 389
HIESRODT..................Vol 77: 539—Vol 81: 430
HIESS..................Vol 34: 538
HIGBEE...Vol 45: 109, 192—Vol 62: 585—
Vol 65: 59—Vol 82: 936
HIGBY..................Vol 65: 59
HIGGINBOTHAM...Vol 44: 236—Vol 59: 763
—Vol 76: 401—Vol 80: 583, 588
HIGGINS...Vol 17: 570—Vol 22: 375, 376—
Vol 32: 163—Vol 35: 57—Vol 47: 397—Vol
55: 109—Vol 58: 173, 330—Vol 64: 714—
Vol 68: 241, 487—Vol 69: 243—Vol 73: (4-
83)—Vol 80: 45, 511
HIGHBERGER..................Vol 39: 328
HIGHFIELD...Vol 76: 653—Vol 77: 117—Vol
78: 554—Vol 80: 277—Vol 81: 430
HIGHLAND..................Vol 83: 171
HIGHTOWER..................Vol 37: 69
HIGLEY...Vol 35: 57—Vol 54: 536—Vol 58:
452—Vol 62: 307—Vol 71: 462
HILBUN..................Vol 84: 705
HILBURN..................Vol 84: 705
HILDEBRAND..................Vol 54: 591—Vol 65: 160
HILDRETH...Vol 28: 161—Vol 30: 61—Vol
44: 233, 311—Vol 56: 44
HILEY..................Vol 84: 245
HILL...Vol 19: 207—Vol 23: 324—Vol 24:
543—Vol 28: 61, 262—Vol 29: 714—Vol 31:
412, 414, 666, 861—Vol 32: 61, 164, 720—Vol

35: 1265—Vol 36: 578, 756—Vol 37: 153—
Vol 38: 331—Vol 39: 226—Vol 41: 69—Vol
42: 193—Vol 43: 416, 424, 495, 546—Vol
45: 25—Vol 46: 21, 152, 159, 337, 387, 393—
Vol 48: 203—Vol 49: 46, 47, 187—Vol 50:
67, 354—Vol 52: 52—Vol 53: 179—Vol 54:
110, 174, 539—Vol 56: 176, 318, 481, 689, 691
—Vol 57: 691, 692—Vol 58: 501, 701—Vol
59: 315, 587—Vol 60: 747—Vol 61: 231, 473,
545—Vol 63: 571, 572—Vol 64: 713, 758,
759—Vol 65: 571—Vol 66: 251, 365, 669—
Vol 67: 242, 443, 515—Vol 68: 373, 553—
Vol 69: 242—Vol 71: 1025—Vol 72: (1-65)
—Vol 73: (2-65), (9-68)—Vol 75: (9-37)—
Vol 78: 695—Vol 79: 332, 561—Vol 80: 84
—Vol 82: 499—Vol 83: 171
HILLAN..................Vol 43: 492
HILLEARY..................Vol 45: 120
HILLHOUSE..................Vol 30: 539—Vol 60: 571
HILLIARD...Vol 31: 861—Vol 33: 474—Vol
49: 49—Vol 70: 1166
HILLIKER..................Vol 66: 461
HILLIS...Vol 42: 81, 189—Vol 44: 82, 84, 383
—Vol 45: 27, 323—Vol 56: 562—Vol 60:
698—Vol 71: 675—Vol 72: (2-62)—Vol 80:
85—Vol 82: 141—Vol 83: 944
HILLMAN...Vol 36: 354—Vol 55: 208—Vol
84: 966
HILLS...Vol 28: 364—Vol 30: 257—Vol 39:
327—Vol 48: 307—Vol 57: 312—Vol 70: 207
HILLYARD..................Vol 49: 49
HILSABECK..................Vol 60: 157
HILTON...Vol 39: 227—Vol 60: 573, 746—Vol
61: 154—Vol 66: 538, 827—Vol 67: 575—
Vol 72: (3-71)—Vol 83: 442
HIMES..................Vol 80: 657
HINCKLEY...Vol 22: 373—Vol 36: 579—Vol
42: 268—Vol 49: 395—Vol 50: 356—Vol 52:
170—Vol 54: 226—Vol 56: 222—Vol 64:
443—Vol 72: (3-70)
HINDALE..................Vol 39: 20
HINDMAN...Vol 45: 122, 197, 327—Vol 46:
237, 245—Vol 47: 25—Vol 51: 355—Vol 55:
713—Vol 56: 113—Vol 60: 249
HINDS...Vol 44: 236—Vol 46: 241—Vol 57:
173—Vol 65: 439, 570
HINE...Vol 42: 336—Vol 58: 331—Vol 76:
401
HINEMAN..................Vol 82: 314
HINES..................Vol 57: 217—Vol 61: 705
HINKLEY..................Vol 27: 889—Vol 49: 45, 395
HINKLY..................Vol 74: (2-41)
HINKSON..................Vol 60: 572
HINLEY..................Vol 83: 945
HINMAN...Vol 26: 240—Vol 31: 588, 667—
Vol 36: 579—Vol 37: 160—Vol 38: 272—
Vol 55: 711—Vol 57: 352, 745—Vol 71: 161
HINSDALE..................Vol 38: 219—Vol 45: 104
HINSEY..................Vol 72: (2-63)
HINSHAW..................Vol 64: 160
HINSON...Vol 25: 966—Vol 27: 43, 44—Vol
30: 145—Vol 84: 632
HINSSY..................Vol 72: (2-63)
HINTON...Vol 37: 488—Vol 38: 328—Vol 39:
326—Vol 40: 224—Vol 45: 27, 105—Vol 46:
328—Vol 57: 216—Vol 64: 122—Vol 77: 603
HINZE..................Vol 72: (2-63)
HIPSHIRE..................Vol 45: 112—Vol 53: 56
HIRE..................Vol 75: (11-70)—Vol 77: 481
HIRST..................Vol 52: 320, 731—Vol 53: 332

HISCOCK_____Vol 54: 536
HISER_____Vol 58: 330
HISLE_____Vol 49: 191
HISSOM_____Vol 41: 127—Vol 46: 393
HITCHBORN_____Vol 24: 543
HITCHCOCK___Vol 1: 334—Vol 5: 466—Vol
25: 38, 966—Vol 28: 159—Vol 30: 440—Vol
33: 476—Vol 40: 78—Vol 42: 139—Vol 49:
285—Vol 56: 318, 562—Vol 58: 372, 586—
Vol 66: 55—Vol 67: 146, 713—Vol 83: 259
HITCHMAN_____Vol 78: 247
HITE___Vol 38: 221—Vol 44: 150—Vol 60:
506—Vol 63: 58—Vol 64: 160, 386—Vol 65:
297—Vol 68: 372, 623—Vol 83: 173—Vol
84: 69
HITER_____Vol 49: 283
HITT___Vol 77: 480—Vol 83: 871—Vol 84: 159
HIVNER_____Vol 44: 84
HIX_____Vol 45: 242, 321—Vol 66: 121
HIXSON_____Vol 45: 22, 322—Vol 54: 709
HOAG_____Vol 58: 241
HOAGLAND_____Vol 55: 714—Vol 75: (6-40)
HOAR_____Vol 70: 356
HOARD_____Vol 49: 135
HOBART___Vol 23: 168—Vol 32: 62, 719—Vol
37: 158—Vol 40: 227—Vol 63: 246—Vol
66: 366—Vol 68: 735—Vol 69: 120
HOBBS___Vol 45: 199—Vol 47: 268—Vol 63:
699—Vol 68: 243—Vol 82: 794, 797—Vol
83: 794, 871
HOBBY_____Vol 62: 388
HOBER_____Vol 75: (6-38)
HOBSON___Vol 41: 121, 127—Vol 45: 127—
Vol 54: 537—Vol 55: 602
HOCHERMILLER_____Vol 61: 157
HOCK_____Vol 84: 447
HODGDON_____Vol 68: 241
HODGE ___Vol 26: 244—Vol 30: 541—Vol 37:
155—Vol 42: 270—Vol 45: 111—Vol 53:
745—Vol 58: 452—Vol 79: 35—Vol 80: 556
HODGES___Vol 31: 588—Vol 39: 23—Vol 47:
194—Vol 52: 358—Vol 55: 108—Vol 57:
175, 480—Vol 62: 500—Vol 63: 699—Vol
69: 244—Vol 84: 771
HODGKINS_____Vol 59: 525—Vol 81: 570
HODGSON_____Vol 43: 419—Vol 66: 600
HODSON_____Vol 69: 243—Vol 83: 93, 443
HOFF___Vol 29: 511—Vol 43: 425—Vol 56:
688—Vol 73: (9-68)—Vol 83: 335, 523
HOFFMAN___Vol 43: 600—Vol 61: 784 Vol
62: 503—Vol 67: 241—Vol 73: (12-63)—Vol
78: 53
HOGABORN_____Vol 45: 117
HOGAN___Vol 60: 248—Vol 70: 353—Vol 83:
872
HOGE___Vol 64: 523—Vol 74: (7-53), (8-53)—
Vol 77: 240
HOGG___Vol 33: 1032—Vol 75: (10-65)—Vol
83: 93
HOGUE___Vol 74: (7-53), (8-53)—Vol 77: 184
HOHNES_____Vol 40: 76
HOISINGTON_____Vol 73: (11-69)
HOIT___Vol 29: 650—Vol 30: 65—Vol 33: 955,
958
HOKES_____Vol 41: 70
HOLBERT_____Vol 84: 522
HOLBROOK___Vol 45: 117—Vol 47: 198—Vol
54: 535—Vol 60: 699—Vol 66: 251—Vol 84:
521

HOLBROOKS_____Vol 82: 397
HOLCOMB___Vol 22: 374—Vol 26: 244—Vol
27: 379—Vol 28: 482—Vol 29: 714—Vol 37:
271—Vol 38: 34, 114, 217—Vol 39: 20, 104—
Vol 50: 62—Vol 63: 508—Vol 64: 445—Vol
65: 761—Vol 66: 119, 362—Vol 82: 935—
Vol 83: 945
HOLCOMBE_____Vol 32: 720—Vol 41: 31
HOLDEN___Vol 43: 482—Vol 45: 193—Vol
54: 54—Vol 63: 59, 293—Vol 67: 292—Vol
75: (9-41)—Vol 84: 636
HOLDER_____Vol 78: 53
HOLDERBAUM_____Vol 42: 78, 189
HOLDREN_____Vol 59: 113
HOLDRIDGE_____Vol 44: 234—Vol 47: 392
HOLEMAN_____Vol 64: 258
HOLESAPPLE_____Vol 50: 281
HOLETON_____Vol 76: 62
HOLGAT_____Vol 74: (11-56)
HOLIDAY___Vol 46: 389—Vol 48: 366—Vol
74: (4-50)—Vol 82: 220
HOLIMAN_____Vol 52: 733
HOLISTER_____Vol 75: (12-64)
HOLLABAUGH_____Vol 81: 630
HOLLADAY_____Vol 48: 366—Vol 78: 108
HOLLAND___Vol 21: 336—Vol 27: 383—Vol
31: 749—Vol 43: 496—Vol 44: 388—Vol 45:
21, 236, 322—Vol 46: 22—Vol 49: 131, 134—
Vol 54: 589—Vol 55: 110—Vol 56: 226, 372
—Vol 58: 650—Vol 66: 535—Vol 67: 43—
Vol 68: 285—Vol 70: 1267—Vol 76: 928—
Vol 83: 336
HOLLEMAN_____Vol 36: 214—Vol 71: 356
HOLLENBECK___Vol 65: 763—Vol 74: (4-50)
HOLLES_____Vol 58: 372—Vol 65: 506
HOLLESTER_____Vol 29: 513
HOLLEY___Vol 19: 433—Vol 48: 308—Vol
54: 464—Vol 60: 49
HOLLIDAY___Vol 20: 62—Vol 23: 326—Vol
45: 194, 327—Vol 47: 191, 194, 265—Vol
50: 64, 185—Vol 54: 175—Vol 74: (4-50)
HOLLINGER_____Vol 82: 501, 654
HOLLINGSWORTH___Vol 9: 498—Vol 28: 61
—Vol 55: 166—Vol 57: 353—Vol 63: 166—
Vol 71: 464—Vol 78: 695—Vol 83: 439—
Vol 84: 246
HOLLINSHEAD_____Vol 67: 713
HOLLIS_____Vol 69: 58
HOLLISTER___Vol 21: 335—Vol 22: 54—Vol
50: 66—Vol 56: 319—Vol 63: 59, 167, 698—
Vol 70: 1171
HOLLMAN_____Vol 45: 326
HOLLODAY_____Vol 53: 572
HOLLOMAN_____Vol 64: 444
HOLLOWAY___Vol 29: 715—Vol 38: 330—Vol
45: 124—Vol 48: 370—Vol 55: 397, 445—Vol
57: 353—Vol 61: 551—Vol 64: 714—Vol
73: (11-69)
HOLLY___Vol 48: 307, 308—Vol 64: 387—Vol
84: 246
HOLLYDAY_____Vol 46: 101
HOLMAN___Vol 41: 214—Vol 42: 14—Vol 44:
25, 28, 82—Vol 56: 627, 628—Vol 68: 373—
Vol 71: 356, 959—Vol 73: (9-64)—Vol 75:
(9-37)—Vol 82: 653—Vol 83: 944—Vol 84:
70
HOLME_____Vol 45: 237—Vol 61: 155
HOLMEAD_____Vol 61: 152, 274
HOLMES___Vol 17: 181, 388—Vol 35: 1263,

HOUSH__Vol 43: 423, 483—Vol 44: 148—Vol 45: 242—Vol 46: 21
HOUSMAN_____Vol 37: 69
HOUSTEN_____Vol 43: 486—Vol 57: 172, 479
HOUSTON__Vol 28: 365—Vol 36: 757—Vol 37: 69, 70—Vol 38: 219—Vol 41: 124—Vol 46: 246, 390—Vol 47: 191—Vol 50: 69—Vol 53: 628—Vol 54: 225, 311, 588—Vol 55: 106, 107, 653—Vol 59: 237, 587—Vol 63: 104 —Vol 64: 446—Vol 72: (10-97)—Vol 78: 52, 245—Vol 82: 861, 935—Vol 83: 522
HOUSTONA_____Vol 26: 53
HOVEY__Vol 42: 75—Vol 43: 546—Vol 44: 25, 80—Vol 45: 104, 111, 239, 325—Vol 56: 176—Vol 68: 57—Vol 74: (6-38)—Vol 81: 631—Vol 83: 872
HOVIS_____Vol 43: 600
HOW_____Vol 28: 160—Vol 38: 34
HOWARD__Vol 22: 272—Vol 30: 147—Vol 39: 102, 324—Vol 40: 274—Vol 42: 76, 190 —Vol 43: 486, 544—Vol 44: 150, 315—Vol 45: 107—Vol 46: 235, 236, 243—Vol 47: 27, 268—Vol 49: 355—Vol 50: 348, 351—Vol 53: 177, 244, 247—Vol 54: 174, 420, 539—Vol 55: 285—Vol 56: 176, 629, 742__Vol 57: 113, 172, 213, 432—Vol 58: 452—Vol 59: 48—Vol 60: 116—Vol 61: 66, 698—Vol 63: 371, 738—Vol 64: 520—Vol 65: 759—Vol 67: 118, 645—Vol 68: 242, 372—Vol 70: 56, 205—Vol 71: 557, 673, 1024—Vol 72: (3-71) —Vol 74: (11-56)—Vol 75: (6-40)—Vol 77: 331—Vol 78: 246—Vol 80: 277—Vol 81: 431, 571—Vol 82: 313, 653, 798—Vol 83: 260, 442, 1014
HOWARTH_____Vol 30: 67
HOWD_____Vol 31: 54—Vol 32: 283
HOWE__Vol 23: 167—Vol 28: 164—Vol 30: 66, 440—Vol 33: 1033—Vol 34: 69, 199—Vol 38: 329—Vol 39: 224—Vol 41: 70, 161—Vol 42: 76—Vol 43: 481—Vol 44: 81, 150, 313—Vol 45: 194—Vol 46: 241—Vol 47: 391 —Vol 50: 60, 62, 190—Vol 53: 493—Vol 54: 537—Vol 56: 479—Vol 59: 112—Vol 61: 552 —Vol 64: 587—Vol 67: 576—Vol 71: 958—Vol 74: (11-58)
HOWELL__Vol 21: 335—Vol 22: 52, 372—Vol 28: 158, 363, 482—Vol 29: 44, 287—Vol 30: 339—Vol 31: 587—Vol 34: 66—Vol 48: 450—Vol 50: 354—Vol 52: 484—Vol 53: 117, 626—Vol 57: 480, 567—Vol 58: 171, 172 —Vol 62: 54, 159, 390—Vol 64: 712—Vol 67: 41, 576—Vol 77: 184—Vol 80: 45, 46, 84, 155
HOWER_____Vol 59: 239—Vol 82: 63
HOWERINGTON_____Vol 45: 103
HOWERTON__Vol 68: 372—Vol 69: 58—Vol 70: 202—Vol 76: 144
HOWES__Vol 46: 237—Vol 57: 693—Vol 70: 56
HOWIE_____Vol 50: 190
HOWISON_____Vol 61: 606
HOWLAND__Vol 31: 749—Vol 32: 160—Vol 38: 274—Vol 39: 323—Vol 62: 307—Vol 68: 443—Vol 70: 133, 355—Vol 74: (11-56)—Vol 76: 63
HOWLETT_____Vol 67: 118
HOWORTH_____Vol 57: 629
HOWS_____Vol 70: 56
HOWSE__Vol 39: 275—Vol 41: 68, 71—Vol 70: 56

HOWSER_____Vol 57: 174
HOWZE_____Vol 74: (11-57)
HOXEY_____Vol 69: 121
HOXIE__Vol.38: 332—Vol 39: 141, 323—Vol 56: 480—Vol 57: 37, 564, 690—Vol 58: 176 —Vol 60: 51—Vol 69: 121, 287—Vol 75: (1-54)
HOYE_____Vol 46: 104
HOYSRODT_____Vol 58: 452
HOYT__Vol 22: 52—Vol 28: 482—Vol 30: 65, 529—Vol 33: 955, 958—Vol 34: 322—Vol 39: 222—Vol 41: 32, 67—Vol 42: 74—Vol 43: 491, 723—Vol 44: 79, 150—Vol 45: 18, 237—Vol 49: 285, 392—Vol 56: 373, 559, 560—Vol 57: 687, 744—Vol 64: 758—Vol 70: 880
HUBBARD__Vol 17: 569—Vol 21: 169—Vol 25: 383—Vol 27: 45—Vol 28: 365—Vol 29: 288, 510—Vol 30: 256—Vol 31: 414—Vol 33: 955—Vol 36: 77—Vol 37: 152—Vol 39: 143—Vol 42: 194—Vol 43: 488—Vol 44: 83, 227, 383—Vol 47: 29—Vol 50: 353—Vol 56: 560, 688, 740—Vol 57: 114, 743—Vol 60: 157, 290—Vol 65: 572—Vol 66: 366—Vol 67: 443, 712—Vol 68: 285—Vol 70: 878—Vol 71: 1110—Vol 72: (8-86)—Vol 81: 430 —Vol 82: 397—Vol 84: 68, 444
HUBBEL_____Vol 67: 42
HUBBELL__Vol 25: 798—Vol 37: 350—Vol 38: 85—Vol 39: 140—Vol 49: 45—Vol 50: 352—Vol 54: 536—Vol 74: (4-48)—Vol 75: (5-45)
HUBBLE__Vol 37: 350, 353—Vol 41: 70—Vol 76: 309—Vol 82: 62—Vol 83: 945
HUBER__Vol 21: 335—Vol 59: 441—Vol 60: 634
HUBERT_____Vol 57: 175
HUBLER_____Vol 58: 241
HUCKINS_____Vol 45: 324
HUDDLESTON__Vol 43: 421, 422—Vol 63: 507—Vol 68: 552—Vol 72: (12-68)
HUDDLESTONE_____Vol 23: 441
HUDGELL_____Vol 60: 365
HUDNALL_____Vol 46: 386
HUDSON__Vol 18: 181—Vol 31: 863—Vol 37: 69, 70, 154, 395, 488—Vol 41: 212—Vol 42: 342—Vol 43: 496—Vol 44: 28—Vol 45: 126, 185—Vol 48: 370—Vol 54: 710—Vol 55: 396—Vol 56: 110—Vol 57: 743—Vol 63: 60—Vol 65: 634—Vol 67: 115, 647—Vol 72: (10-95)—Vol 74: (5-42)—Vol 76: 60—Vol 77: 602—Vol 81: 630—Vol 82: 503, 794
HUDSONPILLAR_____Vol 61: 472
HUDSPETH_____Vol 77: 768
HUE_____Vol 43: 419
HUEY__Vol 42: 80—Vol 43: 425, 597—Vol 47: 196—Vol 55: 602
HUFF__Vol 30: 441—Vol 44: 26—Vol 48: 205—Vol 55: 602—Vol 56: 368—Vol 57: 567, 588—Vol 58: 170, 174—Vol 59: 525, 763
HUFFER__Vol 43: 605—Vol 58: 502—Vol 77: 768
HUFFINGTON_____Vol 71: 463
HUFFMAN__Vol 46: 27—Vol 55: 602—Vol 57: 177—Vol 59: 762—Vol 64: 761—Vol 67: 241—Vol 68: 285—Vol 75: (2-60)—Vol 79: 161—Vol 83: 1015
HUFFNER_____Vol 78: 247
HUFFORD_____Vol 82: 501—Vol 83: 261

HUGG................Vol 57: 217
HUGGINS....Vol 44: 316—Vol 45: 125, 188, 192
HUGHES....Vol 33: 961—Vol 39: 276—Vol 41: 69, 128—Vol 42: 76, 139—Vol 45: 25—Vol 46: 97, 98, 246, 337, 392—Vol 47: 32, 87, 95, 198—Vol 49: 354—Vol 50: 189, 276, 346—Vol 52: 52—Vol 53: 52, 248, 628—Vol 55: 286—Vol 57: 176, 431—Vol 63: 243—Vol 65: 506—Vol 67: 117, 648—Vol 68: 487, 489 —Vol 70: 454—Vol 71: 1026—Vol 74: (7-53), (8-53)—Vol 76, 655, 860—Vol 77: 184, 239—Vol 80: 193—Vol 81: 316, 429—Vol 82: 653—Vol 83: 173, 628, 872—Vol 84: 632
HUGHEY....Vol 42: 80—Vol 43: 597—Vol 44: 236
HUGHS................Vol 65: 505—Vol 67: 575
HUGHY................Vol 49: 282
HUIT................Vol 30: 336—Vol 31, 411, 412
HULBERT....Vol 46: 389—Vol 65: 760—Vol 67: 242
HULBURT................Vol 43: 424
HULET................Vol 83: 259
HULETT....Vol 22: 373—Vol 42: 140—Vol 82: 140
HULIGAN................Vol 56: 225
HULING................Vol 27: 382—Vol 82: 862
HULL....Vol 24: 151, 457—Vol 25: 968—Vol 26: 240—Vol 27: 734, 739, 809—Vol 28: 548 —Vol 31: 589—Vol 32: 631—Vol 33: 1032—Vol 37: 149—Vol 39: 143, 274, 276—Vol 40: 75, 275—Vol 41: 33, 66, 128—Vol 42: 12, 138, 268—Vol 43: 416—Vol 44: 383—Vol 49: 285—Vol 50: 66, 278—Vol 52: 561—Vol 56: 43—Vol 57: 480, 745—Vol 58: 109—Vol 61: 473—Vol 63: 373—Vol 65: 760—Vol 66: 825, 826—Vol 70: 573—Vol 72: (2-63)—Vol 81: 517—Vol 82: 220, 863
HULLIHAN................Vol 45: 107
HULLS................Vol 43: 423
HULME................Vol 71: 463
HULSART................Vol 58: 174—Vol 63: 508
HULTY................Vol 58: 172—Vol 62: 776
HUMBARGER................Vol 19: 628
HUMBERT................Vol 84: 518
HUME....Vol 43: 488—Vol 44: 25, 233, 383—Vol 45: 106, 193, 325
HUMES................Vol 61: 274
HUMISTON................Vol 29: 800
HUMPHREIS................Vol 39: 104
HUMPHREY....Vol 23: 243—Vol 36: 218—Vol 42: 75—Vol 52: 733—Vol 53: 379—Vol 62: 247, 305—Vol 70: 879
HUMPHREYS....Vol 31: 55—Vol 32: 162—Vol 46: 328—Vol 57: 352—Vol 76: 309—Vol 78: 695—Vol 82: 797
HUMPHREYVILLE....Vol 21: 336—Vol 34: 66—Vol 49: 285
HUMPHRIES....Vol 55: 521—Vol 56: 112—Vol 65: 367—Vol 81: 19
HUNDLEY....Vol 60: 507—Vol 77: 539—Vol 81: 216—Vol 84: 70
HUNGATE................Vol 47: 341
HUNGERFORD....Vol 22: 997—Vol 28: 263—Vol 39: 23—Vol 44: 225—Vol 77: 242
HUNKINS................Vol 31: 670
HUNN................Vol 34: 539
HUNNICUT................Vol 82: 221
HUNNICUTT................Vol 78: 600
HUNSACHER................Vol 67: 43

HUNSAKER................Vol 82: 138
HUNSINGER................Vol 47: 268
HUNT....Vol 24: 543—Vol 26: 55, 142, 336—Vol 30: 259—Vol 31: 669—Vol 37: 72, 156, 159—Vol 42: 190, 341—Vol 43: 420, 540—Vol 44: 85—Vol 46: 99—Vol 47: 28—Vol 48: 304—Vol 52: 109—Vol 53: 744—Vol 54: 418—Vol 55: 339—Vol 56: 744—Vol 57: 435—Vol 58: 371, 700—Vol 59: 681—Vol 62: 648—Vol 64: 716—Vol 65: 160, 762—Vol 67: 751—Vol 68: 243, 492, 734, 735—Vol 70: 134, 454, 571—Vol 72: (3-70)—Vol 75: (9-41)—Vol 80: 658—Vol 81: 264—Vol 82: 141
HUNTER....Vol 17: 569—Vol 19: 530—Vol 21: 169—Vol 26: 142, 560—Vol 30: 339—Vol 33: 1032—Vol 34: 424—Vol 41: 34—Vol 43: 601—Vol 44: 233—Vol 45: 117, 327—Vol 46: 27, 328—Vol 47: 197—Vol 48: 204, 306, 440—Vol 50: 356—Vol 54: 420—Vol 56: 372, 479—Vol 63: 107—Vol 65: 758—Vol 67: 48—Vol 72: (9-88)—Vol 77: 389, 538—Vol 79: 35, 194—Vol 83: 718
HUNTING................Vol 30: 64
HUNTINGDON................Vol 22: 154
HUNTINGTON....Vol 27: 671—Vol 28: 549—Vol 29: 649—Vol 36: 218—Vol 37: 489—Vol 38: 113—Vol 39: 101—Vol 40: 271—Vol 46: 237—Vol 49: 43—Vol 53: 243, 492 —Vol 55: 339—Vol 63: 58—Vol 82: 863—Vol 84: 520, 706
HUNTLEY....Vol 31: 54—Vol 38: 332—Vol 39: 22—Vol 56: 746—Vol 84: 67, 325
HUNTOM................Vol 15: 350—Vol 30: 441
HUNTON....Vol 44: 23—Vol 50: 69
HUNTRESS................Vol 28: 60
HUNTSBERRY................Vol 60: 248
HUNTT................Vol 43: 425
HUNTTING................Vol 31: 751
HUPP....Vol 40: 172—Vol 44: 226—Vol 58: 453
HURD....Vol 26: 57—Vol 31: 585, 861—Vol 38: 33—Vol 43: 497—Vol 44: 24—Vol 50: 190—Vol 54: 420—Vol 56: 627—Vol 57: 481—Vol 66: 251—Vol 68: 627—Vol 70: 707—Vol 72: (11-58)—Vol 82: 220
HURDLE................Vol 61: 607
HURLBURT....Vol 32: 162—Vol 40: 26—Vol 49: 136—Vol 57: 566—Vol 70: 574
HURLBUT....Vol 27: 381, 670, 671—Vol 32: 162—Vol 49: 389—Vol 58: 451
HURST....Vol 42: 138, 267—Vol 44: 85—Vol 52: 320—Vol 63: 166, 244, 425—Vol 66: 249—Vol 74: (4-50)—Vol 78: 295—Vol 84: 632
HURT................Vol 38: 331—Vol 54: 53
HURTT................Vol 68: 243
HUSE................Vol 49: 136, 185
HUSKIN................Vol 82: 930
HUSON................Vol 50: 69
HUSSEY................Vol 66: 308
HUSTACE................Vol 37: 151
HUSTEAD................Vol 49: 188
HUSTED....Vol 47: 392—Vol 64: 716—Vol 75: (5-43)
HUSTON....Vol 42: 193—Vol 46: 153—Vol 47: 191—Vol 49: 134—Vol 50: 356, 416—Vol 51: 166—Vol 55: 396—Vol 56: 626, 629, 691 —Vol 61: 544—Vol 65: 571—Vol 66: 361, 534, 600—Vol 69: 243, 564—Vol 70: 708—

Vol 71: 763—Vol 73: (7-70)—Vol 77: 243—
Vol 84: 446
HUTCHASON..............................Vol 56: 175
HUTCHENS..................................Vol 60: 573
HUTCHERSON...Vol 61: 788—Vol 67: 575.
645
HUTCHESON..........Vol 37: 69—Vol 72: (4-82)
HUTCHINGS...Vol 43: 601—Vol 45: 242—
Vol 52: 173—Vol 58: 112—Vol 60: 419
HUTCHINS....Vol 22: 155—Vol 31: 587—Vol
37: 397—Vol 41: 122—Vol 53: 54—Vol 54:
56—Vol 56: 416—Vol 57: 689—Vol 58: 449
—Vol 63: 60, 741—Vol 66: 600—Vol 68: 121
—Vol 69: 121—Vol 82: 500—Vol 83: 717
HUTCHINSON....Vol 18: 181—Vol 22: 155—
Vol 30: 258, 337—Vol 37: 67—Vol 42: 81—
Vol 43: 494—Vol 44: 24, 26, 228—Vol 45:
105—Vol 46: 386—Vol 47: 341, 395—Vol
50: 193—Vol 54: 709—Vol 55: 519—Vol
62: 503—Vol 66: 251—Vol 67: 43—Vol 70:
707—Vol 72: (4-82)—Vol 73: (7-69)—Vol
75: (2-58)—Vol 76: 928—Vol 78: 53—Vol
82: 726, 797
HUTLET..............................Vol 29: 511
HUTSELL..............................Vol 83: 523, 524
HUTSON...Vol 36: 218—Vol 44: 27—Vol 74:
(5-38)
HUTTON....Vol 37: 487—Vol 55: 286—Vol 57:
745—Vol 65: 439—Vol 67: 647—Vol 82:
501
HUYCK..............................Vol 83: 873
HYATT...Vol 41: 72—Vol 49: 188—Vol 50:
353—Vol 52: 358—Vol 57: 39—Vol 59: 238
—Vol 72: (10-95)—Vol 78: 246—Vol 81:
631
HYCHE..............................Vol 80: 556
HYDE...Vol 23: 168—Vol 26: 244—Vol 28:
164—Vol 32: 634—Vol 36: 218—Vol 38: 272
—Vol 41: 68—Vol 42: 14, 15—Vol 43: 417
—Vol 45: 117—Vol 46: 389—Vol 48: 121—
Vol 50: 354—Vol 52: 112, 566—Vol 54: 538
—Vol 55: 598, 653—Vol 56: 46, 314, 412—
Vol 57: 353—Vol 60: 418—Vol 62: 305, 715
—Vol 73: (11-66)—Vol 79: 517—Vol 81:
517
HYDECKER..............................Vol 67: 45
HYDER..............................Vol 65: 247
HYDORN..............................Vol 45: 113
HYER..............................Vol 44: 27
HYNDSHAW..............................Vol 59: 588
HYNE..............................Vol 39: 327—Vol 58: 331
HYNES..............................Vol 63: 104
HYNSON..............................Vol 30: 145, 146
HYRE..............................Vol 60: 248
HYRNE..............................Vol 64: 156, 385
HYSLOP..............................Vol 61: 279

I

ICKES..............................Vol 46: 30—Vol 49: 284
IDDINGS..............................Vol 48: 56
IDE..............................Vol 80: 657
IDLE..............................Vol 23: 326
IJAIMS..............................Vol 53: 575
IJAMS..............................Vol 53: 116—Vol 57: 312, 687
IKARD..............................Vol 52: 173—Vol 54: 595
IMBODEN..............................Vol 58: 650
IMGRAM..............................Vol 39: 273—Vol 46: 389
IMLAY..............................Vol 46: 160, 332—Vol 71: 1110
INGALL..............................Vol 25: 968
INGALLS...Vol 26: 140, 243—Vol 35: 1265—

Vol 36: 73, 348, 753—Vol 38: 221—Vol 40:
170—Vol 43: 419—Vol 47: 394—Vol 48:
200—Vol 79: 467
INGE..............................Vol 43: 496—Vol 46: 102
INGELL...Vol 26: 558—Vol 27: 735—Vol 36:
354
INGERSOLL....Vol 22: 153—Vol 29: 514—Vol
30: 334—Vol 46: 237—Vol 48: 120, 445—
Vol 49: 127, 192, 353—Vol 54: 308—Vol 71:
1110—Vol 72: (6-79)—Vol 74: (12-52)
INGILL..............................Vol 24: 57
INGLES..............................Vol 77: 113
INGLETON..............................Vol 48: 446
INGRAHAM....Vol 32: 720—Vol 42: 270, 340,
341—Vol 43: 420, 544—Vol 45: 106—Vol
53: 244—Vol 55: 339, 603—Vol 59: 762—
Vol 65: 124, 636—Vol 67: 442
INGRAM....Vol 53: 493—Vol 57: 116—Vol
63: 166—Vol 70: 1167—Vol 74: (1-50)—
Vol 75: (9-40)—Vol 79: 194—Vol 82:: 863
—Vol 83: 174
INGRAMS..............................Vol 32: 720—Vol 68: 551
INMAN....Vol 29: 43—Vol 47: 32—Vol 48: 305
—Vol 49: 191
IRBY..............................Vol 41: 72—Vol 44: 152
IRELAND....Vol 22: 156—Vol 23: 244—Vol
47: 392—Vol 55: 397—Vol 67: 753—Vol
74: (2-43)—Vol 77: 241
IRICK..............................Vol 54: 591
IRISH....Vol 45: 124—Vol 48: 305—Vol 49:
41—Vol 54: 109—Vol 79: 36
IRONS..............................Vol 60: 699—Vol 80: 335
IRVIN....Vol 41: 33—Vol 44: 236—Vol 62:
587—Vol 67: 575
IRVINE...Vol 25: 719—Vol 26: 54—Vol 27:
668, 669—Vol 31: 669—Vol 44: 154, 283—
Vol 48: 448—Vol 50: 68—Vol 56: 744—Vol
61: 152—Vol 67: 440—Vol 70: 455—Vol 74:
(2-42)
IRVING..............................Vol 28: 547—Vol 73: (9-67)
IRWIN....Vol 21: 252—Vol 52: 556—Vol 54:
174—Vol 56: 744—Vol 57: 352—Vol 58:
174—Vol 60: 51—Vol 64: 59, 259, 443, 586—
Vol 68: 243—Vol 69: 160—Vol 84: 635
ISAAC..............................Vol 43: 489
ISAACS...Vol 20: 279—Vol 22: 153—Vol 45:
26—Vol 78: 245
ISAAK..............................Vol 59: 763
ISBELL..............................Vol 50: 280—Vol 82: 397
ISBORN..............................Vol 71: 1111
ISGARD..............................Vol 41: 69
ISGREG..............................Vol 80: 413—Vol 83: 871
ISH..............................Vol 48: 60
ISHAM...Vol 50: 352—Vol 51: 166—Vol 60:
572—Vol 64: 257
ISLER..............................Vol 53: 329
ISRAEL..............................Vol 17: 283, 389—Vol 31: 749
ISREAL..............................Vol 82: 314
IVERSON..............................Vol 76: 62
IVES...Vol 25: 968—Vol 29: 718—Vol 38:
329—Vol 43: 496—Vol 44: 24, 232, 383—
Vol 45: 127, 185—Vol 46: 104—Vol 58: 152
—Vol 60: 573—Vol 74: (11-55)
IVEY..............................Vol 62: 121, 248—Vol 63: 245, 425
IVINS..............................Vol 45: 25
IZARD....Vol 33: 708—Vol 41: 69—Vol 83:
258

J

JACK—Vol 36: 757—Vol 54: 51—Vol 56: 45,
478—Vol 60: 248—Vol 78: 457—Vol. 83:

32: 505—Vol 43: 427, 484—Vol 46: 154, 385
—Vol 57: 311—Vol 73: (8-84)—Vol 83: 91,
438
JOHNS....Vol 25: 718—Vol 41: 164—Vol 44:
25, 82—Vol 69: 764—Vol 70: 1019—Vol 74:
(12-53)
JOHNSON....Vol 18: 300—Vol 20: 1064—Vol
22: 157, 998—Vol 23: 244, 400—Vol 24: 544
—Vol 25: 38, 382—Vol 26: 56, 143, 338, 339
—Vol 27: 45—Vol 28: 262—Vol 29: 46, 290,
800—Vol 30: 63—Vol 31: 413, 751—Vol 32:
59, 60, 719—Vol 34: 657—Vol 36: 217, 218
—Vol 37: 68, 488—Vol 38: 35, 36, 217, 218,
276—Vol 39: 104, 141, 274—Vol 40: 227,
274—Vol 41: 33, 215—Vol 42: 78, 81, 335,
337, 338—Vol 43: 487, 488, 491, 545, 602,
603—Vol 44: 85, 152, 154, 310, 311—Vol 45:
17, 22, 24, 121, 124, 128, 188, 200, 236, 240—
Vol 46: 23, 102, 239, 240, 245, 246, 390—Vol
48: 53, 61, 445—Vol 49: 45, 286—Vol 50:
64, 67, 69, 185, 186, 190—Vol 52: 435, 559,
629—Vol 53: 181, 244, 378, 627, 747—Vol
54: 466, 648, 709—Vol 55: 599, 600—Vol 56:
109, 370, 480, 482—Vol 57: 116, 175, 433,
481, 686, 745—Vol 58: 171, 331, 372, 453—
Vol 59: 238, 524, 586, 679, 681, 765—Vol 60:
50, 250, 506—Vol 61: 66, 153, 156, 157, 547
—Vol 62: 502—Vol 63: 295, 373, 572, 632,
739, 742—Vol 64: 158, 758, 760—Vol 65:
438—Vol 66: 54, 361—Vol 67: 114, 242, 290,
293, 715—Vol 68: 373, 443, 489, 553,
554—Vol 69: 160, 564—Vol 70: 355, 356,
1016—Vol 71: 358, 463, 673, 674, 760, 959—
Vol 72: (1-63), (10-94)—Vol 73: (7-70),
(10-75), (11-66)—Vol 74: (4-51), (7-53),
(8-53)—Vol 75: (2-59), (4-54), (9-37), (11-
69)—Vol 76: 219, 581—Vol 77: 240, 539,
664—Vol 80: 657—Vol 81: 130, 569, 631—
Vol 82: 220, 796, 934—Vol 83: 92, 172, 794,
873, 945—Vol 84: 893
JOHNSTON....Vol 28: 159—Vol 32: 720—Vol
38: 86—Vol 41: 71—Vol 42: 79, 265—Vol
44: 22, 313—Vol 45: 122—Vol 46: 157, 388—
Vol 47: 95, 197, 266—Vol 52: 108—Vol 54:
54, 464, 594—Vol 55: 600, 714—Vol 56:
690—Vol 60: 366—Vol 68: 489—Vol 71:
460, 674—Vol 72: (1-63), (7-75), (8-89)—
Vol 74: (12-48)—Vol 75: (10-67)—Vol 82:
62, 500, 931—Vol 83: 944—Vol 84: 632
JOHNSTONE....Vol 43: 491—Vol 47: 82—
Vol 64: 59
JOICE..............................Vol 25: 967
JOINER.............Vol 75: (10-66)—Vol 76: 928
JOLINE...............................Vol 22: 53
JOLLY....Vol 61: 472, 610—Vol 62: 587—Vol
63: 427, 696—Vol 66: 55
JONAS..............................Vol 59: 47
JONES....Vol 1: 444—Vol 7: 174—Vol 14: 279
—Vol 19: 532—Vol 20: 278—Vol 22: 156—
Vol 24: 151—Vol 25: 799, 965—Vol 26: 240,
243—Vol 27: 735, 740—Vol 28: 363—Vol
29: 46, 289—Vol 31: 586, 749—Vol 32: 61,
164, 505—Vol 34: 202, 423, 656—Vol 35:
1101, 1103—Vol 36: 575, 576, 755—Vol 37:
65, 70—Vol 38: 35, 87—Vol 39: 102, 103,
275, 328—Vol 40: 73, 107—Vol 41: 124, 125,
165, 213—Vol 42: 14, 78, 136, 139, 193, 335,
340—Vol 43: 427, 482, 484, 495, 596, 599,
603—Vol 44: 25, 81, 236—Vol 45: 105, 108,
183, 190, 191, 200, 324—Vol 46: 22, 237, 243,

390—Vol 47: 29, 195, 265, 267, 392—Vol 48:
54, 372, 441, 448—Vol 49: 49, 125, 190, 191,
280, 354, 356, 393, 394—Vol 50: 63, 68, 69,
277, 351—Vol 52: 52, 319—Vol 53: 117, 224,
328, 447, 745, 747—Vol 54: 227, 420, 466, 589
Vol 55: 107, 285—Vol 56: 175, 318, 373, 374,
416, 742—Vol 57: 113, 117, 173, 311, 629—
Vol 58: 172, 174, 241, 331, 451, 586, 587, 648,
650—Vol 59: 176, 238, 589, 652—Vol 60: 51,
248—Vol 61: 158, 278, 707, 708, 911—Vol
62: 56, 460, 502, 583, 647—Vol 63: 59, 246,
635—Vol 64: 124, 257, 521, 713—Vol 65:
508, 571—Vol 66: 161, 365, 534, 535—Vol
67: 148, 388, 716—Vol 68: 154, 155, 374,
443, 448, 735—Vol 69: 56, 58—Vol 70: 572,
577, 1167, 1168—Vol 71: 1026—Vol 72:
(2-64), (4-83)—Vol 74: (4-48), (5-42), (9-
50), (11-58)—Vol 75: (2-59), (5-45), (11-
70), (12-63)—Vol 76: 309—Vol 78: 295—
Vol 79: 614—Vol 80: 657—Vol 81: 130, 630
—Vol 82: 220, 503, 797, 936—Vol 83: 93,
523, 628—Vol 84: 324, 632, 633, 702, 966
JOPLING........................Vol 45: 109, 325
JOPSON...........................Vol 68: 443, 623
JORDAN....Vol 1: 605—Vol 22: 679—Vol 50:
66—Vol 62: 122, 457—Vol 63: 168—Vol 67:
752—Vol 70: 707—Vol 77: 479—Vol 79:
562—Vol 82: 396, 794—Vol 83: 871
JORDEN............................Vol 34: 200
JOSEPH...............Vol 45: 200—Vol 73: (8-83)
JOSLIN....Vol 28: 58—Vol 45: 105, 124—Vol
47: 32—Vol 48: 305—Vol 49: 191—Vol 66:
364—Vol 70: 135
JOSLYN.............Vol 50: 352—Vol 58: 369
JOUET.............................Vol 70: 1168
JOUETT........Vol 64: 649—Vol 65: 160, 440
JOUETTE...........................Vol 46: 103
JOUITT............................Vol 43: 596
JOURDAN...........................Vol 63: 168
JOURNEYCAKE......................Vol 46: 393
JOWELL...........................Vol 45: 118
JOY....Vol 44: 79—Vol 56: 562—Vol 57: 38—
Vol 60: 505—Vol 72: (4-83)
JOYNER..........................Vol 75: (10-66)
JUDD....Vol 21: 335—Vol 30: 61—Vol 56: 177,
416—Vol 57: 564, 687—Vol 58: 109—Vol
61: 610—Vol 65: 760—Vol 74: (4-48)
JUDKINS....Vol 43: 542—Vol 44: 23, 315—
Vol 45: 187—Vol 49: 192—Vol 67: 45, 576
JUDSON.................Vol 40: 227—Vol 53: 54
JULIAN....Vol 45: 194—Vol 74: (9-50)—Vol
75: (6-39)—Vol 76: 62
JULIEN...........................Vol 75: (6-39)
JUNG.......................Vol 83: 440, 718
JURDINE...........................Vol 65: 367
JUSTICE....Vol 20: 1064—Vol 25: 36—Vol
26: 244—Vol 56: 745—Vol 60: 573—Vol
71: 960
JUSTIS............................Vol 79: 35
JUSTISS....Vol 44: 313—Vol 45: 110—Vol 74:
(5-42)
JUSTUS...........................Vol 71: 960

K

KAGLE............................Vol 76: 860
KAHLER...........................Vol 56: 373
KAIGLER..........................Vol 84: 633
KALB.............................Vol 50: 189
KALMORE..........................Vol 45: 103
KANARD...........................Vol 71: 674

KERCHEVAL_____Vol 39: 326
KERLEY_____Vol 28: 58
KERLIN___Vol 38: 331—Vol 39: 222—Vol 49: 283
KERN_____Vol 37: 50, 395—Vol 58: 173
KERR___Vol 21: 334—Vol 32: 163—Vol 41: 123—Vol 45: 25, 122—Vol 50: 280—Vol 51: 301—Vol 53: 630—Vol 67: 388, 712—Vol 70: 205, 453, 454, 572, 875, 1167—Vol 73: (11-66)—Vol 75: (10-66)—Vol 78: 53, 247—Vol 81: 517—Vol 82: 397
KERRICK_____Vol 49: 354
KESSLER_____ Vol 39: 22
KESTER_____Vol 72: (4-83)
KETCHAM___Vol 31: 587—Vol 40: 275—Vol 56: 628—Vol 59: 652—Vol 72: (2-62)
KETCHUM___Vol 28: 164—Vol 40: 26—Vol 45: 28—Vol 58: 588—Vol 59: 49—Vol 70: 1168
KETELHUYN_____Vol 69: 120
KEY___Vol 41: 211—Vol 42: 13—Vol 44: 388 —Vol 45: 109—Vol 47: 273—Vol 48: 64— Vol 53: 242—Vol 56: 689—Vol 57: 115—Vol 58: 52—Vol 63: 697—Vol 65: 300—Vol 68: 373—Vol 75: (11-70)—Vol 76: 860—Vol 77: 51, 664—Vol 82: 139
KEYES _Vol 31: 587, 751—Vol 46: 21—Vol 49: 393—Vol 52: 564—Vol 53: 247, 574— Vol 54: 351—Vol 63: 698—Vol 75: (9-37)— Vol 80: 511
KEYS___Vol 30: 65—Vol 39: 225—Vol 42: 79 —Vol 56: 318—Vol 63: 508
KEYSER___Vol 53: 177, 632—Vol 55: 522— Vol 56: 114
KIBBE___Vol 38: 34, 86—Vol 42: 339—Vol 71: 674, 677
KIBBY___Vol 38: 34—Vol 44: 225—Vol 52: 563
KICE_____Vol 67: 147
KIDD___Vol 37: 353—Vol 45: 109—Vol 53: 691—Vol 68: 284—Vol 71: 241
KIDDER _Vol 43: 540—Vol 45: 241—Vol 54: 421—Vol 59: 681—Vol 78: 246, 456
KIDNEY___Vol 43: 424—Vol 50: 190—Vol 55: 286—Vol 63: 373—Vol 84: 447
KIDWELL_____Vol 58: 54
KIEFER_____Vol 20: 351
KIERSTED_____Vol 33: 472
KIETHLUN_____Vol 21: 251
KIGER_____Vol 73: (0 65)
KILBORN_____Vol 43: 599
KILBOURN_____Vol 38: 330—Vol 49: 45
KILBOURNE_____Vol 47: 273
KILBUCK_____Vol 46: 393
KILBURN___Vol 22: 53, 270—Vol 23: 323— Vol 45: 199—Vol 46: 102
KILCREASE_____Vol 80: 589
KILE_____Vol 62: 460
KILER_____Vol 42: 80
KILGORE___Vol 42: 193—Vol 43: 724—Vol 45: 107—Vol 47: 23—Vol 49: 395—Vol 50: 70—Vol 56: 225—Vol 59: 176—Vol 63: 59
KILLAM___Vol 27: 381—Vol 30: 66—Vol 40: 273—Vol 57: 480
KILLCUT_____Vol 59: 46—Vol 71: 558
KILLER_____ Vol 42: 80
KILLEY_____Vol 27: 44—Vol 70: 353
KILLGORE_____Vol 50: 70—Vol 83: 173
KILLIAN_____Vol 45: 129

KILLINGSWORTH___Vol 67: 41, 576—Vol 82: 797
KILLION_____Vol 67: 243
KILLOUGH_____Vol 67: 442
KILMER_____Vol 82: 794
KILPATRICK_____Vol 60: 698
KILSEY__´_____ Vol 40: 108
KIMBALL___Vol 22: 373—Vol 26: 339—Vol 33: 954—Vol 37: 74—Vol 43: 497—Vol 45: 184, 191, 242, 321—Vol 46: 98, 245—Vol 47: 196—Vol 48: 54—Vol 49: 355, 385, 392— Vol 50: 355—Vol 52: 564—Vol 53: 116, 242, 575—Vol 54: 55, 310—Vol 56: 373—Vol 57: 217, 687—Vol 61: 543—Vol 66: 307, 733— Vol 70: 1168—Vol 76: 860—Vol 84: 702
KIMBERLAND_____Vol 59: 315
KIMBERLIN_____Vol 59: 315
KIMBERLY_____Vol 49: 49
KIMBLE___Vol 43: 483—Vol 44: 309—Vol 54: 422
KIMBROUGH___Vol 37: 158—Vol 53: 117, 380 —Vol 54: 225—Vol 62: 306
KIMES_____Vol 67: 242
KIMMELL_____Vol 55: 285
KINAGO_____Vol 83: 874
KINCAID___Vol 41: 33—Vol 47: 269—Vol 56: 43—Vol 61: 472—Vol 67: 386
KINCAIDE_____Vol 48: 446
KINCHELOE___Vol 53: 242—Vol 72: (6-77)
KINCHEN_____Vol 83: 628
KINCHLOE_____Vol 25: 719
KINCONNON_____Vol 82: 313
KINDRICH_____Vol 68: 241
KING___Vol 23: 470—Vol 28: 60—Vol 30: 539, 543—Vol 31: 55, 588—Vol 32: 284—Vol 33: 709—Vol 36: 574, 577, 759—Vol 37: 154, 160—Vol 40: 226—Vol 41: 126, 163, 165 —Vol 42: 76, 77, 78, 186, 265—Vol 43: 487, 599—Vol 44: 83, 235—Vol 45: 27, 123, 195— Vol 46: 21, 100, 152, 160, 240, 329, 337, 338— Vol 47: 86, 199—Vol 48: 119, 120, 205, 444— Vol 49: 46, 285, 286, 352, 391, 395, 396—Vol 50: 116, 351—Vol 52: 433, 483, 559—Vol 53: 177, 181, 244, 330, 377, 632—Vol 54: 591— Vol 55: 209, 446—Vol 58: 52, 173, 371, 500, 698—Vol 59: 109, 113, 439, 587, 764—Vol 60: 113, 290—Vol 61: 699—Vol 62: 460, 586 —Vol 63: 56, 165, 633, 635, 696—Vol 64: 308, 384, 387, 445, 521, 522—Vol 65: 58, 124, 367, 633—Vol 66: 249, 461, 825—Vol 67: 515, 577 —Vol 68: 241, 240, 487, 491, 627, 085, 732— Vol 69: 242, 245—Vol 70: 354—Vol 72: (1-66), (4-82)—Vol 74: (11-57), (11-61)— Vol 77: 183—Vol 79: 613—Vol 80: 191, 588 —Vol 81: 571, 630—Vol 82: 142, 314, 727, 934—Vol 83: 93, 442—Vol 84: 68, 327
KINGSBURY_____Vol 37: 156—Vol 45: 193
KINGSLEY___Vol 20: 277—Vol 21: 250, 336— Vol 46: 156—Vol 49: 192—Vol 57: 435, 565 —Vol 59: 765—Vol 70: 707—Vol 73: (9-63)
KINKEAD_____Vol 72: (4-83)
KINLOCH_____Vol 44: 228
KINMAN_____ Vol 64: 716
KINNAM_____Vol 74: (5-38)
KINNARD_____Vol 71: 674
KINNE___Vol 42: 73, 80—Vol 49: 390—Vol 50: 356—Vol 52: 52, 230—Vol 66: 307— Vol 67: 113—Vol 75: (5-44)
KINNEAR_____Vol 57: 312
KINNER_____Vol 30: 65
KINNEY___Vol 24: 543—Vol 25: 798, 967—

Vol 26: 240—Vol 36: 352—Vol 49: 285—
Vol 66: 537—Vol 67: 113—Vol 70: 708—Vol
82: 499
KINNIE..Vol 49: 284
KINNY................Vol 48: 371—Vol 58: 700
KINSAUL................................Vol 56: 745
KINSEY................................Vol 69: 631
KINSMAN................................Vol 83: 523
KINSTEAD................................Vol 43: 547
KINTER................................Vol 75: (9-41)
KINTNER................................Vol 45: 187
KINTZER................................Vol 59: 237
KINYON................................Vol 56: 171
KINZIE................................Vol 31: 860
KIP................Vol 26: 559—Vol 39: 275
KIPP................................Vol 39: 275
KIRBY....Vol 37: 70, 397—Vol 42: 140—Vol
43: 426, 723—Vol 75: (9-37)—Vol 82: 862
KIRCHEVAL................................Vol 57: 113
KIRK...Vol 31: 669—Vol 38: 331—Vol 44:
312—Vol 45: 190—Vol 74: (1-49)—Vol 83:
627, 874
KIRKE................................Vol 33: 958
KIRKENBOWER................................Vol 77: 479
KIRKENDALL................Vol 65: 508, 668
KIRKLAND...Vol 67: 516—Vol 71: 162—Vol
72: (1-65)—Vol 73: (2-65), (9-66)—Vol 82:
142
KIRKMAN................................Vol 76: 61
KIRKPATRICK...Vol 43: 491—Vol 46: 385—
Vol 47: 392—Vol 48: 199, 200, 308—Vol 49:
42, 124, 355—Vol 50: 58—Vol 53: 330—Vol
55: 601—Vol 58: 702—Vol 63: 373—Vol 82:
793, 859—Vol 84: 636
KIRKSUM................................Vol 43: 495
KIRTLAND...Vol 31: 51—Vol 40: 74—Vol
58: 700—Vol 83: 259
KIRTLEY................Vol 37: 66—Vol 68: 374
KISER................................Vol 67: 645
KISINGER................Vol 38: 276
KISLING................................Vol 57: 218
KITCHELL...Vol 20: 166—Vol 21: 60, 333—
Vol 38: 88—Vol 55: 601
KITTEL................................Vol 69: 433
KITTLE...Vol 27: 380—Vol 36: 573, 576—
Vol 69: 120
KITTREDGE................................Vol 46: 332
KLAARWATER................................Vol 83: 523
KLECKLEY................................Vol 66: 734
KLECKNER................................Vol 66: 827
KLEES................Vol 45: 22, 322
KLEIN...Vol 54: 175—Vol 56: 175—Vol 57:
353—Vol 58: 501—Vol 64: 523—Vol 65:
758—Vol 84: 523
KLIEN................................Vol 54: 420
KLINE...Vol 38: 220—Vol 49: 188—Vol 56:
175—Vol 57: 353—Vol 58: 501
KNAP................................Vol 63: 697
KNAPP...Vol 30: 541—Vol 31: 863—Vol 32:
60, 506—Vol 41: 29, 65—Vol 42: 191, 270—
Vol 43: 418, 422, 493—Vol 44: 24—Vol 46:
29—Vol 50: 115, 279—Vol 52: 231—Vol 53:
245—Vol 55: 337—Vol 63: 572—Vol 64:
158, 386—Vol 75: (9-46), (10-67)—Vol 79:
656—Vol 81: 510
KNAPPS................................Vol 32: 61
KNEPPER................Vol 74: (1-51)
KNERR................................Vol 53: 493
KNICKERBOCKER...Vol 39: 326—Vol 40:
227—Vol 53: 690—Vol 54: 353—Vol 71: 462
KNIFFEN................Vol 70: 356—Vol 83: 521

KNIGHT...Vol 15: 506—Vol 24: 149, 544—
Vol 25: 797—Vol 31: 55—Vol 45: 241—Vol
54: 591—Vol 57: 214, 219, 432, 746—Vol 58:
701—Vol 67: 46, 750—Vol 69: 160—Vol 71:
240, 760—Vol 72: (4-83)—Vol 73: (7-70)—
Vol 75: (9-46)—Vol 77: 663, 768—Vol 83:
171, 627, 874
KNISKERN................................Vol 47: 28
KNIVER................................Vol 65: 442
KNODLER................................Vol 80: 46
KNOKES................................Vol 36: 354
KNOTT...Vol 26: 54—Vol 66: 307—Vol 78:
246—Vol 80: 190
KNOTTS................................Vol 38: 221
KNOWLES...Vol 47: 391—Vol 55: 286—Vol
58: 330, 764—Vol 67: 43—Vol 73: (1-62)
KNOWLTON...Vol 23: 63—Vol 32: 282—Vol
33: 959—Vol 35: 1267—Vol 36: 74, 754, 762
—Vol 40: 25, 170—Vol 45: 28—Vol 47: 391
—Vol 49: 285, 391—Vol 50: 63—Vol 57:
743—Vol 60: 635—Vol 65: 759—Vol 75:
(1-54)—Vol 84: 324
KNOX...Vol 22: 157—Vol 23: 324, 400—Vol
24: 57—Vol 32: 506—Vol 37: 149—Vol 38:
87, 331—Vol 39: 141—Vol 40: 77—Vol 43:
486—Vol 45: 111—Vol 46: 388—Vol 47: 86
—Vol 48: 62, 448—Vol 49: 28, 129, 281—
Vol 50: 192, 278—Vol 54: 538—Vol 55: 109
—Vol 57: 686—Vol 61: 63, 545—Vol 64:
521, 714—Vol 65: 300—Vol 67: 714—Vol
68: 554—Vol 69: 362—Vol 72: (6-78)—Vol
80: 335—Vol 82: 140
KOCH................................Vol 36: 215
KOCHER................................Vol 41: 128
KOGLER................................Vol 83: 945
KOHER................................Vol 77: 664
KOHLMAN................................Vol 45: 115
KOLB...Vol 60: 698—Vol 61: 63—Vol 83: 261,
718
KONING................................Vol 62: 307
KOON................................Vol 71: 461
KOONTZ................................Vol 48: 204
KORN ....Vol 56: 690—Vol 63: 633, 749
KORNEGAY...Vol 62: 159, 160—Vol 64: 384
—Vol 84: 327
KORNMAN................................Vol 68: 285
KORNS................................Vol 68: 492, 732
KORTRIGHT................Vol 64: 157, 309, 385, 442
KOUNTZ................................Vol 43: 493
KRAKE................................Vol 34: 202
KRAMER................Vol 41: 28—Vol 57: 215
KRAUS................................Vol 65: 124
KRAUSE................................Vol 31: 54
KRAUT................................Vol 45: 28, 191
KRAUZE................................Vol 65: 124
KREAMER................Vol 43: 604—Vol 50: 61
KRESLER................................Vol 19: 307
KRIEDER................................Vol 45: 240
KRONK................................Vol 38: 85
KRONKHEIT................................Vol 37: 271
KRONKHITE................................Vol 70: 1170
KRUNK................................Vol 84: 69
KUHN...Vol 76: 783—Vol 79: 561
KUHNS................................Vol 52: 51—Vol 83: 628
KUNTZ................................Vol 43: 493—Vol 55: 600
KURTZ...Vol 39: 274—Vol 40: 25—Vol 41:
125—Vol 42: 15—Vol 45: 27—Vol 54: 55—
Vol 59: 524, 653—Vol 61: 473
KUTZ................................Vol 65: 759—Vol 69: 564, 565
KUYKENDALL................................Vol 65: 663
KUYPER................................Vol 67: 147

KYGER..................Vol 45: 24, 322
KYLE....Vol 25: 719—Vol 26: 54—Vol 29: 290
—Vol 41: 125—Vol 45: 102, 107, 324—Vol
46: 235—Vol 47: 189—Vol 48: 372—Vol 67:
648—Vol 69: 361—Vol 70: 358—Vol 75:
(9-41)—Vol 78: 457—Vol 81: 518—Vol 83:
717, 947
KYNER..................Vol 57: 116
KYSAR..................Vol 43: 493, 543

L

LA BAR..................Vol 83: 522
LABASIEUR..................Vol 84: 445
LABAZEILE..................Vol 84: 445
LABBAN..................Vol 44: 310
LABEZIUS..................Vol 68: 122
LACKEY....Vol 44: 310—Vol 79: 113—Vol 82:
398—Vol 83: 793
LACKLAND..........Vol 45: 236—Vol 67: 441
LA COUNT..................Vol 44: 28
LACY....Vol 27: 672—Vol 29: 715—Vol 40: 26
—Vol 44: 387—Vol 53: 117, 633
LADD...Vol 25: 967—Vol 27: 739—Vol 29:
718—Vol 40: 275—Vol 66: 308—Vol 82: 574
LADIEU..................Vol 22: 680
LAFFERTY..................Vol 44: 21—Vol 46: 391
LAFFOON..................Vol 56: 745—Vol 71: 763
LAHR..................Vol 78: 554
LAIR..................Vol 57: 745
LAIRD...Vol 27: 739—Vol 39: 104—Vol 48:
307—Vol 67: 753—Vol 83: 262
LAKE...Vol 52: 436—Vol 80: 431—Vol 82:
502—Vol 84: 245, 446
LAKES..................Vol 68: 243
LAKIN..................Vol 43: 488
LAMAR...Vol 40: 76—Vol 44: 314—Vol 45:
120—Vol 60: 249—Vol 82: 398, 725
LAMAS..................Vol 55: 597
LAMASTERS..................Vol 50: 65
LAMB...Vol 19: 207—Vol 22: 53—Vol 23: 24
—Vol 26: 139—Vol 29: 45—Vol 30: 542—
Vol 34: 67– Vol 35: 1102—Vol 38: 88—Vol
43: 601—Vol 44: 315—Vol 47: 265—Vol 49:
135—Vol 55: 338—Vol 56: 172—Vol 57:
629—Vol 58: 702, 761—Vol 59: 765—Vol 64:
159—Vol 66: 826—Vol 68: 372—Vol 69:
629—Vol 70: 133, 576—Vol 77: 244—Vol
78: 600—Vol 82: 262
LAMBDIN..................Vol 72. (1-64)
LAMBERT...Vol 31: 412—Vol 44: 234—Vol
45: 24, 322—Vol 47: 392—Vol 48: 61 Vol
53: 329—Vol 57: 481—Vol 61: 473, 706—
Vol 62: 501—Vol 65: 247—Vol 70: 574—
Vol 71: 1109—Vol 84: 635
LAMBETH...Vol 67: 386—Vol 75: (11-70)—
Vol 79: 560
LAMBKIN...Vol 19: 207—Vol 21: 336—Vol
45: 106
LAMBORN..................Vol 45: 190
LAMEREAUX..................Vol 30: 540
LAMERICK..................Vol 30: 540
LAMKIN...Vol 47: 23—Vol 54: 535—Vol 67:
576—Vol 74: (5-41)
LAMME...Vol 43: 485, 487, 488—Vol 44: 233
—Vol 45: 186
LAMOREAUX..................Vol 56: 174
LAMPHEAR...Vol 52: 687—Vol 53: 379—Vol
56: 562—Vol 69: 432
LAMPHERE..................Vol 45: 240—Vol 76: 218
LAMPHIER..................Vol 41: 122
LAMPKIN........Vol 33: 960—Vol 72: (10-95)

LAMPMAN..................Vol 60: 418
LAMPREY..................Vol 47: 193
LAMPTON....Vol 67: 648—Vol 69: 119, 432—
Vol 77: 480
LAMROCK..................Vol 30: 540
LAMSON....Vol 50: 61—Vol 58: 372—Vol 60:
697
LANCASTER....Vol 43: 494, 605—Vol 58: 331
—Vol 81: 631
LANDER...Vol 52: 360—Vol 53: 378—Vol 55:
286
LANDERS..................Vol 50: 350—Vol 55: 286
LANDFEAR..................Vol 49: 46
LANDIS....Vol 56: 480—Vol 64: 587—Vol 65:
507
LANDON..................Vol 45: 105—Vol 46: 100
LANDRAM..................Vol 74: (11-57)
LANDRETH..................Vol 80: 382
LANDRETHS..................Vol 50: 350
LANDRUM..................Vol 74: (11-57)
LANE...Vol 19: 532—Vol 20: 164—Vol 25:
717—Vol 26: 242—Vol 27: 740—Vol 28:
263—Vol 32: 283—Vol 38: 220—Vol 41:
164—Vol 42: 13—Vol 43: 495, 604, 723—
Vol 44: 25, 314—Vol 45: 103, 105, 108, 124,
125, 199—Vol 46: 100, 236, 328, 386—Vol 47:
195, 267—Vol 48: 61, 438—Vol 49: 279, 286
—Vol 50: 66—Vol 51: 302—Vol 53: 176,
244—Vol 56: 319—Vol 57: 312, 313, 479,
686, 688—Vol 59: 442, 651—Vol 60: 698—
Vol 61: 158, 606—Vol 65: 440—Vol 66: 366,
731—Vol 68: 239—Vol 69: 120—Vol 70:
133—Vol 72: (1-65)—Vol 74: (6-37)—Vol
76: 402—Vol 77: 389, 480—Vol 80: 277—
Vol 83: 258—Vol 84: 634
LANFORD..................Vol 76: 581
LANG..................Vol 43: 540—Vol 84: 325
LANGDON....Vol 31: 668—Vol 44: 81—Vol
53: 246—Vol 54: 535, 710—Vol 56: 688—
Vol 67: 289
LANGFORD....Vol 60: 506—Vol 77: 118—Vol
84: 158
LANGLEY..................Vol 43: 423—Vol 44: 26
LANGRIDGE..................Vol 82: 725
LANGSTAFF..................Vol 27: 46
LANGSTON....Vol 17: 283, 389—Vol 67: 115
LANGWORTHY..................Vol 49: 284
LANHAM....Vol 43: 489—Vol 49: 186—Vol
53: 572—Vol 64: 715—Vol 83: 260—Vol 84:
633, 703
LANHAMS..................Vol 50: 350
LANICH..................Vol 57: 116
LANIER....Vol 23: 243—Vol 44: 388—Vol 45:
183—Vol 47: 266—Vol 50: 62—Vol 54: 176
LANK..................Vol 45: 125
LANNING.......Vol 48: 448—Vol 67: 291, 712
LANSDALE..................Vol 61: 469—Vol 84: 327
LANSING..................Vol 43: 422
LAPHAM..................Vol 18: 299
LAQUIER..................Vol 80: 557
LARAMORE..................Vol 83: 259
LARDNER..................Vol 61: 228
LA REEDS..................Vol 65: 440
LAREY..................Vol 64: 522
LARGE..................Vol 26: 141
LARISON..................Vol 80: 154
LARK..................Vol 55: 46—Vol 75: (5-44)
LARKIN....Vol 41: 214—Vol 62: 501—Vol 82:
933
LARKINS.........Vol 42: 194—Vol 74: (4-50)
LARN..................Vol 49: 133

Vol 66: 535—Vol 72: (4-83)—Vol 78: 107, 155
LIND.........Vol 48: 58—Vol 74: (7-53), (8-53)
LINDABERRY..................................Vol 55: 286
LINDAMOND..................................Vol 63: 165
LINDE...Vol 31: 51
LINDLEY....Vol 23: 326, 470—Vol 29: 651—
    Vol 45: 108, 238—Vol 46: 22—Vol 49: 395—
    Vol 60: 249—Vol 73: (7-71)
LINDSAY...Vol 27: 383—Vol 43: 546, 599—
    Vol 47: 269—Vol 48: 306—Vol 50: 193—
    Vol 59: 441—Vol 68: 242—Vol 70: 574—Vol
    74: (1-49)
LINDSEY...Vol 34: 660—Vol 36: 762—Vol
    42: 269—Vol 61: 66—Vol 80: 84
LINDSLEY..........................Vol 26: 340, 560
LINE.......................Vol 43: 486, 598—Vol 47: 264
LINEBARGER..................................Vol 56: 176
LINEBERGER..................................Vol 56: 317
LINENSHEET..........................Vol 56: 173, 317
LINES...Vol 30: 61—Vol 46: 160—Vol 50:
    116—Vol 56: 415—Vol 60: 366, 503
LINGENFELTER..................................Vol 82: 860
LINGLE...Vol 65: 297
LINGO......................Vol 48: 306—Vol 49: 41
LINIES..Vol 46: 239
LINK...Vol 37: 397—Vol 47: 271—Vol 57:
    218—Vol 60: 418—Vol 68: 155—Vol 74:
    (11-60)—Vol 82: 794
LINN....Vol 44: 387—Vol 46: 242—Vol 47:
    395—Vol 53: 52, 248, 574, 631—Vol 57: 353
    —Vol 59: 651—Vol 60: 507—Vol 69: 684—
    Vol 73: (11-68)—Vol 74: (7-53), (8-53)—
    Vol 75: (3-41)
LINNELL..Vol 22: 375
LINSEY...Vol 62: 647
LINTON....Vol 47: 266—Vol 56: 625—Vol 58:
    369
LINUS...Vol 30: 61
LINVILLE..Vol 52: 173
LIPPENCOTT..................................Vol 84: 324
LIPPINCOTT............Vol 77: 241—Vol 84: 324
LIPPS...Vol 69: 564
LIPSCOMBE..................................Vol 64: 58
LISCOMB...Vol 30: 148—Vol 61: 65—Vol
    63: 60—Vol 64: 715—Vol 82: 796
LISLE...............................Vol 18: 300—Vol 69: 160
LISTER......................Vol 53: 246—Vol 83: 260
LITCHFIELD..................................Vol 43: 426
LITHERLAND..................................Vol 29: 47
LITTELL..................Vol 45: 22—Vol 56: 319
LITTLE...Vol 3: 383—Vol 21: 496—Vol 28:
    363—Vol 29: 511—Vol 31: 863—Vol 47: 30
    —Vol 49: 47, 354—Vol 55: 444, 597, 600—
    Vol 56: 314, 476—Vol 58: 502—Vol 61:
    451, 610—Vol 62: 54, 55, 458—Vol 63: 570—
    Vol 65: 442—Vol 70: 203—Vol 73: (9-65)—
    Vol 75: (9-41)—Vol 83: 872
LITTLEFIELD....Vol 26: 54—Vol 33: 1030—
    Vol 59: 114, 315
LITTLEPAGE...Vol 57: 312, 434—Vol 70:
    207—Vol 71: 839, 961, 1025—Vol 84: 703
LITTLER....Vol 49: 130, 185—Vol 50: 343—
    Vol 51: 355—Vol 69: 118, 434, 625, 683—
    Vol 77: 239
LITTLETON..............Vol 41: 165—Vol 63: 107
LITTON......................Vol 63: 247, 569
LIVERMORE..............Vol 32: 59—Vol 45: 198
LIVESAY..........................Vol 41: 34, 68, 119
LIVINGSTON....Vol 3: 681—Vol 4: 305—Vol

22: 680—Vol 23: 397—Vol 24: 261—Vol 26:
    55—Vol 29: 288, 715—Vol 37: 149—Vol 40:
    275—Vol 43: 423, 597—Vol 45: 113—Vol
    52: 486—Vol 57: 480, 744—Vol 62: 390—
    Vol 66: 121—Vol 71: 163—Vol 78: 456—
    Vol 82: 934—Vol 83: 944—Vol 84: 325
LIVINGSTONE..................................Vol 33: 959
LLEWELLYN..................................Vol 57: 173
LLOYD...Vol 30: 148—Vol 36: 214—Vol 50:
    66—Vol 58: 587—Vol 64: 59—Vol 67: 440—
    Vol 68: 734—Vol 84: 68
LOBDELL................Vol 30: 441—Vol 39: 328
LOCHBRIDGE..................................Vol 33: 475
LOCHRY...Vol 39: 323
LOCK..........................Vol 55: 712—Vol 71: 672
LOCKE...Vol 32: 632—Vol 41: 123—Vol 42:
    11—Vol 44: 25, 236—Vol 46: 155—Vol 52:
    321—Vol 67: 752—Vol 68: 240, 241—Vol
    69: 117, 361
LOCKERMAN..................................Vol 32: 163
LOCKETT............Vol 36: 755—Vol 67: 148
LOCKHART............Vol 43: 545—Vol 44: 22
LOCKMON..Vol 84: 635
LOCKRIDGE..................................Vol 70: 577
LOCKRY...Vol 38: 274
LOCKWOOD...Vol 19: 70—Vol 37: 156, 352—
    Vol 38: 329—Vol 39: 222, 275—Vol 46: 21—
    Vol 55: 600—Vol 56: 412, 480—Vol 59: 47,
    238—Vol 75: (9-46)—Vol 77: 52—Vol 84:
    521
LODER..Vol 27: 737
LOFLAND..Vol 80: 46
LOFTIN...Vol 30: 260
LOFTUS..Vol 45: 187
LOGAN....Vol 28: 161, 547—Vol 29: 802—Vol
    38: 35—Vol 43: 424—Vol 45: 112—Vol 46:
    392—Vol 47: 32—Vol 52: 435—Vol 53: 493
    —Vol 55: 519, 713—Vol 61: 552, 707—Vol
    63: 741—Vol 64: 586, 587—Vol 65: 299—
    Vol 73: (10-75)—Vol 74: (1-49)—Vol 77:
    243—Vol 80: 383—Vol 84: 67
LOGSDON..Vol 72: (7-74)
LOGSTON..Vol 41: 69, 72
LOGWOOD..Vol 46: 153
LOLLER..............................Vol 75: (10-65)
LOMAX....Vol 33: 710—Vol 63: 634, 740—Vol
    66: 249
LOMBARD..Vol 82: 863
LONDON....Vol 43: 490, 497, 542—Vol 68: 374
LONG....Vol 26: 52—Vol 27: 45, 671—Vol 37:
    74, 396—Vol 38: 34—Vol 40: 26, 74, 108—
    Vol 41: 32,33, 121, 162, 211—Vol 42: 185—
    Vol 43: 495—Vol 44: 21, 382—Vol 47: 28—
    Vol 48: 55, 58—Vol 49: 48—Vol 50: 343,
    356—Vol 51: 358—Vol 52: 169—Vol 54:
    174, 589, 648—Vol 55: 599—Vol 58: 371—
    Vol 65: 367—Vol 68: 285—Vol 72: (1-66)—
    Vol 75: (6-39)—Vol 81: 629—Vol 82: 861—
    Vol 83: 439
LONGAN..Vol 80: 511
LONGEE..Vol 29: 47, 799
LONGFELLOW....Vol 55: 520—Vol 56: 224—
    Vol 57: 114, 351
LONGLEY..Vol 61: 472
LONGNECKER..................................Vol 45: 326
LONGSHORE..................................Vol 38: 225
LONGSTRETH..................................Vol 33: 42
LONGWELL....Vol 43: 422—Vol 48: 445—Vol
    84: 444
LONGYEAR............Vol 58: 700—Vol 70: 571

LONK................................Vol 29: 652
LOOFBORROW...................Vol 63: 373
LOOK................................Vol 84: 966
LOOKER...Vol 17: 390, 568—Vol 50: 349—
Vol 52: 318
LOOKWOOD.......................Vol 21: 61
LOOMER................................Vol 22: 52
LOOMIS...Vol 27: 668—Vol 36: 349, 353—Vol
39: 327—Vol 42: 343—Vol 43: 599—Vol 46:
237—Vol 50: 66, 186—Vol 61: 912—Vol 63:
106
LOONEY................................Vol 83: 260
LOOPER................................Vol 71: 1111
LOPER................................Vol 64: 716
LORAINE................................Vol 43: 493
LORANCE................................Vol 81: 629
LORD...Vol 24: 262—Vol 25: 384—Vol 26:
558—Vol 29: 651—Vol 35: 436—Vol 42: 340
—Vol 49: 43—Vol 56: 564—Vol 57: 312—
Vol 61: 544—Vol 68: 551—Vol 71: 956—Vol
75: (4-53)—Vol 80: 336
LOREY................................Vol 70: 573
LORING...Vol 19: 207—Vol 29: 653—Vol 46:
242—Vol 84: 893, 894
LORTON................................Vol 70: 454
LOSEE...Vol 50: 349—Vol 74: (2-43), (11-
55)
LOSEY................................Vol 74: (11-55)
LOTHROP...........Vol 64: 258—Vol 74: (6-37)
LOTHROPE................................Vol 39: 142
LOTSHAW................................Vol 57: 480
LOTT...Vol 26: 54—Vol 29: 44, 45—Vol 44:
233—Vol 50: 281, 415—Vol 52: 171—Vol
58: 452—Vol 61: 228—Vol 70: 879—Vol 80:
556—Vol 81: 310, 316
LOUD................................Vol 56: 47
LOUDEN...Vol 38: 328—Vol 42: 76, 77, 189,
265
LOUDERMILCH................................Vol 63: 59
LOUDON...Vol 44: 23, 24—Vol 66: 309—Vol
67: 387
LOUFBOURROW...................Vol 68: 732
LOUGHHEAD................................Vol 56: 47
LOUGHRIDGE................................Vol 36: 214
LOUGHRY................................Vol 76: 218
LOUIS................................Vol 68: 492
LOUKS................................Vol 36: 215
LOULINSON................................Vol 53: 330
LOUNDSBURY................................Vol 43: 543
LOUNSBURY...Vol 29: 46, 650—Vol 30: 61,
62—Vol 33: 707—Vol 43: 493—Vol 44: 80
LOUTHER................................Vol 70: 1168
LOVE...Vol 36: 353—Vol 43: 496—Vol 54:
226, 465, 650—Vol 65: 59—Vol 66: 249, 361
—Vol 67: 117—Vol 68: 551—Vol 71: 676,
677—Vol 73: (10-77)—Vol 74: (11-55)—
Vol 77: 480—Vol 78: 456
LOVEBERRY................................Vol 68: 732
LOVEGROVE................................Vol 53: 242
LOVEJOY...Vol 30: 149—Vol 44: 26, 151—
Vol 56: 690—Vol 82: 861
LOVELACE................................Vol 83: 1014
LOVELAND...Vol 39: 23, 275—Vol 66: 309—
Vol 75: (3-41)
LOVELL...Vol 64: 443—Vol 73: (2-65)—Vol
74: (4-49)—Vol 82: 397
LOVERIDGE................................Vol 60: 115
LOVES................................Vol 64: 257
LOVETT...Vol 21: 168—Vol 27: 670—Vol 43:
421, 422—Vol 45: 321—Vol 48: 445—Vol

56: 558—Vol 57: 113—Vol 63: 428
LOVETTMAR................................Vol 56: 318
LOVEWELL................................Vol 77: 539
LOVIN................................Vol 84: 521
LOVING...........Vol 53: 572—Vol 67: 241, 289
LOW...Vol 22: 998—Vol 24: 57—Vol 47: 196
—Vol 77: 481—Vol 80: 44
LOWDER................................Vol 82: 63, 500, 574
LOWE...Vol 39: 275—Vol 41: 124—Vol 43:
490—Vol 44: 234—Vol 45: 194—Vol 46:
99—Vol 48: 65—Vol 50: 70—Vol 54: 225—
Vol 57: 435—Vol 58: 453—Vol 73: (9-65)—
Vol 83: 439
LOWELL...........Vol 35: 655—Vol 45: 321
LOWER................................Vol 80: 503
LOWERY...Vol 53: 570—Vol 81: 264—Vol
82: 139
LOWMASTER................................Vol 84: 634
LOWNLEY................................Vol 39: 328
LOWNSBURY................................Vol 56: 561
LOWREY................................Vol 48: 444
LOWRIE...........Vol 28: 362—Vol 45: 325
LOWRY...Vol 45: 107, 109—Vol 49: 189—Vol
54: 420—Vol 55: 519, 652—Vol 57: 630—Vol
58: 763—Vol 59: 48—Vol 61: 715—Vol 64:
158—Vol 66: 162—Vol 68: 552—Vol 70: 136
—Vol 73: (11-67)—Vol 74: (4-49), (6-37)—
Vol 80: 193—Vol 83: 1015
LOY................................Vol 30: 148
LOYALLESS................................Vol 44: 234
LOYD................................Vol 49: 40
LOYLESS................................Vol 45: 327
LUBLETT................................Vol 84: 964
LUCAS...Vol 25: 716—Vol 35: 653—Vol 37:
351—Vol 38: 33—Vol 43: 544—Vol 44: 79
—Vol 45: 20—Vol 48: 57—Vol 49: 187—Vol
52: 51—Vol 56: 175, 227—Vol 57: 114, 351
—Vol 64: 258—Vol 67: 45, 576—Vol 68:
154—Vol 71: 356—Vol 73: (8-82), (9-65)—
Vol 74: (4-51)—Vol 75: (2-57)—Vol 82:
503—Vol 83: 522—Vol 84: 702, 705
LUCE...Vol 36: 575—Vol 41: 120, 124—Vol
43: 416, 417—Vol 49: 49—Vol 50: 190, 278—
Vol 52: 485—Vol 56: 560—Vol 60: 634, 747
—Vol 61: 154, 155, 911—Vol 62: 123—Vol
74: (1-50)—Vol 75: (1-54)—Vol 83: 872
LUCKETT...........Vol 62: 773—Vol 68: 243
LUCKIE................................Vol 84: 518
LUDDEN...........Vol 46: 237—Vol 58: 588
LUDDIN................................Vol 19: 627
LUDEN................................Vol 46: 23
LUDGWIG................................Vol 59: 389
LUDINGTON................................Vol 70: 708
LUDLOW...........Vol 41: 214—Vol 63: 700
LUDLOWE................................Vol 28: 479
LUDWIG...Vol 56: 627—Vol 74: (7-53), (8-
53)
LUFER................................Vol 55: 597
LUFKIN...........Vol 81: 131—Vol 83: 945
LUGGETT................................Vol 41: 125
LUGENBEEL................................Vol 79: 284
LUKE...Vol 54: 465—Vol 55: 107, 208—Vol
71: 356
LUKENS................................Vol 55: 597
LUKER................................Vol 50: 349
LULY................................Vol 20: 279
LUM...Vol 46: 328—Vol 47: 30, 264—Vol 56:
625
LUMBARD................................Vol 33: 476
LUMIS................................Vol 84: 446

LUMM....Vol 43: 421, 422—Vol 48: 445—Vol
58: 648
LUMPKIN....Vol 26: 142, 143—Vol 44: 24, 26
—Vol 49: 352
LUMSDEN..Vol 62: 583
LUMSFORD..Vol 49: 135
LUNCEFORD..Vol 49: 135
LUND...Vol 44: 79
LUNDIE.. Vol 35: 57
LUNDY..Vol 83: 336
LUNSFORD....Vol 33: 710—Vol 42: 78—Vol
76: 655
LUNT....Vol 27: 382—Vol 31: 668—Vol 68:
374, 623—Vol 69: 360
LUPFER..Vol 57: 686
LUPHER..Vol 55: 597
LUPPER..Vol 59: 312
LUPTON..Vol 47: 394
LURVER..Vol 46: 102
LUSK....Vol 45: 20—Vol 55: 711—Vol 59: 523
—Vol 60: 596—Vol 61: 609—Vol 79: 112—
Vol 84: 702, 705
LUTES..Vol 48: 55
LUTON..Vol 55: 338
LUTTIG..Vol 52: 564
LUTTRELL........Vol 46: 101—Vol 74: (2-40)
LUTZ........Vol 56: 481, 627—Vol 73: (1-63)
LYATT..Vol 43: 604
LYCAN..Vol 66: 161
LYKINS..Vol 67: 293
LYLE........Vol 55: 338—Vol 69: 566
LYLES........Vol 82: 63—Vol 83: 262
LYMAN....Vol 25: 38—Vol 28: 262—Vol 34:
539—Vol 35: 650—Vol 38: 88—Vol 40: 76,
108—Vol 44: 152—Vol 48: 55—Vol 54: 537
LYNCH....Vol 19: 206—Vol 28: 366—Vol 44:
151, 229, 230—Vol 46: 100, 386—Vol 47: 86
—Vol 54: 420—Vol 56: 474—Vol 58: 561—
Vol 59: 54—Vol 60: 48—Vol 64: 113—Vol
78: 650, 696
LYNDE..Vol 21: 61
LYNE.. Vol 75: (2-57)
LYNES........................Vol 45: 199—Vol 60: 503
LYNN....Vol 45: 191—Vol 48: 445—Vol 54:
55—Vol 57: 352—Vol 59: 651—Vol 60: 507
—Vol 68: 243—Vol 69: 684—Vol 71: 759
LYON....Vol 20: 607—Vol 21: 169—Vol 28:
158, 549—Vol 31: 669—Vol 45: 17, 113, 189
—Vol 49: 283—Vol 50: 65—Vol 62: 651—
Vol 74: (7-54), (8-54)—Vol 80: 85—Vol 82:
502, 503—Vol 83: 93
LYONS....Vol 24: 58—Vol 37: 159—Vol 45:
237—Vol 48: 59—Vol 54: 465—Vol 56: 415
—Vol 62: 651—Vol 64: 759—Vol 75: (8-43)
—Vol 76: 144—Vol 80: 511
LYSTER..Vol 53: 246
LYTLE....Vol 30: 257, 258—Vol 37: 353—Vol
38: 113—Vol 44: 236—Vol 53: 570—Vol 58:
709—Vol 60: 568—Vol 61: 64—Vol 65: 757
—Vol 81: 569—Vol 83: 946

Mc

McADAMS................Vol 66: 162—Vol 80: 192
McADORY................Vol 50: 352—Vol 54: 110
McAFEE........................Vol 61: 472, 867
McALHANEY..Vol 63: 428
McALISTER....Vol 49: 353—Vol 50: 184—Vol
68: 735—Vol 72: (8-84)
McALLASTER..Vol 35: 439
McALLISTER....Vol 31: 590, 414, 862—Vol

35: 11—Vol 47: 87—Vol 48: 442—Vol 58:
451—Vol 70: 206—Vol 72: (2-63)—Vol 74:
(11-56)—Vol 75: (2-61)—Vol 76: 654
McALWEE..Vol 80: 336
McARTHUR....Vol 30: 540—Vol 39: 103—Vol
42: 78, 139—Vol 44: 152—Vol 52: 109
McARTOR..Vol 63: 738
McAULEY........................Vol 43: 425, 543
McBRAYER..Vol 35: 654
McBRIDE....Vol 43: 602—Vol 53: 693—Vol
55: 47—Vol 56: 742—Vol 60: 157—Vol
67: 713—Vol 82: 860—Vol 83: 441
McCABE..Vol 55: 598
McCAFFERTY..Vol 68: 373
McCAFFREY..Vol 67: 290
McCAGUE..Vol 58: 702
McCAIN........................Vol 57: 116—Vol 66: 121
McCALEB..Vol 67: 647
McCALL....Vol 25: 967—Vol 27: 672—Vol 29:
647—Vol 43: 421—Vol 50: 64—Vol 53: 178
—Vol 55: 520—Vol 56: 171, 319—Vol 63:
373—Vol 64: 761—Vol 76: 711—Vol 82: 861
McCALLIE..Vol 83: 718
McCALLUM........................Vol 80: 330, 331
McCALLY..Vol 58: 764
McCAMPBELL..Vol 46: 99
McCANE..Vol 61: 61
McCANLESS..Vol 46: 157
McCANN........................Vol 55: 165—Vol 77: 333
McCANTS..Vol 77: 242
McCARRELL..Vol 61: 158
McCARROLL.. Vol 82: 798
McCART........................Vol 32: 161—Vol 77: 243
McCARTER........................Vol 30: 149—Vol 52: 109
McCARTHY....Vol 45: 237—Vol 50: 67—Vol
83: 442
McCARTNEY....Vol 43: 542—Vol 54: 650—
Vol 56: 475, 563—Vol 59: 47—Vol 78: 398
—Vol 79: 283—Vol 83: 172, 439—Vol 84:
634
McCARTY....Vol 29: 653—Vol 34: 660—Vol
37: 269—Vol 57: 177, 744—Vol 67: 576,
752—Vol 73: (8-85)—Vol 80: 432—Vol 81:
71—Vol 82: 798—Vol 83: 94, 944
McCASKEL..Vol 84: 520
McCASLAN..Vol 47: 271
McCAUGHEY....Vol 34: 69—Vol 43: 542—Vol
53: 747
McCAULEY........................Vol 63: 56—Vol 64: 120
McCAY..Vol 53: 747
McCHEDMEY..Vol 78: 600
McCHESNEY....Vol 37: 487—Vol 78: 245, 600
McCHORD..Vol 45: 235
McCHUGO..Vol 56: 688
McCITCHEON..Vol 37: 155
McCLAFLIN..Vol 84: 69
McCLAIN........................Vol 50: 354—Vol 55: 109
McCLAINE..Vol 84: 245
McCLANAHAN....Vol 60: 697—Vol 70: 709—
Vol 84: 69
McCLANANHAN..Vol 60: 507
McCLANE....Vol 41: 212—Vol 42: 192—Vol
50: 354
McCLARE..Vol 73: (7-70)
McCLEAN....Vol 43: 491—Vol 45: 116—Vol
49: 49, 185—Vol 50: 188—Vol 58: 331—
Vol 72: (4-88)
McCLEARY..Vol 50: 188
McCLELLAN....Vol 29: 803—Vol 35: 653,
1103—Vol 39: 143—Vol 42: 15, 76, 139, 338,

McDOUGALL__Vol 46: 391—Vol 83: 442, 874
McDOW_____Vol 56: 690
McDOWELL__Vol 8: 886—Vol 9: 395—Vol
  28: 547—Vol 45: 101, 323—Vol 49: 40, 285
  —Vol 50: 70, 187—Vol 59: 112—Vol 66: 366,
  669—Vol 67: 517—Vol 70: 351, 708—Vol
  73: (2-64)—Vol 76: 310—Vol 80: 432—Vol
  82: 725—Vol 83: 260, 337—Vol 84: 633
McDUFFEE_____Vol 66: 160
McDUFFIE_____Vol 46: 27
McDURMIT_____Vol 33: 1032
McELFRESH_____Vol 74: (4-48)
McELHANEY_____Vol 45: 25
McELHENEY_____Vol 61: 158
McELHERRON_____Vol 42: 139
McELNAY_____Vol 56: 372
McELRATH_____Vol 48: 447
McELROY__Vol 23: 326—Vol 31: 669—Vol
  42: 337—Vol 49: 190—Vol 52: 108—Vol 53:
  594
McELWEE_____Vol 42: 15—Vol 81: 569
McELWRATH_____Vol 48: 447
McENTIRE_____Vol 75: (5-46)
McEWAN_____Vol 44: 82
McEWEN__Vol 28: 479—Vol 48: 448—Vol
  84: 636
McFADDEN__Vol 33: 274—Vol 42: 72—Vol
  63: 572
McFARLAND__Vol 17: 61—Vol 27: 668, 669
  —Vol 45: 103, 323—Vol 56: 225—Vol 67:
  716—Vol 70: 879—Vol 76: 582—Vol 78: 457
  —Vol 79: 161
McFEATERS_____Vol 48: 445
McGAFFEE_____Vol 54: 468
McGAFFREY_____Vol 54: 172
McGAHA_____Vol 35: 57
McGAMMON_____Vol 22: 375
McGARITY_____Vol 62: 588
McGARY_____Vol 65: 439
McGEE__Vol 47: 27—Vol 48: 59, 122—Vol
  57: 434—Vol 65: 438—Vol 70: 1167—Vol
  75: (9-37)—Vol 76: 400
McGHEE_____Vol 64: 259, 757
McGHEES_____Vol 21: 498
McGHIRK_____Vol 59: 524
McGILL_____Vol 43: 539—Vol 83: 793
McGLACHLIN_____Vol 30: 260
McGLAUGHLIN_____Vol 66: 308
McGLOCHLIN_____Vol 82: 795
McGOUGHEY_____Vol 35: 57
McGOWAN_____Vol 47: 197
McGOWEN_____Vol 64: 56
McGOWENS_____Vol 66: 249
McGOWN_____Vol 68: 374
McGRAW_____Vol 63: 571
McGREGIER_____Vol 26: 244
McGREGOR_____Vol 82: 139
McGREGORY_____Vol 35: 435, 436
McGREW_____Vol 63: 571
McGRUDER_____Vol 65: 299
McGUIRE__Vol 53: 626—Vol 56: 373—Vol
  60: 507—Vol 79: 161—Vol 80: 155
McGUNNEGLE_____Vol 81: 630
McHAFFEY_____Vol 60: 51
McHANEY_____Vol 47: 31—Vol 59: 588
McHENRY__Vol 40: 76—Vol 51: 303—Vol
  55: 522—Vol 57: 217
McHUGH_____Vol 56: 688
McILLWEE_____Vol 68: 490
McILRATH_____Vol 84: 966

McILROY_____Vol 82: 221
McILVAINE _____Vol 69: 160—Vol 73: (8-84)
McINTIRE__Vol 28: 478—Vol 45: 193—Vol
  64: 388—Vol 70: 1266—Vol 76: 400
McINTOSH__Vol 18: 181—Vol 26: 55—Vol
  30: 258—Vol 41: 126—Vol 45: 106—Vol 70:
  207, 1265—Vol 82: 936
McINTYRE__Vol 20: 62—Vol 43: 418—Vol
  48: 199, 444—Vol 50: 192, 354—Vol 59: 588
McISSACKS_____Vol 55: 108
McIVER_____Vol 70: 878
McJUNKIN_____Vol 42: 15, 192—Vol 44: 226
McKAMIE_____Vol 59: 763
McKAY__Vol 29: 513, 716—Vol 39: 277—Vol
  46: 27—Vol 48: 205—Vol 49: 189—Vol 50:
  113—Vol 52: 173—Vol 54: 51—Vol 70: 136
  —Vol 84: 520
McKEAN__Vol 24: 459—Vol 39: 225—Vol 55:
  521—Vol 56: 774
McKEE__Vol 41: 70, 162—Vol 46: 335—Vol
  56: 172—Vol 58: 52—Vol 67: 752—Vol 84:
  244, 520
McKEEN_____Vol 55: 109—Vol 62: 586
McKEITHEN_____Vol 65: 367
McKEMIE_____Vol 58: 649
McKENNA_____Vol 43: 539
McKENNEY_____Vol 46: 100
McKENSIE_____Vol 37: 396
McKENZIE__Vol 43: 425—Vol 66: 305—Vol
  67: 146—Vol 70: 206—Vol 78: 650
McKEOWN_____Vol 82: 794
McKIBBEN_____Vol 66: 160—Vol 82: 861
McKIE_____Vol 55: 46
McKILLIP_____Vol 69: 629
McKIM_____Vol 43: 489—Vol 46: 242
McKINLEY__Vol 41: 126, 163—Vol 43: 543
  —Vol 54: 223, 540—Vol 56: 109—Vol 60:
  635
McKINNA_____Vol 76: 62
McKINNEY__Vol 36: 757—Vol 41: 123—Vol
  45: 196—Vol 46: 287—Vol 49: 46—Vol 54:
  312—Vol 65: 633, 762—Vol 70: 708, 1168—
  Vol 71: 959—Vol 72: (3-73)
McKINNIE_____Vol 48: 121—Vol 66: 248
McKINNON_____Vol 33: 1032—Vol 58: 652
McKINNY_____Vol 58: 173
McKISSACK_____Vol 55: 284—Vol 56: 373
McKISSICK_____Vol 27: 740
McKITRICK_____Vol 83: 522
McKNIGHT__Vol 26: 560—Vol 38: 34—Vol
  41: 128—Vol 44: 388—Vol 49: 136—Vol 56:
  171—Vol 57: 175, 744—Vol 61: 707—Vol
  81: 518—Vol 83: 260
McKNITT_____Vol 82: 574
McKUNE_____Vol 18: 181
McLACHLAN_____Vol 56: 372
McLAIN__Vol 32: 720—Vol 35: 1266—Vol
  43: 491—Vol 82: 221—Vol 84: 245
McLANAHAN_____Vol 70: 709
McLANE_____Vol 79: 160
McLAUGHLIN__Vol 36: 350—Vol 47: 33—
  Vol 62: 503—Vol 82: 501—Vol 83: 1014
McLEAN__Vol 31: 862—Vol 39: 226—Vol 43:
  491—Vol 46: 384—Vol 51: 301—Vol 55:
  598—Vol 59: 525—Vol 61: 704—Vol 69: 160
  —Vol 76: 217—Vol 83: 945
McLELLAN_____Vol 45: 102
McLEMORE__Vol 57: 743—Vol 63: 373—Vol
  64: 587
McLENDON_____Vol 83: 90

McLENE................Vol 34: 199—Vol 79: 160
McLEOD..........Vol 83: 944—Vol 84: 444, 520
McLEROY...........................Vol 83: 1014
McLESTER..........................Vol 34: 66
McLIN....Vol 45: 128—Vol 68: 733—Vol 69: 158
McLOUD..............................Vol 45: 189
McMACHEN...........................Vol 83: 872
McMAHAN.........................Vol 59: 524
McMAHON....Vol 43: 489—Vol 54: 351—Vol 59: 523—Vol 60: 250, 570—Vol 65: 508—Vol 70: 207
McMAKEN............................Vol 79: 283
McMANN........................Vol 74: (2-42)
McMASTER...........Vol 46: 154—Vol 49: 395
McMASTERS.......................Vol 65: 248
McMECHEN....Vol 46: 387—Vol 47: 388—Vol 80: 71
McMICHAEL..........................Vol 64: 522
McMILAN............................Vol 79: 35
McMILLAN....Vol 55: 285—Vol 62: 774—Vol 80: 432—Vol 84: 67
McMILLEN....Vol 32: 720—Vol 33: 959—Vol 54: 464—Vol 57: 480—Vol 60: 418—Vol 68: 243—Vol 82: 931
McMINN........................Vol 59: 111, 521
McMORRIS.........................Vol 67: 147
McMULLEN....Vol 17: 61—Vol 32: 630—Vol 58: 173—Vol 64: 714—Vol 67: 148—Vol 75: (10-66)—Vol 80: 276—Vol 83: 335—Vol 84: 634
McMULLIN.......Vol 45: 112, 238—Vol 50: 61
McMURRAY......................Vol 33: 1032
McMURTRIE.........................Vol 43: 604
McMURTRY....Vol 40: 275—Vol 55: 599—Vol 56: 687—Vol 60: 51, 247
McMURTY...........................Vol 38: 328
McNAB.............................Vol 82: 139
McNABB ....Vol 53: 329—Vol 84: 247
McNAIR....Vol 27: 736—Vol 28: 258—Vol 60: 157—Vol 64: 588
McNAIRY...........................Vol 62: 308
McNALL............................Vol 22: 52
McNARY............................Vol 62: 54
McNATT............................Vol 83: 521
McNEAL.......Vol 64: 650—Vol 70: 335, 1017
McNEEL....Vol 44: 381—Vol 45: 186, 119—Vol 80: 84
McNEELEY..........................Vol 63: 428
McNEELY...........................Vol 70: 575
McNEER............................Vol 83: 173
McNEIL....Vol 46: 103—Vol 45: 119—Vol 48: 448—Vol 58: 241, 586—Vol 67: 646, 751
McNEILL..................Vol 58: 451—Vol 80: 382
McNEIS............................Vol 41: 124
McNICKLE..........................Vol 77: 333
McNITT............................Vol 57: 744
McNUTT....Vol 35: 1265—Vol 42: 342—Vol 43: 420
McPHERSON....Vol 28: 365—Vol 53: 242—Vol 55: 47—Vol 67: 753—Vol 74: (2-41)—Vol 84: 325
McPHIETERS.........Vol 43: 422—Vol 48: 445
McPIKE............................Vol 20: 607
McQUEEN....Vol 42: 341—Vol 43: 420—Vol 77: 479
McQUILLAN.........................Vol 57: 629
McRAE....Vol 32: 61—Vol 33: 42—Vol 36: 217—Vol 37: 486—Vol 38: 275
McRARY............................Vol 36: 354

McREE.............................Vol 66: 599
McREES............................Vol 64: 257
McREYNOLDS....Vol 43: 482—Vol 49: 133—Vol 75: (1-54)
McROY.............................Vol 82: 141
McSPADDEN.........................Vol 70: 454
McSPADDIN.........................Vol 51: 354
McSWAIN...........................Vol 83: 172
McTEER............................Vol 67: 711
McTYLER...........................Vol 63: 700
McVEAN............................Vol 39: 102
McVEY..............Vol 60: 115, 363—Vol 66: 55
McVICKER..........................Vol 81: 631
McWHIRTER...........Vol 57: 564—Vol 82: 396
McWHORTER....Vol 34: 659—Vol 56: 480—Vol 67: 147
McWILLIAMS....Vol 74: (1-50)—Vol 82: 859—Vol 83: 93

M

MABEY............................Vol 43: 420
MABIE....Vol 60: 634, 747—Vol 74: (4-52)—Vol 75: (6-37)
MABRY....Vol 45: 126—Vol 74: (1-48)—Vol 79: 332
MACAFEE...........Vol 28: 364—Vol 30: 338
MacALISTER........................Vol 59: 315
MACALLISTER.......................Vol 31: 414
MacCALL...........................Vol 28: 61
MACCLAINE.........................Vol 44: 152
MacCONNELL........................Vol 39: 102
MacCORKLE.........................Vol 44: 236
MacCRILLIS........................Vol 67: 43
MACCUBBIN.................Vol 39: 142, 325
MacDILL...........................Vol 59: 589
MacDONALD....Vol 36: 355—Vol 37: 394—Vol 47: 397—Vol 48: 201—Vol 53: 247
MacdONOUGH....Vol 36:217, 572, 754—Vol 66: 306
MacDOUGALL....Vol 57: 352—Vol 60: 507—Vol 63: 742
MACE....Vol 33: 707—Vol 41: 32—Vol 64: 714—Vol 68: 373
MacGREGOR........................Vol 83: 521
MACHEN............................Vol 82: 141
MACHETTE..........................Vol 82: 863
MacINTYRE.......................Vol 74: (3-45)
MACKALL...........................Vol 61: 607
MACKAY....Vol 34: 68—Vol 37: 148—Vol 52: 560, 731—Vol 61: 66, 913
MACKENZIE.........................Vol 69: 118
MACKEY....Vol 30: 339—Vol 46: 104—Vol 52: 52, 109—Vol 54: 592—Vol 56: 745—Vol 58: 452—Vol 61: 66, 913—Vol 71: 763—Vol 78: 696—Vol 82: 220—Vol 84: 633
MACKGEHEE...........Vol 67: 385—Vol 83: 521
MACKLIN....Vol 49: 286—Vol 68: 733—Vol 69: 158
MACLIN....Vol 44: 235, 384—Vol 68: 733—Vol 69: 158
MacNEIL ....Vol 65: 570—Vol 66:363
MACOMB............................Vol 71: 759
MACOMBER....Vol 60: 698—Vol 80: 656—Vol 82: 860
MACON....Vol 26: 336—Vol 45: 101—Vol 54: 55—Vol 62: 648—Vol 67: 647
MacPEAKE..........................Vol 45: 194
MacPHERSON........................Vol 6: 702
MACUBBIN..........................Vol 31: 52
MACUMBER ....Vol 50: 349

MARCLAY..................Vol 26: 340
MARCUM...................Vol 83: 794
MARCUS........Vol 60: 248—Vol 68: 155
MARCY......................Vol 48: 306
MARDEN.....................Vol 39: 102
MARDERS....................Vol 82: 862
MARET...................Vol 84: 326
MARICLE....................Vol 57: 217
MARIETTA.........Vol 49: 43—Vol 56: 416
MARINER...Vol 36: 355, 580—Vol 56: 176, 414
MARION...Vol 31: 413—Vol 35: 436—Vol 43: 601—Vol 44: 313—Vol 45: 241—Vol 52: 626
MARIS............Vol 46: 389—Vol 47: 191, 264
MARKHAM...Vol 24: 149—Vol 32: 631—Vol 38: 327—Vol 42: 77—Vol 46: 386—Vol 58: 173—Vol 60: 505, 572—Vol 63: 246
MARKLAND.......Vol 75: (5-46)—Vol 81: 570
MARKLEY....Vol 55: 520—Vol 60: 699—Vol 71: 240
MARKS...Vol 29: 648—Vol 42: 75—Vol 52: 110, 356—Vol 54: 421—Vol 74: (11-58)— Vol 77: 769
MARLATT....................Vol 65: 124
MARLEY............... Vol 69: 58, 158
MARLIN........Vol 46: 26, 157—Vol 48: 63, 440
MARLOW...................Vol 56: 175
MARMADUKE.......Vol 32: 718—Vol 66: 252
MARPLE........... .. Vol 61: 473
MARQUETTE................Vol 68: 121
MARQUIS...Vol 50: 354—Vol 52: 112, 169— Vol 64: 523—Vol 66: 366—Vol 79: 467
MARR.....................Vol 82: 932
MARRIOTT..................Vol 65: 296
MARROW................... Vol 45: 24
MARSDEN................ ....Vol 70: 1170
MARSH..Vol 6: 180—Vol 19: 627—Vol 21: 169—Vol 22: 375—Vol 29: 803—Vol 30: 63 —Vol 31: 53, 669—Vol 40: 75—Vol 41: 30— Vol 43: 543—Vol 49: 46, 395—Vol 53: 378— Vol 54: 112—Vol 56: 628—Vol 65: 248, 762 —Vol 66: 120—Vol 67: 388—Vol 68: 241— Vol 69: 57—Vol 70: 707, 1165—Vol 77: 241 —Vol 82: 726
MARSHALL...Vol 19: 308—Vol 26: 337—Vol 28: 547—Vol 31: 860, 862—Vol 32: 160— Vol 34: 658—Vol 47: 149, 396, 397—Vol 39: 104—Vol 42: 79. 80, 194—Vol 44: 82, 85— Vol 45: 189—Vol 46: 27, 389—Vol 48: 203, 448—Vol 52: 626—Vol 53: 179—Vol 54: 176 —Vol 55: 444, 600, 601, 603—Vol 56: 47, 113, 227, 688—Vol 57: 113, 116, 172, 174, 691—Vol 58: 331, 452—Vol 60: 573—Vol 61: 470, 471, 610, 708, 869, 911—Vol 62: 124, 503—Vol 66: 535—Vol 67: 45, 713—Vol 68: 155, 239, 623—Vol 69: 241, 242—Vol 72: (11-58)—Vol 71: 243—Vol 78: 697—Vol 79: 560—Vol 80: 432—Vol 81: 216—Vol 82: 140, 795—Vol 83: 336, 1014
MARSTERS..................Vol 72: 4, 83
MARSTON...Vol 31: 750—Vol 34: 660—Vol 36: 579—Vol 49: 48, 348
MARTIN...Vol 19: 207—Vol 21: 336—Vol 26: 561—Vol 29: 46, 650, 651—Vol 30: 258— Vol 32: 633, 719—Vol 34: 423—Vol 36: 218, 761—Vol 37: 149, 396, 486—Vol 39: 22, 274, 324—Vol 40: 229—Vol 41: 120, 124, 145— Vol 42: 80—Vol 43: 596, 603—Vol 44: 153, 316—Vol 45: 22, 125—Vol 46: 153, 157, 243 —Vol 47: 22, 25, 33, 95, 193, 199, 270, 395—

Vol 48: 444—Vol 49: 47, 131, 132, 183, 190, 281, 287, 395—Vol 50: 58, 280, 354, 414— Vol 52: 112, 558, 561—Vol 53: 54, 56, 241, 242, 377, 378, 446—Vol 54: 109, 227, 351, 465, 536, 650—Vol 55: 106, 713—Vol 56: 222, 474, 481, 560, 625, 627, 689, 744—Vol 57: 214, 689, 742—Vol 58: 172, 502, 585, 586— Vol 59: 239, 682—Vol 60: 50, 250, 417, 634— Vol 61: 472, 708, 788, 907, 913—Vol 63: 60, 294, 570, 742—Vol 64: 713—Vol 65: 247, 442, 760—Vol 66: 308, 365—Vol 67: 42, 117, 385, 448, 716—Vol 70: 355, 714, 1166— Vol 71: 239, 843—Vol 72: (2-69), (9-88), (12-68)—Vol 73: (7-70), (10-75), (10-76)— Vol 74: (2-40)—Vol 75: (1-54), (2-61), (12-63)—Vol 76: 401, 861—Vol 77: 184, 240, 332—Vol 79: 656—Vol 80: 277—Vol 81: 517 —Vol 82: 139, 140, 653, 862, 931—Vol 83: 172—Vol 84: 246, 631, 964, 966
MARTINDALE...Vol 49: 136—Vol 55: 711— Vol 84: 521
MARTYN.....................Vol 39: 222
MARVEL....................Vol 41: 163
MARVIN...Vol 43: 418—Vol 44: 312—Vol 46: 389—Vol 48: 54, 56, 300—Vol 52: 432, 433— Vol 53: 56—Vol 56: 45—Vol 60: 365—Vol 61: 552, 786—Vol 68: 373—Vol 75: (9-37)
MASK......................Vol 65: 245
MASON...Vol 23: 168—Vol 26: 143—Vol 30: 337—Vol 35: 1037—Vol 37: 70—Vol 38: 274, 327—Vol 39: 272—Vol 41: 215—Vol 42: 70, 140, 189, 267, 333—Vol 43: 424, 539, 540, 600, 723—Vol 44: 230—Vol 45: 200— Vol 52: 565—Vol 53: 178—Vol 55: 47, 165, 166—Vol 56: 416, 482, 625, 745—Vol 59: 48, 175, 314, 524—Vol 60: 248, 634—Vol 62: 390 —Vol 63: 508, 636, 740—Vol 65: 305—Vol 67: 388—Vol 74: (2-40)—Vol 75: (8-43)— Vol 76: 581—Vol 83: 443—Vol 84: 158
MASSENGALE...Vol 49: 356—Vol 50: 59— Vol 83: 439—Vol 84: 520
MASSER....................Vol 48: 63
MASSEY...Vol 29: 289—Vol 35: 1265—Vol 46: 385, 390—Vol 68: 243, 372—Vol 74: (7-54), (8-54)—Vol 80: 190—Vol 82: 141, 795—Vol 84: 445, 632
MASSIE..Vol 41: 120, 125—Vol 45: 109, 115 —Vol 52: 50—Vol 53: 748—Vol 70: 707— Vol 72: (10-94)—Vol 75: (2-61)—Vol 83: 794
MASSINGILL.................Vol 49: 356
MASSON.................. Vol 32: 163
MASTERS..........Vol 61: 607—Vol 64: 651
MASTERTON.................Vol 58: 174
MASTON...................Vol 43: 546
MATCHET...................Vol 63: 426
MATCHETT.......Vol 22: 157—Vol 65: 58
MATCHETTE................Vol 64: 587
MATER.....................Vol 37: 157
MATHENY...................Vol 76: 860
MATHER...Vol 2: 294—Vol 13: 67—Vol 46: 388—Vol 50: 355—Vol 59: 589—Vol 68: 735
MATHERS........Vol 55: 600—Vol 61: 382
MATHES.........Vol 68: 283—Vol 70: 358
MATHESON..................Vol 66: 670
MATHEWS...Vol 26: 244—Vol 28: 161—Vol 33: 676—Vol 37: 67—Vol 42: 16—Vol 43: 424—Vol 53: 56—Vol 56: 373—Vol 62: 121, 246, 456—Vol 63: 508, 634—Vol 65: 763 —Vol 66: 305, 537—Vol 70: 358—Vol 71:

959—Vol 82: 653—Vol 83: 92
MATHEWSON...Vol 38: 219—Vol 44: 236—
Vol 57: 628—Vol 70: 877
MATHIS...Vol 50: 354—Vol 77: 52—Vol 83: 90
MATKIN...........Vol 74: (11-55)—Vol 78: 456
MATLACK.................Vol 25: 383
MATLOCK........Vol 75: (10-64)—Vol 76: 309
MATNEWSON....................Vol 57: 742
MATSON...............Vol 28: 479—Vol 31: 586
MATTERSON.........................Vol 84: 445
MATTESON...Vol 42: 191—Vol 44: 236—Vol
53: 176—Vol 54: 176—Vol 59: 113—Vol 63:
699—Vol 64: 309, 523—Vol 67: 388—Vol
75: (9-37)—Vol 76: 310
MATTHAIS...................Vol 53: 181, 634
MATTHEW..........................Vol 43: 546
MATTHEWS...Vol 26: 561—Vol 27: 383, 807
—Vol 28: 263—Vol 29: 653—Vol 45: 19,
114, 120, 237, 239, 329—Vol 47: 272—Vol
49: 45—Vol 50: 67, 115, 350—Vol 51: 235,
354—Vol 53: 181—Vol 55: 600—Vol 59: 315
—Vol 61: 518—Vol 64: 57, 446—Vol 66:
733—Vol 68: 373, 487—Vol 69: 158, 242—
Vol 75: (5-47)—Vol 76: 709—Vol 77: 664
—Vol 82: 862—Vol 83: 717—Vol 84: 158
MATTHEWSON.......Vol 29: 648—Vol 64: 759
MATTHIAS.................Vol 83: 943, 1015
MATTHIS................Vol 64: 256, 384
MATTHRES.........................Vol 50: 189
MATTICE............................Vol 41: 34
MATTINGLY.......................Vol 48: 204
MATTISON...Vol 31: 587—Vol 41: 163, 164—
Vol 70: 1169
MATTIX...Vol 55: 165—Vol 78: 696—Vol 82: 139, 140
MATTOCKS.........................Vol 59: 763
MATTOON...Vol 29: 800—Vol 48: 443—Vol 57: 353
MATTOS...........................Vol 64: 758
MATTOX...Vol 52: 562—Vol 58: 702—Vol
63: 571—Vol 65: 159—Vol 72: (8-86)
MAULDIN...............Vol 49: 46—Vol 51: 356
MAULSBY...............Vol 7: 442—Vol 29: 512
MAUND..............................Vol 58: 451
MAUPIN...Vol 35: 1265—Vol 37: 74—Vol 42:
137—Vol 43: 596
MAURON...........................Vol 64: 259
MAURY...............Vol 32: 161—Vol 80: 277
MAUZY.............................Vol 61: 552
MAWNEY...........Vol 26: 561—Vol 27: 735
MAXEY...Vol 48: 56—Vol 53: 178—Vol 54:
589—Vol 64: 761—Vol 68: 374, 731—Vol
73: (5-88)
MAXFIELD........................Vol 46: 390
MAXHAM...........................Vol 80: 383
MAXIE.............................Vol 44: 386
MAXON............................Vol 77: 603
MAXSON...Vol 42: 338—Vol 45: 24, 27, 111—
Vol 47: 196—Vol 58: 172—Vol 62: 390—
Vol 73: (2-65), (9-68)—Vol 81: 517
MAXWELL...Vol 17: 569—Vol 28: 158, 362—
Vol 29: 44, 652—Vol 30: 256—Vol 36: 215,
463, 755, 758—Vol 37: 487—Vol 39: 226—
Vol 40: 24—Vol 43: 492—Vol 44: 388—Vol
45: 117—Vol 48: 202—Vol 55: 714—Vol 56:
368—Vol 59: 109, 314—Vol 60: 249—Vol
62: 122—Vol 63: 59, 168—Vol 67: 613, 752—
Vol 69: 631—Vol 82: 931
MAY...Vol 32: 633—Vol 35: 655—Vol 36: 571

—Vol 37: 270—Vol 42: 343—Vol 43: 541—
Vol 45: 19—Vol 47: 28—Vol 49: 43—Vol
56: 690—Vol 61: 376—Vol 71: 674—Vol 84: 447
MAYBANK..........................Vol 62: 53
MAYBERRY...Vol 26: 141—Vol 82: 313, 575,
797—Vol 83: 171
MAYDOLE...Vol 59: 112—Vol 66: 669—Vol 70: 351
MAYER............................Vol 64: 442
MAYES...Vol 39: 103—Vol 66: 534—Vol 67:
385—Vol 80: 44—Vol 82: 798
MAYFIELD...Vol 39: 273—Vol 42: 192—Vol 46: 328
MAYHALL..................Vol 58: 701
MAYHEW...Vol 34: 537—Vol 45: 188, 240—
Vol 53: 242—Vol 55: 522—Vol 72: (2-62)—
Vol 82: 138
MAYNARD...Vol 23: 400—Vol 29: 290—Vol
36: 577—Vol 39: 273—Vol 40: 274—Vol 48:
307—Vol 53: 377—Vol 70: 1166—Vol 83: 337
MAYNE...................Vol 36: 758—Vol 37: 394
MAYO...Vol 36: 575—Vol 38: 113—Vol 42:
194—Vol 45: 109—Vol 46: 152, 242—Vol
47: 270—Vol 65: 298—Vol 67: 441—Vol 68: 488
MAYPOLE.........................Vol 37: 153
MAYS...Vol 33: 959—Vol 43: 494—Vol 59:
314—Vol 72: (10-94)—Vol 77: 241—Vol 82: 500
MEACHAM...Vol 32: 164, 508—Vol 40: 73,
225, 228—Vol 54: 420—Vol 56: 688—Vol 59:
589—Vol 70: 358
MEAD...Vol 27: 669—Vol 33: 42—Vol 35:
1100—Vol 37: 488—Vol 38: 113, 328—Vol
48: 308—Vol 50: 350—Vol 51: 355—Vol 52:
560—Vol 55: 712—Vol 56: 413, 561—Vol 59:
765—Vol 65: 438, 569—Vol 67: 711—Vol
74: (5-42)—Vol 76: 309—Vol 77: 538—Vol
80: 191, 432—Vol 82: 654—Vol 83: 94
MEADE...Vol 36: 352—Vol 44: 228—Vol 55:
109—Vol 62: 309—Vol 64: 159
MEADOWS...Vol 44: 235—Vol 81: 71—Vol 82: 313
MEAKIN...........................Vol 65: 763
MEANLEY...............Vol 82: 397—Vol 83: 91
MEANS...Vol 42: 191—Vol 61: 230—Vol 68:
626—Vol 82: 863
MEARS...............Vol 61: 279—Vol 71: 673
MEBANE............................Vol 50: 70
MEDARY..........................Vol 82: 141
MEDBURY.............Vol 28: 548—Vol 84: 325
MEDCALF.............Vol 57: 177—Vol 58: 329
MEDLEY...Vol 41: 120, 125—Vol 43: 422—
Vol 44: 26, 82—Vol 70: 574
MEDLOCK.........................Vol 76: 309
MEECH...............Vol 45: 123—Vol 57: 215
MEEK...Vol 26: 142—Vol 28: 478—Vol 41:
31—Vol 43: 418—Vol 44: 230, 232—Vol 67:
148, 574—Vol 83: 262, 795
MEEKER...Vol 31: 53—Vol 44: 231—Vol 53:
176—Vol 55: 47, 209—Vol 56: 372, 558—
Vol 75: (9-41)—Vol 82: 932
MEEKES..........................Vol 28: 162
MEEKS...Vol 43: 485, 486—Vol 44: 27—Vol
45: 104—Vol 52: 559—Vol 53: 182—Vol
67: 385—Vol 75: (2-58)
MEEMS...........................Vol 43: 421
MEESE...........................Vol 78: 108

MEGOWN..............Vol 43: 422—Vol 48: 445
MEHAFFEY............Vol 60: 570—Vol 61: 749
MEHRLING.......................Vol 60: 573
MEIGGS...................... ....Vol 37: 151
MEIGS....Vol 36: 350, 463, 754—Vol 61: 376—
Vol 71: 163
MELICK....Vol 67: 713—Vol 68: 239—Vol 69:
764
MELLEN.............................Vol 28: 547
MELLET..............................Vol 80: 191
MELLETT....................... ....Vol 58: 329
MELETTE...........................Vol 46: 157
MELLOTT...........................Vol 61: 706
MELVILLE..........................Vol 67: 387
MELVIN..............Vol 47: 341—Vol 77: 438
MENDALL...........................Vol 68: 154
MENDELL...........................Vol 68: 154
MENDENHALL....Vol 26: 242—Vol 53: 691
—Vol 59: 761—Vol 64: 308—Vol 77: 538
MENEFFEE.........Vol 46: 389—Vol 58: 452
MENET..............................Vol 30: 337
MENG..............................Vol 31: 411
MERCER....Vol 20: 60, 352—Vol 29: 803—Vol
37: 149—Vol 42: 193—Vol 43: 422—Vol 55:
47—Vol 65: 247—Vol 66: 162—Vol 68: 242
—Vol 70: 878—Vol 79: 160—Vol 82: 727,
795, 796
MERCEREAU.......................Vol 84: 703
MERCHANT....Vol 64: 307—Vol 75: (9-40)—
Vol 82: 200
MEREDITH....Vol 39: 104—Vol 43: 421—Vol
49: 134—Vol 64: 257—Vol 65: 438, 572—
Vol 66: 362, 535, 828—Vol 67: 114, 443—
Vol 72: (8-86)—Vol 75: (2-51)—Vol 84: 68
MERIHAM..........................Vol 77: 239
MERITHEW.........................Vol 53: 376
MERIWETHER....Vol 36: 351—Vol 40: 274—
Vol 41: 29—Vol 42: 10—Vol 46: 240—Vol
47: 394—Vol 55: 46—Vol 72: (1-66)—Vol
76: 62—Vol 77: 183
MERKELL..........................Vol 36: 575
MERNISTER.......................Vol 82: 397
MERREILL.........................Vol 28: 366
MERRELL............Vol 52: 435—Vol 58: 371
MERRIAM....Vol 45: 21—Vol 47: 22—Vol 56:
564—Vol 57: 38, 480
MERRICK....Vol 6: 599—Vol 28: 548—Vol
58: 588—Vol 59: 45—Vol 75: (2-58)—Vol
83: 523
MERRIDITH........................Vol 67: 116
MERRIFIELD.......Vol 56: 627—Vol 64: 259
MERRIL....................... ....Vol 77: 725
MERRILL....Vol 20: 61, 278—Vol 21: 59—Vol
22: 154—Vol 29: 647—Vol 30: 64, 441—Vol
31: 585, 586, 749—Vol 32: 59—Vol 33: 1032
—Vol 35: 55, 56, 1038, 1262—Vol 36: 214—
Vol 40: 25—Vol 42: 269—Vol 44: 79, 230,
231, 233, 234, 383, 384—Vol 45: 101, 102, 191
—Vol 46: 104—Vol 47: 29—Vol 48: 203, 368
—Vol 49: 192—Vol 52: 435—Vol 59: 239—
Vol 61: 546—Vol 63: 699—Vol 65: 758—
Vol 71: 1025—Vol 80: 190
MERRILLS.........................Vol 31: 53
MERRILLS.........................Vol 43: 544
MERRIMAN....Vol 20: 277—Vol 21: 60—Vol
22: 157—Vol 24: 262—Vol 26: 142—Vol 27:
739, 890—Vol 29: 47—Vol 38: 84, 272, 329—
Vol 40: 223—Vol 43: 497—Vol 44: 24, 232,
383—Vol 46: 185—Vol 59: 174—Vol 73:
(9-66)—Vol 74: (7-51), (8-51)—Vol 83: 794

MERRIT.............................Vol 56: 46
MERRITHEN.......................Vol 80: 335
MERRITT....Vol 21: 168—Vol 37: 150—Vol
40: 74—Vol 43: 493—Vol 44: 314—Vol 54:
589—Vol 60: 507—Vol 61: 62—Vol 67: 293
—Vol 74: (2-43)—Vol 82: 795—Vol 83: 93
MERRIWETHER.....................Vol 80: 191
MERRY....Vol 41: 121, 125—Vol 42: 11—Vol
82: 139
MERRYMAN....Vol 43: 489, 542—Vol 44: 23
—Vol 81: 631
MERSEREAU.......................Vol 55: 710
MERSHON.........................Vol 46: 387
MERWIN........Vol 27: 735, 806—Vol 43: 481
MESERVEY........................Vol 57: 566
MESSENGER....Vol 45: 118, 239—Vol 52: 50
—Vol 54: 536, 710—Vol 83: 172
MESSER........................Vol 48: 63, 303
MESSIER..........................Vol 67: 114
MESSIT...........................Vol 32: 163
METCALF....Vol 34: 538—Vol 37: 148—Vol
44: 85—Vol 45: 117—Vol 47: 197—Vol 52:
435—Vol 54: 351—Vol 58: 329—Vol 84: 69
METCALFE....Vol 50: 193—Vol 51: 355—Vol
84: 68
METLIN..........................Vol 57: 311
METZ.............................Vol 55: 444
METZGAR.........................Vol 45: 110
MEVDER..........................Vol 31: 862
MEYER....Vol 40: 228—Vol 55: 338, 603—Vol
64: 160, 442, 443—Vol 81: 570—Vol 82: 142,
934
MEYERS....Vol 22: 996—Vol 58: 501—Vol 59:
587—Vol 81: 570—Vol 83: 794
MIARS............................Vol 58: 453
MICHAEL....Vol 24: 152—Vol 57: 174—Vol
65: 763—Vol 81: 20
MICHELLE........................Vol 29: 802
MICHENER........................Vol 72: (4-83)
MICHIE............Vol 35: 1266—Vol 36: 73
MIDDAGH.........................Vol 38: 221
MIDDAUGH........Vol 52: 51—Vol 66: 733
MIDDLEBROOK.....................Vol 25: 38
MIDDLEDITCH......Vol 48: 372—Vol 49: 124
MIDDLESWART....Vol 46: 387—Vol 47: 86—
Vol 49: 187—Vol 64: 160
MIDDLETON....Vol 24: 458—Vol 45: 195—
Vol 46: 104—Vol 56: 743—Vol 61: 469—
Vol 62: 457, 458—Vol 64: 57—Vol 66: 248—
Vol 67: 292—Vol 68: 243—Vol 72: (10-96),
(11-62)—Vol 73: (2-64)—Vol 83: 258—Vol
84: 445
MIERS....Vol 39: 224—Vol 41: 70—Vol 46:
27—Vol 53: 55—Vol 58: 453—Vol 80: 336
MIFFLIN.........................Vol 56: 370
MILAN.......................... Vol 46: 104
MILBURN.........................Vol 56: 561
MILES....Vol 21: 252—Vol 27: 380—Vol 30:
67—Vol 45: 102—Vol 47: 22, 82—Vol 48:
59—Vol 52: 359—Vol 53: 182—Vol 60: 49—
Vol 64: 649, 716—Vol 81: 73—Vol 83: 872,
873
MILFORD.........................Vol 70: 134
MILHORN.........................Vol 82: 397
MILIRON.........................Vol 62: 584
MILLAR............Vol 48: 58—Vol 75: (2-57)
MILLARD....Vol 23: 326—Vol 28: 263—Vol
47: 392—Vol 54: 592—Vol 55: 336—Vol 56:
46—Vol 58: 368—Vol 63: 60
MILLEISON............... ....Vol 62: 584

MILLEN___Vol 28: 162—Vol 49: 131, 285, 348
MILLER___Vol 2: 45—Vol 19: 628—Vol 21:
168—Vol 22: 997—Vol 26: 54—Vol 27: 668,
890—Vol 28: 263, 479—Vol 30: 62—Vol 31:
52, 414—Vol 33: 475—Vol 38: 87, 220—Vol
39: 223, 273, 274—Vol 40: 25—Vol 41: 32,
124—Vol 42: 76, 193, 194, 341—Vol 43: 420,
540, 543, 493, 496, 544, 600, 723,—Vol 44: 84
—Vol 45: 112, 116, 117, 128, 198, 199, 240,
329—Vol 46: 99, 103, 104, 157, 237, 242, 329,
384, 387,—Vol 47: 28, 192, 264, 270—Vol
48: 371, 449, 450—Vol 49: 187, 286—Vol 50:
61, 355—Vol 52: 53, 322, 626, 734—Vol 53:
56, 246, 493—Vol 54: 110, 111, 310, 352, 465
—Vol 55: 46, 47, 164, 286, 397, 446, 521, 598,
655—Vol 56: 44, 225, 557—Vol 57: 116, 174,
177,628, 746—Vol 58: 241, 701—Vol 59: 442,
588—Vol 60: 114, 157, 290, 633—Vol 61:
158, 472, 607—Vol 62: 54, 247—Vol 63: 165,
168, 699, 741—Vol 64: 258—Vol 65: 247,
367, 439, 670, 762—Vol 66: 159, 250, 309,
535, 828—Vol 67: 44, 239, 385, 387, 443, 575,
648—Vol 68: 241, 243, 489—Vol 69: 119,
160, 360, 361, 566, 567, 762—Vol 70: 360,
457, 1020, 1167—Vol 71: 462, 762, 959—Vol
74: (1-50), (11-60)—Vol 75: (1-57), (2-60),
(3-41), (4-52), (9-41)—Vol 76: 219—Vol
77: 52, 244—Vol 78: 108, 156, 246, 554—Vol
79: 332, 613—Vol 80: 155, 277—Vol 81: 20,
130, 429, 518, 629—Vol 82: 499, 501, 726,
727, 863—Vol 83: 259, 522, 717, 1014—Vol
84: 68, 70, 158, 325, 706, 966
MILLIGAN___Vol 47: 30—Vol 74: (11-55)—
Vol 83: 173
MILLIKEN___Vol 34: 200—Vol 43: 602—Vol
45: 105, 324—Vol 50: 345
MILLIMAN_____Vol 43: 493
MILLIN_____Vol 49: 131, 285—Vol 51: 354
MILLINER_____Vol 50: 354
MILLING_____Vol 19: 432—Vol 61: 230
MILLINGTON_____Vol 37: 161
MILLIONS_____Vol 50: 193
MILLIS_____Vol 77: 331
MILLS___Vol 6: 188—Vol 30: 148—Vol 32:
162, 632—Vol 33: 39—Vol 35: 652, 655—Vol
36: 351—Vol 37: 65, 159, 270, 488—Vol 45:
104, 110, 120, 123, 192, 324—Vol 46: 104—
Vol 47: 266—Vol 48: 123—Vol 50: 61—Vol
41: 302, 303—Vol 53: 330—Vol 54: 110, 537
—Vol 55: 399—Vol 56: 45, 629, 691—Vol
57: 310—Vol 58: 112, 588—Vol 59: 45, 48,
589, 651—Vol 61: 157—Vol 66: 825—Vol
67: 240—Vol 69: 121—Vol 82: 793—Vol 83:
173
MILLSAPS_____Vol 38: 275
MILLSLAGLE_____Vol 40: 230
MILNER___Vol 34: 422—Vol 47: 269—Vol 66:
121
MILSAP_____Vol 83: 258
MILSLAGLE_____Vol 46: 153
MILTON_____Vol 44: 28—Vol 62: 307
MIMME_____Vol 54: 311
MIMMES_____Vol 53: 628, 631
MIMS___Vol 54: 588—Vol 55: 49—Vol 56: 227
MINOR _____Vol 65: 572
MINARD _____ _____ Vol 23: 470
MINDWELL_____Vol 32: 633
MINER . Vol 25: 799—Vol 28: 259—Vol 32:
632—Vol 36: 217—Vol 57: 353—Vol 58:

54, 449, 500—Vol 61: 64—Vol 81: 430—Vol
82: 220
MINERS_____Vol 33: 39, 40, 474
MINES_____Vol 44: 24
MINGE_____Vol 43: 422—Vol 61: 149
MINIER_____Vol 65: 440, 668
MINIS_____Vol 30: 148
MINIUM_____Vol 38: 35—Vol 43: 496
MINNEY_____Vol 49: 287
MINNIS_____Vol 43: 459—Vol 44: 149
MINOR___Vol 31: 749, 860—Vol 41: 164—Vol
48: 63—Vol 55: 712—Vol 56: 174—Vol 58:
53, 329, 368, 452—Vol 61: 867, 908—Vol 67:
444
MINOT_____Vol 45: 126—Vol 48: 369
MINOTT_____Vol 41: 123
MINTER_____Vol 43: 545
MINTHORN_____ Vol 28: 262
MINTON___Vol 28: 262—Vol 45: 104—Vol
47: 33—Vol 66: 461—Vol 75: (4-53)
MINTURN_____Vol 30: 542—Vol 73: (8-82)
MIRES_____ _____ Vol 53: 55
MITCHELL___Vol 25: 383—Vol 27: 382, 736—
Vol 28: 480—Vol 36: 354—Vol 39: 226, 276—
Vol 43: 485, 487—Vol 44: 25, 27, 82, 152, 230,
314—Vol 45: 18, 117—Vol 46: 241—Vol 47:
340—Vol 48: 447—Vol 49: 47, 135, 190—Vol
50: 64—Vol 53: 116, 242—Vol 54: 647, 650
—Vol 55: 336, 397, 444—Vol 56: 227, 475,
743—Vol 57: 174, 434, 629—Vol 58: 501—
Vol 59: 315—Vol 60: 366, 504, 507, 747—
Vol 61: 607—Vol 62: 390, 715—Vol 63: 106,
636, 699—Vol 66: 122—Vol 67: 118—Vol 69:
244, 363, 565, 683—Vol 70: 1019—Vol 71:
240, 672, 762—Vol 72: (11-59)—Vol 74:
(1-51)—Vol 75: (6-40), (9-37), (9-41), (10-
67)—Vol 79: 195, 518—Vol 82: 314—Vol
83: 871, 873—Vol 84: 68, 446, 894, 965
MITCHIE_____Vol 43: 596
MIX___Vol 26: 241—Vol 27: 670—Vol 30: 61
—Vol 33: 476—Vol 43: 485—Vol 77: 768
MIXER_____Vol 79: 467
MIZE_____Vol 42: 336—Vol 82: 934
MOASMAN_____Vol 52: 624
MOBERLY_____ Vol 49: 46
MOBLEY___Vol 49: 46—Vol 56: 373—Vol 68:
58
MOFFATT_____Vol 22: 271—Vol 46: 30
MOFFET_____ _____Vol 69: 363
MOFFETT_____Vol 75: (8-62)
MOFFETTE_____Vol 68: 122
MOFFITT_____Vol 56: 47
MOFFITT___Vol 43: 545—Vol 46: 328, 196—
Vol 77: 332
MOHLER___Vol 36: 577—Vol 37: 68—Vol 43:
487—Vol 44: 28, 229—Vol 45: 185
MOIS_____Vol 56: 690
MOISER_____Vol 58: 329
MOLAH_____Vol 36: 577
MOLBY_____Vol 48: 442
MOLER_____Vol 37: 68
MOLING_____Vol 71: 1109—Vol 72: (6-78)
MOLTON_____Vol 63: 105
MONCHET_____Vol 47: 262
MONCRIEF_____Vol 67: 442
MONEY_____Vol 60: 113
MONFOORT_____Vol 59: 589
MONFORT _____ Vol 33: 474—Vol 71: 164
MONG_____Vol 60: 573
MONIGER_____Vol 82: 141

MONK....Vol 17: 569—Vol 54: 648—Vol 55: 397—Vol 80: 656

MONNET....................Vol 54: 465—Vol 69: 630

MONNETT..Vol 54: 114

MONRO..Vol 59: 588

MONROE....Vol 26: 560—Vol 38: 331—Vol 40: 26—Vol 43: 541, 544—Vol 45: 183—Vol 46: 331—Vol 58: 111—Vol 63: 508—Vol 69: 501, 680, 681—Vol 71: 760—Vol 74: (1-49)—Vol 75: (9-41)—Vol 76: 653—Vol 83: 520—Vol 84: 325

MONSEY..Vol 77: 118

MONTAGUE....Vol 29: 801—Vol 30: 539—Vol 46: 240—Vol 57: 113—Vol 59: 175—Vol 83: 522

MONTAZUN..............................Vol 30: 439

MONTFORD................Vol 31: 859—Vol 41: 72

MONTFORT............Vol 31: 414—Vol 54: 649

MONTGOMERY....Vol 1: 451—Vol 19: 207— Vol 23: 326—Vol 27: 668—Vol 28: 547— Vol 30: 439—Vol 31: 584—Vol 33: 1031— Vol 36: 351—Vol 37: 152, 153—Vol 38: 34, 36—Vol 40: 172, 230, 272—Vol 42: 9, 138, 192, 264, 339, 343—Vol 43: 420, 597, 598— Vol 44: 28, 82, 225, 388—Vol 45: 25, 189— Vol 46: 28, 153, 390—Vol 47: 199, 266, 271, 273—Vol 48: 56, 61—Vol 52: 560—Vol 53: 378—Vol 54: 54, 225—Vol 55: 106, 714— Vol 56: 110, 412, 562—Vol 58: 369, 649— Vol 59: 45—Vol 62: 651—Vol 63: 59—Vol 64: 757—Vol 65: 122—Vol 67: 514—Vol 71: 460—Vol 72: (4-82)—Vol 80: 382—Vol 82: 798—Vol 83: 93—Vol 84: 67, 246, 444

MONTIER..Vol 76: 219

MOODY....Vol 45: 193—Vol 46: 23—Vol 49: 134—Vol 57: 177—Vol 60: 506—Vol 64: 446—Vol 66: 122, 160—Vol 69: 361—Vol 70: 205, 353, 355—Vol 72: (8-86)—Vol 73: (11-64)—Vol 74: (5-39)—Vol 81: 429—Vol 84: 522

MOOK....................................Vol 77: 241, 538

MOON....Vol 43: 492—Vol 46: 103, 242—Vol 50: 354—Vol 53: 447—Vol 54: 176—Vol 57: 173, 215—Vol 69: 629—Vol 77: 183— Vol 82: 862

MOONEY....Vol 30: 339—Vol 43: 600, 601— Vol 47: 397—Vol 48: 302

MOOR....Vol 42: 76, 189—Vol 62: 558—Vol 64: 385—Vol 65: 634—Vol 66: 160, 364— Vol 70: 1165, 1170—Vol 71: 677

MOORE....Vol 1: 604—Vol 2: 404—Vol 19: 307, 432—Vol 22: 54, 375—Vol 23: 397— Vol 24: 55—Vol 26: 339—Vol 27: 44—Vol 28: 60, 160, 162—Vol 30: 64—Vol 32: 161, 284—Vol 34: 200—Vol 35: 1264—Vol 36: 217, 354, 762—Vol 37: 267—Vol 41: 32, 67, 121, 125—Vol 42: 75, 76, 189, 337—Vol 43: 416, 426, 489, 605—Vol 44: 28, 81, 151, 230, 234, 314—Vol 45: 26, 101, 102, 198, 242, 184 —Vol 46: 28, 243, 246, 331, 333, 392—Vol 47: 198, 199, 266, 271—Vol 48: 64—Vol 49: 46, 188, 355—Vol 52: 108, 563, 687—Vol 53: 117, 241, 248, 570, 692—Vol 55: 338—Vol 56: 176, 414, 563, 626, 745, 746—Vol 57: 311, 743—Vol 58: 330, 372, 650, 700, 763— Vol 59: 48, 113, 312, 387—Vol 60: 573, 697— Vol 61: 450, 699, 708, 912—Vol 62: 500—Vol 63: 570—Vol 64: 521, 715, 756—Vol 65: 246, 366, 440, 634—Vol 66: 55, 123, 160, 460,

537, 600, 827—Vol 67: 241, 293—Vol 68: 121, 284, 372, 490—Vol 70: 205, 353, 354, 1165, 1167, 1169, 1170—Vol 71: 86, 674, 761, 1110—Vol 73: (4-83)—Vol 74: (2-40), (5-38)—Vol 75: (1-53), (2-61)—Vol 77: 117, 239, 539—Vol 78: 246, 295, 600—Vol 79: 35, 283, 284, 562, 613—Vol 80: 43, 46, 277, 512—Vol 82: 139, 221, 396, 502, 795, 861, 931—Vol 83: 173, 260, 441, 793, 795—Vol 84: 247, 445, 521

MOOREHEAD....Vol 47: 196—Vol 48: 443— Vol 49: 182—Vol 57: 116

MOOREHOUSE........Vol 48: 371—Vol 64: 389

MOORHEAD................Vol 81: 130—Vol 84: 705

MOORMAN....Vol 41: 215—Vol 42: 80, 189— Vol 43: 604—Vol 44: 153—Vol 46: 28, 238— Vol 50: 64

MOORS..............................Vol 33: 42—Vol 66: 827

MOOSER..Vol 56: 373

MORAINE....................................Vol 81: 430

MORAN..................Vol 64: 259—Vol 84: 965

MORE..Vol 81: 570

MOREHEAD....Vol 2: 192—Vol 30: 439—Vol 45: 17—Vol 52: 560—Vol 53: 247—Vol 60: 250, 570—Vol 82: 934

MOREHOUSE....Vol 41: 123—Vol 55: 338— Vol 59: 315—Vol 64: 522, 389—Vol 68: 554

MOREING..Vol 67: 45

MORELAND....Vol 36: 214—Vol 66: 599—Vol 79: 160, 284—Vol 81: 431

MOREMUS......................................Vol 51: 301

MORENAS..Vol 54: 592

MOREY....Vol 31: 54—Vol 38: 221—Vol 43: 416—Vol 49: 284—Vol 57: 114—Vol 58: 172 —Vol 73: (8-84)—Vol 80: 45—Vol 84: 326

MORGAN....Vol 1: 342—Vol 5: 58—Vol 15: 349—Vol 19: 307—Vol 21: 403, 497—Vol 22: 156, 997, 998—Vol 25: 966—Vol 31: 669— Vol 32: 284—Vol 33: 1032—Vol 34: 65, 657, 661—Vol 35: 651—Vol 37: 68, 349—Vol 38: 331—Vol 39: 21, 275, 276, 327—Vol 40: 74, 172—Vol 41: 28—Vol 42: 137—Vol 43: 418, 604—Vol 44: 152, 311—Vol 45: 18, 24, 100, 101, 187—Vol 47: 27—Vol 48: 56, 62, 199, 305, 371—Vol 49: 39, 132—Vol 50: 63, 70— Vol 51: 354—Vol 53: 494—Vol 54: 223, 229, 350, 592—Vol 55: 598, 711—Vol 56: 227— Vol 57: 743—Vol 58: 108, 173, 370, 451, 648, 652, 698—Vol 59: 109—Vol 60: 113, 157, 289, 363, 505—Vol 61: 60—Vol 62: 503— Vol 63: 246, 699, 700—Vol 66: 55—Vol 67: 42, 243, 388—Vol 68: 155, 241, 492, 627— Vol 70: 206—Vol 72: (12-70)—Vol 79: 36, 333, 613—Vol 80: 193—Vol 82: 313, 931

MORGANDOLLAR......................Vol 46: 245

MORGANTHALER............................Vol 25: 968

MORGART................................Vol 84: 247

MORING..Vol 28: 162

MORLATT..Vol 65: 124

MORLEY..Vol 57: 312

MORLY..Vol 41: 31

MORNIER..Vol 31: 414

MORPHAT......................................Vol 71: 1024

MORRELL....Vol 45: 20, 111—Vol 46: 100— Vol 47: 95—Vol 58: 54, 240, 449, 588, 699— Vol 59: 174—Vol 63: 508

MORRILL....Vol 20: 61—Vol 32: 632—Vol 48: 60—Vol 56: 172—Vol 71: 464—Vol 75: (4-55)

MORRIS—Vol 25: 716, 966—Vol 26: 55—Vol 31: 53—Vol 35: 58—Vol 36: 352, 355, 754—Vol 38: 84, 219, 272—Vol 39: 21, 140, 227, 325—Vol 40: 24, 226—Vol 42: 264—Vol 43: 427, 484, 546—Vol 44: 82, 85, 150, 154, 309, 311—Vol 47: 395—Vol 48: 204, 370, 446—Vol 50: 190—Vol 52: 51, 360—Vol 53: 53, 116, 547—Vol 55: 286—Vol 56: 46, 481, 625—Vol 57: 116—Vol 58: 330—Vol 59: 314—Vol 63: 60, 428—Vol 65: 439—Vol 66: 54, 534, 600, —826—Vol 67: 441, 648, 751—Vol 68: 489, 626—Vol 69: 631—Vol 70: 353—Vol 71: 763—Vol 72: (2-64), (4-83)—Vol 73: (5-88) —Vol 74: (6-35), (9-50)—Vol 75: (6-39)— Vol 78: 53, 650—Vol 82: 727—Vol 84: 326

MORRISON—Vol 20: 116—Vol 22: 678—Vol 30: 339, 541—Vol 31: 50—Vol 43: 491, 542 —Vol 44: 236, 313, 315, 382—Vol 45: 114— Vol 49: 355—Vol 55: 444—Vol 57: 552— Vol 58: 111, 651—Vol 60: 115—Vol 61: 708 —Vol 66: 670—Vol 67: 114, 145, 645—Vol 69: 247—Vol 74: (4-52)—Vol 80: 511

MORROW—Vol 31: 588—Vol 53: 244—Vol 60: 418—Vol 64: 758—Vol 67: 516—Vol 68: 120, 684—Vol 69: 244—Vol 70: 205— Vol 74: (2-43), (5-39)—Vol 75: (1-54)— Vol 80: 154—Vol 82: 397—Vol 83: 440

MORRS_____Vol 67: 387

MORSE—Vol 22: 52—Vol 31: 55—Vol 36: 758—Vol 39: 22, 103—Vol 42: 270—Vol 43: 482—Vol 45: 121—Vol 46: 99—Vol 52: 435 —Vol 56: 624—Vol 57: 40, 112, 174, 213— Vol 58: 108, 586—Vol 59: 176, 650—Vol 60: 51—Vol 68: 122—Vol 70: 576, 878—Vol 73: (11-69)—Vol 79: 467—Vol 82: 313—Vol 83: 441

MORTIMER—Vol 22: 268—Vol 40: 274—Vol 43: 539—Vol 75: (10-66)

MORTON—Vol 6: 699—Vol 14: 265—Vol 37: 74, 350—Vol 43: 427, 494—Vol 49: 43, 281— Vol 57: 115, 313—Vol 62: 647—Vol 63: 295, 700—Vol 67: 48, 383, 386, 440—Vol 68: 57— Vol 76: 709—Vol 81: 517—Vol 82: 140—Vol 84: 632

MOSBY_____ Vol 60: 248, 504—Vol 80: 276

MOSELEY—Vol 28: 162—Vol 34: 423—Vol 45: 104—Vol 53: 180—Vol 57: 113—Vol 60: 698—Vol 63: 104, 373, 428—Vol 66: 248— Vol 68: 123, 488—Vol 70: 453—Vol 72: (2-62)

MOSELY—Vol 39: 104—Vol 44: 236—Vol 54: 588—Vol 56: 45—Vol 58: 372—Vol 77: 481

MOSER—Vol 55: 521—Vol 56: 373—Vol 81: 517

MOSES_____Vol 34: 661—Vol 54: 588

MOSHER—Vol 28: 263—Vol 41: 127—Vol 43: 494—Vol 46: 237—Vol 53: 242—Vol 56: 175—Vol 58: 329, 764—Vol 64: 388—Vol 65: 437—Vol 66: 307—Vol 67: 118—Vol 69: 121—Vol 70: 877

MOSIER_____Vol 56: 373—Vol 71: 163

MOSS—Vol 22: 50, 52—Vol 24: 151—Vol 27: 892—Vol 29: 652—Vol 41: 33, 120, 123, 125 —Vol 42: 72, 134—Vol 43: 545—Vol 44: 314—Vol 45: 101—Vol 47: 27, 95—Vol 48: 54, 61—Vol 49: 135—Vol 50: 57—Vol 52: 435—Vol 55: 165, 712—Vol 58: 241—Vol 69: 584—Vol 70: 56, 353—Vol 71: 241, 1024

—Vol 72: (10-94)—Vol 82: 397—Vol 84: 632

MOSSBARGER_____ _____Vol 75: (4-54)

MOSSER_____Vol 42: 337—Vol 63: 247

MOSSOM_____Vol 71: 959

MOTHERAL_____Vol 36: 215

MOTHERSHED_____Vol 58: 173

MOTHERWELL_____Vol 36: 575

MOTLEY—Vol 39: 224—Vol 48: 443—Vol 49: 182, 352—Vol 56: 44—Vol 67: 712—Vol 83: 872

MOTT—Vol 15: 349—Vol 20: 60—Vol 30: 259 —Vol 37: 70—Vol 38: 275—Vol 39: 141— Vol 40: 23, 78—Vol 45: 112—Vol 56: 174, 370—Vol 59: 49—Vol 74: (2-52), (8-52)— Vol 82: 794

MOTTE_____Vol 10: 65

MOULD_____Vol 82: 313—Vol 84: 445

MOULTON—Vol 22: 157—Vol 23: 400—Vol 33: 954—Vol 42: 342—Vol 43: 486—Vol 45: 24, 242—Vol 47: 267—Vol 61: 546—Vol 62: 160, 161—Vol 63: 165—Vol 80: 335—Vol 81: 430

MOUNGER_____Vol 37: 159

MOUNIER_____Vol 22: 53

MOUNT—Vol 71: 356, 957—Vol 73: (11-66)— Vol 74: (1-49)

MOUNTAIN_____ _____Vol 20: 607

MOUNTJOY_____Vol 41: 125

MOUNTS_____ _____Vol 75: (1-55)

MOURNING_____Vol 50: 64—Vol 56: 690

MOWATT_____Vol 20: 61

MOWERY_____Vol 70: 1019—Vol 77: 479

MOWLS_____Vol 67: 577

MOWREY_____Vol 29: 43—Vol 70: 1019

MOWRY_____Vol 47: 273—Vol 70: 1019

MOXLEY—Vol 31: 413—Vol 49: 49—Vol 52: 52—Vol 55: 521—Vol 56: 224—Vol 69: 565, 681

MOYER—Vol 37: 157—Vol 54: 591—Vol 55: 108, 338—Vol 58: 453—Vol 59: 525—Vol 64: 160, 442—Vol 65: 124—Vol 81: 130— Vol 82: 796

MOYERS_____Vol 79: 193

MUCHMORE_____Vol 69: 564

MUCKENFUSS_____Vol 33: 42

MUDD_____Vol 49: 130

MUDGE —Vol 60: 248—Vol 61: 62—Vol 83: 521

MUDGETT_____Vol 83: 794

MUELLER_____Vol 45: 110—Vol 54: 173

MUFFLEY_____Vol 63: 59

MUFFLY_____Vol 32: 160—Vol 60: 50, 635

MUFFY_____Vol 31: 668

MUIRE_____Vol 61: 783

MUIS_____Vol 49: 191

MULCHER_____Vol 63: 107—Vol 66: 828

MULFORD—Vol 29: 514—Vol 44: 228—Vol 81: 569

MULHERIN_____Vol 17: 283, 389

MULHERRIN_____Vol 37: 65

MULKEY_____Vol 69: 363

MULLEN—Vol 44: 84, 229, 383—Vol 58: 452

MULLENS_____Vol 44: 386

MULLER—Vol 28: 262—Vol 43: 541—Vol 55: 47, 336

MULLIKEN_____Vol 35: 57—Vol 50: 67

MULLINER_____Vol 26: 57

MULLINGTON_____Vol 68: 552

MULLINS—Vol 22: 996—Vol 36: 355—Vol

40: 275—Vol 41: 66—Vol 58: 329—Vol 82: 502
MULLISON...............Vol 33: 473
MUMFORD...........Vol 46: 332—Vol 63: 742
MUNDELL...........................Vol 66: 537
MUNDY.......................Vol 25: 800
MUNFORD...................Vol 66: 459
MUNGER...Vol 37: 395—Vol 41: 122—Vol 44: 315—Vol 54: 223
MUNHOLLAND.................Vol 29: 799
MUNN...Vol 25: 967—Vol 33: 474—Vol 46: 100—Vol 48: 64, 303—Vol 74: (7-54), (8-54) —Vol 81: 316
MUNRO...Vol 33: 957—Vol 60: 157—Vol 63: 508—Vol 70: 455
MUNROE.................Vol 37: 159—Vol 39: 273
MUNSELL...Vol 41: 122—Vol 42: 343—Vol 62: 587
MUNSEY...........................Vol 77: 118
MUNSON...Vol 23: 399—Vol 31: 862—Vol 33: 476, 955—Vol 41: 71, 213—Vol 46: 238— Vol 47: 32—Vol 75: (5-45)—Vol 79: 36— Vol 80: 85
MURDOCH...Vol 21: 169—Vol 28: 258—Vol 37: 489—Vol 38: 113—Vol 39: 101—Vol 40: 271—Vol 54: 709
MURDOCK...Vol 53: 745—Vol 54: 354—Vol 59: 48—Vol 64: 157
MURPHEY...Vol 18: 181—Vol 36: 77—Vol 46: 102—Vol 56: 563—Vol 76: 61
MURPHY...........Vol 58: 587, 764—Vol 84: 244
MURRAY...Vol 27: 668—Vol 31: 588—Vol 38: 274—Vol 41: 124—Vol 43: 493—Vol 46: 28, 386—Vol 47: 191—Vol 48: 446—Vol 55: 602, 712—Vol 56: 315, 625—Vol 57: 744— Vol 61: 910—Vol 63: 700—Vol 64: 757—Vol 66: 461—Vol 68: 284—Vol 74: (11-60)— Vol 79: 113—Vol 83: 793—Vol 84: 445
MURROW.............Vol 54: 649—Vol 74: (12-53)
MUSCHETTE........................Vol 64: 588
MUSE...Vol 43: 603—Vol 44: 81—Vol 46: 27, 238
MUSGROVE...Vol 41: 127—Vol 48: 370—Vol 57: 213—Vol 72: (4-83)
MUSICK.................Vol 65: 636—Vol 78: 554
MUSSELWHITE........................Vol 79: 35
MUSSER...Vol 54: 709—Vol 79: 518—Vol 80: 191
MUSSIE.............................Vol 53: 329
MUSTIN...Vol 76: 61—Vol 77: 389, 664—Vol 78: 696—Vol 80: 335
MUZZY...Vol 7: 447—Vol 26: 338—Vol 27: 381—Vol 31: 669
MYER...Vol 42: 138—Vol 55: 600—Vol 56: 626
MYERS...Vol 27: 892—Vol 39: 327—Vol 40: 108—Vol 41: 70—Vol 47: 396—Vol 48: 448 —Vol 53: 447—Vol 59: 47—Vol 60: 573, 634, 698—Vol 65: 572—Vol 66: 824—Vol 67: 444—Vol 71: 1110—Vol 76: 860—Vol 77: 243, 539, 664—Vol 81: 430—Vol 82: 795
MYLER.............................Vol 54: 466
MYLES.............Vol 53: 627—Vol 54: 466
MYNEER............................Vol 31: 414
MYRICK...Vol 36: 579—Vol 40: 75—Vol 42: 16, 80, 265—Vol 43: 542, 603—Vol 46: 98
MYRTLE.............Vol 72: (7-75)—Vol 77: 602

N

NABIOR...........................Vol 68: 243

NAGEL...........................Vol 81: 71
NAGLE...........................Vol 52: 360
NAGLEY..........................Vol 58: 450
NAIL............................Vol 65: 759
NAILER..........................Vol 39: 225
NAILOR..........................Vol 63: 103
NALLEY..........................Vol 61: 608
NANCE...Vol 30: 260—Vol 49: 131—Vol 59: 682—Vol 63: 427
NAPIER...Vol 57: 310—Vol 63: 244, 636— Vol 65: 441
NASH...Vol 24: 544—Vol 27: 807—Vol 29: 46, 801—Vol 31: 52—Vol 33: 42—Vol 36: 577—Vol 37: 64, 147—Vol 38: 84, 329—Vol 39: 21—Vol 40: 273—Vol 41: 33, 209—Vol 42: 73, 79—Vol 43: 492—Vol 44: 234, 311, 384—Vol 46: 241—Vol 49: 129, 189, 354— Vol 57: 352—Vol 64: 390—Vol 70: 358— Vol 75: (2-57)—Vol 76: 402—Vol 80: 155, 657—Vol 81: 429—Vol 82: 503, 861—Vol 83: 946
NASON...Vol 47: 192—Vol 62: 587—Vol 65: 440—Vol 84: 246
NATCHEZ.........................Vol 37: 66
NATHAN..........................Vol 45: 21
NATHON.........................Vol 82: 139
NATION...Vol 64: 390—Vol 74: (4-51)—Vol 75: (2-57), (2-58), (9-36)—Vol 77: 481— Vol 80: 588
NATUS...........................Vol 19: 627
NAUGHTON........................Vol 59: 238
NAVEN..........................Vol 71: 1025
NAY............................Vol 45: 109
NAYLOR...Vol 43: 419—Vol 54: 592—Vol 59: 765—Vol 64: 520—Vol 67: 516—Vol 84: 522
NEADELS.............Vol 81: 631—Vol 82: 221
NEAL...Vol 27: 892—Vol 30: 260—Vol 39: 100, 101—Vol 47: 191, 388—Vol 50: 355— Vol 53: 176—Vol 54: 536, 650—Vol 55: 209 —Vol 56: 371—Vol 57: 630—Vol 59: 48— Vol 60: 571, 598—Vol 64: 712—Vol 65: 763 Vol 66: 308, 364, 459, 671, 731, 733—Vol 67: 242, 715—Vol 68: 285—Vol 69: 119, 764—Vol 70: 132—Vol 71: 461—Vol 73: (9-66)—Vol 75: (3-41)—Vol 77: 332—Vol 82: 502
NEALE...Vol 44: 78—Vol 48: 123—Vol 54: 111—Vol 57: 177—Vol 66: 249
NEASON.........................Vol 84: 246
NEAVIL..........................Vol 62: 714
NEBEKER.........................Vol 68: 243
NEEDHAM...Vol 31: 412—Vol 41: 165—Vol 43: 486
NEEDLES...Vol 66: 252—Vol 70: 353—Vol 81: 631—Vol 82: 221
NEEL...........................Vol 81: 518
NEELY...Vol 39: 227—Vol 41: 123—Vol 56: 227—Vol 84: 69, 246
NEER...........................Vol 59: 238
NEEVAL..........................Vol 45: 26
NEFF...Vol 40: 227—Vol 64: 523—Vol 65: 249, 508—Vol 81: 71—Vol 83: 262
NEGUS...........Vol 68: 242—Vol 72: (4-83)
NEHER...........................Vol 59: 238
NEIFERT.........................Vol 47: 268
NEIL...Vol 70: 359—Vol 80: 45—Vol 82: 747
NEILL...Vol 40: 229—Vol 43: 419—Vol 57: 313—Vol 63: 699—Vol 64: 588, 651
NEILSON...........Vol 35: 1038—Vol 76: 218

NOEL ___Vol 26: 340, 560—Vol 41: 120, 124–Vol 48: 449
NOGGLE___Vol 35: 1103—Vol 54: 649—Vol 81: 71
NOGLE___Vol 58: 111—Vol 71: 845—Vol 76: 60
NOKES___Vol 36: 354, 572
NOLAN___Vol 46: 331
NOLAND___Vol 70: 709, 713—Vol 82: 930
NOONAN___Vol 82: 726
NOONEY___Vol 82: 726
NOONIN___Vol 82: 726
NOOKER___Vol 56: 481
NORBEL___Vol 57: 310
NORCROSS___Vol 27: 808—Vol 35: 655—Vol 38: 33—Vol 57: 689
NORMAN___Vol 27: 382—Vol 45: 17—Vol 46: 385—Vol 59: 764—Vol 62: 52, 53, 54—Vol 63: 372—Vol 77: 331
NORRED___Vol 45: 190
NORRIS___Vol 37: 488—Vol 40: 226—Vol 46: 393—Vol 47: 28, 388—Vol 49: 49, 280, 281—Vol 50: 193—Vol 56: 47, 173, 316—Vol 57: 114, 172, 432—Vol 60: 49—Vol 61: 65, 610—Vol 64: 257—Vol 65: 160—Vol 67: 388, 443, 713—Vol 68: 283—Vol 72: (9-87)—Vol 78: 553—Vol 83: 173
NORTH___Vol 23: 243, 469—Vol 24: 55—Vol 32: 162—Vol 38: 274—Vol 39: 21—Vol 46: 21—Vol 47: 95—Vol 52: 360—Vol 56: 746—Vol 80: 154—Vol 82: 860
NORTHCROSS___Vol 57: 628
NORTHCUTT___Vol 47: 396—Vol 48: 301—Vol 84: 523
NORTHROP___Vol 18: 299
NORTHRUP___Vol 30: 441—Vol 33: 957—Vol 49: 134—Vol 50: 64—Vol 57: 117—Vol 61: 473—Vol 63: 508—Vol 82: 863
NORTHWAY___Vol 28: 61—Vol 61: 610
NORTMAN___Vol 38: 274
NORTON___Vol 21: 403—Vol 27: 670—Vol 34: 66—Vol 39: 275—Vol 41: 71—Vol 49: 191—Vol 50: 61—Vol 55: 286—Vol 56: 174—Vol 57: 628—Vol 59: 238—Vol 66: 306, 460
NORVELL___Vol 27: 738—Vol 29: 47—Vol 50: 68
NORWOOD___Vol 42: 75, 79—Vol 56: 562—Vol 57: 351—Vol 58: 108—Vol 60: 571
NOSE___Vol 74: (5-39)
NOTT___Vol 26: 54—Vol 46: 124—Vol 57: 216
NOURSE___Vol 16: 356—Vol 54: 174, 539
NOWE___Vol 67: 386
NOWLANE___Vol 56: 226
NOWLEN___Vol 59: 239—Vol 82: 63
NOXON___Vol 22: 156
NOYES___Vol 10: 183—Vol 28: 259—Vol 30: 147, 438—Vol 31: 584—Vol 54: 308—Vol 58: 650—Vol 75: (5-45)
NUNN___Vol 34: 68
NUNNALLY___Vol 83: 794
NUSS___Vol 82: 795
NUSSEN___Vol 26: 244
NUTCHELL___Vol 58: 174
NUTT___Vol 44: 230
NUTTER___Vol 75: (2-58)
NUTTING___Vol 22: 375—Vol 49: 284—Vol 68: 156—Vol 76: 580
NYCE___Vol 61: 66
NYE___Vol 57: 174—Vol 69: 631—Vol 70: 708, 1017—Vol 74: (5-39)

O

OAKES___Vol 34: 67—Vol 38: 88—Vol 55: 338—Vol 58: 451—Vol 80: 589
OAKLEY___Vol 70: 204
OATMAN___Vol 43: 599
O'BANNON___Vol 45: 322—Vol 50: 63
O'BRIEN___Vol 43: 421—Vol 84: 68
O'BRYAN___Vol 48: 444
O'BRYANT___Vol 72: (4-83)
O'DANIEL___Vol 62: 500—Vol 63: 56—Vol 72: (12-68)
ODELL___Vol 32: 719—Vol 38: 221—Vol 39: 23—Vol 43: 488—Vol 45: 125—Vol 83: 442, 794
ODEN___Vol 35: 655—Vol 48: 450
ODLE___Vol 77: 241
ODOM___Vol 37: 396—Vol 64: 759—Vol 71: 358, 841
ODUM___Vol 64: 759
OFFICER___Vol 62: 248
OFFILL___Vol 83: 335
OFFUTT___Vol 41: 121, 125
OGBORN___Vol 43: 422—Vol 63: 572—Vol 64: 59—Vol 66: 537
OGBURN___Vol 43: 545—Vol 74: (6-38)—Vol 76: 928
OGDEN___Vol 28: 479—Vol 40: 76—Vol 42: 137—Vol 45: 189—Vol 48: 448—Vol 58: 331—Vol 75: (4-53)—Vol 81: 430—Vol 82: 863
OGILVIE___Vol 30: 338—Vol 61: 606
OGLE___Vol 46: 236—Vol 59: 239—Vol 61: 276—Vol 67: 145
OGLESBY___Vol 45: 195—Vol 69: 121—Vol 71: 464—Vol 83: 871
OGLETHORPE___Vol 26: 56, 57
OGLEVEE___Vol 50: 348—Vol 52: 54
O'HAIR___Vol 45: 120
O'HARA___Vol 5: 566—Vol 26: 244—Vol 45: 109, 192—Vol 83: 945
O'KEEFE___Vol 26: 55 –Vol 72: (4-84)
OLCOTT___Vol 21: 166—Vol 22: 155—Vol 27: 735—Vol 28: 549—Vol 30: 256—Vol 74: (4-48)—Vol 80: 383
OLDFIELD___Vol 50: 192
OLDHAM___Vol 20: 352—Vol 21: 61—Vol 26: 241—Vol 28: 58—Vol 43: 596—Vol 48: 369—Vol 49: 124, 182—Vol 77: 184—Vol 83: 521, 524—Vol 84: 521
OLDS___Vol 23: 325—Vol 28: 548—Vol 48: 306—Vol 49: 41
OLIN___Vol 48: 119
OLIPHANT___Vol 45: 27—Vol 75: (10-67)
OLIVER___Vol 22: 54—Vol 42: 194—Vol 43: 600—Vol 56: 318, 479—Vol 57: 214, 310, 311—Vol 61: 783—Vol 63: 246—Vol 68: 486—Vol 69: 241—Vol 74: (5-42)—Vol 75: (9-36)—Vol 79: 283
OLMSTEAD___Vol 19: 433—Vol 23: 324, 469—Vol 35: 1100—Vol 42: 15—Vol 46: 160—Vol 49: 282, 283—Vol 50: 58—Vol 61: 912—Vol 65: 245—Vol 69: 121—Vol 72: (2-62)
OLNEY___Vol 56: 564—Vol 77: 769
OMANS___Vol 46: 156
ONDERDUNK___Vol 38: 86
O'NEAL___Vol 57: 116—Vol 74: (4-52)—Vol 84: 324, 325
O'NEIL___Vol 39: 142—Vol 41: 122—Vol 46: 156—Vol 60: 114—Vol 67: 116
ONSTINE___Vol 53: 744—Vol 54: 53, 418

PAINTER....Vol 40: 228—Vol 45: 24, 190—
Vol 59: 653—Vol 64: 523—Vol 76: 709—
Vol 77: 241—Vol 82: 396
PAISLEY.................Vol 47: 270—Vol 67: 753
PALATINES.................Vol 20: 62, 165
PALM.................Vol 39: 143—Vol 40: 228
PALMATIER.................Vol 57: 351
PALMER....Vol 17: 181, 479—Vol 19: 628—
Vol 27: 890—Vol 28: 162, 259—Vol 29: 715
—Vol 30: 146, 441—Vol 31: 413—Vol 33:
40—Vol 34: 200, 538—Vol 35: 438, 1038—
Vol 36: 77, 214—Vol 39: 142, 325—Vol 40:
25—Vol 44: 28, 148—Vol 45: 114, 115, 119,
194—Vol 46: 23, 157, 266, 331—Vol 49: 393
—Vol 50: 190, 278, 356—Vol 51: 358—Vol
52: 170, 229, 437, 485, 565—Vol 53: 377,
745—Vol 54: 350, 351—Vol 55: 601—Vol
57: 689—Vol 59: 388—Vol 60: 632—Vol 64:
715—Vol 67: 146—Vol 69: 242, 764—Vol
71: 86, 461—Vol 73: (7-70)—Vol 74: (5-
43)—Vol 75: (5-45)—Vol 78: 53—Vol 82:
139, 654—Vol 83: 91, 439, 628
PALMINTER.................Vol 45: 127
PALMORE.................Vol 67: 146
PALTON.................Vol 66: 54
PANCAKE.................Vol 56: 742
PANCOAST.................Vol 63: 247, 373
PANGBORN.................Vol 54: 650—Vol 60: 698
PANGBURN.................Vol 55: 163
PANGMAN.................Vol 43: 486
PANKEY.................Vol 67: 443
PARAMORE.................Vol 65: 440
PARAMOURE.................Vol 79: 35
PARCEL.................Vol 30: 337—Vol 54: 709
PARCELL.................Vol 81: 263
PARDEE....Vol 25: 799, 887—Vol 59: 314—
Vol 60: 570
PARDON.................Vol 53: 378
PARHAM....Vol 48: 62, 438—Vol 49: 45—Vol
57: 116—Vol 58: 587
PARIS.................Vol 58: 451, 649
PARISH....Vol 26: 336—Vol 42: 339—Vol 63:
56
PARK....Vol 23: 470—Vol 29: 513—Vol 36:
573, 577—Vol 37: 394—Vol 38: 332—Vol
43: 420, 494—Vol 45: 111—Vol 48: 372—
Vol 49: 124—Vol 50: 354—Vol 52: 112—
Vol 54: 592—Vol 63: 507—Vol 65: 438—
Vol 71: 162—Vol 75: (6-37)
PARKE....Vol 19: 70, 205—Vol 26: 243—Vol
27: 735—Vol 44: 381—Vol 48: 372—Vol 50:
280—Vol 52: 359—Vol 54: 226, 710—Vol
63: 426—Vol 66: 828—Vol 74: (2-42)—
Vol 77: 480
PARKER....Vol 14: 439—Vol 20: 60—Vol 22:
272, 375, 679—Vol 24: 450—Vol 27: 380,
671, 739, 806—Vol 28: 260, 549—Vol 30:
64, 338—Vol 32: 59, 717—Vol 33: 958—Vol
34: 68—Vol 35: 1100—Vol 36: 757—Vol 38:
88, 328, 331—Vol 39: 223—Vol 40: 77, 172—
Vol 41: 34, 124, 210, 212—Vol 42: 76, 335,
337—Vol 43: 488—Vol 44: 83, 382—Vol 45:
101, 104, 107, 118—Vol 47: 23, 271—Vol 48:
121, 307—Vol 49: 49, 132, 185—Vol 50: 69,
190, 280, 351, 354—Vol 52: 111,321,687—Vol
53: 181, 244—Vol 55: 108, 164—Vol 56: 44,
109, 177, 319, 370, 626, 742—Vol 57: 566,
744—Vol 58: 451—Vol 59: 314—Vol 62:
52, 53, 774—Vol 63: 571, 700—Vol 64: 124,
387, 523, 650, 712—Vol 68: 728—Vol 70: 56,

136, 354, 454, 710, 880, 1168—Vol 71: 840—
Vol 73: (9-63), (11-67), (11-69)—Vol 74:
(5-41)—Vol 76: 62, 144, 581—Vol 77: 240—
Vol 78: 107—Vol 79: 369—Vol 80: 432—
Vol 82: 142, 860—Vol 83: 260—Vol 84: 325,
705
PARKHILL.................Vol 67: 442
PARKHURST....Vol 34: 660—Vol 45: 240—
Vol 57: 565—Vol 73: (4-83)—Vol 81: 571
—Vol 82: 935
PARKINSON....Vol 43: 543—Vol 45: 22—Vol
63: 636—Vol 64: 58
PARKMAN.................Vol 37: 158—Vol 45: 22, 321
PARKS....Vol 21: 251—Vol 26: 240—Vol 36:
757, 758—Vol 37: 266—Vol 41: 68, 124—Vol
42: 15, 77—Vol 44: 234—Vol 45: 23, 126,
184, 198—Vol 46: 154, 385—Vol 47: 22, 198
—Vol 50: 70—Vol 52: 359—Vol 53: 328,
693—Vol 56: 370, 475—Vol 59: 47—Vol 73:
(2-64)—Vol 74: (5-39)—Vol 77: 242—Vol
80: 379, 432—Vol 84: 325, 524
PARMELE.................Vol 56: 416
PARMELEE....Vol 23: 398—Vol 24: 56, 148,
342—Vol 25: 798—Vol 26: 54—Vol 33: 956
—Vol 40: 78—Vol 77: 240
PARMENTER....Vol 39: 226—Vol 44: 25, 28,
82—Vol 77: 538
PARMINTER.................Vol 45: 104
PARNEL.................Vol 78: 156
PARNELL.................Vol 45: 122
PARR....Vol 35: 1102—Vol 39: 226—Vol 76:
784—Vol 84: 247
PARRETT.................Vol 59: 441
PARRICK.................Vol 30: 338
PARRISH....Vol 40: 274—Vol 41: 29—Vol 43:
486—Vol 44: 84—Vol 46: 98—Vol 48: 57—
Vol 50: 69—Vol 59: 111—Vol 64: 384
PARROTT.................Vol 57: 692—Vol 76: 928
PARRY.................Vol 60: 507—Vol 67: 575
PARSELS.................Vol 77: 479
PARSHALL.................Vol 31: 751—Vol 55: 522
PARSLER.................Vol 26: 339
PARSON.................Vol 28: 365—Vol 71: 1110
PARSONS....Vol 2: 295—Vol 39: 23, 222—Vol
40: 76—Vol 43: 485, 488—Vol 44: 233—
Vol 47: 196, 396—Vol 48: 201—Vol 49: 356
—Vol 52: 53—Vol 55: 521, 522, 599—Vol
56: 226—Vol 57: 691—Vol 58: 452, 586, 648
—Vol 59: 589—Vol 64: 445, 587—Vol 65:
57—Vol 71: 357—Vol 74: (3-44)—Vol 79:
560—Vol 82: 798
PARTESON.................Vol 56: 482
PARTLOW.................Vol 62: 307—Vol 69: 431
PARTRIDGE.................Vol 30: 336—Vol 50: 352
PARVIN.................Vol 52: 51
PASCAL.................Vol 69: 631
PASCHAL.................Vol 57: 629
PASCO.................Vol 64: 521
PASS.................Vol 55: 397
PASSMORE....Vol 45: 123—Vol 48: 205—Vol
49: 352
PASTEUR.................Vol 44: 85—Vol 45: 101
PATCH....Vol 33: 41—Vol 74: (7-54), (8-54)
PATCHEN.................Vol 45: 200
PATCHIN.................Vol 39: 276—Vol 55: 598
PATE.................Vol 60: 419—Vol 71: 1026
PATHE.................Vol 75: (9-37)
PATILLO....Vol 43: 491—Vol 48: 304—Vol
83: 259
PATISON.................Vol 72: (4-83)

PATMAN....Vol 45: 103—Vol 46: 28—Vol 48: 60—Vol 51: 354—Vol 67: 712
PATON............Vol 78: 246—Vol 82: 522
PATRICK....Vol 48: 62—Vol 59: 588—Vol 68: 687—Vol 70: 359—Vol 73: (8-88)
PATSEY............................Vol 49: 43, 44
PATSY............................Vol 49: 44
PATTEE............................Vol 29: 653, 800
PATTEN............Vol 43: 597—Vol 83: 1013
PATTERSON....Vol 27: 380—Vol 29: 288— Vol 30: 338, 439—Vol 36: 756—Vol 37: 266 —Vol 38: 87—Vol 39: 277, 327—Vol 41: 32 —Vol 44: 25, 232, 233, 310—Vol 45: 184, 185, 186—Vol 47: 32, 184, 185, 186, 264, 395 —Vol 48: 119—Vol 49: 47, 190, 353—Vol 53: 178—Vol 54: 224—Vol 55: 599—Vol 58: 174—Vol 59: 49—Vol 62: 122, 387, 389, 390, 456, 460—Vol 65: 437, 442, 572, 633—Vol 66: 361—Vol 68: 734—Vol 69: 158—Vol 70: 206—Vol 71: 463—Vol 72: (1-65)—Vol 76: 401—Vol 80: 276, 658—Vol 83: 172, 944
PATTON....Vol 11: 6—Vol 20: 352—Vol 21: 494—Vol 23: 324—Vol 29: 801—Vol 33: 42, 475—Vol 36: 215—Vol 40: 226, 274—Vol 43: 597—Vol 45: 117—Vol 48: 58, 204—Vol 50: 66—Vol 53: 571—Vol 54: 113—Vol 57: 311—Vol 63: 371, 372—Vol 65: 759—Vol 72: (1-66)—Vol 77: 183—Vol 80: 190, 191— Vol 81: 518—Vol 82: 930—Vol 83: 171
PATTY............................Vol 49: 43, 44
PAUL....Vol 32: 62—Vol 43: 485—Vol 48: 59 —Vol 49: 189—Vol 50: 188—Vol 52: 556— Vol 64: 389—Vol 70: 203—Vol 75: (10-64) —Vol 84: 635
PAULDING............Vol 50: 66—Vol 84: 325
PAULETT............................Vol 37: 488
PAULL............................Vol 49: 188
PAVERY............................Vol 25: 967
PAXON............................Vol 51: 303
PAXSON............................Vol 45: 21, 321
PAXTON....Vol 28: 263—Vol 35: 1266—Vol 43: 543—Vol 46: 100—Vol 48: 203, 438— Vol 50: 280—Vol 58: 173, 330—Vol 61: 913 —Vol 79: 283
PAYNE....Vol 22: 51—Vol 31: 861—Vol 37: 157, 268—Vol 39: 274—Vol 41: 33, 71, 121, 125—Vol 42: 186, 342—Vol 43: 483—Vol 44: 25, 150—Vol 45: 20, 107, 127—Vol 46: 390—Vol 47: 189, 195, 394—Vol 52: 564— Vol 53: 52—Vol 54: 54—Vol 55: 599, 603— Vol 56: 44—Vol 57: 218—Vol 58: 172, 328, 700—Vol 60: 505—Vol 61: 153, 156, 607, 912—Vol 65: 508—Vol 67: 292—Vol 70: 577—Vol 71: 960—Vol 72: (1-66)—Vol 73: (7-69)—Vol 75: (3-41)—Vol 76: 710—Vol 77: 183—Vol 79: 332—Vol 80: 191, 193— Vol 81: 71—Vol 82: 934—Vol 83: 945—Vol 84: 69, 519
PAYNSFORD............................Vol 41: 30
PAYNTER............................Vol 84: 326
PEABODY....Vol 43: 604—Vol 45: 43—Vol 67: 750—Vol 68: 684
PEACE............................Vol 39: 226
PEACH............Vol 63: 635—Vol 80: 46
PEACOCK....Vol 36: 574—Vol 38: 275—Vol 45: 113, 192—Vol 46: 152—Vol 76: 62
PEADON............................Vol 75: (4-55)
PEAGRAM............Vol 45: 194, 195
PEAK............................Vol 43: 485—Vol 49: 45

PEAKE............................Vol 80: 46—Vol 84: 631
PEALE....Vol 45: 17, 236—Vol 57: 743—Vol 58: 240
PEARCE....Vol 27: 44—Vol 29: 514—Vol 42: 270—Vol 48: 308—Vol 50: 193—Vol 54: 420 —Vol 56: 480, 744—Vol 57: 215, 691—Vol 58: 51—Vol 59: 315—Vol 61: 66—Vol 67: 293, 711—Vol 69: 119, 432—Vol 77: 184
PEARL............Vol 46: 98—Vol 61: 788
PEARMAN............................Vol 43: 493, 543
PEARSALL....Vol 58: 329—Vol 63: 245, 424— Vol 64: 121
PEARSON....Vol 26: 143—Vol 28: 365—Vol 32: 58—Vol 37: 66—Vol 42: 9—Vol 48: 203, 368, 370—Vol 54: 223—Vol 56: 174— Vol 59: 681—Vol 69: 120—Vol 71: 1110— Vol 82: 796—Vol 83: 717
PEART............................Vol 36: 353
PEASE....Vol 35: 1101—Vol 41: 210—Vol 42: 134—Vol 43: 601—Vol 49: 190—Vol 56: 625—Vol 59: 237
PEASLEE............................Vol 77: 240
PECK....Vol 17: 181—Vol 19: 628—Vol 22: 50—Vol 26: 139—Vol 27: 670—Vol 28: 260 —Vol 29: 652—Vol 30: 64, 149—Vol 33: 42, 706, 1032—Vol 37: 161—Vol 42: 190—Vol 44: 234—Vol 47: 28, 268—Vol 48: 305, 307, 372, 449—Vol 49: 348—Vol 50: 192, 355— Vol 53: 241, 692—Vol 56: 175, 372—Vol 58: 372—Vol 60: 249, 250—Vol 61: 704—Vol 63: 247—Vol 68: 554—Vol 70: 1020, 1168
PECKHAM....Vol 30: 149—Vol 35: 55—Vol 42: 338—Vol 43: 604—Vol 54: 110—Vol 67: 576
PECKINPAUGH............................Vol 77: 539
PEEBLES....Vol 47: 197—Vol 60: 572, 746— Vol 63: 106—Vol 84: 634
PEED............Vol 45: 126—Vol 74: (3-45)
PEEK............Vol 43: 485—Vol 84: 635
PEEKKE............................Vol 64: 712
PEEL............................Vol 63: 636
PEELE............................Vol 50: 280
PEELER............................Vol 38: 219
PEEPLES....Vol 30: 259—Vol 49: 188—Vol 56: 629—Vol 84: 157
PEET....Vol 62: 651—Vol 63: 59—Vol 81: 315
PEEVEY............................Vol 84: 705
PEGRAM............................Vol 60: 157
PEGUES............................Vol 79: 613
PEHN............................Vol 65: 367
PEIFER............................Vol 67: 711
PEIFFER............Vol 43: 496—Vol 67: 711
PEIRCE............................Vol 32: 59
PEIROT............................Vol 45: 26
PELL............................Vol 84: 446
PELLET............Vol 26: 242, 243—Vol 27: 672
PELTON............................Vol 70: 577
PEMBERTON....Vol 46: 160—Vol 54: 174— Vol 67: 44
PEMBROKE............................Vol 27: 382
PENCE....Vol 45: 104—Vol 49: 49—Vol 57: 218
PENCILLE............Vol 76: 653—Vol 79: 561
PENDERSON............................Vol 50: 65
PENDLETON....Vol 30: 540—Vol 31: 751— Vol 37: 395, 487—Vol 43: 493, 543—Vol 46: 337—Vol 47: 396—Vol 48: 60, 201, 302, 366 —Vol 49: 39—Vol 52: 358—Vol 70: 1167— Vol 71: 956

PENFIELD..............Vol 54: 591—Vol 55: 108
PENGRA....Vol 41: 164, 212—Vol 42: 13, 14—
Vol 45: 107
PENGRAY..............Vol 58: 501
PENICK..............Vol 73: (9-64)
PENN....Vol 26: 241—Vol 45: 114, 118—Vol
54: 649—Vol 55: 162, 163—Vol 59: 314—
Vol 67: 515—Vol 71: 88—Vol 79: 613
PENNELL..............Vol 59: 521, 525
PENNEPACKER..............Vol 39: 143
PENNFIELD..............Vol 47: 32—Vol 48: 54
PENNIMAN..............Vol 18: 181—Vol 57: 565
PENNINGER..............Vol 48: 449
PENNINGTON....Vol 23: 169—Vol 54: 111—
Vol 62: 460, 502—Vol 65: 635—Vol 74:
(4-52)
PENNOCH..............Vol 72: (10-94)
PENNY..............Vol 55: 599
PENNYPACKER..............Vol 37: 154
PENS..............Vol 45: 199
PENTECOST ..Vol 43: 423, 483—Vol 44: 148
—Vol 67: 385
PENTLAND..............Vol 83: 260
PENTON..............Vol 43: 494
PEOPLES..............Vol 49: 188—Vol 84: 634
PEPPER....Vol 15: 349—Vol 35: 1100—Vol
38: 329—Vol 45: 117—Vol 50: 357—Vol 62:
309—Vol 67: 711
PEPPLE..............Vol 67: 516
PERCELL..............Vol 29: 715
PERCEY..............Vol 71: 558
PERCIVAL....Vol 17: 389, 569—Vol 54: 590—
Vol 81: 518—Vol 82: 575
PERCY..............Vol 71: 558
PERDUE..............Vol 44: 26—Vol 80: 193
PEREGO..............Vol 71: 957
PERHAM..............Vol 8: 889—Vol 56: 627
PERKINS....Vol 7: 264—Vol 24: 343—Vol 26:
241—Vol 28: 161, 162—Vol 30: 61—Vol 32:
632—Vol 33: 958—Vol 34: 424—Vol 36:
216, 217, 572—Vol 37: 71, 73—Vol 40: 172—
Vol 42: 77—Vol 43: 598—Vol 44: 235, 313—
Vol 45: 20, 28, 237—Vol 47: 269—Vol 49:
393—Vol 50: 189—Vol 51: 354—Vol 53:
627, 690, 693—Vol 54: 354, 421—Vol 55:
339, 521—Vol 56: 224—Vol 57: 628—Vol
60: 507—Vol 62: 587—Vol 64: 388, 446,
585, 714—Vol 65: 437—Vol 68: 121, 441—
Vol 70: 353—Vol 73: (1-63), (11-66)
PERLEE..............Vol 54: 308—Vol 55: 444
PERMAN..............Vol 57: 218
PERRIN..Vol 21: 62—Vol 23: 326—Vol 30:
148—Vol 32: 163—Vol 45: 25—Vol 48: 441
—Vol 49: 353—Vol 55: 335—Vol 61: 275—
Vol 65: 298, 632
PERRITT..............Vol 29: 290
PERRY....Vol 21: 58, 498—Vol 22: 52, 53, 270
—Vol 23: 325—Vol 24: 458—Vol 26: 54—
Vol 27: 380—Vol 28: 60—Vol 32: 162—Vol
34: 322, 538—Vol 35: 54, 437—Vol 36: 76—
Vol 37: 151, 157, 158, 397—Vol 39: 104,
275—Vol 40: 271—Vol 41: 214—Vol 42: 15,
75, 78, 191, 349—Vol 43: 418, 494, 545, 604—
Vol 45: 20—Vol 48: 122—Vol 50: 352—Vol
51: 235—Vol 52: 560—Vol 53: 178, 247,
494, 571—Vol 54: 110, 647—Vol 56: 46, 115,
689—Vol 57: 215, 312—Vol 58: 111, 453,
586—Vol 63: 373, 699—Vol 67: 46—Vol 70:
205, 360, 1019—Vol 75: (9-40)—Vol 76: 860

—Vol 77: 183—Vol 81: 518—Vol 82: 63,
797—Vol 84: 158
PERRYMAN..............Vol 41: 125—Vol 63: 246
PERSIFUL..............Vol 81: 518
PERSON....Vol 59: 175—Vol 70: 456—Vol 71:
1110
PERSONS....Vol 66: 307—Vol 78: 553—Vol
84: 445
PETER..............Vol 50: 64, 352—Vol 61: 470, 705
PETERFISH..............Vol 45: 128—Vol 47: 83
PETERS....Vol 23: 325—Vol 24: 151—Vol 36:
353—Vol 40: 274—Vol 41: 123—Vol 43: 542
—Vol 50: 64, 352—Vol 53: 242—Vol 61:
788—Vol 62: 55—Vol 65: 758—Vol 77: 183,
724—Vol 81: 71—Vol 82: 797—Vol 84: 518
PETERSON....Vol 46: 237—Vol 47: 266—Vol
52: 322—Vol 54: 310—Vol 68: 686—Vol 72:
(6-78)—Vol 80: 657—Vol 82: 793—Vol 83:
337, 439, 628, 795
PETRIE..............Vol 45: 122—Vol 80: 192
PETTEGREW....Vol 54: 535—Vol 55: 283—
Vol 82: 501, 654—Vol 84: 158, 245, 706
PETTIBONE....Vol 2: 46—Vol 50: 355—Vol
51: 304—Vol 52: 113, 229—Vol 59: 763—Vol
60: 112
PETTINGILL....Vol 30: 147—Vol 45: 109, 325
PETTIPOOL....Vol 45: 105, 235, 324—Vol 47:
195
PETTIS..............Vol 41: 122—Vol 45: 322
PETTIT....Vol 27: 807—Vol 48: 59—Vol 64:
649—Vol 77: 242
PETTITT..............Vol 45: 191
PETTUS....Vol 41: 164—Vol 45: 25—Vol 46:
157, 391—Vol 55: 713—Vol 56: 413, 743—
Vol 57: 348—Vol 61: 868—Vol 64: 759—Vol
65: 121, 437—Vol 68: 487
PETTWAY..............Vol 58: 329, 647
PETTY....Vol 39: 22, 324—Vol 55: 520—Vol
63: 373, 741—Vol 66: 364—Vol 67: 48, 715
PETWAY..............Vol 58: 329, 647
PEURIFOY..............Vol 31: 752
PEVA..............Vol 36: 356
PEVELER..............Vol 32: 162
PEYSER..............Vol 84: 635
PEYTON....Vol 22: 54—Vol 75: (2-58)—Vol
78: 398
PFOST..............Vol 83: 336
PFOUTZ..............Vol 45: 123
PHARES..............Vol 47: 198—Vol 67: 753
PHARR..............Vol 82: 794—Vol 83: 337
PHELPS....Vol 22: 53—Vol 23: 400—Vol 25:
798—Vol 28: 259—Vol 35: 57—Vol 36: 217,
576—Vol 37: 269, 348—Vol 39: 272—Vol 40:
75—Vol 43: 418, 486—Vol 45: 23, 108—Vol
46: 387—Vol 49: 135—Vol 50: 64, 66—Vol
53: 53, 493—Vol 54: 465—Vol 63: 700—Vol
67: 48—Vol 71: 1109—Vol 72: (11-59)—
Vol 76: 581, 582—Vol 82: 314—Vol 83: 441
PHIEFER..............Vol 41: 214—Vol 42: 135, 188
PHILABOR..............Vol 68: 492
PHILBERT..............Vol 21: 335
PHILBRICK..............Vol 41: 214—Vol 68: 554
PHILIP..............Vol 68: 242—Vol 69: 158
PHILIPS....Vol 45: 192—Vol 54: 110, 111, 226,
465—Vol 57: 310—Vol 67: 647
—Vol 72: (4-83)
PHILIPSE..............Vol 56: 43
PHILLER..............Vol 63: 373
PHILLEY..............Vol 45: 115
PHILLIPPS..............Vol 71: 959

PLUMLEY..............................Vol 45: 123
PLUMLY..............................Vol 46: 153
PLUMMER....Vol 21: 335—Vol 22: 53—Vol
  23: 64—Vol 34: 201—Vol 44: 234—Vol 47:
  392—Vol 54: 590—Vol 55: 711—Vol 57:
  216, 431, 478, 745—Vol 65: 636, 668
PLUNKETT....Vol 57: 177—Vol 62: 388—Vol
  83: 92
PLYLEY..............................Vol 84: 326
POAGE.............Vol 44: 147—Vol 45: 185, 186
POBLETZ..............................Vol 31: 589
POCOCK..............................Vol 45: 123
POCOHONTAS..............................Vol 37: 72
POE....Vol 45: 26—Vol 48: 121—Vol 57: 630
  —Vol 83: 717
POFFIN..............................Vol 31: 751—Vol 32: 60
POFFINO..............................Vol 32: 60, 719
POGUE.............Vol 71: 675—Vol 74: (4-48)
POINDEXTER....Vol 44: 22—Vol 48: 450—
  Vol 49: 283—Vol 79: 614—Vol 84: 245
POLAND..............................Vol 40: 77—Vol 46: 386
POLHEMUS....Vol 9: 287—Vol 40: 228—Vol
  46: 104—Vol 67: 384
POLIN..............................Vol 46: 100
POLK....Vol 11: 621—Vol 35: 57, 1036—Vol
  36: 217, 572, 756—Vol 37: 72, 394, 486—
  Vol 38: 217, 274—Vol 39: 141—Vol 41: 70—
  Vol 43: 603—Vol 44: 232—Vol 45: 185—Vol
  48: 441—Vol 55: 444, 711, 713—Vol 62: 460,
  775—Vol 64: 445—Vol 78: 398—Vol 83: 946,
  1014—Vol 84: 328
POLLAND..............................Vol 39: 103—Vol 53: 242
POLLARD....Vol 38: 218—Vol 39: 103—Vol
  41: 215—Vol 44: 228—Vol 46: 385—Vol 49:
  283—Vol 50: 69—Vol 54: 52, 467—Vol 58:
  587—Vol 59: 111—Vol 67: 714—Vol 76: 144
  —Vol 81: 264—Vol 82: 574
POLLICK..............................Vol 55: 711
POLLITT..............................Vol 74: (11-60)
POLLOCK....Vol 30: 259—Vol 40: 78—Vol 53:
  245—Vol 57: 310—Vol 64: 121—Vol 76: 653
  —Vol 79: 561
POLLY..............................Vol 22: 272—Vol 26: 338
POLOGUE..............................Vol 74: (4-48)
POLOKE..............................Vol 74: (4-48)
POLSEY..............................Vol 42: 139
POLYTHRESS ....Vol 64: 522
POMEROY....Vol 22: 155—Vol 23: 398—Vol
  24: 342—Vol 26: 54, 139—Vol 27: 735—Vol
  31: 670—Vol 46: 237—Vol 55: 284
POND....Vol 55: 519—Vol 56: 224, 372, 558,
  740—Vol 63: 427
POOL....Vol 31: 862—Vol 32: 283, 720—Vol
  42: 192—Vol 44: 386—Vol 46: 102—Vol 55:
  166—Vol 56: 172, 226—Vol 58: 764—Vol
  74: (4-50)—Vol 82: 142—Vol 83: 628
POOLE....Vol 41: 122—Vol 48: 120—Vol 63:
  168—Vol 82: 139
POOR....Vol 44: 232—Vol 45: 185—Vol 53:
  628, 631—Vol 54: 311, 558, 588, 710—Vol 55:
  48—Vol 82: 503
POORBAUGH..............................Vol 56: 746
POORE....Vol 26: 143, 243—Vol 34: 322—Vol
  39: 225—Vol 84: 68
POORMAN..............................Vol 42: 343
POPE....Vol 22: 270—Vol 29: 288—Vol 41: 34,
  68—Vol 42: 16—Vol 43: 426, 541—Vol 44:
  23, 315—Vol 46: 104, 238, 335—Vol 49: 396
  —Vol 57: 745—Vol 58: 174—Vol 60: 572—
  Vol 61: 274—Vol 63: 374, 425—Vol 66: 366

—Vol 70: 708—Vol 73: (8-83)—Vol 78:
  155—Vol 82: 502
POPHAM..............................Vol 22: 271
POPINO..............................Vol 39: 22, 324
POPPINO..............................Vol 32: 719
PORTER....Vol 18: 58—Vol 22: 154, 373—Vol
  30: 148, 338, 439, 440—Vol 31: 587, 862—
  Vol 32: 162, 282—Vol 33: 41, 954, 955, 958,
  1033—Vol 35: 1266—Vol 36: 463, 464, 755—
  Vol 38: 328—Vol 40: 25, 274—Vol 41: 124,
  127, 165, 212—Vol 43: 420, 421, 485, 486,
  487, 493, 540, 541, 543, 599—Vol 44: 27, 152
  —Vol 45: 26, 27, 116—Vol 46: 155, 158—Vol
  48: 202—Vol 49: 189—Vol 50: 67, 188—Vol
  51: 301—Vol 52: 559—Vol 53: 117, 631—
  Vol 54: 353, 536—Vol 55: 601—Vol 56: 47,
  109, 478, 742—Vol 58: 502, 586, 761, 764—
  Vol 59: 314—Vol 60: 418—Vol 61: 66—Vol
  63: 167, 742—Vol 64: 259—Vol 66: 307, 536,
  537, 825—Vol 67: 41, 241, 575—Vol 68: 58,
  734—Vol 69: 564—Vol 71: 86, 956, 1108—
  Vol 75: (2-60), (10-60)—Vol 76: 653—Vol
  79: 283—Vol 80: 383—Vol 81: 571—Vol 82:
  141, 575, 727—Vol 83: 522—Vol 84: 246,
  444, 521
PORTERFIELD....Vol 23: 325—Vol 24: 457—
  Vol 26: 559—Vol 50: 62—Vol 63: 427
PORTERVENT..............................Vol 64: 257
PORTLOCK..............................Vol 39: 326—Vol 67: 752
PORTMAN..............................Vol 34: 659—Vol 35: 435
PORTRESS..............................Vol 58: 587
POSEY....Vol 48: 204—Vol 65: 634—Vol 67:
  386, 512—Vol 71: 838
POST....Vol 31: 863—Vol 33: 958—Vol 35: 58
  —Vol 38: 221, 331—Vol 39: 22—Vol 41:
  213—Vol 42: 134—Vol 43: 494, 543—Vol
  45: 25—Vol 50: 116, 281—Vol 52: 626—Vol
  53: 248—Vol 54: 351—Vol 55: 442—Vol 57:
  115—Vol 59: 239—Vol 64: 756—Vol 69: 764
  —Vol 73: (9-65)—Vol 77: 52—Vol 83: 173,
  336
POTEET..............................Vol 81: 629
POTTER....Vol 31: 62, 497—Vol 23: 471—Vol
  27: 381, 382, 735, 891—Vol 28: 158, 482—
  Vol 29: 44, 800—Vol 31: 55, 587—Vol 34:
  27—Vol 36: 75—Vol 44: 27—Vol 47: 27, 33
  —Vol 49: 285—Vol 53: 181, 246—Vol 56:
  319—Vol 57: 311—Vol 59: 315—Vol 66: 536
  —Vol 70: 1266—Vol 71: 557, 957, 1026—Vol
  72: (3-70)—Vol 74: (4-48), (5-40), (5-43)—
  Vol 75: (9-46)—Vol 82: 931—Vol 83: 337
POTTERF..............................Vol 40: 26
POTTLE..............................Vol 36: 757
POTTS ..Vol 41: 72—Vol 45: 101—Vol 55:
  521—Vol 56: 226—Vol 59: 238—Vol 77: 241,
  333—Vol 81: 130
POULMIN..............................Vol 30: 540
POULSON..............................Vol 64: 156
POULTNEY..............................Vol 54: 308
POUNCEY..............................Vol 84: 704
POUND..............................Vol 42: 137, 268, 335
POVALL....Vol 41: 31, 125—Vol 42: 12—Vol
  46: 22—Vol 59: 442—Vol 60: 156
POWE..............................Vol 38: 332
POWELL....Vol 26: 336—Vol 28: 57—Vol 29:
  511—Vol 36: 76, 356, 762—Vol 38: 330—Vol
  43: 493, 547, 599—Vol 45: 119—Vol 46: 27,
  385—Vol 47: 31—Vol 48: 203, 307—Vol 53:
  244, 630—Vol 54: 224, 312—Vol 56: 47, 560
  —Vol 58: 701—Vol 59: 387—Vol 60: 418,

419—Vol 63: 57, 294—Vol 64: 444, 587, 649 —Vol 66: 162, 534—Vol 67: 517—Vol 68: 734—Vol 69: 160, 431, 631—Vol 71: 466, 468 —Vol 73: (11-68)—Vol 74: (4-50), (4-52), (5-38), (7-51), (8-51)—Vol 76: 309—Vol 79: 194—Vol 82: 653, 654—Vol 83: 92, 794, 872

POWER....Vol 58: 501—Vol 72: (11-58)—Vol 79: 160, 331

POWERS....Vol 21: 62—Vol 26: 143—Vol 28: 365—Vol 30: 148—Vol 31: 587—Vol 43: 491—Vol 45: 26—Vol 46: 244—Vol 48: 306 —Vol 54: 535—Vol 55: 283, 713—Vol 56: 558—Vol 59: 588—Vol 61: 546—Vol 70: 360 Vol 74: (11-61)—Vol 75: (5-47)—Vol 81: 130—Vol 82: 798—Vol 83: 521—Vol 84: 446, 447, 703

POYNER............................Vol 55: 600
POYTHRESS...............Vol 52: 51—Vol 68: 488
PRALL.................................Vol 56: 688
PRATER...........................Vol 74: (2-43)
PRATHER ..Vol 52: 436—Vol 53: 629—Vol 58: 702—Vol 60: 697—Vol 61: 63—Vol 72: (12-67)—Vol 73: (3-86)—Vol 75: (2-57)
PRATOR............................Vol 74: (2-43)
PRATT....Vol 19: 627—Vol 26: 56—Vol 27: 45, 735, 737—Vol 28: 263, 479—Vol 30: 339 —Vol 31: 51—Vol 32: 161—Vol 33: 1033— Vol 34: 423—Vol 37: 159—Vol 39: 273—Vol 40: 108—Vol 41: 214—Vol 43: 423—Vol 45: 106, 112, 324—Vol 48: 444—Vol 50: 66, 67, 186—Vol 52: 52—Vol 53: 247—Vol 55: 599 —Vol 56: 108—Vol 57: 115, 216, 349, 432, 745—Vol 58: 54—Vol 63: 635—Vol 64: 389 —Vol 65: 240, 248, 505, 507, 632—Vol 69: 116, 630—Vol 70: 876, 1170—Vol 71: 462— Vol 72: (11-59)—Vol 78: 156, 502—Vol 80: 44, 276—Vol 81: 569—Vol 83: 523
PRAUL...............................Vol 43: 424, 597
PRAY...................Vol 52: 625—Vol 80: 277
PRAYS.................................Vol 47: 273
PRAYTOR............................Vol 74: (2-43)
PREBLE................................Vol 56: 372
PRECISE..............................Vol 53: 246
PREDMORE...........................Vol 42: 138
PRENET...............................Vol 53: 247
PRENTICE....Vol 26: 338—Vol 30: 539—Vol 44: 83—Vol 71: 164, 760
PRENTIS........................Vol 71: 760
PRENTISS..... ....Vol 71: 760—Vol 82: 933
PRESCOTT....Vol 37: 153—Vol 45: 104, 323— Vol 50: 70—Vol 56: 413
PRESNELL..............................Vol 83: 944
PRESSEY...........Vol 32: 718—Vol 56: 479
PRESSLER.................. ....Vol 57: 351
PRESSLEY............Vol 55: 714—Vol 82: 397
PRESSON.............................Vol 82: 397
PRESTON....Vol 27: 668, 669—Vol 28: 161— Vol 39: 224—Vol 45: 106—Vol 46: 101—Vol 49: 49—Vol 52: 320—Vol 56: 45—Vol 57: 217, 431—Vol 59: 523, 653—Vol 60: 51—Vol 70: 878—Vol 71: 676—Vol 76: 860—Vol 78: 156—Vol 79: 160, 518—Vol 81: 316— Vol 82: 397, 860, 933—Vol 84: 245
PRETTYMAN...........................Vol 64: 712
PREUIT...............................Vol 53: 631
PREVOST..............................Vol 54: 535
PREWET...........Vol 59: 653—Vol 73: (11-66)
PREWETT...............Vol 61: 913—Vol 68: 243

PREWITT....Vol 23: 169—Vol 24: 260—Vol 53: 247, 631—Vol 54: 53—Vol 57: 215—Vol 59: 653—Vol 61: 153—Vol 67: 115, 239, 293 —Vol 83: 336
PRICE....Vol 22: 53—Vol 29: 512—Vol 30: 62, 147, 542—Vol 31: 589—Vol 36: 761—Vol 37: 67, 266, 397, 487—Vol 38: 275—Vol 41: 121, 126—Vol 42: 12—Vol 44: 313—Vol 45: 25, 128—Vol 46: 22—Vol 47: 273—Vol 53: 117, 380—Vol 54: 465—Vol 55: 714—Vol 56: 44, 315, 624—Vol 57: 177, 219—Vol 58: 451—Vol 59: 441—Vol 70: 135, 878—Vol 74: (5-40), (12-52)—Vol 78: 295—Vol 83: 261, 628, 874, 946—Vol 84: 244, 702
PRICKET..................Vol 43: 424—Vol 44: 148
PRIDE.................Vol 22: 268—Vol 80: 193, 276
PRIDGEON................................Vol 49: 190
PRIEST...Vol 31: 51—Vol 63: 699—Vol 67: 713—Vol 68: 623, 685—Vol 70: 356—Vol 78: 245
PRIESTLY...............................Vol 82: 312
PRILL.................................Vol 46: 160
PRIME ....Vol 70: 360
PRINCE....Vol 39: 22—Vol 53: 54—Vol 57: 116—Vol 59: 238—Vol 63: 428, 633—Vol 81: 571—Vol 82: 727
PRINDLE....Vol 22: 157—Vol 26: 241, 336— Vol 27: 735—Vol 31: 670, 750—Vol 45: 106 —Vol 60: 699—Vol 61: 787, 788—Vol 62: 55, 56, 249—Vol 73: (12-63)—Vol 74: (5-39)
PRINGLE....Vol 40: 228—Vol 46: 243—Vol 48: 300—Vol 50: 280
PRINKEY.................................Vol 83: 793
PRIOR...................Vol 27: 668—Vol 66: 600
PRITCHARD....Vol 44: 26—Vol 45: 25—Vol 46: 100, 101—Vol 49: 188—Vol 63: 427— Vol 67: 290
PRITCHETT....Vol 25: 39—Vol 46: 335—Vol 59: 314—Vol 84: 893
PRITLOE................................Vol 79: 613
PRIVETT.........................Vol 75: (5-44)
PROBASCO...............................Vol 50: 348
PROCTOR....Vol 27: 670—Vol 38: 332—Vol 44: 234—Vol 46: 246, 381—Vol 50: 189— Vol 70: 878—Vol 75: (7-36)—Vol 82: 794
PROFFITT...............................Vol 69: 363
PROFITT................................Vol 69: 363
PROTSMAN...............................Vol 56: 109
PROTZMAN.........................Vol 56: 478, 739
PROUDFIT.............................Vol 33: 1033
PROUT.................Vol 28: 60, 363—Vol 38: 320
PROUTY................................Vol 43: 541
PROVENCE.........................Vol 75: (10-67)
PROVINCE....... ....Vol 75: (10-67)
PROVOOST..............................Vol 54: 535
PROWELL...............................Vol 76: 61
PRUDDEN....Vol 44: 154, 236, 309—Vol 48: 58, 202—Vol 71: 1025
PRUDEN....................Vol 40: 226—Vol 48: 58
PRUET.................................Vol 57: 215
PRUIT....Vol 54: 55—Vol 59: 653—Vol 61: 153—Vol 67: 239
PRUITT...Vol 52: 564—Vol 53: 247, 631—Vol 67: 115, 293—Vol 73: (11-66)—Vol 79: 369 —Vol 82: 221, 934
PRUNTY..................Vol 50: 350—Vol 53: 57
PRYER.................................Vol 64: 651
PRYOR....Vol 41: 68, 72—Vol 43: 604—Vol 49: 190—Vol 62: 715—Vol 66: 600—Vol 83: 945

—Vol 70: 136—Vol 75: (10-65)—Vol 78: 398—Vol 80: 190—Vol 82: 142, 726
RANEY............................Vol 83: 173
RANKIN....Vol 45: 27—Vol 56: 371, 558—Vol 64: 756—Vol 66: 54, 537—Vol 67: 116—Vol 71: 240—Vol 72: (6-78)—Vol 80: 193, 335—Vol 81: 569, 630
RANSOM...Vol 9: 46, 174—Vol 22: 998—Vol 36: 356—Vol 40: 273—Vol 56: 562, 741—Vol 57: 350—Vol 58: 170—Vol 59: 388—Vol 71: 461—Vol 73: (1-62), (11-69)—Vol 82: 139
RANSOME....Vol 42: 16—Vol 63: 59—Vol 82: 139
RANSON...................Vol 56: 481—Vol 65: 245
RAPALJE...Vol 47: 267—Vol 70: 135—Vol 82: 930
RAPE...............Vol 53: 630—Vol 81: 571
RAPPELEYE...........................Vol 46: 239
RASOR.........................Vol 83: 628
RATCLIFFE ....Vol 72: (8-86)—Vol 83: 1015
RATHBONE..............Vol 50: 191—Vol 70: 575
RATHBUN...Vol 40: 229—Vol 41: 29—Vol 74: (12-53)—Vol 81: 570
RATHBURN...Vol 41: 161—Vol 43: 491, 542
RAUB................................Vol 57: 434
RAULSTON.........................Vol 67: 386
RAWLES............................Vol 79: 35, 613
RAWLEY...............................Vol 75: (6-40)
RAWLING.............................Vol 28: 547
RAWLINGS ...Vol 19: 205, 430—Vol 36: 215—Vol 48: 63—Vol 57: 746—Vol 58: 174—Vol 59: 387, 681—Vol 63: 373, 569—Vol 64: 756—Vol 65: 438—Vol 72: (11-58)
RAWLINS...Vol 40: 75—Vol 53: 572—Vol 77: 43
RAWSON...Vol 42: 268—Vol 43: 481—Vol 45: 184—Vol 48: 64—Vol 54: 352—Vol 57: 745
RAY....Vol 23: 64—Vol 26: 54—Vol 37: 149—Vol 42: 191—Vol 43: 421, 422, 423, 483, 539, 724—Vol 44: 84—Vol 46: 385, 389—Vol 47: 198—Vol 48: 447—Vol 52: 109—Vol 53: 571—Vol 56: 416—Vol 57: 629—Vol 61: 470—Vol 67: 646—Vol 72: (1-66)—Vol 84: 704
RAYBURN............................Vol 44: 27
RAYFIELD...........................Vol 82: 934
RAYLAND............................Vol 48: 62
RAYMOND...Vol 20: 352—Vol 21: 250—Vol 22: 270—Vol 23: 63—Vol 36: 756—Vol 37: 394—Vol 41: 33—Vol 42: 191—Vol 43: 425, 481, 492—Vol 44: 82—Vol 45: 116—Vol 50: 280, 414—Vol 51: 357—Vol 57: 175, 312—Vol 58: 173, 452—Vol 61: 552, 911—Vol 68: 495—Vol 70: 135—Vol 71: 357—Vol 74: (5-42)—Vol 80: 190—Vol 84: 325, 524
RAYNER..............................Vol 74: (5-41)
RAYNOR..............Vol 41: 212—Vol 44: 226
REA...Vol 44: 152, 230—Vol 46: 28—Vol 48: 300—Vol 50: 190—Vol 52: 53—Vol 56: 45
READ...Vol 34: 540—Vol 35: 1038, 1103, 1266—Vol 36: 73—Vol 42: 16—Vol 43: 427, 484, 489—Vol 44: 149, 383—Vol 52: 53, 54, 358—Vol 53: 246—Vol 54: 420—Vol 56: 624—Vol 67: 576—Vol 70: 1166—Vol 71: 356—Vol 84: 446
READE...Vol 43: 426—Vol 44: 148—Vol 58: 450—Vol 75: (9-37)—Vol 82: 862
READING............................Vol 69: 361

REAGAN...Vol 38: 330—Vol 51: 301—Vol 60: 747—Vol 68: 488
REAGER............................Vol 44: 154
REAL.............................Vol 45: 28
REAM...........Vol 58: 112—Vol 66: 600, 732
REAMES...........................Vol 72: (4-84)
REAMS..............................Vol 58: 53
REASMOOR.........................Vol 62: 501
REASONER.....Vol 46: 388—Vol 66: 537, 733
REAVES.............................Vol 39: 22
RECORD.........................Vol 48: 306
RECTOR...Vol 37: 69—Vol 57: 566—Vol 75: (2-59)—Vol 77: 51
REDD....Vol 28: 548—Vol 36: 760—Vol 46: 23—Vol 48: 62—Vol 49: 188
REDDE ....Vol 45: 25
REDDICK...........................Vol 75: (1-53)
REDDING...Vol 20: 61—Vol 44: 153—Vol 75: (1-53)—Vol 80: 45
REDFIELD—Vol 39: 276—Vol 40: 108—Vol 74: (12-53)
REDMAN...Vol 53: 244—Vol 73: (9-64)—Vol 82: 502, 727
REDMON...Vol 44: 153—Vol 75: (6-37)—Vol 78: 650
REDMOND...........................Vol 82: 501
REDSICKER........................Vol 56: 373
REDUS..............................Vol 45: 118
REECE...Vol 21: 253—Vol 65: 437—Vol 73: (10-77)—Vol 83: 628
REED...Vol 19: 627—Vol 21: 57—Vol 27: 382—Vol 31: 53, 751—Vol 32: 62—Vol 33: 41—Vol 34: 539—Vol 36: 73, 74—Vol 39: 22—Vol 41: 34—Vol 43: 417, 492, 602—Vol 44: 27, 79, 316—Vol 45: 28, 111, 124, 190—Vol 46: 29, 100, 159—Vol 47: 194—Vol 48: 58, 123, 305—Vol 49: 135—Vol 50: 353—Vol 52: 322—Vol 54: 110, 175, 223, 310, 351, 420, 651—Vol 55: 339, 519, 532, 713—Vol 56: 44, 175, 226, 481, 627, 746—Vol 57: 115, 116—Vol 58: 173, 450—Vol 59: 176, 442, 523—Vol 60: 157, 366—Vol 64: 651—Vol 65: 123, 759—Vol 66: 826—Vol 67: 388, 514—Vol 69: 245—Vol 70: 135—Vol 71: 677—Vol 73: (1-63), (10-76)—Vol 77: 239, 480—Vol 78: 696—Vol 80: 85, 192, 336, 657—Vol 83: 173—Vol 84: 446
REEDE ....Vol 58: 450
REEDER...Vol 26: 142—Vol 28: 478—Vol 41: 31, 164—Vol 45: 22, 193—Vol 46: 103—Vol 47: 22—Vol 49: 45, 281, 285, 287—Vol 54: 109—Vol 57: 481—Vol 58: 327—Vol 61: 855—Vol 64: 445—Vol 65: 59, 441
REEDY.............................Vol 34: 423
REES...Vol 56: 744—Vol 64: 715—Vol 67: 116
REESE...Vol 47: 272—Vol 48: 306, 441—Vol 56: 373, 416—Vol 57: 743—Vol 59: 111, 387—Vol 60: 571—Vol 71: 87—Vol 73: (10-77)—Vol 82: 63, 931, 935
REEVE...Vol 30: 540—Vol 32: 58—Vol 42: 490—Vol 48: 443—Vol 50: 350—Vol 55: 522—Vol 48: 443—Vol 50: 350—Vol 55: 522
REEVES...Vol 24: 458—Vol 27: 736—Vol 39: 102—Vol 42: 194—Vol 44: 85—Vol 57: 174—Vol 58: 649—Vol 62: 648—Vol 68: 492—Vol 69: 631—Vol 70: 204—Vol 79: 613
REGAN......................Vol 56: 371—Vol 58: 110
REGAR ....Vol 60: 417
REGER ....Vol 60: 417

Vol 75: (2-60), (9-41)—Vol 76: 928—Vol
82: 141, 797—Vol 83: 93, 335, 336, 440, 1015
—Vol 84: 67, 445
RICHARESON..Vol 48: 62
RICHBOURG..Vol 82: 934
RICHE...Vol 54: 55
RICHEY...Vol 26: 340—Vol 43: 602—Vol 50:
355, 415—Vol 55: 521—Vol 70: 210
RICHMOND...Vol 22: 272—Vol 23: 399—Vol
32: 283—Vol 39: 23—Vol 41: 164—Vol 45:
115, 326—Vol 46: 337—Vol 61: 471—Vol
72: (5-67)—Vol 83: 261, 717
RICHTER......................Vol 33: 1032—Vol 82: 794
RICKETSON...Vol 40: 78
RICKETTS...Vol 27: 672—Vol 58: 502—Vol
. 83: 336
RICKMAN..Vol 66: 160
RICKS...Vol 27: 669
RIDDICK...........................Vol 61: 156—Vol 83: 336
RIDDLE...Vol 45: 27, 323—Vol 60: 50—Vol
68: 283—Vol 82: 798
RIDENOUR........................Vol 40: 26—Vol 43: 604
RIDER...Vol 26: 139—Vol 34: 538—Vol 36:
761—Vol 39: 22—Vol 40: 25—Vol 41: 32—
Vol 50: 349—Vol 64: 443
RIDGELEY...Vol 30: 63
RIDGEWAY...Vol 56: 627—Vol 57: 112—Vol
67: 515
RIDGLEY............Vol 29: 512, 715—Vol 32: 160
RIDGWAY.....................Vol 54: 51—Vol 64: 712
RIDLEY...Vol 38: 220—Vol 39: 222—Vol 42:
79—Vol 47: 272—Vol 48: 372
RIDLOW...Vol 84: 324
RIDPATH...Vol 45: 24, 322—Vol 65: 439—
Vol 66: 56—Vol 67: 647
RIEBSOM..Vol 63: 635
RIEGAL...Vol 64: 160
RIFE...................................Vol 55: 284—Vol 74: (11-58)
RIFFLE..Vol 28: 478
RIFLE...Vol 75: (8-43)
RIGBY...Vol 64: 648
RIGGAN.........................Vol 37: 150—Vol 48: 441
RIGGIN...Vol 36: 76—Vol 51: 301—Vol 70:
356
RIGGINS...Vol 66: 309
RIGGS...Vol 37: 74—Vol 42: 16—Vol 52: 686
—Vol 55: 109—Vol 56: 371, 558—Vol 63:
632, 633—Vol 64: 389—Vol 65: 124—Vol
67: 293—Vol 76: 653
RIGHTER..Vol 37: 71
RIGHTOR..Vol 33: 1032
RIGNEY.......................Vol 67: 387—Vol 71: 163
RIGSBY..Vol 72: (11-58)
RILEY...Vol 44: 236—Vol 46: 104, 330—Vol
47: 194—Vol 55: 164, 654—Vol 56: 688,
743—Vol 65: 246—Vol 82: 502
RIMEL..................Vol 72: (4-83)—Vol 78: 107
RINEHART................Vol 48: 203—Vol 82: 500
RINER...Vol 61: 65
RINEVAULT...Vol 83: 1015
RING..Vol 74: (4-48)
RINGLE...Vol 56: 416
RINGLER..Vol 45: 121
RINGO...Vol 76: 310
RIPLEY......................Vol 27: 380—Vol 58: 174
RIPPEY...Vol 43: 492—Vol 64: 308—Vol 83:
171, 337
RIPPLE..Vol 47: 27
RIPSOME...Vol 63: 635

RISH...Vol 41: 214—Vol 44: 25—Vol 60: 698
—Vol 71: 844
RISHER..Vol 71: 557
RISING.........................Vol 30: 147—Vol 39: 327
RISLEY...Vol 27: 889—Vol 57: 567—Vol 62:
584
RISSER..Vol 22: 271
RITCHEY...............Vol 67: 385—Vol 74: (4-50)
RITCHIE.............Vol 43: 604—Vol 73: (11-67)
RITE..Vol 48: 63
RITTENHOUSE...Vol 58: 369—Vol 68: 489
—Vol 80: 44
RITTER...Vol 55: 519—Vol 67: 293—Vol 74:
(4-51)
RIVERS...Vol 41: 213
RIVES...Vol 47: 270—Vol 52: 51—Vol 53:
176, 179, 633—Vol 59: 110
RIX...Vol 46: 102—Vol 50: 356—Vol 54: 353
RIXEY...Vol 43: 421
ROACH...Vol 38: 219—Vol 39: 21, 140—Vol
79: 613
ROADCAP..Vol 71: 763
ROADEN..Vol 83: 947
ROADMAN...Vol 56: 371
ROADS...Vol 65: 248
ROAK..Vol 54: 111
ROAN..Vol 67: 384
ROANE...............................Vol 33: 1033—Vol 39: 102
ROATH..Vol 68: 122
ROBARDS...................Vol 39: 104—Vol 42: 263
ROBB...................Vol 55: 166—Vol 73: (1-62)
ROBBERSE...Vol 83: 523
ROBBINS...Vol 29: 650—Vol 38: 35—Vol 39:
327—Vol 41: 210, 212—Vol 42: 270, 341—
Vol 45: 125—Vol 47: 193—Vol 48: 306—
Vol 58: 330, 369—Vol 61: 788—Vol 62: 55
—Vol 64: 588—Vol 71: 838—Vol 74: (4-53)
—Vol 75: (6-40)—Vol 77: 539—Vol 82: 139
—Vol 83: 262, 717, 795—Vol 84: 705
ROBERSON..Vol 64: 257
ROBERT...Vol 56: 415
ROBERTS...Vol 20: 352—Vol 22: 50—Vol 23:
398—Vol 28: 263—Vol 30: 149—Vol 42: 76
—Vol 43: 486, 541, 601—Vol 46: 388—Vol
47: 95, 193—Vol 48: 65, 121, 444, 448—Vol
49: 188, 189—Vol 50: 280, 356—Vol 53: 241
—Vol 54: 308, 421—Vol 55: 337—Vol 56:
415, 563, 564, 624—Vol 57: 567, 689—Vol 58:
51, 53, 450, 501, 587—Vol 59: 113, 764—Vol
60: 698—Vol 62: 500—Vol 63: 508—Vol 66:
122, 160—Vol 67: 293, 442—Vol 70: 355,
454—Vol 75: (6-39)—Vol 77: 389—Vol 79:
193, 369—Vol 80: 153, 191, 589—Vol 82:
574, 861—Vol 83: 262
ROBERTSON...Vol 16: 181—Vol 25: 383—
Vol 26: 550—Vol 30: 338—Vol 36: 353, 580
—Vol 40: 229—Vol 41: 212—Vol 43: 494,
541—Vol 44: 21—Vol 45: 114, 187—Vol 48:
121—Vol 49: 45, 396—Vol 54: 52—Vol 55:
597, 713—Vol 57: 310, 480—Vol 60: 573—
Vol 61: 606, 708—Vol 63: 294—Vol 64: 649
—Vol 65: 365, 367—Vol 69: 246—Vol 70:
457—Vol 71: 468, 957—Vol 74: (5-40)—
Vol 75: (8-43)—Vol 79: 561—Vol 80: 432—
Vol 82: 141—Vol 83: 92
ROBESON..Vol 42: 190
ROBIDEAU...Vol 30: 257
ROBIE...Vol 44: 315—Vol 45: 114
ROBINETT..Vol 47: 262
ROBINS...........Vol 49: 287—Vol 70: 354

ROBINSON....Vol 5: 59, 573—Vol 22: 997—
Vol 27: 808—Vol 31: 667—Vol 32: 281, 507
—Vol 33: 476—Vol 35: 656, 1037—Vol 36:
215, 576, 580—Vol 40: 59, 60, 64—Vol 41:
164, 212—Vol 42: 191, 269—Vol 43: 425,
481, 482, 546, 602—Vol 44: 79, 82—Vol 45:
107, 127, 197, 238—Vol 46: 97—Vol 47: 27,
29, 31—Vol 49: 132, 134, 287—Vol 50: 113,
184, 193, 344—Vol 52: 359—Vol 53: 56, 331,
493, 571, 628, 747—Vol 54: 113, 230, 353,
651—Vol 55: 108, 597, 602—Vol 56: 43, 480
—Vol 57: 114, 173, 313, 434, 745—Vol 58:
111, 651, 764—Vol 59: 388—Vol 60: 114, 699
—Vol 61: 64, 153, 158—Vol 62: 121—Vol
63: 60—Vol 64: 156, 158, 649—Vol 65: 247,
759—Vol 66: 306—Vol 67: 115, 118, 240,
647, 713—Vol 68: 120, 241, 373, 627, 735—
Vol 69: 56, 244, 246, 433, 683—Vol 70: 354,
573, 1165—Vol 71: 358, 1111—Vol 73:
(9-66), (11-68)—Vol 74: (2-43), (3-45)—
Vol 75: (5-46), (9-37, 41), (10-64)—Vol 78:
108—Vol 80: 335, 432—Vol 81: 71, 631—
Vol 82: 139, 142, 762, 862, 932—Vol 84: 68,
702
ROBISON...Vol 43: 481—Vol 74: (9-66)—Vol
83: 523
ROBUCK............................Vol 58: 450, 650
ROBY....Vol 30: 66—Vol 45: 119—Vol 84: 445
ROCHELLE............................Vol 35: 436, 438
ROCHESTER....Vol 1: 341—Vol 26: 243—Vol
52: 108
ROCK....Vol 22: 157—Vol 29: 803—Vol 70:
135
ROCKEFELLER.....Vol 26: 141—Vol 63: 697
ROCKHILL............................Vol 56: 743—Vol 78: 108
ROCKMORE............................Vol 59: 49
ROCKWELL....Vol 20: 60—Vol 36: 218, 352—
Vol 41: 215—Vol 42: 270—Vol 45: 127—
Vol 46: 29—Vol 48: 371—Vol 53: 627—Vol
57: 312—Vol 58: 173—Vol 59: 176—Vol 60:
505—Vol 62: 501—Vol 66: 122—Vol 75:
(5-44)—Vol 79: 332
RODDY............................Vol 43: 483—Vol 48: 450
RODER............................Vol 56: 739—Vol 68: 239
RODERICK............................Vol 56: 480
RODES...Vol 34: 538—Vol 37: 488—Vol 43:
485, 487, 596, 598—Vol 44: 310—Vol 67: 712
RODGERS...Vol 52: 733—Vol 55: 322—Vol
64: 586, 602, 758—Vol 67: 293—Vol 69: 564
—Vol 70: 56—Vol 71: 460—Vol 82: 397
RODMAN...Vol 66: 734—Vol 67: 115—Vol
71: 958
ROE...Vol 20: 60—Vol 29: 287—Vol 40: 74—
Vol 44: 314—Vol 54: 225—Vol 58: 331—
Vol 61: 705—Vol 68: 551—Vol 70: 1020—
Vol 71: 161—Vol 75: (10-64)—Vol 79: 332
—Vol 82: 933—Vol 84: 521
ROEBUCK............................Vol 58: 540, 650—Vol 83: 946
ROELOF............................Vol 68: 491, 732
ROEMER............................Vol 53: 448—Vol 68: 554
ROERBACK............................Vol 74: (11-61)
ROFF............................Vol 61: 783—Vol 69: 564
ROGAN............................Vol 84: 444
ROGER............................Vol 70: 359
ROGERS...Vol 1: 334—Vol 19: 432—Vol 22:
268—Vol 26: 337—Vol 27: 381, 737—Vol
28: 61, 549—Vol 29: 287, 649—Vol 30: 540
—Vol 31: 670—Vol 32: 282—Vol 37: 66—
Vol 40: 77—Vol 41: 33—Vol 42: 269, 340—

Vol 43: 419, 482, 486, 540, 601—Vol 44: 152,
153, 230, 235—Vol 45: 21, 28, 113, 119, 238,
322—Vol 48: 119,' 370—Vol 49: 354—Vol
51: 301—Vol 52: 172, 322—Vol 53: 328—
Vol 56: 175, 318, 480, 743—Vol 57: 114, 312,
626—Vol 58: 176, 451, 588, 649, 761—Vol
59: 588, 681, 762—Vol 60: 51, 112, 507—Vol
62: 460, 588, 775—Vol 63: 58, 428—Vol 64:
57—Vol 65: 245, 298, 365, 437, 507, 762—
Vol 68: 491—Vol 69: 58—Vol 70: 576, 707
—Vol 71: 356, 460—Vol 74: (2-40), (9-50)
—Vol 79: 368, 561—Vol 80: 84—Vol 82:
653, 795, 936—Vol 83: 439—Vol 84: 893, 894
ROICE............................Vol 27: 380
ROKER............................Vol 52: 320
ROLAND............................Vol 42: 338—Vol 45: 126
ROLFE...Vol 21: 169—Vol 32: 719—Vol 40:
76—Vol 71: 161
ROLGONE............................Vol 28: 479
ROLLINGTON............................Vol 81: 571
ROLLINS...Vol 43: 488—Vol 44: 79, 149—Vol
83: 944
ROLLIS............................Vol 45: 24, 322
ROLLISTON............................Vol 73: (8-83)
ROLLOW............................Vol 69: 160
ROLPH............................Vol 41: 70—Vol 69: 564
ROMANS............................Vol 33: 1030
ROMER............................Vol 47: 271—Vol 53: 495
ROMIG............................Vol 32: 160—Vol 45: 23
RONEY...Vol 49: 136—Vol 54: 110—Vol 56:
222—Vol 77: 242
ROOD...Vol 34: 538, 657—Vol 42: 76—Vol
47: 27, 32—Vol 56: 373, 625
ROOKE............................Vol 30: 338
ROOKER...Vol 52: 320—Vol 66: 601—Vol 67:
387
ROOME............................Vol 43: 424
ROOP...Vol 35: 437—Vol 36: 74—Vol 54: 650
ROOS............................Vol 65: 299
ROOSA...Vol 60: 573, 746—Vol 61: 154, 383—
Vol 70: 206, 1020
ROOSEVELT............................Vol 44: 312
ROOT...Vol 30: 149—Vol 31: 51—Vol 44: 26
—Vol 45: 194—Vol 46: 237—Vol 58: 241—
Vol 61: 912—Vol 62: 124—Vol 63: 373—
Vol 69: 160—Vol 72: (3-71)
ROOTE............................Vol 53: 692
ROPER...Vol 55: 166—Vol 67: 442, 753—Vol
82: 139
ROQUEMORE............................Vol 59: 49
RORABAUGH............................Vol 45: 326
ROSBERRY............................Vol 41: 209
ROSCHONG............................Vol 83: 628
ROSCOE...Vol 57: 310—Vol 65: 441—Vol 68:
486
ROSCOW............................Vol 57: 310—Vol 63: 636
ROSE...Vol 21: 62—Vol 27: 807—Vol 33: 707
—Vol 37: 270, 487—Vol 38: 85, 87—Vol 39:
23—Vol 41: 32—Vol 42: 78—Vol 43: 423,
427, 497—Vol 44: 148, 225—Vol 46: 336—
Vol 47: 85—Vol 53: 243—Vol 60: 572—Vol
64: 714—Vol 65: 366—Vol 68: 373—Vol 70:
1020—Vol 82: 500—Vol 83: 441, 872
ROSEBERRY...Vol 41: 69, 120—Vol 47: 32—
Vol 57: 176, 431, 629
ROSECRANS............................Vol 84: 634
ROSECRANTZ............................Vol 35: 652
ROSENKRANCE .....Vol 45: 191—Vol 46: 159
ROSENKRANS............................Vol 50: 190

ROSEKRANTS............................Vol 53: 53
ROSS....Vol 22: 269—Vol 23: 398—Vol 27:
382—Vol 28: 366—Vol 33: 957—Vol 34: 65,
68—Vol 41: 70—Vol 43: 542—Vol 44: 232—
Vol 45: 27, 188—Vol 46: 386—Vol 47: 191
—Vol 51: 354—Vol 55: 286—Vol 56: 560—
Vol 58: 649—Vol 64: 588—Vol 65: 439—Vol
66: 535, 733—Vol 67: 42, 148, 388, 517—
Vol 68: 687—Vol 69: 118, 243, 432—Vol 70:
204—Vol 71: 161—Vol 72: (2-63)—Vol 76:
861—Vol 80: 154—Vol 81: 630—Vol 84: 446
ROSSEAU..................................Vol 61: 913
ROSSER..................Vol 41: 34—Vol 84: 69
ROSSITER................................Vol 80: 383
ROSSMAN..............Vol 41: 71—Vol 65: 442
ROSSON..................................Vol 77: 479
ROTHBAUST............................Vol 60: 573
ROTHERK................................Vol 60: 250
ROTHROCK......Vol 50: 63—Vol 68: 627—
Vol 82: 220
ROTHS......................................Vol 65: 760
ROTHWELL............................Vol 74: (2-41)
ROUND......................................Vol 24: 542
ROUNDS....Vol 36: 578—Vol 53: 243, 627—
Vol 56: 46, 172, 691—Vol 68: 58
ROUNSAVILLE........................Vol 65: 761
ROUNSAWELL........................Vol 84: 245
ROUSE...Vol 19: 431, 432—Vol 23: 244—Vol
56: 624—Vol 63: 57—Vol 68: 735—Vol 83:
173
ROUSH..................Vol 44: 381—Vol 45: 112
ROUT..Vol 77: 243
ROUTH.................................... Vol 42: 341
ROUTLEDGE....................Vol 63: 57, 105
ROUTT......................................Vol 37: 155
ROW..............Vol 73: (11-69)—Vol 74: (5-43)
ROWAN...Vol 56: 47—Vol 66: 309—Vol 67:
240, 387—Vol 68: 489
ROWE....Vol 25: 888—Vol 37: 158—Vol 42:
77, 343—Vol 45: 189—Vol 48: 123, 365—
Vol 51: 303—Vol 55: 339, 709—Vol 60: 51
—Vol 61: 66, 382—Vol 67: 442—Vol 68: 551
—Vol 70: 351—Vol 77: 480
ROWELL..................Vol 57: 480—Vol 68: 156
ROWEN.................................. Vol 42: 80
ROWLAND...Vol 41: 71, 162—Vol 42: 193,
335—Vol 43: 602—Vol 45: 242—Vol 56: 45
—Vol 57: 114, 351—Vol 58: 53, 763—Vol
59: 49—Vol 61: 473—Vol 63: 570—Vol 67:
648—Vol 68: 155—Vol 74: (1-49)—Vol 76:
309—Vol 79: 35—Vol 82: 932—Vol 84: 703
ROWLET..................................Vol 59: 442
ROWLES..................................Vol 79: 613
ROWLETT.... ....Vol 70: 1167—Vol 72: (3-73)
ROWLEY...Vol 15: 349—Vol 16: 243—Vol
57: 689—Vol 61: 156, 157—Vol 71: 959
ROX..Vol 82: 933
ROXBURGHE ....Vol 48: 55
ROY..Vol 44: 150
ROYAL................Vol 35: 1266—Vol 75: (7-36)
ROYCE...Vol 1: 606—Vol 18: 181—Vol 21:
249—Vol 22: 679—Vol 27: 889—Vol 31:
860—Vol 32: 507—Vol 42: 74—Vol 51: 354
—Vol 52: 357—Vol 70: 876
ROYELL..................................Vol 48: 60
ROYER.................. Vol 62: 585—Vol 67: 117
ROYS..Vol 54: 466
ROYSE......................................Vol 45: 24
ROYSTER................................Vol 58: 111

ROYSTON................................Vol 59: 525
ROZELL....................................Vol 65: 299
RUARK....................................Vol 31: 670
RUBARD..................................Vol 27: 738
RUBELL..................................Vol 64: 757
RUBEY....Vol 36: 578—Vol 37: 64—Vol 61:
913—Vol 62: 651
RUBLE....Vol 41: 213—Vol 46: 242—Vol 54:
464—Vol 64: 757
RUBLEE..................................Vol 55: 600
RUBY..Vol 61: 913
RUCK..Vol 53: 747
RUCKER....Vol 37: 66, 67, 349—Vol 45: 195—
Vol 58: 700—Vol 59: 389—Vol 60: 250, 365,
418, 569, 745, 746—Vol 62: 388—Vol 64: 757
—Vol 72: (9-89)
RUCKMAN................................Vol 30: 439
RUCKS..............................Vol 50: 354, 415
RUDD...Vol 38: 328—Vol 43: 547—Vol 65:
760
RUDDELL..................Vol 44: 82—Vol 60: 50
RUDDER..................................Vol 55: 397
RUDDLE................Vol 60: 50—Vol 61: 148
RUDE...Vol 21: 253—Vol 45: 116—Vol 54:
537
RUDOLPH................................Vol 56: 315
RUDULPH................................Vol 55: 602
RUE...Vol 26: 53—Vol 28: 480, 481—Vol 32:
508
RUFF....Vol 40: 230—Vol 41: 212—Vol 46:
153—Vol 64: 758
RUFFCORN............................Vol 55: 109
RUFFIN...Vol 54: 107, 590—Vol 55: 47, 284—
Vol 83: 947
RUFFNER..........................Vol 56: 47, 226
RUGG...Vol 26: 561—Vol 42: 190—Vol 43:
419—Vol 45: 126—Vol 54: 593—Vol 64:
389, 586—Vol 67: 711—Vol 68: 241
RUGGLES....Vol 26: 140—Vol 30: 64—Vol
54: 593—Vol 83: 258
RUKARD..................................Vol 29: 47
RULE..................Vol 36: 352—Vol 58: 53
RUMMEL..................................Vol 64: 444
RUMNEY..................................Vol 59: 682
RUMPLE..................................Vol 67: 148
RUMSEY..................................Vol 43: 490
RUNDALL................................Vol 76: 783
RUNDEL ....Vol 44: 385—Vol 64: 158
RUNDELL—Vol 41: 29, 65—Vol 45: 194—
Vol 74: (4-48)
RUNDLE...Vol 27: 383—Vol 29: 715—Vol 30:
146, 541—Vol 32: 60, 508—Vol 56: 563—Vol
74: (4-48)
RUNION..................................Vol 77: 538
RUNNELS................Vol 63: 742—Vol 69: 684
RUNNO....................................Vol 52: 172
RUNS..Vol 64: 387
RUNYAN...Vol 43: 489, 542—Vol 46: 154, 385
—Vol 58: 763—Vol 59: 389—Vol 83: 171
RUNYON...Vol 59: 47—Vol 71: 164—Vol 82:
499
RUPEL......................................Vol 64: 757
RUPERT...Vol 54: 52—Vol 60: 635—Vol 70:
876
RUPPERT..................................Vol 62: 586
RUSH...Vol 29: 288—Vol 34: 200, 657—Vol
37: 155, 350—Vol 39: 274—Vol 40: 24—Vol
43: 545—Vol 48: 306—Vol 49: 42—Vol 53:
330—Vol 55: 444—Vol 56: 373, 480—Vol

59: 46, 111—Vol 62: 306—Vol 65: 366—Vol
80: 190, 588
RUSHEBARGER............................Vol 45: 121
RUSHTON..............................Vol 83: 1014
RUSS.....Vol 50: 66—Vol 59: 315—Vol 84: 703
RUSSELL....Vol 6: 593—Vol 8: 881—Vol 20:
61, 277—Vol 21: 169—Vol 22: 997—Vol 29:
716—Vol 30: 66—Vol 36: 759—Vol 34: 201
—Vol 35: 1103—Vol 37: 488—Vol 39: 23,
103, 275—Vol 42: 139—Vol 43: 482, 601—
Vol 45: 28, 104, 118, 323, 324—Vol 46: 160,
384—Vol 47: 27, 29—Vol 48: 306, 370—Vol
49: 131, 280—Vol 50: 66, 281—Vol 57: 114,
117—Vol 58: 370, 702—Vol 59: 112, 314—
Vol 63: 294—Vol 66: 123, 365—Vol 67: 243,
292, 647—Vol 72: (3-71)—Vol 76: 582, 655
—Vol 79: 113, 571—Vol 81: 130, 571—Vol
82: 500, 727, 932
RUST....Vol 17: 282, 388—Vol 20: 278—Vol
29: 45—Vol 53: 244, 747—Vol 54: 353, 539,
591—Vol 55: 163—Vol 56: 373—Vol 61:
382—Vol 62: 459—Vol 67: 443
RUTAN.............................Vol 61: 473, 610, 705
RUTH....Vol 55: 520—Vol 78: 601—Vol 80:
656
RUTHERFORD....Vol 11: 509—Vol 28: 363—
Vol 37: 153—Vol 46: 157—Vol 56: 319—Vol
74: (1-50)—Vol 77: 117, 331—Vol 84: 522
RUTLAND.................................Vol 35: 438
RUTLEDGE....Vol 54: 172—Vol 67: 293—Vol
71: 241—Vol 76: 401
RYALL................................Vol 46: 23
RYAN....Vol 39: 143—Vol 41: 126—Vol 56:
172—Vol 58: 52—Vol 67: 577
RYANHART...........................Vol 44: 229
RYASON..............................Vol 59: 764
RYCKMANN.........................Vol 66: 160
RYDER....Vol 46: 242—Vol 50: 349—Vol 64:
443—Vol 78: 108—Vol 82: 313
RYERSON.............................Vol 59: 764
RYLAND..............................Vol 39: 224
RYON.................................Vol 27: 891

S

SABIN.................Vol 49: 133—Vol 71: 1025
SACHERWELL......................Vol 27: 383
SACHEVERELL....................Vol 28: 164
SACKET....Vol 30: 543—Vol 44: 25—Vol 47:
392
SACKRIDER..........................Vol 28: 262
SADDLER...............Vol 32: 62—Vol 82: 798
SADLER....Vol 35: 438—Vol 41: 123—Vol 57:
680
SAFFLE.................Vol 66: 309—Vol 67: 387
SAFFORD....Vol 41: 164, 212—Vol 45: 28,
184—Vol 50: 356—Vol 54: 353
SAGE....Vol 48: 307—Vol 53: 376—Vol 57:
630—Vol 58: 501—Vol 59: 238—Vol 67:
385
SAGER.................................Vol 82: 793
SAHLER................................Vol 71: 86
SAINE..................................Vol 37: 154
ST. CLAIR....Vol 8: 95—Vol 9: 296—Vol 13:
485—Vol 26: 141—Vol 37: 159—Vol 38: 32
—Vol 47: 194—Vol 68: 554—Vol 70: 55—
Vol 77: 332
ST. JOHN...............................Vol 44: 386
ST. JULIEN.............................Vol 45: 241
SALE....Vol 19: 531—Vol 26: 56—Vol 47: 95
—Vol 54: 113—Vol 74: (11-59)

SALEY.................................Vol 70: 352
SALISBURY.... Vol 27: 807—Vol 28: 545—Vol
45: 198—Vol 46: 243—Vol 47: 270—Vol 52:
625—Vol 55: 714—Vol 56: 113, 628—Vol
57: 690—Vol 58: 499—Vol 72: (11-59)—
Vol 84: 702
SALKELD....Vol 61: 707—Vol 62: 123—Vol
69: 432
SALLARD............Vol 82: 140, 313—Vol 83: 94
SALLE...............................Vol 73: (9-64)
SALLEE...............................Vol 54: 589
SALMON....Vol 36: 573, 576—Vol 37: 153—
Vol 38: 217—Vol 53: 492—Vol 56: 745—
Vol 57: 353—Vol 67: 577—Vol 70: 206—
Vol 72: (2-69)
SALSBURY.............................Vol 55: 714
SALTAR................................Vol 49: 355
SALTER....Vol 28: 262—Vol 30: 62—Vol 57:
630—Vol 67: 516
SALTONSTALL....Vol 46: 241—Vol 47: 265—
Vol 48: 55
SALTSMAN.........................Vol 72: (12-69)
SAMMONS.............................Vol 64: 587
SAMPLE....Vol 29: 650—Vol 48: 204—Vol
65: 636
SAMPSON....Vol 42: 270, 335—Vol 45: 112,
122, 197, 240, 327—Vol 46: 29—Vol 47: 197,
263, 266—Vol 49: 192—Vol 50: 355, 357—
Vol 51: 235, 303, 358—Vol 52: 113—Vol 53:
54, 574—Vol 54: 308, 647—Vol 55: 711—
Vol 59: 388—Vol 63: 293—Vol 64: 158—
Vol 66: 309
SAMS.................................Vol 38: 328—Vol 70: 354
SAMSON....Vol 51: 235, 358—Vol 61: 546
SAMUEL................................Vol 48: 447
SANBORN....Vol 23: 168—Vol 34: 322—Vol
35: 1266—Vol 36: 74, 461—Vol 37: 159—
Vol 41: 127—Vol 44: 315—Vol 45: 114—
Vol 56: 318, 415, 624, 627—Vol 57: 213—
Vol 75: (9-41)—Vol 83: 441
SANBORNTON.........................Vol 42: 12
SANDER...............................Vol 71: 86
SANDERLIN........................Vol 74: (11-61)
SANDERS....Vol 32: 284—Vol 41: 126—Vol
43: 491, 597—Vol 44: 25, 85, 153—Vol 47:
273—Vol 63: 375—Vol 65: 633—Vol 67:
443—Vol 79: 112
SANDERSON....Vol 22: 217—Vol 42: 337—
Vol 43: 419
SANDIDGE...........Vol 47: 194—Vol 53: 574
SANDIFER.............................Vol 68: 874
SANDRIDGE...........Vol 52: 732—Vol 57: 174
SANDS.................Vol 45: 200—Vol 81: 516
SANDY.................................Vol 48: 203
SANFORD....Vol 23: 244—Vol 28: 365—Vol
30: 337—Vol 35: 655—Vol 41: 35—Vol 42:
16—Vol 43: 545—Vol 44: 313—Vol 47: 397
—Vol 48: 56, 201—Vol 49: 136—Vol 52:
436, 686—Vol 53: 180, 332, 634—Vol 54:
228—Vol 55: 711—Vol 60: 51, 418—Vol 69:
241, 681—Vol 72: (1-65)—Vol 77: 239—
Vol 81: 630—Vol 82: 796—Vol 83: 171, 261
SANGER.............Vol 50: 348—Vol 52: 321
SANKEY...............Vol 69: 120—Vol 70: 1018
SANSBURY.............................Vol 70: 577
SANSEBAUGH.........................Vol 58: 111
SAPPERLEY...........................Vol 70: 1165
SAPPINGTON....Vol 35: 1104—Vol 44: 54—
Vol 60: 568—Vol 62: 583
SAPPLINGTON......................Vol 84: 633

Vol 41: 125—Vol 43: 489, 497, 543, 546, 598, 599, 604—Vol 44: 150, 234, 315—Vol 45: 111, 121, 122, 127, 236, 300, 325—Vol 46: 97, 104, 155, 335—Vol 47: 82, 266, 267, 271— Vol 48: 56, 64, 124, 450—Vol 49: 43, 131, 135, 190, 350, 394, 395—Vol 50: 61, 354, 356 —Vol 52: 112, 626—Vol 54: 350—Vol 55: 181, 247—Vol 56: 46, 109, 114, 416—Vol 57: 175, 214, 313, 688, 744—Vol 58: 52, 54, 501, 502, 587—Vol 59: 111, 176, 388—Vol 60: 632, 635—Vol 61: 149, 607, 867—Vol 62: 246, 248, 500, 773—Vol 63: 243—Vol 64: 59, 158, 445—Vol 65: 248, 440—Vol 66: 460, 826, 827—Vol 67: 48, 145, 146, 148, 385, 577, 645—Vol 68: 122, 551—Vol 69: 247, 629— Vol 70: 203, 572—Vol 71: 676, 1025—Vol 72: (1-65)—Vol 75: (6-40), (10-66)—Vol 76: 710, 860—Vol 77: 117—Vol 79: 194, 561 —Vol 80: 85, 154, 382, 589—Vol 81: 130— Vol 82: 139, 142, 930, 934—Vol 83: 335, 795 —Vol 84: 247, 625

SCOUT...Vol 45: 242
SCONTEN..Vol 45: 121
SCOVIL...Vol 36: 77
SCOVILL.................Vol 40: 227—Vol 41: 70
SCRAMBLING...........Vol 58: 453—Vol 59: 652
SCRANTON......................................Vol 50: 63
SCREWS......................................Vol 73: (8-83)
SCRIBER.................Vol 42: 192—Vol 45: 187
SCRIBNER....Vol 43: 542—Vol 57: 628—Vol 59: 111, 312—Vol 83: 1015
SCROGGINS..................................Vol 53: 630
SCROGGS............Vol 23: 244—Vol 77: 241, 333
SCROGGY............Vol 27: 736—Vol 28: 362
SCROGIN...............Vol 44: 235—Vol 56: 152
SCOVAIL..Vol 34: 423
SCOVILLE..Vol 33: 960
SCRIPTURE....................................Vol 58: 60
SCRUGGS.................Vol 53: 180—Vol 83: 717
SCUDDER...Vol 24: 152—Vol 26: 142—Vol 33: 709, 1030—Vol 67: 386
SCULL...Vol 64: 444—Vol 73: (11-67)—Vol 78: 696
SCURLOCK..Vol 43: 546
SCURRY.................Vol 62: 503—Vol 64: 256
SCYPERT..Vol 77: 389
SEABOLT..Vol 55: 711
SEABORN..Vol 70: 136
SEABRING..Vol 70: 136
SEABURY..Vol 40: 26
SEAGARD..Vol 55: 285
SEAGARDIN ....Vol 55: 285
SEAL.......................Vol 70: 1019—Vol 71: 672
SEALE..Vol 82: 934
SEALEY..Vol 46: 159
SEAMAN...............Vol 43: 545—Vol 58: 53, 328
SEAMON..Vol 19: 307
SEAMONDS......................................Vol 59: 237
SEARCH..Vol 75: (9-37)
SEARCHMAN....................................Vol 63: 38
SEARCY...............Vol 26: 54—Vol 70: 878
SEARING..Vol 76: 62
SEARL..Vol 50: 192
SEARLE...Vol 1: 339—Vol 67: 645—Vol 68: 442
SEARLES..Vol 49: 395
SEARLS..Vol 50: 192
SEARS...Vol 44: 84—Vol 46: 29—Vol 63: 427—Vol 64: 650—Vol 65: 124—Vol 66: 55

SEATON....Vol 45: 22, 195—Vol 48: 63—Vol 53: 446
SEAVER.................Vol 34: 323—Vol 48: 57
SEAVEY...................Vol 55: 284—Vol 56: 110
SEAWARD....................Vol 16: 192—Vol 52: 321
SEAWRIGHT..................................Vol 60: 417
SEAY...Vol 41: 123—Vol 83: 717—Vol 84: 893
SEBASTIAN....................................Vol 48: 59
SEBOR..Vol 45: 26
SEBREE..Vol 53: 180
SEBRELL..Vol 49: 354
SECOR....Vol 42: 139—Vol 45: 323—Vol 72: (1-65)
SECORD..Vol 45: 103
SEDGWICK....Vol 27: 379—Vol 30: 542—Vol 61: 158, 787—Vol 67: 41, 511—Vol 71: 461— Vol 74: (11-61)
SEE....................................Vol 64: 159, 386, 443
SEEBOLT..Vol 55: 711
SEECHRIST....................................Vol 46: 154
SEEKEL..Vol 44: 148
SEELEY...Vol 22: 680—Vol 24: 58—Vol 25: 716—Vol 31: 863—Vol 34: 322—Vol 43: 605—Vol 44: 151—Vol 54: 649—Vol 55: 162, 208—Vol 63: 572, 696—Vol 65: 366— Vol 67: 117—Vol 68: 685—Vol 71: 164—Vol 72: (10-94)—Vol 77: 538—Vol 84: 519, 523
SEELY....................Vol 72: (3-78)—Vol 81: 570
SEELYE....Vol 54: 649—Vol 55: 208, 445— Vol 57: 175
SEERIGHT..Vol 60: 249
SEEVER..Vol 57: 481
SEFTON..Vol 62: 714
SEGAR..Vol 64: 160
SEGUIN..Vol 45: 194
SEHL.......................Vol 70: 1019—Vol 71: 672
SEHORN...Vol 46: 153—Vol 56: 44, 109—Vol 58: 53
SEIDEL..Vol 41: 125
SEIFERT..Vol 82: 140
SEIGLE..Vol 44: 25
SEITER..Vol 82: 220
SELBY...Vol 42: 192, 270, 335—Vol 49: 286 —Vol 61: 606—Vol 70: 356—Vol 71: 673— Vol 73: (10-76)—Vol 74: (2-42)—Vol 76: 309—Vol 78: 553—Vol 80: 46
SELDEN...Vol 19: 206, 531—Vol 22: 155— Vol 27: 735—Vol 30: 256—Vol 42: 138— Vol 45: 191—Vol 59: 589—Vol 82: 861
SELDON..Vol 59: 442
SELF....................Vol 39: 227—Vol 83: 440, 946
SELFRIDGE....................................Vol 45: 326
SELKIRK..Vol 35: 1103
SELKRIG..................Vol 35: 1263, 1266
SELLARD...............Vol 36: 216—Vol 43: 598
SELLARS..Vol 55: 519
SELLECK................Vol 48: 371—Vol 59: 175
SELLER..Vol 61: 469
SELLERD..Vol 43: 496
SELLERS................Vol 67: 45, 144, 388
SELLON..Vol 53: 372
SELLS..Vol 49: 188
SELOVER....Vol 73: (1-62), (9-64)—Vol 75: (5-43)
SELSER....Vol 42: 336—Vol 43: 419—Vol 81: 518
SELTZER..Vol 78: 53
SEMAN..Vol 58: 171

SENCERBOUGH......Vol 34: 202—Vol 42: 263
SENEKER..................................Vol 50: 281
SENGER......................................Vol 21: 404
SENSSENENDORFER....................Vol 59: 45
SENTER....................................Vol 42: 270
SERCOMBE................................Vol 84: 523
SERGEANT..............................Vol 70: 1165
SESSIONS...Vol 36: 353—Vol 38: 88, 113,
   114—Vol 41: 213—Vol 45: 189
SESSUMS..................................Vol 53: 746
SETTLE...Vol 54: 172—Vol 66: 600—Vol 68:
   56, 121—Vol 79: 332—Vol 82: 63—Vol 84:
   704
SETTLETON..............................Vol 44: 230
SEVERANCE...Vol 64: 161, 385—Vol 67: 146
SEVERNS................................Vol 74: (1-50)
SEVIER...Vol 8: 248—Vol 30: 543—Vol 46:
   337—Vol 47: 264—Vol 55: 166, 337—Vol
   56: 313
SEWALL....................................Vol 47: 86—Vol 48: 437
SEWARD...Vol 28: 60—Vol 45: 237—Vol 47:
   196—Vol 56: 480—Vol 71: 959
SEWELL...Vol 34: 203—Vol 46: 386—Vol 84:
   636
SEXTON...Vol 22: 374—Vol 34: 67, 321—
   Vol 40: 225, 226—Vol 59: 176
SEYLE..Vol 49: 192
SEYMOUR...Vol 27: 890—Vol 29: 45—Vol
   34: 201—Vol 39: 327—Vol 40: 108—Vol
   49: 131—Vol 62: 776—Vol 70: 707—Vol
   75: (3-41)
SEYPRET..................................Vol 58: 699
SHACKELFORD...Vol 47: 394—Vol 50: 193
   —Vol 59: 49, 521—Vol 82: 140, 313
SHACKFORD............................Vol 48: 305
SHACKLEFORD...Vol 63: 373, 741—Vol 64:
   123—Vol 66: 825
SHADDINGER........................Vol 43: 422
SHADOWHURST....................Vol 26: 560
SHAEFFER............Vol 43: 599—Vol 44: 150
SHAFER...Vol 56: 743—Vol 67: 241—Vol
   84: 445
SHAFFER...Vol 43: 493, 546, 599, 605—Vol
   44: 386—Vol 49: 135—Vol 50: 70—Vol 60:
   419—Vol 67: 241—Vol 68: 243—Vol 71: 87
SHAILER..................................Vol 52: 360
SHALER............Vol 43: 487, 542—Vol 81: 569
SHALL......................................Vol 34: 659
SHALLCOP..............................Vol 27: 807
SHANE......................................Vol 42: 343
SHANER....................................Vol 66: 537
SHANK................Vol 34: 68—Vol 83: 628
SHANKLE..................................Vol 49: 396
SHANKLIN................................Vol 54: 465
SHANLY....................................Vol 61: 704
SHANNON...Vol 24: 458—Vol 39: 140—Vol
   44: 312—Vol 48: 446—Vol 53: 179—Vol 56:
   689—Vol 65: 247, 636, 757—Vol 68: 552—
   Vol 82: 794
SHAON......................................Vol 58: 173
SHAORN....................................Vol 65: 507
SHARES....................................Vol 43: 603
SHARK......................................Vol 79: 112
SHARKEY..............................Vol 73: (11-68)
SHARON...Vol 29: 716—Vol 37: 70—Vol 65:
   365
SHARP...Vol 31: 414—Vol 36: 75, 352, 755—
   Vol 37: 348—Vol 44: 141, 231—Vol 47: 199
   —Vol 55: 286—Vol 57: 348—Vol 59: 314—
   Vol 62: 713—Vol 63: 373, 507—Vol 67: 613

—Vol 69: 631—Vol 71: 959—Vol 72: (4-82)
   —Vol 75: (7-36), (11-69)—Vol 76: 710—
   Vol 77: 481—Vol 79: 161—Vol 82: 797—Vol
   83: 523
SHARPE...Vol 32: 62—Vol 36: 757—Vol 37:
   151—Vol 38: 328—Vol 47: 272—Vol 49: 135
   —Vol 72: (11-58)
SHARRETTS..............................Vol 56: 174
SHARWOOD..............................Vol 26: 337
SHATTUCK...Vol 30: 149—Vol 53: 55—Vol
   57: 177—Vol 75: (10-67)—Vol 76: 218
SHAUB......................................Vol 55: 335
SHAUN......................................Vol 49: 285
SHAURBORN..........................Vol 82: 501
SHAVER............Vol 55: 165—Vol 67: 516
SHAW...Vol 24: 542—Vol 25: 716—Vol 26:
   53, 54—Vol 28: 57, 262—Vol 30: 259, 334—
   Vol 33: 709, 1030, 1033—Vol 34: 658—Vol
   35: 57—Vol 37: 157—Vol 39: 143—Vol 41:
   30—Vol 43: 540, 542—Vol 45: 106—Vol 46:
   27—Vol 48: 446—Vol 52: 52, 321—Vol 56:
   174, 372—Vol 63: 247—Vol 64: 158—Vol 67:
   385, 575—Vol 68: 551—Vol 71: 240, 284,
   1025, 1027—Vol 73: (3-86), (7-70)—Vol 75:
   (4-52)—Vol 80: 557—Vol 82: 139—Vol 83:
   943
SHAWEN....................................Vol 49: 285
SHAWHAN..............................Vol 75: (2-58)
SHAWM....................................Vol 70: 1168
SHAWN......................................Vol 49: 285
SHAY..Vol 59: 765
SHAYLER..................................Vol 43: 542
SHAYLOR............Vol 8: 402—Vol 43: 487
SHAYS......................................Vol 61: 869
SHEADS....................................Vol 49: 284
SHEAFF....................................Vol 31: 54
SHEARER...Vol 48: 64—Vol 60: 418—Vol
   80: 383
SHEARMAN..........................Vol 73: (10-75)
SHEARON..................................Vol 37: 72
SHECKEL..................................Vol 52: 109
SHECKELLS..............................Vol 64: 390
SHECKLE............Vol 46: 390—Vol 72: (1-66)
SHEELEY..................................Vol 45: 199
SHEERER..................................Vol 49: 356
SHEETS...Vol 29: 288—Vol 45: 123—Vol 60:
   250
SHEFFER..................................Vol 62: 712
SHEFFIELD...Vol 45: 105—Vol 48: 306—
   Vol 56: 44, 318
SHEIK..Vol 43: 602
SHEKELS..................................Vol 47: 193
SHELBY...Vol 7: 176, 267—Vol 32: 508—Vol
   33: 475, 956—Vol 39: 275—Vol 40: 108—
   Vol 41: 126—Vol 42: 12—Vol 46: 101, 246,
   335—Vol 47: 190, 267—Vol 48: 304—Vol 49:
   132—Vol 53: 630—Vol 55: 285, 443, 523—
   Vol 56: 110—Vol 57: 434—Vol 62: 247—Vol
   65: 759—Vol 77: 184
SHELDEN............Vol 38: 331—Vol 39: 23
SHELDON...Vol 21: 62—Vol 26: 56, 562—
   Vol 47: 273—Vol 54: 420—Vol 56: 175, 563
   —Vol 59: 442—Vol 79: 161
SHELEY................Vol 73: (8-83), (9-66)
SHELHAMER............................Vol 59: 47
SHELL..Vol 63: 427
SHELLEY...Vol 71: 673—Vol 83: 442, 443
SHELLMAN..............................Vol 54: 648
SHELLY....................................Vol 65: 124
SHELTON...Vol 25: 716—Vol 37: 66, 67—Vol

43: 696—Vol 46: 155—Vol 47: 341—Vol 48:
62, 438—Vol 49: 45, 396—Vol 56: 45, 474,
477—Vol 57: 219—Vol 58: 50—Vol 61: 157
—Vol 62: 387, 649—Vol 66: 160, 600, 732—
Vol 68: 285—Vol 71: 673—Vol 73: (4-84)—
Vol 74: (11-59)—Vol 81: 20—Vol 82: 935
SHENK..Vol 84: 328
SHEPARD....Vol 20: 61—Vol 21: 251—Vol
25: 799—Vol 33: 43—Vol 38: 275—Vol 44:
154—Vol 46: 389—Vol 52: 360—Vol 57:
215, 219—Vol 59: 112—Vol 61: 706—Vol
64: 57—Vol 79: 614—Vol 84: 522
SHEPARDSON....Vol 46: 28, 388—Vol 48: 449
SHEPHARD................Vol 27: 738—Vol 58: 111
SHEPARS..Vol 26: 57
SHEPHERD....Vol 21: 60, 400—Vol 22: 154—
Vol 32: 162—Vol 35: 654—Vol 37: 70—Vol
41: 127—Vol 43: 482, 604—Vol 47: 30, 264,
271—Vol 48: 122—Vol 56: 226, 560, 561, 740
—Vol 57: 478—Vol 58: 652—Vol 59: 315—
Vol 63: 427—Vol 64: 258—Vol 65: 297—
Vol 70: 206—Vol 84: 247
SHEPPARD....Vol 39: 273—Vol 55: 339, 712—
Vol 56: 45, 413, 477, 557—Vol 60: 744—Vol
62: 390
SHEPLER................................Vol 58: 453
SHERALD................................Vol 37: 150
SHERBURNE ...Vol 27: 671—Vol 28: 60—Vol
37: 153—Vol 44: 83—Vol 55: 446—Vol 57:
565—Vol 60: 697—Vol 80: 556
SHERETT..Vol 26: 57
SHERIDAN..Vol 39: 326
SHERIFF..............Vol 78: 295—Vol 84: 894
SHERLEY..Vol 53: 178
SHERMAN....Vol 1: 342—Vol 5: 58—Vol 19:
207—Vol 21: 61—Vol 24: 57—Vol 26: 243—
Vol 27: 382—Vol 31: 585—Vol 32: 159, 719
—Vol 34: 424—Vol 36: 213—Vol 37: 32,
68, 160, 332, 394—Vol 38: 32, 272, 332—Vol
39: 141, 273, 323—Vol 43: 497—Vol 44: 234
—Vol 46: 332—Vol 47: 27, 30, 391—Vol
48: 443—Vol 49: 284—Vol 50: 58, 113—Vol
54: 222—Vol 55: 165—Vol 58: 502—Vol
59: 238—Vol 62: 307—Vol 63: 60, 295—Vol
68: 686—Vol 69: 56, 246, 631—Vol 71: 161
—Vol 70: 352, 708—Vol 72: (1-64)—Vol
74: (11-60)—Vol 78: 155—Vol 80: 383—Vol
82: 220
SHERRARD................Vol 45: 105—Vol 76: 655
SHERRILL................................Vol 84: 634
SHERRITS................................Vol 61: 867
SHERRY..................................... Vol 25: 967
SHERWIN....Vol 37: 488—Vol 45: 237—Vol
46: 241, 385—Vol 47: 191—Vol 81: 630
SHERWOOD....Vol 26: 141—Vol 41: 211, 213
—Vol 42: 14—Vol 49: 192—Vol 56: 479—
Vol 57: 114, 627—Vol 58: 651, 762—Vol 59:
764—Vol 60: 247, 633—Vol 65: 570, 571—
Vol 66: 363—Vol 67: 715—Vol 70: 457—Vol
79: 36
SHETTERLY................................Vol 67: 716
SHETTLE................Vol 78: 456, 650
SHEWELL................................Vol 37: 157
SHIDLER................................Vol 39: 225
SHIELD ....Vol 36: 216, 349—Vol 37: 66, 73
SHIELDS....Vol 37: 349, 350, 351—Vol 38:
35, 113, 219—Vol 44: 309, 310—Vol 55: 520
—Vol 56: 371
SHIGLEY................................Vol 82: 795
SHILLITS ....Vol 40: 274—Vol 45: 22

SHINN....Vol 41: 163, 166—Col 48: 202, 368—
Vol 54: 51, 419—Vol 67: 515—Vol 83: 872
SHION.....................................Vol 39: 274
SHIPLEY....Vol 47: 268—Vol 60: 249—Vol
62: 713
SHIPMAN....Vol 21: 498—Vol 40: 74—Vol 50:
357—Vol 55: 285—Vol 58: 700—Vol 60: 507
—Vol 67: 713
SHIPP....Vol 43: 542—Vol 58: 329—Vol 59:
315
SHIPPEN................Vol 27: 44—Vol 30: 145, 146
SHIPPY..Vol 54: 51
SHIRES ....Vol 74: (12-53)
SHIREY......................................Vol 84: 635
SHIRK................Vol 38: 331—Vol 39: 222
SHIRLEY....Vol 37: 154—Vol 43: 423—Vol
62: 207—Vol 63: 373
SHITE................................Vol 61: 155
SHIVERS..Vol 61: 785
SHOBE....Vol 75: (9-46), (10-64), (11-70)—
Vol 77: 481
SHOCFORD................................Vol 48: 305
SHOCK..Vol 69: 243
SHOCKLEY................................Vol 46: 246
SHOEMAKER....Vol 36: 218—Vol 42: 335—
Vol 44: 149, 153—Vol 59: 387—Vol 62: 388
—Vol 68: 552
SHOMAKER................................Vol 42: 269
SHONSE..Vol 68: 285
SHONTZ..Vol 46: 99
SHOOK....Vol 47: 273—Vol 54: 537—Vol 60:
417
SHOOP.....................................Vol 38: 87
SHOOPMAN................Vol 53: 744—Vol 54: 174
SHOOT................................Vol 55: 711
SHORES....Vol 44: 310—Vol 46: 100—Vol 58:
331—Vol 61: 547—Vol 77: 603
SHORT....Vol 25: 718—Vol 27: 739—Vol 31:
589—Vol 38: 274—Vol 41: 124—Vol 43:
546—Vol 45: 17—Vol 48: 120, 370, 446—
Vol 49: 42—Vol 52: 733—Vol 53: 574—Vol
56: 173—Vol 59: 47—Vol 64: 651—Vol 65:
759—Vol 83: 628
SHOUP....Vol 50: 62—Vol 54: 351, 710—Vol
55: 335—Vol 57: 691—Vol 76: 653
SHOWER..Vol 67: 47
SHRADER................................Vol 83: 90
SHREIBER................................Vol 83: 794
SHRENE................Vol 46: 387—Vol 77: 481
SHREWDER................................Vol 82: 575
SHRIMPLIN................................Vol 70: 572
SHRIVER................................Vol 48: 63
SHROPSHIRE....Vol 43: 544—Vol 53: 178,
633—Vol 54: 353, 593—Vol 58: 764—Vol
69: 121
SHROYER................................Vol 66: 827
SHRYOCK ....Vol 82: 794
SHUBRICK................................Vol 44: 229
SHUCK..Vol 57: 114
SHUFF..Vol 76: 653
SHUFFELL................................Vol 62: 160
SHUGART....Vol 28: 548—Vol 29: 799—Vol
43: 489—Vol 46: 242—Vol 47: 388
SHULL....Vol 40: 230—Vol 46: 28, 30
SHULTZ................Vol 27: 737—Vol 84: 634
SHUMATE....Vol 48: 203—Vol 70: 1165—Vol
73: (2-65)
SHUMWAY................................Vol 72: (2-64)
SHUNK....Vol 59: 175—Vol 65: 246
SHUNNARD................................Vol 43: 425

SHUPE..Vol 57: 69
SHURBURNE...............................Vol 25: 798
SHURTLEFF............Vol 58: 370—Vol 61: 612
SHUTE....Vol 48: 444—Vol 49: 127—Vol 56: 371
SHUTTS.....................................Vol 61: 158
SIAS..Vol 54: 590
SIBERT..............................Vol 53: 243, 747
SIBERTS..Vol 69: 631
SIBLEY....Vol 30: 64—Vol 35: 437—Vol 43: 601—Vol 54: 55, 590—Vol 55: 107—Vol 58: 500—Vol 74: (11-61)—Vol 83: 794
SICK...Vol 82: 501
SICKLES................Vol 41: 30—Vol 55: 714
SICKMAN..................................Vol 43: 602
SIDDLE.......................................Vol 45: 17
SIDMORE...................................Vol 58: 329
SIDWELL....Vol 60: 50—Vol 69: 245—Vol 76: 582
SIEBE...Vol 42: 192
SIEBERT......................................Vol 60: 573
SIETHERLIN...............................Vol 26: 339
SIGNOR.......................................Vol 32: 160
SIGSBEE......................................Vol 43: 422
SIKES..Vol 22: 156
SILBAUGH...................................Vol 47: 33
SILBORN......................................Vol 64: 308
SILCOAT....................................Vol 75: (6-40)
SILER...Vol 82: 862
SILK..Vol 45: 101
SILL.........Vol 2: 297—Vol 27: 45—Vol 44: 312
SILLCOCKS...................................Vol 67: 44
SILLIMAN....Vol 31: 669—Vol 38: 220—Vol 40: 107—Vol 66: 460
SILLOWAY.................................Vol 76: 310
SILLS..Vol 49: 188
SILVER..Vol 21: 253
SILVERNAIL...............................Vol 45: 240
SILVERTHORNE.........................Vol 80: 84
SIMERS.............Vol 25: 968—Vol 43: 544
SIMIRAL.....................................Vol 66: 671
SIMKINS.....................................Vol 45: 120
SIMMERMAN....Vol 77: 479, 602—Vol 79: 614
SIMMERON.................................Vol 68: 373
SIMMONDS.................................Vol 59: 47
SIMMONS....Vol 21: 252—Vol 26: 339—Vol 30: 441—Vol 36: 351—Vol 37: 65—Vol 38: 329—Vol 40: 26—Vol 41: 211—Vol 44: 313 —Vol 45: 110—Vol 50: 61—Vol 52: 52—Vol 53: 570—Vol 54: 649—Vol 55: 338, 655— Vol 56: 367, 624—Vol 57: 690—Vol 58: 110 —Vol 59: 315—Vol 67: 292—Vol 69: 631— Vol 70: 54—Vol 71: 672—Vol 72: (3-79)— Vol 74: (2-41)—Vol 75: (9-40), (11-70)— Vol 80: 382—Vol 81: 630—Vol 83: 628
SIMMS....Vol 21: 496—Vol 51: 354—Vol 61: 231, 471—Vol 65: 758—Vol 77: 768
SIMONDS....Vol 26: 143—Vol 47: 271—Vol 59: 681
SIMONS....Vol 47: 32—Vol 48: 444—Vol 49: 394—Vol 58: 371
SIMONSON...............Vol 37: 149—Vol 84: 520
SIMPKINS....Vol 43: 496, 543, 599—Vol 74: (7-53), (8-53)
SIMPSON....Vol 25: 383, 718—Vol 32: 634, 718, 719—Vol 33: '959—Vol 37: 150—Vol 38: 34, 217, 220—Vol 39: 327—Vol 43: 493, 495, 543, 596—Vol 44: 225—Vol 45: 191— Vol 46: 30, 101—Vol 48: 123, 369, 442—Vol 49: 124, 188, 354—Vol 55: 46, 285—Vol 56:

742—Vol 57: 114, 175—Vol 58: 702—Vol 61: 231—Vol 66: 600—Vol 67: 515—Vol 68: 242—Vol 69: 363—Vol 70: 206, 360—Vol 72: (9-87)—Vol 74: (5-41)—Vol 80: 193
SIMPTON..Vol 82: 795
SIMS....Vol 43: 546—Vol 45: 113—Vol 51: 354 —Vol 53: 331—Vol 56: 479—Vol 59: 523— Vol 60: 49—Vol 66: 123—Vol 75: (11-70)
SINCLAIR....Vol 29: 653, 800—Vol 41: 124— Vol 65: 762—Vol 66: 250—Vol 67: 44—Vol 76: 400
SINGER....Vol 21: 404—Vol 43: 493—Vol 53: 630
SINGLETON....Vol 21: 251—Vol 41: 128—Vol 42: 76, 340—Vol 43: 422—Vol 45: 110—Vol 46: 100, 331—Vol 49: 283—Vol 58: 364— Vol 71: 1109—Vol 72: (6-78)—Vol 73: (9-64)—Vol 75: (4-53)
SINK...Vol 83: 945
SINKEY................Vol 69: 120—Vol 70: 1018
SINKLER......................................Vol 81: 570
SINNEX......................................Vol 81: '517
SINSABAUGH...............................Vol 52: 563
SIPE...Vol 54: 172
SIPES..Vol 40: 77
SIRLOTT....................................Vol 73: (4-83)
SISK..Vol 40: 226
SISSON....Vol 24: 459—Vol 55: 338—Vol 75: (6-89)
SISSONS......................................Vol 29: 23
SITES...Vol 79: 35
SITTON............Vol 56: 45, 114—Vol 58: 170
SIZER...Vol 59: 524
SKELDING.................Vol 17: 480—Vol 42: 15
SKELTON....Vol 43: 599—Vol 56: 113—Vol 61: 788—Vol 71: 760—Vol 77: 481
SKAGGS......................................Vol 82: 500
SKIDMORE....Vol 42: 75, 188, 264—Vol 53: 177—Vol 59: 525—Vol 84: 521
SKIELS..............................Vol 34: 201, 540
SKIFF.................Vol 45: 184—Vol 53: 446
SKILLINS.....................................Vol 29: 288
SKINNER....Vol 20: 166—Vol 21: 494—Vol 26: 142—Vol 27: 891—Vol 28: 162, 479— Vol 33: 1032—Vol 45: 107, 110—Vol 46: 29, 104—Vol 48: 124—Vol 49: 131—Vol 50: 62—Vol 52: 360—Vol 57: 176—Vol 58: 701 —Vol 61: 470—Vol 64: 120—Vol 66: 308— Vol 70: 576, 1167—Vol 72: (4-82), (7-74)— Vol 73: (4-83)—Vol 76: 928—Vol 79: 161— Vol 80: 84, 193—Vol 81: 629—Vol 82: 575— Vol 83: 628
SKIPP..Vol 81: 571
SKIPURTH............Vol 26: 54—Vol 33: 1030
SKYLES......................................Vol 81: 130
SLACK....Vol 22: 679—Vol 41: 33—Vol 49: 189—Vol 50: 188—Vol 55: 713—Vol 56: 557
SLADE Vol 30: 66—Vol 48: 123—Vol 67: 48
SLAFTER....................................Vol 39: 103
SLARROW.................................Vol 74: (4-52)
SLATE.................Vol 22: 272—Vol 31: 54
SLATER....Vol 64: 520—Vol 66: 365—Vol 67: 387
SLAUFFER...................................Vol 65: 124
SLAUGHT...................................Vol 49: 189
SLAUGHTER....Vol 1: 341—Vol 21: 61—Vol 35: 1101—Vol 37: 270—Vol 38: 274—Vol 39: 323—Vol 40: 274—Vol 42: 339—Vol 43: 420—Vol 44: 227—Vol 65: 762—Vol 67:

442—Vol 69: 245, 247—Vol 80: 511—Vol 81:
630—Vol 82: 221
SLAUSON_____Vol 67: 515
SLAVEN_____Vol 79: 614
SLAVENS_____Vol 74: (2-41)
SLAVIN_____Vol 74: (2-41)
SLAWSON_____Vol 36: 214—Vol 54: 591
SLEATOR_____Vol 82: 796
SLEDGE_____Vol 46: 103
SLEEPER_____Vol 45: 114
SLEETH___Vol 53: 376—Vol 58: 500—Vol 62:
586
SLEIGHT_____Vol 37: 149
SLEMMONS_____Vol 20: 1064—Vol 36: 578
SLITER _____Vol 36: 77
SLOAN___Vol 29: 803—Vol 30: 335—Vol 31:
752—Vol 62: 120, 122, 160, 161, 502, 647—
Vol 63: 57, 373—Vol 64: 385—Vol 73: (7-
70)—Vol 74: (7-52), (8-52)
SLOAT___Vol 58: 452—Vol 75: (1-54)—Vol
83: 717
SLOCUM___Vol 43: 492—Vol 45: 22, 189, 237
—Vol 61: 869—Vol 80: 192
SLOCUMB_____Vol 45: 118—Vol 63: 105
SLONE___Vol 65: 571—Vol 66: 365—Vol 67:
716
SLOVER___Vol 73: (1-62)—Vol 75: (5-43),
(7-35)—Vol 77: 539
SLUNSON_____Vol 36: 77
SMALL___Vol 36: 757—Vol 45: 118—Vol 52:
109—Vol 53: 242—Vol 63: 246—Vol 65:
635—Vol 71: 86—Vol 73: (7-69)—Vol 84:
67
SMALLAGE_____Vol 30: 65
SMART___Vol 29: 652—Vol 30: 334, 335—Vol
32: 507—Vol 75: (5-45)—Vol 84: 635
SMEAD___Vol 21: 252—Vol 26: 139, 140—Vol
45: 106
SMEDES_____Vol 45: 26, 322
SMEDLEY_____Vol 46: 390
SMELLIE_____Vol 66: 734—Vol 71: 461
SMILES_____Vol 63: 635
SMILEY___Vol 62: 502, 650—Vol 66: 734—Vol
70: 1170—Vol 71: 461—Vol 74: (4-53)—Vol
77: 183—Vol 79: 35—Vol 82: 933
SMILIE_____Vol 39: 143—Vol .75: (2-59)
SMITH___Vol 2: 45—Vol 7: 179—Vol 8: 252—
Vol 14: 271—Vol 15: 342—Vol 18: 181—Vol
19: 433—Vol 20: 352—Vol 21: 169—Vol 22:
54, 154, 156, 268, 277, 373—Vol 23: 62, 168
—Vol 24: 459, 542—Vol 25: 382, 717—Vol
26: 55, 143, 242—Vol 27: 44, 383, 670, 672,
808, 891—Vol 28: 58, 61, 161, 163, 365, 366,
547, 549—Vol 29: 46, 47, 287, 288, 512, 513,
648, 714, 716—Vol 30: 66, 67, 148, 256, 336,
337, 540—Vol 31: 412, 413, 414, 585, 587,
588, 589, 666, 668, 752, 862, 863—Vol 32:
60, 61, 160, 161, 162, 282, 284, 631, 720—
—Vol 33: 38, 473, 474—Vol 34: 69, 322, 659
—Vol 35: 653, 1264—Vol 36: 77, 218, 573,
576, 579, 759, 760—Vol 37: 64, 69, 74, 151,
154, 158, 268, 271, 396—Vol 38: 34, 35, 87,
275, 276, 327, 331—Vol 39: 23, 104, 224, 225,
227, 276, 325, 327—Vol 40: 24, 26, 75, 228,
272—Vol 41: 28, 29, 70, 72, 123, 127, 164,
212, 214—Vol 42: 76, 77, 79, 137, 191, 194,
269, 340—Vol 43: 420, 423, 424, 425, 426,
427, 483, 487, 491, 493, 494, 495, 541, 542,
543—Vol 44: 23, 24, 27, 80, 149, 234, 310, 311,
312, 315, 316, 386, 387—Vol 45: 18, 23, 27,

28, 105, 114, 115, 116, 118, 191, 192, 196, 200,
236, 237, 239, 241, 324, 326—Vol 46: 22, 27,
29, 160, 236, 237, 242, 244, 246, 330, 336,
387, 392, 393—Vol 47: 192, 264—Vol 48: 56,
59, 60, 62, 202, 205, 308, 367, 370, 371, 437—
Vol 49: 129, 131, 189, 191, 353, 395—Vol 50:
58, 61, 62, 189, 192, 279, 280, 350, 351, 354—
Vol 51: 303—Vol 52: 172, 319, 320, 321, 360,
559, 686—Vol 53: 55, 179, 182, 242, 331, 746
—Vol 54: 109, 224, 351, 465, 466, 537—Vol
55: 166, 285, 520, 653—Vol 56: 44, 108, 175,
222, 318, 319, 475, 480, 561, 564, 626, 688,
691, 740, 744, 745—Vol 57: 216, 434, 567,
630—Vol 58: 112, 172, 370, 371, 450, 453,
580, 700, 762—Vol 59: 47, 111, 112, 588, 762
—Vol 60: 49, 50, 51, 116, 248, 249, 289, 290,
363, 570, 635—Vol 61: 66, 158, 704, 707, 912
—Vol 62: 20, 52, 120, 121, 122, 387, 389, 390,
456—Vol 63; 60, 295, 372—Vol 64: 160,
309, 446, 713, 758—Vol 65: 120, 297, 366,
438, 636, 762—Vol 66: 57, 161, 250, 308, 534,
600, 732—Vol 67: 115, 292, 514, 517, 645, 713
—Vol 68: 123, 156, 487, 490, 491, 554—Vol
69: 161, 244, 246, 564, 630—Vol 70: 358,
708, 710, 1019, 1165, 1166—Vol 71: 88, 357,
762, 958, 1027—Vol 72: (3-73), (3-79), (5-
67), (7-74), (7-75), (10-94)—Vol 73: (5-89)
—Vol 74: (3-44), (4-53), (11-55), (11-57),
(11-58)—Vol 75: (2-59), (5-46), (5-47),
(6-37), (9-40), (10-67)—Vol 76: 710—Vol
77: 332, 481, 769—Vol 78: 457—Vol 79: 194,
332—Vol 80: 46, 84, 154, 335, 382, 510, 557,
589, 657—Vol 81: 316, 516, 569, 629, 630, 631
—Vol 82: 312, 397, 398, 501, 725, 795, 797, 934
—Vol 83: 171, 173, 261, 440, 441, 521, 523,
524, 718, 873, 944, 946—Vol 84: 69, 247, 324,
326, 521, 523, 632, 633, 702, 705
SMITHERS_____Vol 77: 238, 333
SMITHSON___Vol 19: 628—Vol 21: 58—Vol
65; 506—Vol 68: 686
SMOCK_____Vol 52: 358, 733—Vol 70, 1170
SMOOT___Vol 38: 87, 273—Vol 39: 274—Vol
49: 287—Vol 53: 376—Vol 63: 632
SMYSER_____Vol 39: 225
SMYTH___Vol 49: 287—Vol 53: 55—Vol 58:
453—Vol 63: 507—Vol 82: 930
SMYTHE_____Vol 43: 427
SNAVELEY_____Vol 66: 305
SNEAD___Vol 34: 423—Vol 44: 383—Vol 45:
112, 325—Vol 46: 243—Vol 47: 23—Vol 50:
275—Vol 59: 682
SNEDEKER_____Vol 77: 117
SNEED___Vol 44: 232—Vol 49: 396—Vol 55:
597—Vol 58: 588—Vol 59: 442
SNELL___Vol 38: 330—Vol 44: 150—Vol 64:
257—Vol 70: 1168—Vol 75: (8-43)—Vol
80: 382
SNELLING_____Vol 58: 173—Vol 83: 945
SNIFFEN_____Vol 68: 734
SNIGGERS_____Vol 48: 372
SNIPES_____Vol 45: 114
SNODDY_____Vol 60: 571—Vol 66: 249
SNODGRASS___Vol 48: 55—Vol 53: 53—Vol
67: 514—Vol 79: 561
SNOOK___Vol 38: 219—Vol 39: 275—Vol 47:
29—Vol 82: 502
SNOVER_____Vol 56: 560—Vol 60: 116
SNOW___Vol 21: 496—Vol 23: 166—Vol 30:
257—Vol 41: 125, 210, 213—Vol 48: 202,
305—Vol 50: 357—Vol 53: 243—Vol 55:

166—Vol 56: 172—Vol 58: 648—Vol 60: 365—Vol 61: 707, 869—Vol 67: 145, 514—Vol 75: (2-59)—Vol 80: 155—Vol 81: 629 —Vol 85: 520
SNOWDEN...Vol 39: 276—Vol 61: 152—Vol 69: 565
SNUDER.............................Vol 59: 764
SNUFF...........................…Vol 72: (2-63)
SNUKE...........................Vol 54: 537
SNYDER...Vol 20: 62—Vol 28: 263—Vol 33: 709—Vol 44: 313—Vol 45: 121, 326—Vol 46: 244—Vol 48: 444—Vol 54: 536—Vol 63: 374, 572—Vol 67: 577, 714—Vol 68: 683, 732—Vol 69: 120—Vol 70: 1165—Vol 72: (4-82)—Vol 73: (12-63)—Vol 76: 783, 928 —Vol 78: 53—Vol 81: 430—Vol 83: 793
SODOWSKI........................Vol 38: 220
SOLES.............................Vol 53: 328
SOLLARS......................Vol 71: 86
SOLLERS........................Vol 72: (11-58)
SOLOMON...Vol 54: 650—Vol 57: 353—Vol 60: 114
SOLT.............................Vol 55: 338
SOMERBY......................Vol 24: 150
SOMERS.........................Vol 54: 540
SOMERVILLE...Vol 45: 194, 327—Vol 58: 764
SOMMER...........................Vol 50: 65
SOMMERS.........................Vol 54: 225
SOMMERVILLE.........Vol 66: 366—Vol 67: 387
SONBER.............................Vol 84: 966
SOPER...Vol 8: 253—Vol 44: 234—Vol 48: 65, 202—Vol 49: 131—Vol 54: 224—Vol 59: 315—Vol 60: 698—Vol 66: 306
SOPP.............................Vol 35: 1265
SORREL..........................Vol 45: 124
SORRELLS.........Vol 30: 66—Vol 38: 329
SORSBY..........................Vol 73: (9-66)
SOUBER............................Vol 84: 966
SOUDER............................Vol 19: 205
SOUL...........Vol 22: 156—Vol 32: 162
SOULE...Vol 32: 718—Vol 46: 104—Vol 48: 59—Vol 50: 343—Vol 52: 53—Vol 64: 520—Vol 79: 113
SOULTHEIR.......................Vol 19: 205
SOUSLEY.........Vol 48: 122—Vol 57: 744
SOUTH.........Vol 44: 154—Vol 45: 200, 329
SOUTHARD...Vol 27: 736—Vol 42: 138, 333 —Vol 49: 133—Vol 65: 508
SOUTHBOUTH......................Vol 36: 217
SOUTHERLAND..........Vol 59: 589, 680
SOUTHERN........................Vol 41: 34
SOUTHESLEY......................Vol 48: 122
SOUTHGATE.........Vol 36: 216—Vol 46: 22
SOUTHWICK...Vol 43: 544—Vol 45: 18, 239 —Vol 60: 572, 746
SOUTHWORTH...Vol 19: 206—Vol 20: 59—Vol 26: 241—Vol 58: 502
SOWARD..........................Vol 47: 196
SOWDERM.........................Vol 78: 457
SOWELL..........................Vol 37: 160
SPAFFORD.......Vol 40: 172—Vol 58: 372, 699
SPAHR...........................Vol 77: 603
SPAIN..........Vol 66: 162—Vol 73: (11-66)
SPALDING...Vol 19: 69—Vol 25: 967—Vol 45: 321—Vol 61: 856—Vol 70: 359, 574—Vol 71: 461
SPANGLER...Vol 45: 110—Vol 56: 56, 560—Vol 57: 350—Vol 73: (1-63)
SPANN...........................Vol 58: 502

SPARHAWK...Vol 26: 143, 242, 243, 338—Vol 40: 273
SPARK..............Vol 44: 382—Vol 78: 155
SPARKMAN........................Vol 82: 862
SPARKS...Vol 23: 64—Vol 29: 46—Vol 39: 275—Vol 46: 244—Vol 48: 56—Vol 50: 350 —Vol 51: 353—Vol 56: 45—Vol 72: (7-74) —Vol 76: 62, 859
SPARR...........................Vol 53: 244
SPARRELL.......................Vol 57: 480
SPARROW.......Vol 42: 190, 235—Vol 79: 107
SPATZ...........................Vol 63: 742
SPAULDING...Vol 18: 181—Vol 43: 601—Vol 45: 337—Vol 56: 174—Vol 61: 473—Vol 70: 359, 574—Vol 71: 461
SPAUN...........................Vol 55: 445
SPAWN...........................Vol 76: 860
SPEAKE..........................Vol 61: 608
SPEAKS..........................Vol 55: 713
SPEAR..........Vol 46: 388—Vol 75: (7-35)
SPEARS...Vol 38: 36—Vol 64: 716—Vol 83: 871
SPEER..............Vol 48: 307—Vol 67: 711
SPEIGHT.........................Vol 64: 760
SPELMAN.........Vol 63: 102—Vol 70: 577
SPENCE...Vol 58: 110—Vol 66: 461, 601—Vol 76: 219—Vol 83: 335—Vol 84: 69
SPENCER...Vol 19: 628—Vol 20: 165—Vol 21: 58, 61, 167, 250, 400, 495—Vol 25: 799—Vol 27: 44, 671—Vol 28: 163—Vol 33: 474, 1031—Vol 34: 198, 539—Vol 36: 216, 217, 572—Vol 37: 351, 355, 486, 487—Vol 38: 84—Vol 39: 22—Vol 40: 26—Vol 42: 15, 191, 270—Vol 43: 495, 496, 598, 599—Vol 45: 26, 103, 197, 191, 328—Vol 46: 23, 159—Vol 47: 267, 271, 273—Vol 48: 119, 442—Vol 53: 177—Vol 55: 209, 602—Vol 56: 371 —Vol 57: 746—Vol 60: 157—Vol 61: 869—Vol 62: 53—Vol 64: 758—Vol 65: 366—Vol 67: 42, 146, 240—Vol 70: 352—Vol 71: 762 —Vol 73: (1-63)—Vol 75: (10-65)—Vol 76: 653—Vol 77: 479, 768—Vol 78: 456, 457, 650 —Vol 80: 588—Vol 82: 935—Vol 83: 521—Vol 84: 705
SPENGLER........................Vol 73: (1-63)
SPENSER........................Vol 53: 179, 633
SPERING........................Vol 21: 251
SPERRY...Vol 24: 58, 261—Vol 30: 61—Vol 31: 863—Vol 50: 350—Vol 54: 353—Vol 60: 571, 699
SPICER...Vol 10: 179—Vol 29: 510—Vol 39: 327—Vol 41: 20, 30—Vol 45: 18, 107, 189
SPICKARD.......................Vol 70: 456
SPICKERMAN.....................Vol 53: 629
SPICKNALL......................Vol 74: (4-48)
SPIER...Vol 31: 412—Vol 43: 424—Vol 46: 246
SPIERS...Vol 38: 36—Vol 59: 314, 587, 762
SPILLERS.......................Vol 24: 542
SPILLMAN.......................Vol 51: 354
SPINDLER.........Vol 73: (1-63), (11-66)
SPINK...Vol 27: 382—Vol 28: 58—Vol 31: 52
SPINNEY........................Vol 23: 400
SPINNING.......................Vol 31: 414
SPITLER........................Vol 71: 1024
SPIVEY.........Vol 45: 115—Vol 64: 256
SPODE...........................Vol 60: 573
SPOFFORD...Vol 54: 52—Vol 59: 174—Vol 67: 388
SPOKESFIELD....................Vol 50: 69

SPOONER........Vol '41: 210, 213—Vol 49: 191
SPOOR....Vol 35: 1264—Vol 45: 105—Vol 48:
55, 305—Vol 65: 248
SPOTSWOOD................Vol 62: 501,·650
SPOTTS................Vol 62: 501, 650
SPRAGGINS................ ....Vol 83: 262, 795
SPRAGUE...Vol 22: 272—Vol 26: 53—Vol
28: 164—Vol 31: 750—Vol 34: 537—Vol 35:
54, 265, 652—Vol 36: 216—Vol 45: 24—Vol
50: 356—Vol 56: 225—Vol 63: 168, 293, 741
—Vol 71: 673, 958—Vol 78: 246—Vol 82:
932
SPRAKE................Vol 43: 423, 597
SPRIGG................Vol 65: 247
SPRIMSTEIN................Vol 39: 276
SPRING...Vol 22: 156—Vol 44: 233—Vol 49:
395—Vol 72: (3-80)
SPRINGER...Vol 41: 212—Vol 42: 138, 267—
Vol 44: 148—Vol 64: 520—Vol 69: 245—
Vol 79: 602—Vol 82: 396, 727, 793
SPRINGES................Vol 43: 426
SPRINGSTEEN................Vol 42: 139
SPRINK................Vol 22: 374
SPRONG................Vol 21: 496
SPROTT................Vol 46: 160
SPROUL................Vol 44: 382
SPROULE................Vol 60: 571
SPROWL................Vol 57: 313
SPRY................Vol 44: 225—Vol 54: 172
SPURGIN................Vol 49: 395
SPURLOCK................Vol 80: 154
SQUIER................Vol 48: 306—Vol 57: 116
SQUIERS................ ....Vol 53: 53
SQUIRE...Vol 19: 628—Vol 21: 58—Vol 25:
717—Vol 28: 549—Vol 31: 52, 585—Vol 32:
162—Vol 38: 220—Vol 39: 21, 223—Vol 40:
78—Vol 41: 71—Vol 49: 131—Vol 64: 260
—Vol 81: 429
SQUIRES...Vol 32: 162—Vol 37: 67—Vol 38:
32—Vol 46: 21—Vol 47: 193, 388—Vol 54:
650—Vol 64: 445—Vol 74: (11-57)
STAATS...Vol 46: 332—Vol 56: 108—Vol 57:'
480—Vol 66: 536, 732—Vol 74: (7-53),
(8-53)
STACEY................Vol 50: 354
STACKHOUSE................Vol 46: 384
STACY................Vol 59: 48, 682—Vol 63: 741
STADDEN................Vol 43: 546—Vol 50: 183
STADLER................Vol 45: 119
STAFFORD...Vol 34: 540—Vol 35: 437, 1266
—Vol 56: 480—Vol 61: 913—Vol 70: 877—
Vol 82: 63 Vol 84: 447
STAGG................Vol 83: 793
STAGE................Vol 78: 502
STAHL................Vol 71: 675
STAINS................Vol 80: 432
STAKE................Vol 22: 375
STALCUP................ ....Vol 27: 45
STALEY...Vol 43: 486—Vol 58: 764—Vol 64:
522—Vol 69: 119
STALLCUP................Vol 56: 482
STAMBAUGH........ Vol 62: 459—Vol 83: 628
STAMM...Vol 45: 122—Vol 47: 83—Vol 59:
388
STAMPER...Vol 38: 330—Vol 43: 488—Vol
44: 23
STAMPS................Vol 47: 394
STANDARD................ Vol 24: 542
STANDIFER................Vol 83: 946
STANDISH...Vol 27: 382, 806—Vol 28: 161—

Vol 30: 148—Vol 39: 224—Vol 42: 13, 340—
Vol 43: 604—Vol 44: 147—Vol 58: 500—Vol
60: 506, 696, 745
STANDLY................Vol 82: 726, 727, 793
STANDRING................Vol 27: 891
STANFER................Vol 58: 369
STANFIELD................Vol 69: 119
STANHOPE................Vol 44: 28—Vol 47: 198
STANLEY...Vol 27: 45, 381—Vol 45: 198—
Vol 49: 133, 191—Vol 54: 649—Vol 56: 47—
Vol 57: 114, 310—Vol 67: 576—Vol 68: 56—
Vol 70: 359, 573—Vol 73: (2-64)—Vol 83:
93
STANNARD...Vol 33: 707—Vol 37: 151—Vol
39: 22
STANSBURY...Vol 64: 446—Vol 67: 118, 648
STANSELL................Vol 31:' 670
STANTON...Vol 7: 562—Vol 10: 182—Vol
28: 259, 263—Vol 31: 584—Vol 35: 57—Vol
43: 600—Vol 44: 233, 234, 383—Vol 45: 110
—Vol 46: 239, 240, 331—Vol 47: 32—Vol
61: 150—Vol 70: 355, 1169—Vol 74: (3-44)
—Vol 83: 521. 524
STANYAN................Vol 33: 955
STAPLES...Vol 29: 288—Vol 30: 541—Vol
31: 860—Vol 43: 495, 724—Vol 45: 115, 326
—Vol 47: 31—Vol 66: 122—Vol 74: (11-61)
—Vol 82: 500
STAPLETON...Vol 75: (8-42)—Vol 84: 447
STAPLIN...Vol 50: 352—Vol 58: 369—Vol
74: (9-50)
STARBIRD...Vol 42: 194—Vol 43: 419—Vol
45: 197—Vol 82: 860
STARK...Vol 29: 47, 651—Vol 31: 861—Vol
32: 620, 634—Vol 33: 40, 473—Vol 35: 1266
—Vol 38: 272—Vol 40: 74, 108—Vol 41:
120, 122, 124, 162—Vol 42: 72, 76, 139—Vol
43: 416, 417, 418, 545—Vol 44: 80—Vol·45:
128—Vol 50: 190, 278—Vol 52: 425—Vol
55: 714—Vol 62: 460—Vol 64: 259—Vol 71:
762—Vol 72: (1-63)—Vol 80: 85—Vol 83:
874—Vol 84: 444
STARKE...Vol 45: 106—Vol 57: 435—Vol 58:
764—Vol 61: 707, 911—Vol 62: 55, 56
STARKEY...Vol 46: 332—Vol 59: 764—Vol
61: 275—Vol 76: 709
STARKS................Vol 34: 540—Vol 42: 267
STARKWETHER................Vol 57: 744
STARN................Vol 54: 466
STARNS................Vol 43: 541—Vol 80: 335
STARR...Vol 40: 226—Vol 4b: 200—Vol 49:
187—Vol 57: 113—Vol 70: 206—Vol 79:
368—Vol 82: 862
STARRITT................Vol 71: 1111
STATLER................Vol 55: 444—Vol 59: 312
STATON................Vol 42: 190
STATTEN................Vol 62: 308
STATTS................Vol 64: 713
STAUFFER................Vol 82:·795
STAUNTON................Vol 42: 334—Vol 46: 237
STEADMAN...Vol 45: 127—Vol 80: 335—Vol
82: 797
STEARN................Vol 54: 466
STEARNS...Vol 40: 272—Vol 41: 213—Vol
42: 186, 191—Vol 43: 497, 543—Vol 44:
148, 386—Vol 45: 193, 241—Vol 46: 235—
Vol 58: 453—Vol 68: 239, 553—Vol 69: 764
—Vol 80: 45—Vol 83: 523
STEBBENS................ ....Vol 41: 210
STEBBINS...Vol 30: 539—Vol 42: 13. 134.

269—Vol 43: 482—Vol 49: 190
STEDMAN—Vol 19: 206—Vol 22: 996—Vol 42: 80, 189—Vol 65: 300—Vol 82: 797
STEED—————————————Vol 63: 572
STEEL—Vol 31: 748—Vol 43: 484—Vol 48: 124—Vol 61: 868, 908—Vol 62: 460—Vol 70: 1019—Vol 71: 87, 239—Vol 80: 193
STEELE—Vol 18: 58—Vol 26: 57—Vol 29: 649—Vol 32: 508—Vol 35: 656—Vol 38: 218 —Vol 39: 327—Vol 41: 34—Vol 42: 338— Vol 43: 419, 427, 484, 487, 597—Vol 44: 233 —Vol 46: 22—Vol 47: 269, 270—Vol 49: 133, 284—Vol 50: 351—Vol 51: 301—Vol 54: 175—Vol 55: 522—Vol 59: 314, 587— Vol 60: 363, 635—Vol 61: 868—Vol 63: 59— Vol 65: 245, 634—Vol 68: 686—Vol 70: 1019—Vol 71: 87, 239, 761—Vol 74: (11-59) —Vol 75: (4-52-53)—Vol 77: 479—Vol 80: 45
STEELEMAN————————————Vol 39: 327
STEELY————————Vol 55: 598—Vol 69: 362
STEEN——————————————Vol 48: 61
STEER——————————Vol 56: 744—Vol 57: 627
STEERE——————————————Vol 41: 123
STEFFENHAGEN——————————Vol 83: 945
STEIDLEY————————————Vol 74: (1-49)
STEIN————————Vol 53: 53—Vol 83: 944
STEINBERGER——————————Vol 31: 414
STEINER—Vol 2: 694—Vol 37: 157—Vol 82: 798, 933
STEINHAUER—Vol 67: 241—Vol 74: (3-45) —Vol 75: (3-40)
STEINMETZ————————————Vol 52: 733
STELL—————————————— Vol 27: 46
STELLE——————————————Vol 77: 480
STELLMAN————————————Vol 39: 102
STEMPLE—————————————Vol 69: 565
STEPHEN—————————————Vol 38: 218
STEPHENS—Vol 30: 542—Vol 39: 223—Vol 40:23—Vol 44: 79—Vol 45: 17, 104, 109, 325 —Vol 48: 123—Vol 50: 280—Vol 51: 301, 303—Vol 55: 444, 519—Vol 56: 109, 372, 745—Vol 58: 452—Vol 60: 114, 290, 503— Vol 61: 65, 155—Vol 68: 123—Vol 69: 157— Vol 70: 1266—Vol 77: 243—Vol 81: 631— Vol 83: 1015
STEPHENSON—Vol 21: 403—Vol 29: 513— Vol 58: 450, 650—Vol 65: 296, 297, 760— Vol 66: 362—Vol 77: 117, 663, 725
STEPTOE—Vol 26: 559—Vol 43: 497—Vol 57: 174—Vol 61: 153
STERLING—Vol 28: 262—Vol 53: 241, 694— Vol 57: 691—Vol 84: 325
STERNBERG————————Vol 23: 244—Vol 45: 321
STERNBERGER————————————Vol 24: 55
STERNEMAN————————Vol 73: (11-67)
STERRETT————————————Vol 53: 377
STETSON————————Vol 63: 508—Vol 70: 457
STEUTEL—————————————Vol 29: 717
STEVENS—Vol 17: 570—Vol 18: 181—Vol 19: 430, 628—Vol 20: 165, 351, 1064—Vol 22: 376—Vol 23: 326—Vol 26: 57—Vol 27: 380, 382—Vol 28: 161, 162, 259—Vol 32: 59, 160, 282—Vol 33: 475, 706, 710, 959—Vol 37: 158, 270—Vol 39: 22, 276—Vol 40: 25— Vol 41: 165, 214—Vol 44: 82, 85—Vol 45: 110, 114, 120—Vol 46: 102, 238, 239, 389— Vol 47: 23, 190—Vol 50: 193—Vol 53: 377— Vol 54: 53—Vol 55: 165, 337, 520—Vol 56: 109—Vol 58: 112, 648—Vol 59: 653—Vol

60: 418, 505, 572, 699, 745—Vol 61: 63, 157— Vol 62: 121—Vol 64: 259, 445—Vol 65: 438, 441, 570, 571—Vol 66: 56, 363, 364—Vol 67: 715, 716—Vol 68: 551—Vol 69: 361—Vol 70: 356, 358, 1170—Vol 72: (9-87)—Vol 77: 479, 602—Vol 80: 383—Vol 83: 171
STEVENSON—Vol 29: 513—Vol 30: 63, 441 —Vol 32: 720—Vol 40: 77—Vol 42: 338— Vol 48: 120—Vol 54: 648—Vol 55: 601— Vol 56: 413—Vol 58: 369—Vol 59: 681— Vol 60: 289, 632—Vol 65: 758, 762—Vol 68: 284—Vol 70: 574—Vol 74: (2-43)—Vol 76: 927—Vol 79: 518—Vol 81: 431
STEWARD—————————————Vol 55: 522
STEWART—Vol 20: 60—Vol 21: 58—Vol 24: 149—Vol 27: 668, 807—Vol 30: 439—Vol 33: 40, 475, 959—Vol 34: 199, 422—Vol 36: 218—Vol 37: 68: 486—Vol 39: 326—Vol 40: 75—Vol 41: 32—Vol 43: 421, 422, 604— Vol 44: 25, 310—Vol 45: 23, 26, 105, 184, 191 —Vol 46: 22, 158—Vol 47: 95, 199—Vol 48: 55, 121, 449—Vol 53: 746—Vol 54: 421— Vol 56: 47—Vol 57: 173—Vol 58: 173, 241, 368, 500, 651—Vol 59: 653—Vol 61: 469— Vol 63: 59, 571—Vol 65: 249—Vol 66: 599— Vol 67: 46, 116—Vol 68: 491—Vol 69: 501, 565, 680, 681—Vol 70: 359, 1265—Vol 71: 1025—Vol 74: (11-59)—Vol 76: 401—Vol 78: 107—Vol 79: 332—Vol 81: 429, 518— Vol 82: 861, 935—Vol 83: 260
STHRESHLEY—————————————Vol 61: 909
STICKNEY—Vol 41: 32—Vol 58: 329—Vol 60: 506, 696, 745—Vol 82: 396
STIDHAM—————————Vol 43: 541—Vol 62: 773
STIEGEL——————————————Vol 44: 84
STIENE————————————————Vol 83: 440
STILES—Vol 37: 487—Vol 38: 87—Vol 39: 326—Vol 52: 435—Vol 53: 244, 629, 747— Vol 56: 371—Vol 61: 708—Vol 65: 441, 508 —Vol 66: 56, 363
STILL————————————Vol 46: 240—Vol 77: 480
STILLMAN—Vol 29: 46, 650—Vol 41: 215— Vol 42: 343—Vol 47: 263—Vol 49: 43—Vol 60: 506—Vol 61: 788—Vol 62: 55
STILLSON—Vol 21: 497—Vol 22: 154—Vol 27: 45, 669—Vol 31: 586
STILLWELL—Vol 45: 110—Vol 46: 391— Vol 47: 271—Vol 63: 247—Vol 67: 713—Vol 73: (9-65)
STILSON—————————Vol 53: 692—Vol 54: 650
STILTS—————————————————Vol 64: 759
STIMPSON————————Vol 46: 393—Vol 47: 87
STINSON—Vol 60: 249—Vol 83: 943—Vol 84: 702
STIRE—————————————————Vol 70: 1266
STIRMAN———————————————— Vol 56: 44
STITCH————————————————Vol 45: 101
STITES——————————————————Vol 80: 588
STITH—Vol 41: 72—Vol 45: 101—Vol 48: 62 —Vol 67: 515
STOCKARD—Vol 43: 544—Vol 44: 153, 310— Vol 48: 441
STOCKBRIDGE————————Vol 15: 350—Vol 28: 58
STOCKDALE—Vol 66: 161—Vol 80: 432— Vol 82: 795—Vol 83: 173
STOCKDELL————————————Vol 62: 309
STOCKER————————Vol 45: 23—Vol 75: (5-44)
STOCKETT—————————————Vol 65: 505
STOCKHAM————————————————Vol 59: 389

STOCKING—Vol 22: 157—Vol 46: 23—Vol 66: 308—Vol 67: 113
STOCKINGER .... Vol 51: 355
STOCKMAN .... Vol 83: 442
STOCKTON—Vol 31: 587—Vol 37: 65, 74, 395, 396—Vol 38: 85—Vol 46: 156, 331—Vol 49: 192, 283, 350—Vol 50: 70—Vol 64: 716 —Vol 67: 291, 515—Vol 74: (2-41)—Vol 76: 218—Vol 83: 794—Vol 84: 635
STOCKWELL—Vol 38: 220—Vol 42: 263, 268—Vol 48: 307—Vol 50: 349—Vol 51: 235 —Vol 57: 115—Vol 61: 606—Vol 66: 826— Vol 69: 160—Vol 70: 56, 202
STODDARD—Vol 22: 268—Vol 23: 468—Vol 32: 508—Vol 42: 192—Vol 43: 605—Vol 45: 239—Vol 56: 370, 562—Vol 59: 587—Vol 70: 878—Vol 71: 676—Vol 84: 519
STOEL .... Vol 32: 284
STOKELEY—Vol 29: 801—Vol 33: 955, 1168
STOKES—Vol 43: 488, 542—Vol 46: 337—Vol 50: 280—Vol 56: 561, 741—Vol 61: 788— Vol 66: 825—Vol 72: (9-88)—Vol 74: (11-59)
STOKLEY .... Vol 33: 42
STOLLICKER .... Vol 32: 719
STOLP .... Vol 48: 306
STONE—Vol 17: 480—Vol 23: 64—Vol 26: 338—Vol 28: 366—Vol 32: 284—Vol 38: 88, 114, 328—Vol 39: 21, 103, 222, 327—Vol 41: 71—Vol 42: 341, 343—Vol 43: 422—Vol 44: 83—Vol 45: 28, 102, 112, 114, 323—Vol 46: 103—Vol 47: 195—Vol 48: 54, 372, 447 —Vol 49: 48—Vol 50: 190, 192, 351—Vol 52: 360—Vol 54: 172, 468, 535, 650—Vol 55: 284, 446—Vol 56: 744—Vol 59: 525—Vol 60: 635—Vol 63: 428, 507, 570, 697, 739— Vol 64: 523, 759—Vol 65: 367, 761—Vol 66: 252, 535, 732, 734—Vol 68: 155—Vol 71: 1027—Vol 72: (4-83)—Vol 73: (4-83)—Vol 76: 62—Vol 77: 183—Vol 79: 332, 562, 613 —Vol 80: 557—Vol 81: 315, 517—Vol 82: 935—Vol 83: 945
STONEBARGER .... Vol 31: 414—Vol 43: 493
STONEBREAKER—Vol 21: 335—Vol 56: 44
STONEHAM .... Vol 48: 61
STONEHOUSE .... Vol 47: 32
STONER—Vol 40: 228—Vol 52: 320—Vol 56: 687—Vol 80: 431
STONEUM .... Vol 48: 61
STOOKEY—Vol 75: (10-64), (11-70)—Vol 77: 332
STOOPS .... Vol 38: 221—Vol 68: 285
STOPHET .... Vol 59: 239
STORER—Vol 21: 335, 495—Vol 22: 154— Vol 30: 146
STORES .... Vol 48: 122—Vol 84: 636
STOREY .... Vol 55: 338
STORF .... Vol 27: 44
STORKE .... Vol 53: 632
STORM—Vol 46: 103—Vol 48: 53—Vol 50: 350—Vol 53: 571—Vol 54: 114, 310—Vol 55: 714—Vol 61: 788—Vol 62: 247—Vol 63: 634—Vol 70: 574—Vol 71: 838
STORMS—Vol 19: 432—Vol 31: 587—Vol 53: 629
STORY—Vol 22: 156—Vol 29: 289—Vol 31: 586—Vol 32: 62—Vol 37: 161—Vol 39: 23, 102—Vol 43: 601—Vol 80: 432—Vol 83: 172—Vol 84: 520
STOTESBURY .... Vol 67: 714

STOUFFER .... Vol 46: 99—Vol 49: 188
STOUGH .... Vol 79: 369
STOUGHTON—Vol 26: 340—Vol 27: 380— Vol 43: 418—Vol 59: 765—Vol 63: 570— Vol 75: (8-43)
STOUT—Vol 29: 510—Vol 38: 33—Vol 44: 312, 313—Vol 45: 28, 191—Vol 46: 21—Vol 50: 354—Vol 56: 688—Vol 64: 651—Vol 70: 455, 574—Vol 71: 956—Vol 81: 264
STOVALL .... Vol 65: 635
STOVER—Vol 54: 351—Vol 56: 176—Vol 62: 585—Vol 64: 390—Vol 67: 146—Vol 74: (7-52), (8-52)—Vol 75: (4-55)—Vol 77: 481—Vol 78: 457—Vol 81: 20
STOW—Vol 33: 1033—Vol 59: 314—Vol 61: 278
STOWE—Vol 56: 175—Vol 59: 314—Vol 69: 56
STOWELL .... Vol 42: 80, 266, 268
STOWERS .... Vol 43: 487
STOY .... Vol 23: 398
STRADER .... Vol 78: 107
STRAHL .... Vol 45: 21
STRAIGHT—Vol 21: 648—Vol 44: 235—Vol 67: 514—Vol 77: 52
STRAIN .... Vol 56: 742
STRAINS .... Vol 52: 626
STRAIT .... Vol 67: 514
STRAITS .... Vol 34: 67
STRANAHAN .... Vol 33: 41—Vol 46: 24
STRANG .... Vol 30: 336, 337
STRANGE .... Vol 75: (9-37)—Vol 78: 108
STRANK .... Vol 52: 436
STRATE .... Vol 62: 308
STRATTON—Vol 29: 801—Vol 30: 542—Vol 32: 59—Vol 36: 350—Vol 43: 603—Vol 82: 860—Vol 83: 335
STRAUB .... Vol 47: 395
STRAW .... Vol 48: 60—Vol 60: 115
STRAWN .... Vol 56: 226—Vol 59: 763
STRAWSON .... Vol 42: 191
STRECH .... Vol 80: 587
STREET—Vol 31: 667—Vol 36: 577—Vol 37: 64, 147—Vol 55: 601—Vol 61: 552, 911
STREETER .... Vol 43: 723—Vol 45: 27
STREIGHT .... Vol 67: 514
STRETCH—Vol 40: 76—Vol 45: 188—Vol 67: 383
STRICKLAND—Vol 22: 679—Vol 24: 457— Vol 29: 289—Vol 33: 1032—Vol 50: 190— Vol 52: 231—Vol 53: 53—Vol 65: 571—Vol 66: 364, 730—Vol 67: 716—Vol 75: (3-41), (5-44)—Vol 80: 193
STRICKLER—Vol 43: 496—Vol 45: 101, 107
STRICKLING .... Vol 72: (12-67)
STRIEB .... Vol 52: 436
STRINGER .... Vol 50: 192
STRINGFELLOW .... Vol 76: 400
STRODE .... Vol 45: 187
STROHL .... Vol 29: 512
STROHM .... Vol 49: 192
STROM .... Vol 74: (4-52)
STRONG—Vol 21: 62, 250—Vol 29: 802—Vol 31: 588, 667—Vol 38: 35—Vol 40: 77, 108— Vol 44: 83—Vol 45: 110, 113, 238, 325—Vol 46: 239—Vol 47: 269—Vol 56: 226—Vol 57: 117—Vol 61: 473, 911—Vol 71: 241—Vol 83: 260
STRONT .... Vol 46: 387
STROTHER—Vol 23: 168—Vol 30: 540—Vol

31: 861—Vol 36: 351—Vol 37: 488—Vol 38: 36, 113—Vol 39: 273—Vol 43: 421—Vol 44: 22—Vol 46: 238—Vol 53: 178—Vol 55: 338, 603, 652—Vol 56: 223—Vol 58: 173—Vol 60: 697—Vol 67: 292—Vol 71: 1026—Vol 74: (7-53), (8-53)—Vol 84: 704

STROUD....Vol 26: 242, 559—Vol 66: 825— Vol 79: 369—Vol 81: 264

STROUP....Vol 47: 395—Vol 48: 61—Vol 62: 309

STROUPE..Vol 48: 61

STROUSE...Vol 76: 144

STROUT...............................Vol 49: 187—Vol 52: 53

STRUTHERS...................................Vol 20: 351

STRYKER.................Vol 41: 215—Vol 58: 370

STUART....Vol 22: 54, 154—Vol 26: 336—Vol 33: 40—Vol 39: 104—Vol 41: 32—Vol 43: 421, 422, 602, 604—Vol 44: 314—Vol 45: 27—Vol 55: 108—Vol 56: 47, 370—Vol 57: 629—Vol 61: 610—Vol 63: 571—Vol 65: 249, 367, 507, 568—Vol 69: 120—Vol 70: 1265—Vol 73: (8-83)—Vol 80: 190—Vol 84: 703

STUBBERFIELD...................Vol 74: (5-42)

STUBBLEFIELD....Vol 53: 494—Vol 56: 225 —Vol 80: 46

STUBBS....Vol 53: 179—Vol 79: 518—Vol 80: 46—Vol 82: 931

STUCKER...Vol 39: 274

STUCKEY...Vol 77: 52

STUCKSLAGER...............................Vol 70: 880

STUCKY..Vol 33: 957

STUDLEY................................. Vol 69: 630

STUKES...Vol 35: 438

STULL....Vol 50: 68, 187—Vol 51: 356—Vol 56: 318—Vol 61: 230, 275—Vol 83: 439

STUMP....Vol 64: 159, 386, 387, 443—Vol 77: 241—Vol 83: 1015

STURGEON....Vol 15: 220—Vol 39: 102, 324 —Vol 63: 428

STURGES.......................................Vol 49: 136, 285

STURGIS....Vol 33: 708—Vol 35: 655—Vol 42: 343—Vol 43: 489—Vol 54: 589—Vol 65: 366—Vol 67: 385—Vol 72: (10-94)

STURM...Vol 61: 64

STURMAN............... ....Vol 55: 598

STURR...Vol 84: 636

STURTEVANT........Vol 64: 714—Vol 77: 664

STURTZ.............................Vol 68: 492, 732

STUTSMAN.....................................Vol 43: 493

STUTSON................Vol 59: 387—Vol 63: 508

STUTZMAN...................................Vol 43: 493

STUYVESANT............Vol 59: 525—Vol 64: 59

STYERS...Vol 83: 440

SUBIN...Vol 28: 480

SUBLETT...................................... Vol 49: 189

SUBLETTE..Vol 43: 496

SUDDITH..................Vol 45: 112—Vol 82: 653

SUDDUTH.................................Vol 45: 123, 327

SUETTER..................... ....Vol 40: 227

SUFFRON... Vol 71:675

SUGGETT....Vol 29: 512—Vol 30: 66—Vol 41: 121—Vol 42: 11—Vol 43: 545—Vol 61: 61—Vol 67: 385

SUITER..Vol 80: 191

SULLINS..Vol 51: 354

SULLIVAN....Vol 25: 967—Vol 31: 414, 590— Vol 37: 354—Vol 42: 268, 334—Vol 43: 723—Vol 44: 25—Vol 48: 60—Vol 51: 302—

Vol 52: 483—Vol 74: (2-40)—Vol 81: 264—, Vol 82: 313—Vol 83: 259

SULTAN...Vol 58: 451

SUMMER....Vol 21: 251—Vol 32: 282—Vol 47: 396—Vol 81: 517—Vol 83: 873

SUMMERS....Vol 35: 58—Vol 38: 331—Vol 46: 98—Vol 59: 315—Vol 64: 715—Vol 67: 148—Vol 69: 631—Vol 72: (4-82)—Vol 75: (5-46)—Vol 76: 928—Vol 78: 53—Vol 79: 112, 113, 283

SUMMONS...Vol 63: 571

SUMNER....Vol 21: 400—Vol 34: 538—Vol 40: 75—Vol 46: 153—Vol 49: 356—Vol 50: 62, 115—Vol 56: 561, 741—Vol 58: 52—Vol 75: (4-54)—Vol 78: 107

SUMTER....Vol 22: 53—Vol 23: 396—Vol 45: 123

SUNDERLAND.................................Vol 57: 219

SUPHEN...Vol 28: 260

SUPPLEE...Vol 59: 314

SUSONG........................Vol 50: 281, 415

SUTHERLAND....Vol 25: 37—Vol 41: 34— Vol 43: 603—Vol 44: 310—Vol 45: 194, 195, 243—Vol 53: 246—Vol 54: 649—Vol 67: 516—Vol 82: 863

SUTHERLIN...................................Vol 26: 339

SUTLIFF...........Vol 47: 193, 388—Vol 48: 54

SUTPHEN....Vol 22: 156—Vol 24: 341—Vol 25: 963—Vol 27: 735—Vol 30: 259—Vol 39: 142—Vol 53: 626

SUTPHIN...Vol 39: 276

SUTTENFIELD...............................Vol 67: 116

SUTTER...........................Vol 43: 544—Vol 44: 84

SUTTLE....Vol 66: 600—Vol 82: 63—Vol 84: 158, 328

SUTTLES...Vol 83: 442

SUTTON....Vol 22: 271—Vol 30: 439, 540, 541 —Vol 42: 190—Vol 47: 196, 391, 395—Vol 48: 58—Vol 49: 390—Vol 50: 70—Vol 52: 625—Vol 53: 178, 492—Vol 57: 690—Vol 64: 587, 716, 756—Vol 65: 571—Vol 67: 443 —Vol 68: 242, 373—Vol 70: 1167—Vol 77: 480—Vol 80: 588—Vol 83: 718

SUYDEM...Vol 29: 512

SWAIN....Vol 36: 756—Vol 38: 327—Vol 41: 70, 127—Vol 42: 12—Vol 44: 315—Vol 45: 114—Vol 52: 109—Vol 54: 467—Vol 55: 523, 597—Vol 61: 708—Vol 75: (2-58)—Vol 83: 171, 172—Vol 84: 67, 445

SWAINE.................Vol 31: 861—Vol 55: 285

SWALES..Vol 79: 561

SWALLOW...................................... Vol 23: 397

SWAN....Vol 24: 262—Vol 27: 670—Vol 43: 605—Vol 44: 151—Vol 46: 24, 155—Vol 47: 271—Vol 53: 377—Vol 54: 112, 174—Vol 58: 370, 761—Vol 61: 608—Vol 62: 459— Vol 65: 760—Vol 73: (9-67)—Vol 74: (1-50)—Vol 75: (2-57)

SWANGER..............Vol 67: 116—Vol 69: 121

SWANGO...Vol 79: 112

SWANK....................................... Vol 57: 217

SWANN....Vol 41: 31, 32—Vol 45: 323—Vol 46: 242—Vol 52: 52—Vol 54: 464—Vol 56: 44, 372—Vol 64: 757—Vol 67: 753

SWANSON....Vol 40: 26—Vol 43: 425—Vol 47: 33—Vol 48: 308

SWARTWOOD....Vol 75: (2-60)—Vol 76: 400 —Vol 79: 34

SWARTZ....Vol 43: 602—Vol 76: 709—Vol 83: 93

SWAYNE..Vol 26: 143
SWEADNER..Vol 22: 156
SWEARENGEN....Vol 43: 546, 599—Vol 44: 80, 310, 381
SWEARINGEN....Vol 49: 189—Vol 67: 385—Vol 74: (7-54), (8-54)—Vol 81: 630
SWEAT..Vol 67: 441
SWEATMAN...Vol 67: 441
SWEENEY....Vol 32: 283—Vol 47: 270, 390—Vol 68: 487—Vol 79: 193
SWEESY...Vol 64: 760
SWEET....Vol 24: 149—Vol 25: 384—Vol 27: 667—Vol 31: 51—Vol 43: 545—Vol 45: 102, 241—Vol 46: 329—Vol 53: 53—Vol 56: 319 —Vol 57: 175—Vol 60: 505—Vol 67: 41, 145, 387, 576—Vol 71: 460, 957—Vol 72: (3-70)—Vol 76: 410, 784—Vol 84: 966'
SWEETING...Vol 65: 300
SWEETLAND....Vol 23: 398—Vol 42: 190— Vol 45: 105—Vol 47: 23—Vol 50: 192—Vol 52: 483—Vol 63: 246
SWEETZEN..............Vol 27: 382—Vol 45: 196
SWENEY......................................Vol 82: 314
SWESSY......................................Vol 65: 160
SWETLAND....Vol 39: 222, 223—Vol 40: 23 —Vol 46: 245—Vol 48: 449—Vol 49: 348— Vol 74: (1-49)—Vol 82: 575
SWETT............Vol 68: 374, 623—Vol 74: (3-44)
SWICK......................................Vol 48: 443
SWIFT....Vol 22: 270—Vol 29: 652—Vol 36: 758—Vol 37: 159—Vol 45: 240—Vol 46: 392 —Vol 48: 304—Vol 50: 189, 357—Vol 56: 629—Vol 57: 40, 745—Vol 58: 502—Vol 70: 204
SWIGAR......................................Vol 64: 308
SWIGER......................................Vol 49: 188
SWINEHART.................................Vol 67: 146
SWINERTON....Vol 44: 234—Vol 66: 600
SWINFORD.................................Vol 78: 107
SWINGLE...................................Vol 19: 307
SWINTON....................................Vol 61: 705
SWISHER....Vol 43: 490—Vol 47: 196—Vol 65: 571—Vol 66: 364—Vol 67: 716—Vol 81: 70
SWITZER..........................Vol 43: 490—Vol 77: 51
SWITZLER.................................Vol 53: 571
SWIZAR......................................Vol 64: 308
SWOPE...............Vol 65: 633—Vol 67: 116
SWORDS.....................................Vol 84: 635
SYBLEY......................................Vol 77: 480
SYDENBOTHAM.....................Vol 30: 338
SYKES.........................Vol 54: 225, 593
SYLVESTER....Vol 34: 68—Vol 43: 488—Vol 46: 28—Vol 56: 627
SYME..Vol 48: 440
SYMMES......Vol 43: 422, 599—Vol 58: 451
SYMONDS...........Vol 54: 592—Vol 59: 681
SYPRET....................................Vol 58: 699*
SYRES......................................Vol 67: 290

T

TAAFFEE..................................Vol 56: 226
TABAR......................................Vol 42: 190
TABB...Vol 80: 45
TABOR....Vol 22: 270—Vol 29: 650—Vol 45: 120—Vol 64: 760
TACKELS...................................Vol 81: 571
TACKETT....Vol 42: 79, 189—Vol 71: 558
TAFE..Vol 56: 226
TAFF..Vol 78: 456

TAFFEE............Vol 56: 226—Vol 77: 539
TAFT....Vol 18: 58—Vol 19: 68—Vol 22: 272 —Vol 26: 57—Vol 30: 260—Vol 45: 111— Vol 50: 60, 185—Vol 52: 53—Vol 61: 65— Vol 63: 294—Vol 76: 582—Vol 83: 523—Vol 84: 327
TAGERT..................Vol 38: 331—Vol 39: 141
TAGGART....Vol 37: 266—Vol 43: 488, 542— Vol 44: 149, 388—Vol 48: 122—Vol 84: 244
TAGGERT.................................Vol 36: 756
TAGUE......................................Vol 82: 141
TAILOR......................................Vol 33: 39
TAINTOR..................................Vol 28: 479
TALBERT.................Vol 81: 511—Vol 84: 325
TALBOT....Vol 43: 425—Vol 44: 312—Vol 45: 18, 102, 104, 196, 238, 324—Vol 46: 155— Vol 47: 83—Vol 52: 563—Vol 53: 182—Vol 55: 18, 47, 166, 446, 522—Vol 56: 563—Vol 58: 451—Vol 66: 250—Vol 67: 386—Vol 68: 121, 442, 626—Vol 72: (2-62)—Vol 84: 325
TALBOTT...................................Vol 48: 123
TALCOTT....Vol 22: 52, 372—Vol 40: 77—Vol 49: 287—Vol 63: 295—Vol 82: 397
TALIAFERRO....Vol 23: 471—Vol 26: 559— Vol 44: 151—Vol 48: 306, 440—Vol 53: 177, 178, 632—Vol 59: 48
TALLEY..................................Vol 75: (9-40)
TALLMADGE....Vol 27: 44—Vol 29: 650—Vol 45: 189—Vol 48: 203, 368
TALLMAN....Vol 19: 627—Vol 43: 604—Vol 44: 81—Vol 64: 257—Vol 71: 356, 676—Vol 74: (4-51)
TALMADGE.........Vol 54: 590—Vol 67: 291
TALMA...................................Vol 52: 563
TALMAN...................................Vol 25: 383
TANDY....Vol 56: 46—Vol 58: 170—Vol 70: 57
TANKERSLEY....Vol 57: 746—Vol 58: 649— Vol 82: 796
TANNEHILL............Vol 40: 75—Vol 71: 844
TANNER....Vol 37: 68—Vol 45: 183—Vol 65: 442, 763—Vol 66: 365
TANNYHILL...........................Vol 78: 600
TANSILL....Vol 39: 225—Vol 44: 315—Vol 45: 236
TANTLINGER.........................Vol 80: 588
TAPLEY............Vol 65: 636—Vol 66: 251
TAPPAN....Vol 26: 141—Vol 43: 423, 540— Vol 48: 442—Vol 50: 66, 186—Vol 81: 73
TAPPEN...................................Vol 27: 44
TAPSCOT....Vol 44: 153—Vol 45: 21—Vol 48: 203—Vol 80: 84
TARBELL.................................Vol 26: 243
TARBOX....Vol 27: 382—Vol 69: 160—Vol 81: 571—Vol 84: 246, 444
TARKINGTON....Vol 75: (8-43)—Vol 83: 336
TARLTON...................................Vol 42: 140
TARPENNING.....................Vol 73: (2-64)
TARPLEY....Vol 42: 190—Vol 45: 105, 235— Vol 47: 22, 271—Vol 65: 636—Vol 66: 251
TARR..............Vol 20: 1064—Vol 57: 746
TARRANT............Vol 58: 649—Vol 73: (9-63)
TARVER....Vol 38: 34—Vol 40: 226—Vol 42: 16, 188—Vol 44: 231, 232, 235, 312—Vol 84: 245
TASH......................Vol 23 · 398—Vol 82: 220
TASNETT.................................Vol 56: 173
TATE....Vol 23: 243, 469—Vol 29: 649—Vol 34: 424—Vol 36: 575—Vol 37: 146, 269— Vol 40: 228—Vol 41: 214—Vol 42: 135, 186 —Vol 45: 190—Vol 49: 133, 282—Vol 65:

437—Vol 67: 646—Vol 76: 219—Vol 84: 965
TATMAN....Vol 69: 246—Vol 70: 207—Vol
74: (5-43)
TAUBERMAN................................Vol 48: 447
TAUGHENBAUGH....................Vol 51: 354
TAYLOR....Vol 17: 61, 390—Vol 19: 626—Vol
20: 278—Vol 22: 54, 269, 372—Vol 24: 543
—Vol 25: 716, 964—Vol 26: 53, 55, 336, 560
—Vol 27: 44, 671—Vol 28: 60, 365, 366—
Vol 29: 44, 286, 287—Vol 30: 149—Vol 31:
587—Vol 32: 508, 632—Vol 33: 39, 960—
Vol 34: 67, 656—Vol 35: 1038—Vol 36: 575
—Vol 37: 73, 155—Vol 39: 224—Vol 40:
75, 172—Vol 41: 34, 68, 70, 120, 123, 164,
213, 214—Vol 42: 74, 76, 138, 139, 192, 269,
336, 337—Vol 43: 427, 486, 488, 493, 494,
545, 547—Vol 44: 24, 149, 150, 226, 235,
387—Vol 45: 21, 28, 101, 108, 116, 119, 125,
126, 189, 197, 239, 242, 323—Vol 46: 102,
160, 236, 332, 386—Vol 47: 27, 86, 192, 193,
388—Vol 48: 63, 64, 121, 304, 445, 446—Vol
49: 191, 192, 353—Vol 50: 64, 350, 354—Vol
51: 355—Vol 52: 52, 562—Vol 53: 55, 179,
330, 371, 377, 692, 693, 694, 747—Vol 54: 51,
56, 176, 465, 466, 590, 591, 709—Vol 56: 628,
691, 742—Vol 57: 687, 690, 691, 745—Vol
58: 451, 453, 501, 586, 700, 701, 763—Vol 59:
110, 174, 238, 315, 651, 762—Vol 60: 49,
115—Vol 61: 61, 66, 546, 607, 788—Vol 62:
246, 306, 500—Vol 63: 373, 507, 570—Vol
64: 257, 389, 523, 715, 758, 759—Vol 65:
122, 147, 367, 634, 759—Vol 66: 55—Vol 67:
43, 243, 388, 444, 575, 712, 750—Vol 68:
487, 490, 626—Vol 69: 117, 243, 244, 246,
432—Vol 70: 56, 354, 575, 1018—Vol 71: 357,
676, 761—Vol 73: (9-67), (11-68)—Vol 74:
(2-43), (9-50), (11-55)—Vol 75: (4-54),
(9-41)—Vol 76: 654, 927—Vol 77: 240, 332,
663—Vol 79: 36, 194—Vol 80: 154, 336, 431
—Vol 81: 569—Vol 82: 141, 313, 503, 860—
Vol 83: 92, 173, 261, 944—Vol 84: 158, 326
TAXTER..Vol 77: 537
TEAD..Vol 75: (2-59)
TEAGARDEN................................Vol 70: 133
TEAGLE..Vol 65: 366
TEAGUE ...Vol 20: 62—Vol 44: 230, 231, 383
—Vol 45: 26—Vol 54: 308—Vol 82: 313, 501
TEAL..Vol 59: 762
TEAMAN..Vol 64: 714
TEARS..Vol 34: 67
TEATLE..Vol 62: 502
TEBBETTS......................................Vol 45: 326
TEBBS..Vol 25: 383
TEDFORD......................................Vol 74: (5-39)
TEE..Vol 42: 81
TEED...................................Vol 75: (2-59)—Vol 84: 325
TEEL..Vol 83: 258
TEEPLE....Vol 46: 334—Vol 56: 560—Vol 64:
258
TEETAR..Vol 83: 439, 795
TEETER..Vol 58: 450, 647
TEFFT....Vol 45: 111—Vol 50: 63, 185, 277—
Vol 76: 62
TELFORD...........Vol 30: 256—Vol 49: 45, 184
TELLER..Vol 55: 285, 442
TEMAN..Vol 83: 946
TEMPLE...Vol 43: 495—Vol 45: 104, 238—
Vol 46: 22—Vol 56: 373—Vol 66: 307—Vol
68: 242, 442—Vol 60: 158—Vol 75: (4-54)—
Vol 80: 656

TEMPLEMAN....Vol 45: 192, 193—Vol 57.
349
TEMPLETON....Vol 47: 395—Vol 56: 227—
Vol 57: 174, 630—Vol 64: 522—Vol 67: 145
TENBROCK....................Vol 23: 397—Vol 45: 117
TENBROECK....Vol 28: 364—Vol 65: 758—
Vol 66: 120—Vol 67: 118
TENBROOK..........._Vol 66: 120—Vol 67: 118
TENBROOKE..............................Vol 65: 758
TENEY..Vol 66: 250
TENNANT......................................Vol 50: 189
TENNEY..Vol 33: 40
TENNISON....................................Vol 80: 584
TENNY..Vol 63: 700
TENNYSON....................................Vol 64: 712
TERHUNE......................................Vol 80: 154
TERR..Vol 59: 524
TERREE..Vol 70: 135
TERREL........................Vol 55: 603—Vol 56: 225
TERRELL....Vol 25: 719—Vol 33: 955—Vol
39: 103, 273—Vol 40: 73, 75, 108—Vol 43:
544—Vol 44: 388—Vol 46: 99, 332—Vol 48:
447—Vol 52: 684—Vol 53: 692—Vol 55:
338—Vol 56: 111, 479, 480—Vol 58: 54—
Vol 59: 763—Vol 62: 54, 159—Vol 63: 571—
Vol 67: 387—Vol 70: 1169—Vol 73: (1-64)
—Vol 75: (2-61)—Vol 76: 219—Vol 78:
246, 600—Vol 80: 277, 335
TERRILE..Vol 30: 63
TERRILL....Vol 21: 496—Vol 45: 100—Vol
51: 355—Vol 53: 377—Vol 54: 652—Vol
55: 47—Vol 58: 588, 647—Vol 61: 60, 275—
Vol 84: 69
TERRY....Vol 26: 244—Vol 27: 668—Vol 38:
87—Vol 41: 34, 213—Vol 42: 79—Vol 43:
546—Vol 47: 268—Vol 48: 55, 60—Vol 52:
359—Vol 53: 378—Vol 55: 598—Vol 57:
353—Vol 58: 172—Vol 62: 456, 460, 588—
Vol 67: 147, 574—Vol 68: 550, 552—Vol 69:
56, 161—Vol 70: 455, 876—Vol 71: 464—
Vol 76: 580, 928—Vol 77: 184—Vol 80: 382
TERWILLINGER............................Vol 40: 77
TEUNIS..Vol 28: 164
TEW..Vol 70: 133
THACHER......................................Vol 60: 507
THACKER....Vol 46: 236—Vol 55: 597—Vol
67: 387—Vol 84: 632
THACKSTON................................Vol 63: 428
THARP....Vol 44: 315—Vol 83: 1014—Vol 84:
67
THATCHER....Vol 13: 612—Vol 65: 297, 634,
757—Vol 82: 726, 727
THAYER....Vol 31: 668—Vol 32: 160—Vol
38: 329—Vol 39: 21, 101, 141, 222, 327—Vol
40: 225, 227—Vol 43: 497, 543—Vol 47: 390,
394—Vol 48: 370—Vol 50: 60—Vol 52: 51—
Vol 54: 226—Vol 57: 177, 219, 477—Vol 64:
588—Vol 67: 115—Vol 69: 431—Vol 79:
160—Vol 81: 71—Vol 83: 521
THEALL......................Vol 57: 565—Vol 59: 109
THEUS..Vol 84: 245
THIGPEN......................Vol 56: 563—Vol 84: 68
THOCKMORTON........................Vol 21: 252
THOM..Vol 34: 658
THOMAN..Vol 45: 199
THOMAS....Vol 20: 279—Vol 21: 496—Vol 23:
324—Vol 26: 143—Vol 28: 161—Vol 29: 46,
650—Vol 31: 863—Vol 32: 633—Vol 36:
217, 351—Vol 37: 68—Vol 38: 328—Vol 39:
327—Vol 41: 33, 124—Vol 42: 138, 191—

Vol 43: 424, 427—Vol 44: 226—Vol 45: 119, 120—Vol 46: 98, 153, 392—Vol 47: 271— Vol 48: 58, 59, 62, 442—Vol 49: 48, 281, 284, 285—Vol 50: 275, 281, 350—Vol 52: 54 —Vol 53: 52—Vol 55: 47, 109, 338, 339, 442, 446, 521, 598, 602—Vol 56: 482—Vol 57: 177, 348—Vol 58: 53, 649—Vol 59: 239, 389, 442—Vol 61: 153, 552, 608, 784—Vol 62: 161, 248, 389—Vol 63: 427, 699—Vol 64: 121, 260, 651—Vol 65: 245, 248, 300, 761— Vol 66: 307—Vol 68: 123, 490—Vol 69: 54, 58, 160, 245, 431—Vol 70: 205, 577, 879, 1018, 1267—Vol 71: 87, 673—Vol 72: (4-83) —Vol 73: (2-65), (5-89)—Vol 74: (7-52), (8-52)—Vol 75: (2-59)—Vol 77: 239—Vol 79: 36, 368, 369—Vol 82: 797, 860, 931—Vol 83: 91, 442—Vol 84: 519, 633
THOMASON............Vol 45: 100
THOMASSON......Vol 73: (9-66)—Vol 83: 944
THOMBURGH............Vol 53: 180
THOMPSON....Vol 23: 400—Vol 25: 38, 968— Vol 26: 52—Vol 27: 382, 668, 669, 671, 808— Vol 28: 258, 363—Vol 29: 47, 287—Vol 30: 334—Vol 32: 58—Vol 33: 960—Vol 34: 322, 539—Vol 36: 76—Vol 37: 73, 152, 158, 351, 397—Vol 38: 275, 276—Vol 39: 104—Vol 41: 34, 68, 120, 215—Vol 42: 192, 334, 341— Vol 43: 426, 481, 541, 596, 600, 602, 605— Vol 44: 23, 27, 28—Vol 45: 103, 110, 111, 237—Vol 46: 151, 155, 331—Vol 47: 267, 273 —Vol 48: 57, 121, 204, 304, 449—Vol 49: 46, 134, 283—Vol 50: 60, 67, 113, 190, 278, 353, 356—Vol 52: 359, 485—Vol 53: 182, 494— Vol 54: 113, 225, 589—Vol 55: 164, 285, 521—Vol 56: 112, 173, 174, 625, 626, 628, 688, 743, 744—Vol 57: 172, 218, 566, 627— Vol 58: 329, 372, 698, 700—Vol 61: 157, 158, 469, 912—Vol 62: 503—Vol 63: 59, 294— Vol 64: 259, 520—Vol 65: 367, 634, 762— Vol 66: 120—Vol 67: 118—Vol 68: 488— Vol 69: 564—Vol 70: 355, 707, 1021—Vol 71: 763—Vol 75: (4-53), (4-55), (5-43)— Vol 76: 62, 218, 310, 709, 928—Vol 77: 768, 769—Vol 79: 36, 331—Vol 82: 499, 725, 859, 936—Vol 83: 93, 261, 443
THOMSON....Vol 30: 338—Vol 33: 959—Vol 40: 74—Vol 43: 541, 545—Vol 46: 241—Vol 50: 68, 186—Vol 59: 238—Vol 62: 160 —Vol 64: 156, 260—Vol 65: 762—Vol 66: 249, 250, 534—Vol 82: 141—Vol 83: 93
THORINGTON ....Vol 53: 54
THORLA............Vol 22: 53, 270
THORN.......Vol 39: 143, 224—Vol 45: 241, 329
THORNBURGH............Vol 55: 601
THORNBURG............Vol 22: 375—Vol 84: 522
THORNDIKE............Vol 45: 329
THORNE....Vol 30: 148, 337—Vol 39: 143— Vol 40: 26—Vol 41: 9, 77—Vol 45: 184—Vol 54: 591—Vol 60: 50
THORNHILL............Vol 47: 387
THORNTON....Vol 24: 262, 457—Vol 34: 422, 658—Vol 35: 650—Vol 36: 576—Vol 37: 269—Vol 38: 86—Vol 39: 22, 226, 324—Vol 41: 68, 72—Vol 44: 82—Vol 45: 123, 195— Vol 48: 308, 369, 440—Vol 49: 130, 285— Vol 50: 58, 65—Vol 52: 358—Vol 53: 118— Vol 54: 222—Vol 55: 108, 286—Vol 56: 691—Vol 57: 743—Vol 58: 701—Vol 59: 48 —Vol 62: 309, 586—Vol 63: 107, 168—Vol 64: 757—Vol 68: 241, 443—Vol 75: (4-53),

(10-64), (10-65)—Vol 77: 539—Vol 82: 936
THOROUGOOD............Vol 45: 104
THORP....Vol 34: 67—Vol 44: 312—Vol 48: 371—Vol 49: 135—Vol 72: (8-87)—Vol 76: 144
THORPE....Vol 53: 627—Vol 56: 416—Vol 59: 589—Vol 60: 49
THRALL....Vol 20: 62—Vol 25: 796—Vol 49: 131—Vol 78: 696
THRASHER............Vol 29: 652
THREIKELD............Vol 82: 500
THRELKELD....Vol 57: 117—Vol 75: (1-55) —Vol 83: 92—Vol 84: 247
THRELKILL............Vol 62: 124
THRESKILL............Vol 61: 869
THREWITTS............Vol 44: 227
THRIFT............Vol 45: 196, 328
THROCKMORTON....Vol 45: 237—Vol 51: 355—Vol 58: 701—Vol 65: 296
THROOP....Vol 35: 1038—Vol 36: 214—Vol 39: 223—Vol 83: 1014
THROP............Vol 39: 327
THRUEATT............Vol 83: 628
THURBER....Vol 22: 156, 374—Vol 23: 63— Vol 28: 549—Vol 45: 20—Vol 57: 215, 349
THURBUR............Vol 55: 601
THURLOW............Vol 24: 149
THURMAN Vol 42: 343—Vol 48: 61—Vol 67: 516—Vol 73: (2-65)
THURMOND............Vol 61: 472
THURSTON....Vol 19: 627—Vol 20: 164—Vol 28: 364—Vol 36: 579—Vol 37: 147—Vol 38: 220—Vol 49: 45, 281—Vol 50: 189, 346 —Vol 51: 234—Vol 58: 701
THWARBACK............Vol 67: 241
TIBBALS....Vol 45: 106—Vol 46: 238—Vol 47: 29—Vol 49: 356
TIBBARDS............Vol 58: 112
TIBBET............Vol 73: (2-66)
TIBBITTS....Vol 28: 60—Vol 47: 27—Vol 82: 653
TIBBLES............Vol 58: 112
TIBBS............Vol 25: 797
TICE....Vol 43: 600, 601—Vol 57: 115—Vol 68: 553
TICHENOR............Vol 59: 681—Vol 66: 251
TICKNOR............Vol 45: 241
TIDBALL............Vol 55: 47, 336
TIDD............Vol 75: (2-59)
TIFF............Vol 43: 496, 543
TIFFANY....Vol 37: 395—Vol 39: 223—Vol 40: 23—Vol 48: 449—Vol 58: 111
TIFFY............Vol 45: 117
TIFFT............Vol 50: 63
TIGHLMAN............Vol 43: 492
TIGUE............Vol 72: (1-66)
TILDEN....Vol 1: 333—Vol 5: 466—Vol 29: 269, 511—Vol 31: 586—Vol 39: 102—Vol 83: 872
TILFORD............Vol 30: 543—Vol 81: 429
TILLER............Vol 48: 370
TILLERY............Vol 70: 877
TILLEY............Vol 65: 763
TILLINGHAST....Vol 27: 735—Vol 44: 234— Vol 59: 175—Vol 63: 246
TILLMAN....Vol 34: 540—Vol 54: 590—Vol 80: 277—Vol 83: 1015
TILLOTSON....Vol 44: 85—Vol 45: 193, 241— Vol 47: 272—Vol 48: 205—Vol 68: 374— Vol 80: 383

65: 763—Vol 66: 252, 825—Vol 67: 47—Vol
72: (5-66)—Vol 75: (10-65)—Vol 77: 243—
Vol 79: 560—Vol 83: 943
TOWNSLEY............Vol 33: 473—Vol 39: 143
TOYER..Vol 38: 276
TRABUE....Vol 36: 760—Vol 37: 349—Vol 43:
545—Vol 65: 760—Vol 67: 290—Vol 75:
(3-40)
TRACEY...Vol 34: 661
TRACKETT.........................Vol 71: 960
TRACY....Vol 19: 628—Vol 20: 165—Vol 24:
58—Vol 26: 241—Vol 27: 671—Vol 49: 287
—Vol 51: 354—Vol 52: 357—Vol 58: 452—
Vol 59: 589—Vol 62: 774—Vol 64: 445—
Vol 66: 601, 827—Vol 84: 705
TRAFFARIN.............................Vol 23: 325
TRAFTON....Vol 39: 224, 327—Vol 41: 70,
211—Vol 43: 427
TRAMMELL.............................Vol 50: 189
TRAIN..........................Vol 24: 459—Vol 25: 37
TRAVIS....Vol 38: 219—Vol 49: 191—Vol 52:
359—Vol 55: 445, 709—Vol 60: 418—Vol
63: 428—Vol 70: 205
TRAYLER............................Vol 38: 34
TRAYLOR....Vol 42: 342—Vol 43: 520—Vol
44: 316—Vol 45: 195, 236, 328—Vol 82:
142, 726
TREADWAY....Vol 24: 57—Vol 42: 269—Vol
43: 482—Vol 47: 31
TREADWELL....Vol 61: 275—Vol 62: 52, 120,
160, 585
TREAGLE..............................Vol 78: 600
TREAT....Vol 31: 411—Vol 33: 40—Vol 43:
601
TREATTE.............................Vol 82: 796
TREEN...........................Vol 80: 192—Vol 81: 571
TREES..................Vol 53: 243—Vol 77: 183
TREGO.............................Vol 72: (11-59)
TREMBLY.........................Vol 77: 480, 538
TRENARY....................Vol 64: 756—Vol 76: 310
TRENT....Vol 27: 669—Vol 44: 388—Vol 45:
236—Vol 59: 176
TRETHREM...............................Vol 57: 176
TREUSCH.............................Vol 75: (5-45)
TRIBBLE.............................Vol 46: 243
TRIBBY.............................Vol 81: 569
TRIBLE.....................Vol 49: 354—Vol 70: 574
TRICE....Vol 40: 226—Vol 41: 65—Vol 49:
283—Vol 68: 122—Vol 74: (5-39)—Vol 75:
(9-46)
TRICKEY....................Vol 26: 55—Vol 67: 752
TRICKLE.............................Vol 46: 389
TRIGG....Vol 41: 128—Vol 44: 23, 25, 82, 228
—Vol 45: 184—Vol 70: 359—Vol 82: 934
TRIMBLE....Vol 34: 539—Vol 48: 122—Vol
54: 54—Vol 56: 560—Vol 57: 37—Vol 58:
368—Vol 70: 575
TRINDLE.............................Vol 82: 312
TRIPLETT....Vol 48: 60—Vol 49: 43, 44, 183
—Vol 50: 57—Vol 58: 700—Vol 60: 49
TRIPP....Vol 24: 149—Vol 27: 382—Vol 33:
476—Vol 41: 127—Vol 45: 121, 237—Vol
51: 354—Vol 53: 177—Vol 54: 465, 651—
Vol 56: 562—Vol 57: 175—Vol 60: 698—
Vol 68: 627—Vol 72: (7-76)
TRIPPE................................Vol 18: 58
TRISCOTT.............................Vol 83: 522
TRITCH.............................Vol 69: 247
TROAT.............................Vol 30: 542
TROBAUGH.............................Vol 67: 241

TROPHOGEN.............................Vol 45: 194
TROTTER....Vol 48: 202—Vol 53: 117, 631—
Vol 69: 243, 763—Vol 78: 398—Vol 82: 500
TROUTMAN....Vol 46: 155—Vol 47: 84, 340—
Vol 48: 122, 304—Vol 83: 523, 524
TROUTWINE.............................Vol 57: 310, 691
TROVILAR.............................Vol 82: 863
TROWBRIDGE....Vol 32: 631—Vol 35: 1104
—Vol 46: 387—Vol 53: 179—Vol 83: 335
TROXAL............Vol 75: (5-43)—Vol 78: 457
TROXEL.............................Vol 58: 702
TROXWELL.............................Vol 59: 389
TROYMAN.............................Vol 44: 23
TRUAX....Vol 48: 59—Vol 61: 473, 609, 706,
786
TRUE.....................Vol 43: 602—Vol 44: 79
TRUEHART.............Vol 43: 421—Vol 46: 22
TRUESDALE.............................Vol 53: 180
TRUESDELL....Vol 40: 74—Vol 46: 391—Vol
56: 45, 414—Vol 78: 695
TRUEWORTHY.............................Vol 29: 651
TRUITT................Vol 45: 110—Vol 70: 136
TRUMAN.............................Vol 84: 518
TRUMBLE.................Vol 24: 543—Vol 28: 549
TRUMBULL..........Vol 37: 396—Vol 51: 302
TRUMP.............................Vol 83: 523
TRUSSEL.............................Vol 63: 742
TRUSSELL.............................Vol 61: 757
TRYON....Vol 22: 997—Vol 27: 672—Vol 48:
61—Vol 59: 113—Vol 65: 571—Vol 66: 364
—Vol 67: 716—Vol 82: 220
TSEHORN.............................Vol 56: 44
TUBB.............................Vol 47: 269
TUBBS.............................Vol 47: 391
TUCK.....................Vol 61: 156—Vol 83: 90
TUCKER....Vol 22: 270—Vol 24: 343—Vol 31:
413—Vol 32: 282—Vol 37: 68, 154, 349—
Vol 40: 172, 228—Vol 41: 123—Vol 42: 80,
191, 194—Vol 43: 604, 723—Vol 45: 23—Vol
46: 329, 386—Vol 48: 56, 124—Vol 53: 492
—Vol 56: 46, 47, 115, 225, 319, 563—Vol 59:
114—Vol 62: 309, 460—Vol 66: 734—Vol 67:
43, 441—Vol 68: 155, 550—Vol 70: 205,
1168—Vol 71: 163—Vol 73: (3-86)—Vol 74:
(2-41)—Vol 75: (2-58), (2-61), (4-52), (9-
46), (10-64), (10-65)—Vol 76: 400, 582—
Vol 78: 295—Vol 79: 160—Vol 82: 795, 796
—Vol 83: 172—Vol 84: 327, 519, 520
TUDOR.............................Vol 41: 128
TUESDELL.................Vol 39: 274—Vol 67: 577
TUFTS....Vol 17: 390—Vol 21: 57—Vol 71:
161—Vol 82: 935
TULL.............................Vol 43: 485
TULLEY.............................Vol 77: 239
TUNDA.............................Vol 48: 55
TUNE.............................Vol 68: 372
TUNISON.............................Vol 26: 244
TUNNELL.............................Vol 58: 370, 499
TUNSTALL......Vol 29: 514—Vol 66: 248, 307
TUPPER............Vol 34: 200—Vol 38: 331
TURBEVILLE.............................Vol 77: 241
TURBLEVILLE.............................Vol 84: 327
TURK.............................Vol 37: 159
TURKINGTON.............................Vol 39: 326
TURLEY.............................Vol 34: 540
TURMAN.............................Vol 49: 190
TURNBULL.............................Vol 45: 324
TURNER....Vol 21: 61—Vol 22: 51—Vol 23:
470—Vol 25: 39, 383—Vol 26: 54, 240, 336—
Vol 27: 383, 672, 735, 737, 889—Vol 28: 163

Vol 54: 222—Vol 58: 452—Vol 84: 446
WAITE ...Vol 26: 139—Vol 27: 382—Vol 29: 717—Vol 30: 441—Vol 31: 750—Vol 38: 272—Vol 44: 227—Vol 45: 22, 193—Vol 47: 22, 193—Vol 58: 452—Vol 60: 115—Vol 61: 609—Vol 66: 365, 730—Vol 67: 240—Vol 68: 155—Vol 84: 632
WAITY..Vol 69: 363
WAKEFIELD.............Vol 64: 651—Vol 76: 63
WAKEMAN....Vol 22: 52, 995—Vol 56: 481— Vol 61: 611
WALBRIDGE..................................Vol 22: 373
WALCHER...............- ....Vol 72: (7-75)
WALCOTT.......................................Vol 22: 271
WALDE..Vol 31: 668
WALDEN..Vol 83: 793
WALDO ...Vol 35: 56, 651—Vol 45: 27—Vol 47: 27
WALDRON..............Vol 77: 769—Vol 83: 336
WALDSMITH............... ....Vol 68: 487
WALES...Vol 17: 181—Vol 23: 64—Vol 31: 55—Vol 47: 392—Vol 64: 124
WALGER..Vol 53: 744
WALKER...Vol 20: 1063—Vol 21: 404, 496— Vol 23: 64, 326, 470—Vol 24: 151, 152—Vol 26: 335—Vol 27: 738, 891—Vol 29: 650—Vol 31: 668—Vol 34: 67—Vol 35: 1104—Vol 36: 75, 215, 354, 576, 579, 759—Vol 37: 155— Vol 40: 274—Vol 41: 70—Vol 42: 80, 191, 338, 342, 343—Vol 43: 425, 426, 597, 724— Vol 44, 84, 226, 230, 236, 310—Vol 45: 18— Vol 47: 28, 33, 265, 268, 273, 394—Vol 48: 448—Vol 49: 46, 47, 188, 355—Vol 50: 69— Vol 52: 323, 560—Vol 53: 179, 346, 627, 633, 692, 744—Vol 54: 53, 354, 418, 589—Vol 55: 521—Vol 56: 560, 688, 690—Vol 57: 113, 309 —Vol 58: 172, 173, 174, 330, 371, 451—Vol 59: 113—Vol 61: 153, 231—Vol 62: 389— Vol 63: 60, 293, 426—Vol 64: 159—Vol 66: 461—Vol 67: 388, 646—Vol 68: 374, 487— Vol 69: 244—Vol 70: 573, 878—Vol 71: 761, 1025—Vol 72: (8-88), (12-67)—Vol 73: (3-86), (9-63), (11-65)—Vol 74: (1-49, 51), (2-40), (3-45)—Vol 77: 239, 241—Vol 78: 53, 247, 649—Vol 79: 193—Vol 80: 432— Vol 81: 19, 264, 429—Vol 82: 575, 798, 931, 934—Vol 83: 173, 718—Vol 84: 158, 325, 326, 524, 894
WALKINS..............................Vol 53: 694, 748
WALKUP................................Vol 42: 14, 15
WALL.. Vol 39: 225—Vol 43: 410—Vol 53: 180, 628—Vol 64: 122—Vol 65: 508—Vol 66: 364—Vol 67: 715—Vol 69: 242—Vol 71: 162
WALLACE...Vol 23: 325—Vol 28: 161, 547— Vol 33: 474—Vol 34: 198—Vol 36: 755—Vol 37: 151—Vol 38: 274—Vol 39: 140, 323— Vol 40: 225, 226—Vol 41: 124—Vol 42: 185, 264—Vol 43: 424, 547—Vol 44: 26—Vol 47: 193—Vol 50: 350, 355—Vol 52: 173, 687— Vol 54: 55—Vol 56: 624—Vol 59: 112—Vol 63: 508, 634—Vol 64: 256—Vol 69: 631—Vol 71: 676—Vol 72: (10-98)—Vol 74: (11-55) —Vol 75: (2-57)—Vol 78: 245—Vol 79: 561 —Vol 80: 44—Vol 81: 430—Vol 82: 500— Vol 84: 702, 894
WALLEN...Vol 70: 1166—Vol 71: 1027—Vol 83: 872
WALLER...Vol 38: 220—Vol 43: 486, 490, 495—Vol 44: 84—Vol 49: 47—Vol 50: 183— Vol 64: 388—Vol 67: 750—Vol 70: 880—

Vol 74: (4-52)—Vol 78: 695—Vol 80: 557—
Vol 82: 141—Vol 83: 92, 946—Vol 84: 523
WALLIN...................Vol 70: 1166—Vol 71: 1027
WALLING...Vol 66: 826—Vol 67: 645—Vol 69: 119—Vol 70: 1166
WALLIS....Vol 47: 193—Vol 50: 355—Vol 52: 321—Vol 57: 566—Vol 58: 450
WALLS....Vol 44: 382—Vol 63: 699—Vol 82: 796
WALLSTORE................................Vol 62: 648
WALLSZ...Vol 31: 54
WALMACK.......................................Vol 63: 244
WALMESLEY..........Vol 47: 31—Vol 53: 331
WALMSLEY....................................Vol 54: 353
WALN...Vol 61: 65
WALPOLE.....................................Vol 84: 632
WALRATH....................................Vol 68: 553
WALRAVEN...................................Vol 70: 575
WALROD........................Vol 68: 492, 624
WALSTON...........Vol 47: 32—Vol 66: 56, 734
WALSWORTH...............................Vol 56: 45
WALTENBAUGH....Vol 73: (1-62)—Vol 81: 130
WALTENMIRE..............................Vol 59: 175
WALTER...Vol 28: 546, 547—Vol 30: 67, 258 —Vol 40: 172—Vol 41: 31—Vol 43: 601, 604—Vol 62: 714
WALTERS...Vol 41: 164—Vol 43: 488—Vol 47: 268—Vol 60: 699—Vol 64: 157—Vol 65: 298—Vol 67: 577—Vol 75: (2-57)—Vol 79: 284
WALTHAM...................................Vol 82: 140
WALTON...Vol 10: 1088—Vol 25: 719—Vol 27: 381, 888—Vol 29: 800—Vol 30: 148, 339 —Vol 32: 61, 505—Vol 35: 651, 653—Vol 37: 161, 352—Vol 38: 332—Vol 40: 76— Vol 41: 31, 209, 213—Vol 42: 14, 79—Vol 43: 486, 492, 496—Vol 44: 23—Vol 45: 113, 200, 326—Vol 46: 97, 385, 391—Vol 48: 448 —Vol 49: 394—Vol 50: 69, 187, 345—Vol 51: 354—Vol 52: 686—Vol 53: 117, 243, 692, 694—Vol 54: 353, 537, 590, 651—Vol 56: 373, 479, 628, 689, 743—Vol 57: 630— 635—Vol 67: 148, 513—Vol 68: 488—Vol 79: 613—Vol 81: 20—Vol 82: 797—Vol 84: 632
WALTZ.................................Vol 55: 445, 709
WALWORTH....Vol 4: 199—Vol 33: 473—Vol 45: 128
WAMSLEY.......................................Vol 50: 193
WANAMAKER...................Vol 32: 160, 630
WANDEL...Vol 37: 70
WANDLACE...........Vol 40: 26—Vol 44: 147
WANZER...Vol 30: 339
WAPLES...Vol 46: 100
WARD...Vol 20: 62—Vol 24: 58, 343—Vol 25: 968—Vol 27: 807—Vol 28: 58, 160, 262—Vol 29: 652—Vol 30: 64—Vol 31: 55, 860, 861— Vol 33: 1032—Vol 36: 217—Vol 37: 67, 70— Vol 38: 219, 274—Vol 40: 75—Vol 41: 215— Vol 43: 491, 492, 545, 604, 723—Vol 44: 24, 85, 311—Vol 45: 128, 199, 240, 323—Vol 47: 341—Vol 48: 123—Vol 53: 493—Vol 54: 464, 649—Vol 55: 164, 339—Vol 58: 370, 588, 701—Vol 59: 588, 765—Vol 60: 113, 364, 417—Vol 61: 158, 781, 910—Vol 64: 257—Vol 65: 124—Vol 66: 309—Vol 67: 118 —Vol 70: 573, 574, 575, 1167—Vol 71: 672— Vol 77: 184, 238, 664—Vol 78: 457—Vol 80: 192—Vol 82: 727—Vol 84: 520

WARDELL...Vol 43: 493, 543, 598—Vol 50: 249, 414
WARDEN...Vol 77: 539—Vol 78: 456—Vol 84: 245
WARDER...........Vol 44: 148—Vol 78: 696
WARDLAW.........................Vol 29: 649
WARDWELL.................Vol 44: 26, 151
WARE ...Vol 33: 959, 1032—Vol 37: 71, 394—Vol 38: 219—Vol 40: 229—Vol 42: 76—Vol 45: 109—Vol 46: 390—Vol 48: 445—Vol 49: 46—Vol 50: 60—Vol 53: 181—Vol 56: 627—
—Vol 62: 460, 649—Vol 64: 521—Vol 66: 308—Vol 67: 115, 713—Vol 68: 553—Vol 71: 1024—Vol 80: 155—Vol 83: 259, 443—Voi 84: 634
WARFIELD...Vol 54: 54, 419—Vol 57: 312—Vol 71: 162, 956, 958—Vol 79: 113
WARFORD...Vol 58: 502—Vol 66: 159—Vol 78: 246—Vol 83: 442
WARIN........................Vol 84: 324
WARING...Vol 46: 101—Vol 53: 492—Vol 55: 520—Vol 56: 561—Vol 57: 37—Vol 65: 761 —Vol 72: (2-62)—Vol 73: (2-66)—Vol 75: (10-64)—Vol 82: 935
WARM...........................Vol 59: 387
WARMER........................ ... .Vol 52: 559
WARNE.................Vol 58: 650—Vol 59: 440
WARNER...Vol 6: 188—Vol 22: 272—Vol 23: 326—Vol 25: 717—Vol 27: 892—Vol 29: 648—Vol 30: 541, 542—Vol 31: 668, 669—Vol 37: 395—Vol 39: 142—Vol 43: 418, 597 —Vol 44: 228—Vol 48: 61, 121, 202, 303—Vol 49: 135—Vol 50: 280, 351, 353—Vol 52: 52, 54—Vol 54: 55, 175—Vol 57: 14, 175, 308, 349—Vol 58: 588, 701—Vol 59: 45, 587 —Vol 62: 501—Vol 64: 124, 650—Vol 68: 735—Vol 69: 630—Vol 74: (6-38)—Vol 77: 768—Vol 84: 632
WARNOCK....................Vol 53: 179
WARREN...Vol 19: 627—Vol 20: 278—Vol 21: 62, 403—Vol 23: 325—Vol 27: 889—Vol 28: 61—Vol 29: 511, 651—Vol 30: 542—Vol 31: 750—Vol 32: 59, 61, 163, 282—Vol 33: 475, 1033—Vol 36: 574—Vol 38: 221—Vol 39: 274, 328—Vol 41: 34, 71, 72, 125, 127— Vol·42: 337—Vol 43: 425, 597—Vol 44: 26— Vol 45: 28—Vol 46: 332—Vol 48: 65, 303, 305, 308—Vol 49: 187, 390—Vol 50: 64—Vol 52: 485—Vol 53: 54, 376, 746—Vol 54: 52, 308—Vol 55: 601—Vol 56: 691—Vol 57: 479—Vol 58: 371, 585, 649, 698, 760, 764— Vol 60: 419—Vol 63: 58—Vol 65: 298, 636— Vol 67: 42, 118, 753—Vol 68: 626—Vol 69: 240, 242—Vol 71: 557, 675—Vol 75: (4-55) —Vol 76: 218—Vol 77: 240—Vol 80: 277, 587—Vol 81: 629, 631—Vol 82: 860—Vol 83: 92, 171—Vol 84: 632
WARRIN..........................Vol 84: 324
WARRINER....................Vol 54: 55
WARTH.........................Vol 57: 313
WARWICK...Vol 44: 230—Vol 45: 186—Vol 49: 192—Vol 69: 160, 501—Vol 80: 557
WASHBURN...Vol 31: 50, 860—Vol 39: 227 —Vol 49: 356—Vol 50: 61—Vol 51: 356—Vol 52: 556—Vol 54: 466, 589—Vol 57: 353 —Vol 58: 588—Vol 60: 635—Vol 65: 572— Vol 67: 444, 646—Vol 68: 492—Vol 73: (2-64)—Vol 80: 44—Vol 83: 172, 717
WASHER......................Vol 83: 91
WASHINGTON...Vol 26: 243—Vol 37: 270—

Vol 39: 328—Vol 41: 72—Vol 45: 22, 106— Vol 46: 153—Vol 47: 23—Vol 48: 120—Vol 59: 113—Vol 61: 705, 784—Vol 67: 441— Vol 68: 486, 491—Vol 81: 518—Vol 82: 794 —Vol 83: 871
WASS.........................Vol 26: 143
WASSON................Vol 55: 285, 714
WATER..............................Vol 27: 806
WATERBURY......Vol 60: 418—Vol 83: 91
WATERER...................Vol 41: 164
WATERHOUSE...Vol 31: 861—Vol 34: 202—Vol 45: 199—Vol 67: 209
WATERMAN...Vol 29: 715—Vol 40: 78—Vol 42: 341—Vol 43: 420—Vol 44: 234—Vol 45: 28, 321—Vol 46: 154—Vol 47: 396—Vol 53: 627—Vol 54: 311—Vol 59: 111, 441, 652— Vol 60: 51—Vol 67: 243
WATERS...Vol 20: 60—Vol 25: 887—Vol 28: 59, 159—Vol 34: 423—Vol 36: 756—Vol 38: 219—Vol 39: 20—Vol 40: 25—Vol 41: 121, 126, 127—Vol 45: 18, 239—Vol· 46: 104— Vol 48: 56, 121—Vol 50: 65, 413—Vol 53: 691—Vol 54: 465—Vol 55: 710—Vol 56: 109, 222—Vol 58: 54—Vol 59: 763—Vol 61: 606—Vol 63: 295—Vol 64: 259, 522—Vol 66: 252—Vol 68: 489—Vol 76: 655, 860— Vol 80: 557, 657—Vol 84: 324
WATKENS..........................Vol 65: 505
WATKINS...Vol 22: 52—Vol 26: 55—Vol 32: 284—Vol 33: 1031—Vol 36: 762—Vol 43: 494—Vol 44: 80—Vol 45: 197, 328—Vol 46: 100—Vol 48: 204—Vol 53: 243, 329—Vol 54: 310, 652—Vol 55: 165—Vol 58: 172, 369 —Vol 60: 635—Vol 64: 759—Vol 65: 505— Vol 66: 599—Vol 67: 444—Vol 70: 1168— Vol 74: (6-38)—Vol 80: 46, 557—Vol 81: 130—Vol 82: 863—Vol 83: 172
WATLINGTON...Vol 68: 732—Vol 83: 944— Vol 84: 704
WATRING.......................Vol 45: 108
WATROUS......................Vol 25: 968
WATROUSS....................Vol 73: (1-62)
WATSON...Vol 22: 272—Vol 26: 336—Vol 27: 380—Vol 28: 162, 548—Vol 30: 65—Vol 31: 412—Vol 32: 62—Vol 35: 55, 1267—Vol 36: 756—Vol 37: 269, 394—Vol 38: 276— Vol 39: 22, 224, 276, 277—Vol 42: 342—Vol 43: 420—Vol 44: 154—Vol 45: 110, 241, 329 —Vol 46: 28, 100, 156, 238—Vol 47: 28—Vol 49: 48, 185—Vol 50: 275—Vol 51: 354—Vol 52: 732—Vol 53: 630—Vol 54: 111, 173— Vol 55: 521—Vol 56: 372, 690—Vol 59: 112 —Vol 60: 419—Vol 63: 427—Vol 64: 760— Vol 65: 633, 758—Vol 67: 443—Vol 73: (8-82)—Vol 75: (4-55)—Vol 76: 63—Vol 81: 517, 518—Vol 82: 63—Vol 84: 327, 524, 705
WATT.................Vol 29: 715—Vol 81: 264
WATTERS...........Vol 63: 742—Vol 67: 577
WATTLES...Vol 43: 603—Vol 45: 27, 126— Vol 52: 434, 559
WATTS...Vol 25: 964—Vol 26: 53—Vol 28: 365—Vol 38: 328—Vol 41: 164—Vol 42: 12, 73, 192—Vol 43: 483, 486, 599—Vol 44: 23, 226—Vol 45: 126, 321—Vol 46: 103, 246— Vol 47: 393—Vol 50: 67, 115, 186—Vol 52: 734—Vol 56: 560—Vol 61: 150, 856, 913— Vol 63: 507, 634, 636—Vol 66: 57—Vol 67: 291—Vol 69: 631—Vol 71: 465—Vol 74:

(5-43)—Vol 76: 219—Vol 80: 657—Vol 83: 522—Vol 84: 705
WAUGH............Vol 28: 548—Vol 81: 630
WAULESS...................................Vol 36: 216
WAXHALL...Vol 48: 61
WAXHAW...Vol 48: 61
WAY...Vol 37: 397—Vol 42: 190—Vol 50: 354 —Vol 57: 115, 746—Vol 59: 442—Vol 62: 53
WAYLAND..Vol 32: 159
WAYLES........................... Vol 43: 599
WAYNE...Vol 48: 41, 306—Vol 49: 134—Vol 55: 522—Vol 60: 573—Vol 70: 1168—Vol 74: (4-49)—Vol 82: 499
WEABER...Vol 56: 226
WEAKLEY..............Vol 56: 688—Vol 81: 316
WEARE...Vol 43: 423, 540—Vol 50: 62—Vol 54: 466
WEAST................Vol 37: 68—Vol 44: 28, 229
WEATHERBEE.................Vol 56: 46, 479, 740
WEATHERBY........ ....Vol 42: 76
WEATHERFORD.................... Vol 28: 549
WEATHERHEAD......................Vol 82: 861
WEATHERLY..................................Vol 79: 161
WEATHERS...............................Vol 64: 158
WEATHERSBEE...........................Vol 53: 448
WEATHERWAX...Vol 38: 218—Vol 39: 226 —Vol 58: 588—Vol 64: 651—Vol 65: 120
WEATT....................... ....Vol 24: 458
WEAVER...Vol 24: 58, 261, 542, 543—Vol 25: 382—Vol 30: 147—Vol 33: 960—Vol 37: 152, 396—Vol 39: 225—Vol 40: 274—Vol 41: 65—Vol 42: 270—Vol 43: 425—Vol 44: 27—Vol 45: 103, 112, 199—Vol 46: 27, 238, 242—Vol 47: 24, 33—Vol 48: 54—Vol 50: 281—Vol 60: 573—Vol 67: 242—Vol 70: 354—Vol 74: (7-54), (8-54)—Vol 75: (1-55) —Vol 81: 20—Vol 83: 871—Vol 84: 159, 894
WEBB...Vol 23: 401—Vol 26: 562—Vol 34: 200, 539—Vol 36: 571—Vol 39: 22—Vol 40: 273—Vol 41: 35—Vol 42: 80—Vol 43: 723— Vol 45: 21, 196, 198—Vol 46: 389—Vol 47: 28—Vol 48: 371-442—Vol 49: 135, 193, 283— Vol 53: 693—Vol 54: 421—Vol 55: 444, 710 —Vol 56: 628—Vol 58: 329, 372—Vol 60: 418—Vol 64: 446—Vol 65: 59, 762—Vol 68: 122—Vol 71: 557, 674—Vol 82: 502, 933— Vol 83: 521—Vol 84: 247
WEBBER...Vol 30: 541—Vol 32: 281—Vol 53: 53, 54, 629—Vol 57: 566—Vol 58: 763— Vol 61: 66—Vol 81: 570
WEBER Vol 22: 374—Vol 24: 58, 261—Vol 56: 226
WEBLEY..........................Vol 45: 189—Vol 46: 28
WEBSTER...Vol 16: 69—Vol 37: 153, 395— Vol 38: 88—Vol 39: 328—Vol 43: 491, 542— Vol 44: 23, 26, 84, 151, 227, 315—Vol 45: 116, 128, 187, 326—Vol 46: 22—Vol 48: 55, 204, 445—Vol 49: 124, 136, 181, 186—Vol 54: 421, 590—Vol 50: 166—Vol 57: 116, 216 —Vol 65: 635—Vol 66: 461, 825—Vol 68: 551—Vol 80: 192—Vol 82: 934—Vol 84: 69, 327
WEDGER.................Vol 68: 486—Vol 69: 120
WEDGEWOOD............................Vol 61: 464
WEED...Vol 27: 671—Vol 32: 284—Vol 53: 693—Vol 60: 507—Vol 61: 909—Vol 65: 440—Vol 78: 155—Vol 83: 1015—Vol 84: 245, 328
WEEDEN..............Vol 49: 396—Vol 50: 345
WEEDON.................Vol 49: 396—Vol 82: 502

WEEDS.......................Vol 74: (4-51)
WEEKLEY......................................Vol 56: 688
WEEKS...Vol 28: 366—Vol 29: 716—Vol 34: 322—Vol 36: 215—Vol 44: 386—Vol 45: 20 —Vol 48: 305, 444—Vol 50: 354—Vol 53: 243—Vol 56: 479—Vol 58: 370—Vol 59: 587, 761—Vol 61: 869—Vol 62: 306, 647— Vol 66: 365—Vol 82: 935
WEEMS............Vol 71: 672—Vol 73: (9-66)
WEETER...................................Vol 82: 220
WEGLEY...................................Vol 71: 162
WEICHEL.................................Vol 74: (3-45)
WEIGHT...............Vol 48: 62—Vol 53: 691
WEIR...Vol 26: 339—Vol 64: 588—Vol 68: 120, 684—Vol 69: 244, 433, 566—Vol 74: (2-43)—Vol 81: 570
WEISER................Vol 57: 177—Vol 74: (11-60)
WEISSMER................................Vol 67: 115
WELBORN......................... ...Vol 41: 165
WELCH...Vol 27: 45, 808—Vol 38: 331—Vol 39: 327—Vol 45: 107—Vol 46: 238—Vol 47: 29, 196—Vol 49: 394—Vol 50: 189, 279, 414 —Vol 55: 445—Vol 64: 160—Vol 65: 124— Vol 69: 120, 432—Vol 70: 359—Vol 80: 190 —Vol 82: 653—Vol 83: 1014
WELD...Vol 33: 1033—Vol 34: 198—Vol 42: 79
WELDEN.......................................Vol 37: 155
WELDON...Vol 35: 656—Vol 52: 434—Vol 53: 448—Vol 55: 335—Vol 56: 47—Vol 76: 401
WELLBORN...Vol 50: 350—Vol 51: 358—Vol 52: 228
WELLER—Vol 39: 273—Vol 40: 24, 170—Vol 42: 336—Vol 55: 520
WELLES...Vol 18: 300—Vol 28: 480—Vol 32: 282—Vol 33: 40—Vol 36: 77—Vol 41: 210—Vol 42: 134—Vol 45: 19—Vol 50: 116 —Vol 59: 589, 680, 762—Vol 64: 389
WELLET...................................Vol 38: 329
WELLINGHAM.............................Vol 46: 335
WELLINGTON...Vol 47: 393—Vol 48: 300— Vol 82: 63
WELLMAN...............................Vol 37: 73, 270
WELLS...Vol 3: 686—Vol 19: 206, 431—Vol 20: 278—Vol 22: 154—Vol 23: 64, 326, 398 —Vol 26: 139—Vol 27: 671—Vol 35: 651, 654—Vol 37: 488—Vol 38: 35, 276—Vol 39: 273—Vol 40: 227, 272—Vol 41: 210—Vol 43: 425, 426, 488—Vol 44: 312—Vol 49: 46 —Vol 50: 190, 191—Vol 52: 50—Vol 53: 627, 630—Vol 54: 351—Vol 56: 564, 629, 688—Vol 57: 215, 478, 567, 688—Vol 58: 52, 452, 588, 649—Vol 59: 111, 312, 387, 440, 587, 651—Vol 60: 572—Vol 61: 552—Vol 62: 587—Vol 63: 107—Vol 64: 57, 121, 387, 443—Vol 65: 441—Vol 66: 828—Vol 67: 577—Vol 68: 58, 401, 685—Vol 69: 120—: Vol 70: 129—Vol 71: 463—Vol 73: (11-69) —Vol 75: (6-39)—Vol 76: 63, 709—Vol 78: 246, 650—Vol 80: 154, 382—Vol 82: 138, 397—Vol 83: 172, 522—Vol 84: 245, 247, 323, 633, 964
WELSH...Vol 46: 243—Vol 61: 275—Vol 71: 956—Vol 76: 60—Vol 78: 294—Vol 80: 276 —Vol 82: 141
WELSHEIMER...............................Vol 66: 538
WELTON...Vol 32: 632—Vol 49: 135—Vol 60: 418—Vol 74: (4-51)
WELTY................................... ....Vol 70: 356

WENDEL..Vol 53: 117
WENDELL...........................Vol 60: 572—Vol 65: 124
WENTWORTH...Vol 15: 351—Vol 31: 588,
859—Vol 36: 757—Vol 43: 599—Vol 53: 118
WENZELL.............Vol 43: 492—Vol 44: 80, 150
WERNER...............Vol 67: 47—Vol 82: 860
WERTZ..Vol 84: 706
WERTZER...Vol 48: 122
WESCHLER...Vol 54: 537
WESCOTT..................Vol 52: 51—Vol 58: 331
WESHLER..Vol 54: 537
WESNER...Vol 49: 192
WEST...Vol 21: 497—Vol 23: 325, 398—Vol
24: 456—Vol 25: 885—Vol 26: 57—Vol 30:
541—Vol 34: 656—Vol 36: 574—Vol 38:
276, 331—Vol 39: 22, 222—Vol 43: 598—
Vol 44: 382—Vol 45: 19, 120, 185, 198, 239—
Vol 46: 157, 336, 337, 387—Vol 48: 370—Vol
49: 187, 354—Vol 50: 70, 187, 351, 415—Vol
52: 687, 733—Vol 53: 446—Vol 54: 112, 223,
228—Vol 55: 106, 109, 338—Vol 57: 72, 352
—Vol 58: 53, 370, 500—Vol 59: 238, 653—
Vol 60: 505—Vol 62: 390, 649—Vol 63: 60,
742—Vol 65: 439, 763—Vol 66: 309—Vol
68: 373, 492—Vol 69: 361—Vol 70: 355—
Vol 71: 957—Vol 73: (2-64), (10-76)—Vol
77: 39, 603—Vol 79: 613—Vol 81: 516, 517
—Vol 82: 860, 862—Vol 83: 93, 945—Vol
84: 519
WESTBROOK......................................Vol 80: 272
WESTBROOKE.............................Vol 61: 912
WESTCOTT...Vol 2: 41—Vol 9: 293—Vol
23: 325—Vol 27: 808—Vol 28: 261—Vol 29:
514—Vol 39: 273—Vol 57: 216—Vol 59:
312—Vol 60: 635—Vol 63: 636—Vol 64:
523—Vol 67: 41—Vol 84: 520
WESTEN...Vol 84: 634
WESTER...Vol 37: 72
WESTERVELT....................................Vol 34: 538
WESTFALL..Vol 61: 784
WESTON...Vol 20: 166—Vol 49: 47—Vol 82:
398
WESTOVER..................Vol 28: 259—Vol 43: 496
WESTROPE..Vol 63: 635
WETER..Vol 82: 220
WETHERALL.............Vol 43: 545—Vol 82: 398
WETHERBEE...Vol 26: 339—Vol 42: 12—
Vol 45: 121—Vol 50: 64—Vol 60: 697—Vol
67: 46, 116, 512, 514
WETHERELL...Vol 41: 30—Vol 57: 569, 688
—Vol 65: 246, 298
WETHERILL..Vol 54: 536
WETHINGTON......................................Vol 55: 713
WETMORE..Vol 43: 490
WETZEL...Vol 46: 384
WETZELL...Vol 37: 395
WEYMAN...................Vol 45: 23—Vol 67: 752
WHALEY...Vol 31: 51—Vol 41: 33—Vol 47:
396—Vol 48: 301, 372—Vol 65: 298—Vol
74: (2-40)—Vol 83: 945
WHAREY..Vol 67: 47
WHARTON...Vol 43: 496—Vol 50: 355—Vol
57: 116
WHEADON....................Vol 41: 212—Vol 42: 75
WHEAT.......................Vol 41: 127—Vol 63: 633
WHEATLEY...Vol 44: 84—Vol 57: 630—Vol
69: 764—Vol 78: 155
WHEATON...Vol 45: 112—Vol 46: 21—Vol
55: 165—Vol 74: (5-43)—Vol 79: 113
WHEEDEN..Vol 43: 423

WHEELER...Vol 1: 451—Vol 19: 433—Vol
20: 62—Vol 22: 155—Vol 26: 562—Vol 28:
259, 262, 549—Vol 30: 256—Vol 31: 50,
414—Vol 34: 67, 538—Vol 35: 656—Vol 37:
73—Vol 38: 330—Vol 39: 276—Vol 42: 74,
270—Vol 43: 423—Vol 44: 83, 386—Vol 45:
111, 120, 121, 123, 197—Vol 46: 21, 98, 99,
100, 104, 239, 386—Vol 48: 306, 372, 450—
Vol 50: 62—Vol 52: 436—Vol 53: 52, 243,
448, 493, 690—Vol 54: 229, 353, 465—Vol 55:
106—Vol 56: 561—Vol 57: 37, 218, 219, 349,
350, 478, 481—Vol 58: 54—Vol 62: 307, 387,
456, 684—Vol 63: 59, 373—Vol 65: 249, 442
—Vol 66: 364, 670, 730—Vol 67: 242, 715—
Vol 70: 1265—Vol 74: (5-39)—Vol 76: 401,
653—Vol 77: 664—Vol 82: 796—Vol 83:
259—Vol 84: 635
WHEELOCK...Vol 28: 164, 364—Vol 32: 507
—Vol 46: 102—Vol 54: 53, 422—Vol 56: 110
—Vol 58: 329—Vol 70: 352
WHEELWRIGHT.................................Vol 79: 35
WHELAN...Vol 67: 146
WHELDEN..Vol 84: 159
WHERRY...Vol 31: 410, 752—Vol 32: 60—
Vol 67: 47—Vol 70: 1267
WHIDBEE..Vol 82: 794
WHILBURGER...................................Vol 30: 337
WHINEY.........................Vol 74: (7-54), (8-54)
WHIPPLE...Vol 20: 278, 608—Vol 21: 167—
Vol 41: 125—Vol 42: 139—Vol 43: 424,
495, 496, 596—Vol 50: 190—Vol 52: 321—
Vol 53: 181, 332, 447, 694—Vol 59: 442—Vol
65: 441—Vol 77: 239, 332
WHISTLER...Vol 48: 64—Vol 52: 231—Vol
68: 526
WHITAKER...Vol 39: 223—Vol 44: 26, 381—
Vol 48: 56, 448—Vol 49: 354—Vol 60: 64,
277
WHITBECK..Vol 83: 439
WHITCOMB...Vol 26: 140, 241—Vol 42: 192
—Vol 43: 419—Vol 48: 205, 371, 449—Vol
49: 128—Vol 52: 53
WHITCOME...Vol 29: 514
WHITFIELD.............................Vol 64: 121, 122
WHITE...Vol 6: 595—Vol 20: 278—Vol 22:
373—Vol 23: 244, 471—Vol 24: 149—Vol 25:
39, 800, 888—Vol 26: 55, 140—Vol 27: 381,
736, 805, 806—Vol 28: 161, 260, 365, 366,
482, 546—Vol 29: 44, 287, 290, 648, 652—
Vol 30: 63, 64—Vol 32: 718—Vol 35: 654—
Vol 36: 214, 349, 354, 573—Vol 37: 271—
Vol 38: 35, 86—Vol 39: 21, 227—Vol 40:
75—Vol 41: 212—Vol 42: 341—Vol 44: 314
—Vol 45: 105, 118, 119, 125, 126, 195, 199,
241—Vol 46: 104, 154, 156, 157—Vol 47:
394—Vol 48: 444—Vol 49: 356—Vol 50:
192, 345—Vol 52: 322—Vol 53: 691—Vol
54: 107, 350, 421, 590, 592, 709—Vol 55: 164,
166, 338, 521, 713—Vol 56: 44, 108, 172, 173,
226, 370, 371, 561, 625, 688—Vol 57: 172, 312,
350, 478, 690—Vol 58: 172, 453, 502, 652—
Vol 59: 314, 387, 524—Vol 60: 248, 249, 506,
572—Vol 61: 230, 708, 912—Vol 62: 586,
587, 651—Vol 63: 59, 107, 167, 295, 506, 568
—Vol 64: 651, 714, 716, 757—Vol 65: 299,
300, 437, 759—Vol 66: 308—Vol 67: 517—
Vol 68: 58—Vol 69: 245—Vol 70: 129, 206,
352, 573, 1166, 1169, 1170—Vol 71: 87, 958—
Vol 72: (2-64), (7-72)—Vol 73: (1-63),
(11-68)—Vol 74: (5-41)—Vol 75: (2-57),

(4-53)—Vol 76: 63, 144, 654—Vol 77: 183, 389, 725—Vol 79: 332—Vol 80: 277, 555—Vol 81: 315, 429, 430, 630—Vol 82: 140, 313, 503—Vol 83: 93, 171, 336—Vol 84: 327, 524, 632, 705
WHITEFORD ....Vol 69: 121
WHITEHEAD....Vol 35: 652—Vol 41: 125—Vol 45: 198, 200, 328—Vol 46: 336—Vol 49: 191—Vol 53: 243—Vol 57: 216, 745—Vol 63: 56, 106—Vol 75: (10-65)—Vol 81: 71, 316—Vol 83: 873
WHITEHILL............Vol 48: 202—Vol 59: 442
WHITEHOUSE....................Vol 45: 193
WHITEHURST....................Vol 63: 426
WHITEIS........................Vol 67: 146
WHITELY.........Vol 46: 392—Vol 81: 20, 316
WHITEMAN...Vol 50: 62—Vol 71: 1110—Vol 78: 246
WHITENBURG...........................Vol 57: 435
WHITESIDE....Vol 34: 202—Vol 45: 190—Vol 49: 283, 390—Vol 82: 502
WHITESIDES.......Vol 45: 322—Vol 46: 156, 331
WHITEWOOD....................Vol 61: 704
WHITFIELD....Vol 44: 154—Vol 49: 130, 131, 186, 190—Vol 50: 57, 352—Vol 62: 53, 120, 121—Vol 63: 245
WHITFORD....Vol 42: 191, 341—Vol 46: 154 —Vol 47: 396—Vol 57: 175
WHITHAM.....................Vol 70: 1267
WHITING....Vol 29: 650, 715—Vol 38: 331—Vol 43: 424, 495, 540, 597—Vol 44: 148—Vol 45: 27, 197—Vol 46: 29—Vol 49: 45, 281 —Vol 50: 352—Vol 52: 733—Vol 53: 574, 693—Vol 54: 590—Vol 59: 764—Vol 61: 610 —Vol 65: 245—Vol 73: (2-65)
WHITLACH.......................Vol 48: 57
WHITLEY.............Vol 54: 226—Vol 60: 635
WHITLOCK....Vol 31: 586—Vol 42: 341—Vol 43: 483—Vol 46: 154—Vol 48: 57—Vol 63: 572, 697
WHITMAN....Vol 24: 149—Vol 26: 53, 54—Vol 41: 32—Vol 42: 339—Vol 48: 119, 304—Vol 53: 55—Vol 54: 590—Vol 58: 652—Vol 70: 574—Vol 71: 460—Vol 82: 396
WHITMARSH....Vol 67: 41, 576—Vol 84: 894
WHITMORE....Vol 26: 56, 242—Vol 28: 159—Vol 42: 268—Vol 43: 602—Vol 60: 51—Vol 67: 290—Vol 78: 553—Vol 83: 520
WHITNEY....Vol 4: 31—Vol 25: 888—Vol 28: 159—Vol 30: 540—Vol 31: 54, 586—Vol 32: 59, 161, 282, 283—Vol 33: 475, 959—Vol 34: 322—Vol 39: 274, 328—Vol 40: 74, 76, 108—Vol 41: 213—Vol 43: 602—Vol 44: 311—Vol 46: 98, 243—Vol 48: 443—Vol 49: 45—Vol 57: 435—Vol 70: 135—Vol 73: (11-68)
WHITSEL....................Vol 55: 209—Vol 58: 369
WHITSETT.....................Vol 75: (5-46)
WHITTAKER........Vol 53: 744—Vol 84: 636
WHITTEAR......................Vol 27: 670
WHITTEMORE....Vol 26: 142, 337—Vol 27: 44, 671, 735, 738
WHITTEN....Vol 29: 513—Vol 48: 64—Vol 60: 419—Vol 82: 933
WHITTEREDGE........................Vol 47: 95
WHITTIER....Vol 43: 488, 602—Vol 45: 20, 111—Vol 46: 100—Vol 48: 60, 446
WHITTING.........................Vol 82: 933

WHITTINGTON....Vol 57: 630—Vol 63: 700—Vol 82: 726
WHITTIS...............Vol 65: 247—Vol 69: 362
WHITTLESEY....................Vol 45: 192
WHITTMAN.......................Vol 46: 153
WHOLEBUR......................Vol 41: 34
WIATT.............Vol 72: (7-75)—Vol 81: 631
WIBLE..........................Vol 78: 457
WICKER............Vol 58: 452—Vol 69: 629
WICKERSHAM....................Vol 45: 190
WICKES................Vol 27: 44—Vol 46: 154
WICKHAM..........Vol 35: 653—Vol 83: 873
WICKLIFF.......................Vol 46: 240
WICKLIFFE ......Vol 66: 162—Vol 72: (2-68)
WICKS....Vol 34: 538—Vol 36: 356—Vol 42: 341
WIDDIFIELD.....................Vol 68: 551
WIDDIS.........................Vol 69: 362
WIDDRINGTON......................Vol 33: 473
WIDGER.............Vol 68: 486—Vol 69: 120
WIEDERWAX......................Vol 64: 651
WIELER.........................Vol 55: 522
WIER..........................Vol 67: 516
WIESSE........................Vol 30: 337
WIGFALL..................... Vol 81: 430
WIGGINS....Vol 46: 334—Vol 52: 109—Vol 54: 421—Vol 57: 434, 481—Vol 62: 122, 389—Vol 70: 207
WIGGINTON....Vol 57: 177—Vol 68: 155—Vol 69: 57
WIGHT....Vol 45: 106—Vol 61: 607—Vol 67: 442, 714—Vol 75: (10-67)
WIGHTMAN....Vol 37: 395, 487—Vol 42: 339 —Vol 48: 119, 304—Vol 58: 764—Vol 59: 174, 525
WIGTON........................Vol 36: 577
WIKOFF....Vol 41: 128—Vol 47: 87—Vol 50: 357—Vol 82: 142
WILBANKS......................Vol 50: 65
WILBER........................Vol 42: 81
WILBOIT.......................Vol 30: 65
WILBOR........................Vol 83: 91
WILBOUR...........Vol 39: 327—Vol 53: 377
WILBOURN......................Vol 45: 118
WILBOURNE....................Vol 72: (3-72)
WILBRIGHT.....................Vol 30: 65
WILBUR....Vol 22: 272—Vol 28: 263, 546—Vol 46: 158—Vol 50: 355—Vol 51: 166, 235 —Vol 53: 630
WILBURGER.....................Vol 30: 337
WILCOCK.......................Vol 28: 260
WILCOX....Vol 22: 997—Vol 28: 546—Vol 31: 751—Vol 32: 161—Vol 37: 150—Vol 43: 492—Vol 45: 114—Vol 46: 29—Vol 48: 447, 450—Vol 50: 189, 354—Vol 53: 494—Vol 55: 166, 337, 522—Vol 56: 491, 740, 743 —Vol 57: 352—Vol 58: 372—Vol 60: 51, 507—Vol 63: 270, 508, 569, 740, 742—Vol 68: 120, 488—Vol 70: 359—Vol 74: (4-53), (5-43)—Vol 76: 401—Vol 80: 383—Vol 81: 73—Vol 82: 220—Vol 83: 872
WILCOXEN......................Vol 63: 571
WILCOXON......................Vol 64: 713
WILCOXSON..........Vol 28: 362—Vol 55: 209
WILD............Vol 26: 242—Vol 31: 588
WILDER...Vol 26: 140—Vol 42: 192—Vol 43: 419—Vol 50: 351—Vol 54: 110—Vol 56: 561 —Vol 70: 708
WILDERMAN.....................Vol 60: 571
WILDS.........................Vol 28: 60

WILDY_____Vol 54: 588
WILES_____Vol 64: 161
WILEY___Vol 24: 458—Vol 26: 243—Vol 27:
44, 805—Vol 30: 541—Vol 33: 475, 956,
1031—Vol 38: 87, 275, 332—Vol 55: 110—
Vol 56: 691—Vol 59: 387, 388—Vol 70: 706
—Vol 77: 539—Vol 78: 456—Vol 80: 276—
Vol 82: 141
WILGUS_____Vol 60: 49
WILHELM_____ ____Vol 82: 797
WILHOIT_____Vol 59: 589—Vol 78: 398
WILKERSON___Vol 43: 596—Vol 79: 332—
Vol 83: 1014
WILKES___Vol 22: 997—Vol 68: 686—Vol 69:
54
WILKINS___Vol 21: 496—Vol 27: 671—Vol
30: 441—Vol 45: 20—Vol 48: 372—Vol 49:
192—Vol 53: 330—Vol 55: 710—Vol 58:
54—Vol 59: 682—Vol 60: 417—Vol 62: 774
—Vol 72: (11-58)—Vol 75: (5-47)—Vol 83:
260
WILKINSON___Vol 25: 718—Vol 27: 381—
Vol 30: 147—Vol 36: 353—Vol 38: 87—Vol
40: 228—Vol 42: 194—Vol 43: 598—Vol 45:
125—Vol 57: 746—Vol 63: 59—Vol 68: 553
—Vol 71: 759—Vol 82: 397—Vol 83: 336
WILL__Vol 50: 353, 415—Vol 58: 451
WILLARD___Vol 17: 569—Vol 26: 338—Vol
40: 227—Vol 44: 83—Vol 47: 27—Vol 53:
181—Vol 54: 173—Vol 55: 339—Vol 58:
372—Vol 59: 238, 525—Vol 67: 42, 442—
Vol 68: 551—Vol 69: 58, 434—Vol 70: 130—
Vol 75: (9-46)—Vol 82: 141
WILLCOX_____Vol 64: 520—Vol 68: 492
WILLEMIN_____Vol 34: 538
WILLETS_____Vol 38: 86—Vol 45: 187
WILLETT___Vol 43: 602—Vol 44: 316—Vol
45: 111—Vol 75: (9-46)
WILLETTS___Vol 31: 586—Vol 41: 71—Vol
44: 236
WILLEY___Vol 25: 799—Vol 26: 339—Vol 28:
162, 479—Vol 37: 489—Vol 76: 580
WILLIAM_____Vol 43: 421
WILLIAMS___Vol 2: 192—Vol 7: 45, 170—Vol
10: 183—Vol 15: 224—Vol 17: 282, 390—
Vol 19: 70, 628—Vol 20: 608—Vol 21: 62,
168, 332, 498—Vol 22: 156, 373, 997—Vol
23: 470—Vol 25: 717—Vol 26: 142—Vol 27:
45, 46, 71, 667, 808—Vol 28: 164, 482, 549—
Vol 29: 289, 652—Vol 30: 62, 256, 441, 538,
542—Vol 31: 52, 412, 665, 749, 861—Vol 32:
161, 282—Vol 33: 39, 707, 1168—Vol 34:
66—Vol 36: 1037—Vol 37: 66, 578, 759—Vol
37: 66, 151, 155, 270—Vol 38: 35, 85, 86, 220,
275, 330—Vol 39: 103, 141, 224, 326—Vol
40: 76, 77, 229, 275—Vol 41: 29, 31, 34, 68,
123, 161, 164—Vol 42: 74, 81, 191, 342—Vol
43: 416, 493, 547, 601—Vol 44: 26, 149, 154,
311—Vol 45: 101, 119, 198—Vol 46: 28, 103,
241, 385, 391, 393—Vol 47: 27, 31, 193, 194,
199, 263, 270, 341, 397—Vol 48: 58, 65, 121,
306, 446, 448—Vol 49: 41, 47, 48, 352, 354,
355, 395—Vol 50: 66, 67, 68, 115, 187, 357,
413—Vol 52: 109, 434; 561—Vol 53: 56,
180, 328, 329, 628, 746, 748—Vol 54: 52, 55,
56, 224, 420, 422, 709—Vol 55: 282, 446, 599,
601, 714—Vol 56: 46, 108, 318, 369, 416, 563,
564, 626, 629—Vol 57: 49, 218, 353, 479, 566,
629, 691, 743—Vol 58: 52, 329, 371, 372, 499,
764—Vol 59: 47, 48, 238, 586, 763, 764—Vol

60: 50, 51, 112, 366, 419, 699—Vol 61: 470,
607, 866, 867—Vol 62: 503—Vol 63: 244,
246, 506, 633, 738—Vol 64: 157, 257, 388,
522, 650—Vol 65: 299—Vol 66: 248, 249,
826, 827—Vol 67: 46, 148, 388, 443, 753—
Vol 68: 241, 372, 486, 488, 552, 625—Vol 69:
160, 161—Vol 70: 135, 452, 574—Vol 71:
453, 557, 1108—Vol 72: (1-66), (4-82), (4-
83), (7-73)—Vol 73: (9-65), (9-67)—Vol
74: (2-40), (5-42)—Vol 75: (10-66)—Vol
76: 62, 400, 402, 655, 711—Vol 77: 240—Vol
78: 53—Vol 79: 284—Vol 80: 190, 191, 194,
382, 657—Vol 81: 130, 316, 431, 630—Vol
82: 50, 797, 933—Vol 83: 94, 170, 439, 520,
521, 718, 872—Vol 84: 70, 326, 447, 519, 634,
966
WILLIAMSON___Vol 26: 340—Vol 27: 44, 672,
740—Vol 37: 271—Vol 38: 221—Vol 39:
101, 140, 227—Vol 40: 73—Vol 42: 79—Vol
45: 21, 185, 198—Vol 46: 157, 239, 387—
Vol 47: 191—Vol 49: 49, 353—Vol 53: 55,
249—Vol 54: 226—Vol 57: 435—Vol 59:
589—Vol 61: 470—Vol 62: 123, 712, 713—
Vol 63: 106, 295—Vol 64: 445—Vol 66: 159,
537—Vol 68: 488—Vol 73: (9-64)—Vol 74:
(5-42)—Vol 76: 654—Vol 77: 240
WILLIER_____Vol 67: 42
WILLIFORD_____Vol 57: 312—Vol 71: 461
WILLING_____Vol 43: 601
WILLINGHAM ____Vol 44: 387___Vol 45: 236
WILLIS___Vol 26: 339—Vol 27: 739—Vol 28:
366, 480, 481—Vol 36: 350—Vol 38: 328—
Vol 39: 141, 142, 272—Vol 40: 23, 73, 107,
223—Vol 41: 120—Vol 42: 270—Vol 43:
425, 483—Vol 49: 190, 286, 350—Vol 50: 63
—Vol 53: 448—Vol 55: 653—Vol 59: 239,
387, 679—Vol 66: 305—Vol 67: 47, 117, 293
—Vol 68: 486, 550—Vol 76: 400, 401, 710—
Vol 77: 603—Vol 83: 946
WILLISTON_____Vol 55: 397
WILLOUGHBY___Vol 36: 755—Vol 37: 151—
Vol 45: 116—Vol 68: 687—Vol 69: 56, 631—
Vol 70: 359, 1018—Vol 75: (2-60)
WILLS___Vol 50: 69, 193—Vol 58: 451—Vol
59: 49—Vol 83: 442
WILLSEY_____Vol 76: 218
WILLSON___Vol 45: 239, 241—Vol 47: 193—
Vol 63: 374—Vol 68: 373, 551—Vol 84: 521
WILMOT_____Vol 36: 354—Vol 39: 327
WILSEY_____Vol 38: 35
WILSON___Vol 22: 52—Vol 25: 718, 886—Vol
26: 55, 143—Vol 27: 381, 740, 888, 891—
Vol 28: 162, 366—Vol 29: 647, 716—Vol 30:
147, 258, 335—Vol 31: 413, 586—Vol 32:
507, 631—Vol 33: 953—Vol 36, 76, 573, 576,
755, 760—Vol 37: 69, 149—Vol 38: 36—
Vol 40: 225, 227—Vol 41: 29, 33, 68—Vol
42: 138, 190, 194, 267, 333, 342—Vol 43:
419, 423, 486, 495, 542, 546—Vol 44: 80, 82,
85, 147, 152, 227, 230, 309—Vol 45: 102, 103,
107, 110, 188, 191, 323—Vol 46: 23, 27, 104,
242, 245, 246, 388, 389—Vol 47: 29, 31, 269
—Vol 48: 59, 62, 203, 308, 368, 443—Vol 49:
44, 46, 48, 126, 190, 286, 356, 394—Vol 50:
189—Vol 51: 301—Vol 52: 322, 359—Vol
53: 447—Vol 54: 53, 110, 222, 223, 350, 351,
353—Vol 55: 286, 445, 519, 521—Vol 56:
171, 175, 317, 319, 624, 742, 746—Vol 57:
115, 214, 311, 348, 478, 481, 691, 744—Vol 58:
53: 171, 372—Vol 59: 112, 679, 681, 763—

Vol 60: 50, 157, 419, 571, 572, 697—Vol 61: 156, 274, 276, 708, 866—Vol 62: 713—Vol 63: 246, 371, 374, 632—Vol 64: 716, 759—Vol 65: 297, 366, 634, 760—Vol 66: 248, 251, 365, 538, 599, 827, 828—Vol 67: 148, 242, 289, 577, 753—Vol 68: 58, 120, 121, 242, 683 —Vol 69: 119, 242, 287, 361, 565—Vol 70: 135—Vol 71: 673, 958—Vol 73: (9-66), (10- 77)—Vol 74: (2-43), (3-45), (5-40), (5-41), (11-58), (11-60)—Vol 75: (4-53)—Vol 76: 61, 653, 709—Vol 77: 242—Vol 78: 398— Vol 79: 35, 284, 518—Vol 80: 44—Vol 81: 431—Vol 82: 63, 396, 501, 861, 933, 934, 936 —Vol 83: 441, 717—Vol 84: 69, 325

WILT_____Vol 43: 492
WILTSE_____Vol 45: 121
WIMBERLY__Vol 60: 249—Vol 64: 56—Vol 66: 248
WIMBISH_____Vol 65: 761
WIMBLEDUFF_____Vol 59: 523
WINAN_____Vol 35: 439
WINANS__Vol 25: 37, 383—Vol 30: 62, 146— Vol 39: 224—Vol 40: 25, 26, 73, 107, 223— Vol 56: 43—Vol 74: (12-53)
VINCHELL__Vol 27: 739—Vol 32: 162—Vol 33: 473—Vol 50: 194—Vol 52: 559—Vol 55: 286—Vol 82: 63, 313, 931
WINCHESTER__Vol 68: 242—Vol 69: 118— Vol 72: (4-83)
WINDEMOLD_____Vol 67: 441
WINDER_____Vol 77: 243
WINDROW_____Vol 83: 92
WINDSOR__Vol 35: 437, 1263—Vol 56: 318— Vol 67: 115—Vol 74: (5-43)
WINE__Vol 57: 480—Vol 64: 713—Vol 72: (9-88)
WINEGALL_____Vol 60: 747
WINEGAR_____Vol 59: 764—Vol 60: 49
WINEINGER_____Vol 76: 61
WINES_I_____Vol 73: (10-76)
WINFIELD__Vol 38: 35—Vol 48: 62—Vol 49: 189—Vol 56: 688
WINFREY_____Vol 70: 709
WING__Vol 28: 164—Vol 30: 538—Vol 32: 718—Vol 47: 28—Vol 56: 226, 626—Vol 57: 40—Vol 59: 762—Vol 60: 289, 568, 569, 696
WINGENON_____Vol 46: 393
WINGFIELD__Vol 25: 719—Vol 54: 173, 648 —Vol 56: 688
WINGLEY_____Vol 42: 15
WINGO_____Vol 41: 123
WINKELEY_____Vol 37: 152
WINKS_____Vol 39: 226
WINN__Vol 35: 57—Vol 40: 274—Vol 41: 29—Vol 46: 243, 386—Vol 47: 95, 199, 272, 389, 391—Vol 49: 190—Vol 50: 275—Vol 53: 629—Vol 54: 352—Vol 61: 274—Vol 64: 521—Vol 71: 358, 461—Vol 74: (1-50)—Vol 75: (10-67)—Vol 81: 430
WINNE__Vol 55: 599—Vol 67: 647—Vol 75: (2-59)
WINSHIP_____Vol 40: 26
WINSLIP_____Vol 53: 746
WINSLOW__Vol 2: 45—Vol 4: 29—Vol 32: 632—Vol 42: 269—Vol 45: 24—Vol 48: 372 —Vol 50: 280—Vol 52: 230—Vol 55: 520, 710—Vol 56: 625, 688—Vol 70: 456
WINSOR__Vol 22: 156, 374—Vol 23: 62—Vol 46: 22—Vol 58: 172—Vol 67: 115—Vol 74: (5-43)

WINSTEAD_____Vol 60: 248
WINSTON__Vol 36: 75—Vol 41: 31—Vol 46: 22—Vol 47: 197—Vol 48: 440, 441—Vol 55: 711—Vol 56: 415—Vol 58: 587
WINTER__Vol 36: 350, 760—Vol 37: 349— Vol 38: 328—Vol 40: 76, 108—Vol 58: 369 —Vol 65: 761
WINTERMUTH_____Vol 67: 440
WINTERRINGER_____Vol 68: 687
WINTERS__Vol 48: 119—Vol 57: 481—Vol 59: 681—Vol 62: 775—Vol 67: 47, 144, 145— Vol 71: 839—Vol 76: 928—Vol 84: 636
WINTHROP____Vol 26: 52—Vol 67: 575, 712
WINTON_____Vol 31: 585—Vol 59: 389
WIRDERWAX_____Vol 65: 120
WIRE_____Vol 25: 384—Vol 81: 570
WIRES_____Vol 45: 194
WISDOM_____Vol 61: 552
WISE__Vol 35: 653—Vol 38: 87, 219, 329— Vol 43: 496—Vol 49: 355—Vol 50: 348—Vol 63: 294—Vol 64: 446—Vol 65: 365—Vol 66: 305—Vol 67: 292—Vol 68: 122—Vol 69: 246—Vol 77: 240—Vol 84: 246, 325, 706
WISEBURY_____Vol 28: 159
WISEHART_____Vol 48: 55—Vol 83: 521
WISEMAN__Vol 56: 690—Vol 66: 308, 406, 731—Vol 78: 107—Vol 84: 447
WISMER_____Vol 37: 156
WISNER__Vol 43: 600—Vol 46: 393—Vol 80: 45
WISTER_____Vol 39: 328
WISWALL__Vol 5: 574—Vol 26: 143, 562— Vol 36: 217, 572—Vol 43: 541—Vol 52: 51 WISWELL_____Vol 67: 516
WITCHER_____Vol 52: 434
WITHAM_____Vol 24: 149
WITHERELL__Vol 22: 375—Vol 34: 540— Vol 64: 389—Vol 65: 246, 298—Vol 70: 1266 Vol 77: 389
WITHERILL_____Vol 30: 148
WITHEROW_____Vol 54: 591
WITHERS__Vol 44: 314—Vol 61: 472—Vol 62: 248, 305
WITHERSPOON__Vol 36: 760—Vol 37: 266 —Vol 41: 126—Vol 58: 587—Vol 66: 461, 731—Vol 70: 353—Vol 74: (2-42)—Vol 83: 94, 171—Vol 84: 159, 523
WITHERSTINE_____Vol 22: 996
WITHROW_____Vol 52: 110
WITT__Vol 45: 188—Vol 48: 306—Vol 67: 289
WITTER__Vol 44: 316—Vol 45: 111, 123, 327 —Vol 49: 287—Vol 60: 113
WITTY_____Vol 82: 139
WOBLIVER_____Vol 45: 321
WOLCOTT__Vol 26: 57—Vol 35: 439, 1099— Vol 39: 327—Vol 45: 199—Vol 46: 23, 237— Vol 47: 270—Vol 61: 229—Vol 67: 114— Vol 72: (1-66)—Vol 77: 332—Vol 82: 862— Vol 83: 259
WOLF__Vol 61: 707—Vol 67: 43—Vol 74: (9-49)—Vol 82: 312
WOLFE__Vol 22: 53—Vol 48: 444—Vol 59: 681—Vol 66: 535—Vol 79: 34—Vol 82: 933
WOLFROM_____Vol 55: 339
WOLFSKILL_____Vol 79: 656
WOLLAN_____Vol 64: 161
WOLLASTON_____Vol 59: 239
WOLLEN_____Vol 28: 260—Vol 70: 1166
WOLLSTON_____Vol 71: 760

WOLVERTAN_____Vol 56: 174, 317
WOMACK___Vol 49: 193—Vol 53: 693—Vol
61: 865, 866—Vol 62: 159—Vol 74: (2-42),
(5-42)
WOOD___Vol 25: 37—Vol 26: 57—Vol 27: 736,
890—Vol 28: 478—Vol 29: 288—Vol 31: 586,
861—Vol 32: 160—Vol 34: 423—Vol 35:
436, 1265—Vol 37: 67, 70, 149, 153—Vol 38:
87, 217—Vol 39: 226, 326—Vol 40: 25—Vol
41: 70, 124—Vol 42: 81, 339, 343—Vol 43:
420, 425, 483, 492, 546, 597, 600, 601—Vol
44: 28, 150, 227, 314, 386—Vol 45: 22, 112,
187, 188, 194—Vol 46: 241—Vol 47: 31, 194,
198, 397—Vol 48: 58, 62, 119, 122, 307, 308
—Vol 49: 49, 393—Vol 50: 353—Vol 52:
565—Vol 53: 176—Vol 54: 225, 421, 549—
Vol 55: 443, 445—Vol 56: 175, 373, 479, 563,
628—Vol 57: 174, 175, 688—Vol 58: 500,
651—Vol 59: 49—Vol 60: 250—Vol 61: 552,
783, 911—Vol 62: 647—Vol 64: 59, 161, 259,
389, 587, 759—Vol 65: 160, 248, 440—Vol
66: 252—Vol 67: 575, 647—Vol 68: 492, 553
—Vol 69: 243, 244—Vol 70: 352, 355, 456,
573—Vol 71: 1109—Vol 72: (3-71), (10-94)
—Vol 73: (1-63), (10-76)—Vol 74: (5-37)—
Vol 75: (7-35), (8-56), (10-64), (10-67)—
Vol 76: 709—Vol 77: 769—Vol 79: 560, 656
—Vol 82: 312, 727, 930, 933, 934—Vol 83:
521, 522—Vol 84: 636, 704
WOODBRIDGE___Vol 21: 335—Vol 22: 52—
Vol 83: 1014
WOODBURN___Vol 30: 257—Vol 42: 268—Vol
50: 356—Vol 77: 239
WOODBURY___Vol 27: 45—Vol 29: 289—Vol
34: 657—Vol 45: 118—Vol 84: 445
WOODCOCK___Vol 46: 337—Vol 47: 264—Vol
67: 44—Vol 84: 633
WOODELL_____Vol 46: 98
WOODEN_____Vol 38: 35
WOODFIN___Vol 59: 111, 521—Vol 67: 516—
Vol 68: 57
WOODFOLK___Vol 70: 134—Vol 73: (10-77)
WOODFORD___Vol 21: 496—Vol 29: 800—Vol
44: 234—Vol 54: 352—Vol 56: 227, 479—
Vol 66: 365
WOODHULL_____Vol 18: 181
WOODIN___Vol 25: 717—Vol 42: 140—Vol
51: 301—Vol 56: 745
WOODING___Vol 35: 1264—Vol 56: 225—Vol
60: 418
WOODLY_____Vol 83: 946
WOODMAN_____Vol 29: 647—Vol 44: 315
WOODMANSEE_____Vol 81: 429
WOODROW___Vol 41: 70—Vol 55: 164—Vol
78: 294
WOODRUFF___Vol 3: 301—Vol 21: 404—Vol
22: 155—Vol 29: 717—Vol 30: 146, 147, 335
—Vol 35: 1038—Vol 44: 234—Vol 54: 650—
Vol 57: 434—Vol 67: 48, 444—Vol 74: (1-
51), (3-45), (7-55), (8-55)—Vol 82: 863
WOODRUFFE___Vol 41: 164—Vol 42: 138—
Vol 43: 486
WOODS___Vol 23: 398—Vol 28: 547—Vol 41:
165, 213—Vol 45: 109—Vol 46: 390—Vol
47: 191—Vol 49: 282, 286, 347, 392—Vol 50:
353—Vol 51: 238, 302—Vol 52: 52, 229—Vol
53: 118, 242, 331, 630—Vol 54: 227—Vol
56: 319—Vol 57: 689—Vol 60: 418—Vol 61:
866—Vol 62: 307, 694—Vol 63: 246, 371,
427—Vol 66: 599—Vol 68: 154—Vol 71: 87,

462—Vol 74: (5-39)—Vol 77: 333—Vol 82:
396, 795—Vol 83: 173, 1015
WOODSIDES_____Vol 66: 122
WOODSON___Vol 30: 543—Vol 43: 427, 494,
495—Vol 44: 80, 151—Vol 45: 110—Vol 53:
631—Vol 54: 311, 591—Vol 55: 712—Vol
56: 563—Vol 58: 331—Vol 67: 293, 383, 576
—Vol 71: 358—Vol 75: (1-54)—Vol 76: 709
—Vol 81: 570
WOODSTOCK_____Vol 66: 462
WOODSWORTH_____Vol 59: 681
WOODWARD___Vol 19: 308—Vol 22: 156, 269
—Vol 27: 671, 672—Vol 30: 149, 338, 439—
Vol 32: 163—Vol 36: 579—Vol 37: 348—
Vol 39: 22—Vol 45: 113, 116, 190, 192—Vol
46: 102, 152—Vol 47: 394—Vol 50: 190, 192,
357—Vol 56: 46, 691—Vol 57: 691—Vol 58:
330—Vol 59: 175—Vol 65: 763—Vol 66: 55
—Vol 67: 290—Vol 70: 877, 878—Vol 71:
464—Vol 76: 655—Vol 82: 797, 860
WOODWORTH___Vol 22: 376—Vol 27: 669—
Vol 37: 150—Vol 46: 21—Vol 52: 687—Vol
54: 176—Vol 72: (5-68)
WOODY_____Vol 49: 395
WOODYARD___Vol 50: 187—Vol 80: 276
WOOL_____Vol 49: 44
WOOLDRIDGE_____Vol 43: 545
WOOLEVER_____Vol 77: 664
WOOLEY___Vol 45: 123, 327—Vol 48: 59—Vol
58: 451—Vol 82: 499—Vol 83: 718
WOOLFOLK___Vol 38: 330—Vol 42: 79—Vol
47: 394—Vol 53: 53, 249—Vol 57: 218—Vol
67: 576
WOOLFORD_____Vol 45: 189—Vol 46: 392
WOOLIN_____Vol 28: 260
WOOLLEN_____Vol 82: 933
WOOLMAN_____Vol 75: (9-40)
WOOLS_____Vol 37: 74—Vol 43: 605
WOOLSEY_____Vol 56: 561—Vol 60: 114
WOOLVERTON_____Vol 41: 127—Vol 42: 78
WOOLY_____Vol 82: 502
WOOSTER___Vol 26: 142—Vol 39: 101, 103—
Vol 42: 270—Vol 46: 99
WOOSLEY_____Vol 48: 443
WOOTEN___Vol 26: 142—Vol 73: (1-63)
WORCESTER___Vol 31: 53, 749—Vol 32: 59,
717—Vol 39: 223—Vol 40: 172, 272
WORD_____Vol 58: 52—Vol 68: 154
WORDEN___Vol 31: 751—Vol 55: 520—Vol
65: 763—Vol 68: 285—Vol 74: (9-49)—Vol
77: 602
WORDON_____Vol 55: 710
WORDSON_____Vol 53: 628
WORK_____Vol 19: 532
WORKMAN_____Vol 59: 238
WORLAND_____Vol 84: 445, 703
WORLEY___Vol 50: 281—Vol 53: 328—Vol
66: 600—Vol 76: 654
WORLINE_____Vol 28: 365
WORM_____Vol 59: 387
WORMLEY_____Vol 45: 101
WORNOM_____Vol 84: 444
WORRALL_____Vol 56: 226—Vol 57: 565
WORRELL___Vol 47: 396—Vol 68: 487, 731—
Vol 71: 1026
WORSHAM___Vol 58: 451, 649—Vol 68: 486—
Vol 77: 603
WORSLEY_____Vol 80: 155
WORSTER_____Vol 55: 109
WORTERDYKE_____Vol 59: 176

WORTH................Vol 80: 336—Vol 83: 1014
WORTHINGTON....Vol 30: 147—Vol 39: 102,
327—Vol 42: 80, 189—Vol 45: 110—Vol 47:
32—Vol 58: 587—Vol 65: 300—Vol 74:
(11-57)—Vol 75: (2-61), (8-43)—Vol 81:
569
WORTHY...............................Vol 56: 172
WORTMAN.............................Vol 58: 370
WORTSER..............................Vol 48: 122
WORTZER..............................Vol 82: 932
WOSEMAN.............................Vol 45: 105
WOSLEY................................Vol 54: 174
WOTRING..........Vol 68: 284—Vol 75: (5-43)
WRAY....Vol 29: 802—Vol 66: 308, 671, 731—
Vol 67: 117—Vol 83: 91
WREN..................................Vol 59: 524
WRIGHT....Vol 14: 86—Vol 19: 628—Vol 24:
459—Vol 25: 716—Vol 26: 53, 339, 340—Vol
27: 379, 672, 805, 889—Vol 28: 262, 263—
Vol 29: 45, 290, 650—Vol 30: 149, 538—Vol
31: 55, 411—Vol 32: 60, 162—Vol 33: 957,
958—Vol 34: 659—Vol 35: 1038—Vol 36:
575, 576, 761—Vol 37: 68, 71, 349, 396—Vol
38: 87, 113, 114, 273, 276—Vol 39: 23, 143,
277—Vol 40: 25, 74, 76, 107, 108, 170—Vol
43: 423, 544, 545, 597—Vol 44: 24, 152, 235
—Vol 45: 19, 20, 101, 125, 242, 321, 327—Vol
46: 243, 329, 389—Vol 47: 190, 191, 272, 392
—Vol 48: 65, 122, 305, 440, 448—Vol 50: 62,
357—Vol 51: 166—Vol 52: 52, 172—Vol 53:
330, 332—Vol 54: 110, 225, 468, 648—Vol
55: 285, 601—Vol 56: 172, 315, 318, 629, 690
—Vol 57: 219, 434, 744—Vol 58: 368, 371,
588, 702—Vol 59: 45, 49, 441, 653—Vol 60:
365, 418, 474, 569, 573, 633—Vol 62: 583—
Vol 63: 104—Vol 65: 367, 441, 701—Vol 66:
54—Vol 68: 123, 443, 554, 623, 626—Vol 70:
206, 879, 1018—Vol 71:: 673, 760, 957—Vol
72: (3-70)—Vol 73: (1-63)—Vol 74: (7-54),
(8-54), (11-59)—Vol 75: (7-36)—Vol 77:
183—Vol 78: 295—Vol 79: 34, 193, 561—
Vol 80: 46, 382—Vol 82: 139—Vol 83: 94—
Vol 84: 327, 444
WRIGHTMAN....Vol 22: 53, 374, 678—Vol
58: 652
WYANT...............................Vol 44: 386
WYAT..................................Vol 71: 558
WYATT....Vol 27: 736—Vol 32: 720—Vol 41:
212—Vol 42: 134, 336—Vol 43: 600, 603—
Vol 44: 148, 233—Vol 46: 151, 244, 335—
Vol 47: 198—Vol 48: 441—Vol 53: 179, 243,
694—Vol 54: 228—Vol 56: 482—Vol 57:
690, 745—Vol 63: 293, 506—Vol 64: 57, 258,
522—Vol 74: (5-40)—Vol 79: 195—Vol 81:
631—Vol 84: 158, 446
WYCHE.................Vol 37: 155—Vol 47: 270
WYCKOFF....Vol 47: 87—Vol 48: 448—Vol
73: (2-65)
WYCLIFFE............................Vol 45: 327
WYCOFF....Vol 25: 967—Vol 26: 336—Vol 45:
114, 191—Vol 46: 28, 330, 392—Vol 50: 354
—Vol 52: 229
WYGAL................................Vol 65: 759
WYKE..................................Vol 78: 600
WYKOFF..............................Vol 55: 46
WYLIE....Vol 29: 290—Vol 48: 306—Vol 74:
(5-39)
WYLLIS...........Vol 32: 161, 283—Vol 56: 480
WYLLYS...............................Vol 56: 480

WYMAN....Vol 33: 476, 707—Vol 82: 396, 861,
863
WYNKOOP...........................Vol 43: 422
WYNN...Vol 37: 70—Vol 39: 143—Vol 47: 95,
389—Vol 56: 688—Vol 61: 274—Vol 62: 308
WYNNE.................................Vol 58: 173
WYTHE.................................Vol 56: 225

Y

YAFLE.................................Vol 30: 67
YAGER...............Vol 46: 153—Vol 49: 39
YALE..................Vol 41: 70—Vol 78: 246
YALLALEE...........................Vol 81: 430
YANCEY....Vol 34: 661—Vol 35: 1098—Vol
78: 696—Vol 80: 44
YANCY....Vol 51: 354—Vol 52: 557—Vol 59:
315
YANSEY...............................Vol 81: 431
YARBOROUGH.......Vol 70: 134—Vol 82: 933
YARBROUGH........................Vol 65: 759
YARD..................................Vol 57: 353
YARDLEY.............................Vol 22: 375
YARGON..............................Vol 56: 415
YARNALL...........Vol 5: 277—Vol 74: (4-49)
YARNELL.............................Vol 33: 42
YATES...Vol 35: 57—Vol 37: 488—Vol 42:
337—Vol 43: 539—Vol 49: 47—Vol 50: 355
—Vol 53: 630—Vol 58: 650—Vol 67: 292—
Vol 68: 686—Vol 69: 564—Vol 83: 946
YEAGER...............................Vol 49: 39
YEAMANS....Vol 58: 700—Vol 59: 312—Vol
66: 600
YEATER...............................Vol 68: 155
YEATMAN............................Vol 48: 203
YEATON...............................Vol 47: 341
YEAW..................................Vol 29: 512
YEISER................................Vol 55: 712
YELDELL..............................Vol 48: 369
YELLINGS.............................Vol 28: 158
YELLOTT..............................Vol 29: 512
YELTON...............................Vol 83: 944
YENMORE............................Vol 71: 239
YEOMAN..............................Vol 49: 46
YERGER...............................Vol 34: 659
YERRINGTON.......................Vol 84: 246
YETTER...............................Vol 42: 269
YETTES................................Vol 68: 686
YOCUM................Vol 69: 247—Vol 76: 653
YOE....................Vol 83: 173, 793
YOHN..................Vol 65: 634—Vol 71: 86
YOHO..................................Vol 54: 535
YONGE................................Vol 55: 339
YORK..................Vol 24: 343—Vol 55: 446
YOST...Vol 48: 65—Vol 54: 465—Vol 81: 569
—Vol 83: 440
YOUMANS...........................Vol 45: 109, 191
YOUNG....Vol 19: 532—Vol 22: 52—Vol 24:
542—Vol 26: 340—Vol 27: 670, 806—Vol
29: 289—Vol 31: 586—Vol 32: 62—Vol 33:
959—Vol 35: 57, 1036, 1038—Vol 36: 757—
Vol 37: 160, 266, 353—Vol 38: 331—Vol 39:
102—Vol 41: 71—Vol 43: 492, 604—Vol 44:
153—Vol 45: 18—Vol 46: 152—Vol 48: 120,
205, 368—Vol 49: 134—Vol 50: 63, 348, 351,
356—Vol 51: 354—Vol 52: 109, 434—Vol
53: 116, 746—Vol 54: 224, 465, 594, 650—
Vol 55: 108—Vol 57: 176, 691—Vol 58: 649
—Vol 59: 173, 239—Vol 61: 274, 546, 784—
Vol 62: 159—Vol 64: 388—Vol 66: 307—
Vol 67: 115, 147, 242, 516, 573—Vol 68: 121,

487, 552, 622—Vol 69: 58, 158, 160—Vol 70:
1166—Vol 71: 762—Vol 72: (8-88)—Vol
73: (2-65)—Vol 76: 581, 710—Vol 77: 479,
538, 663—Vol 78: 456—Vol 79: 518—Vol
80: 45—Vol 81: 569—Vol 84: 69, 246
YOUNGBLOOD....Vol 56: 416—Vol 70: 132—
Vol 76: 62
YOUNGE................................Vol 56: 111
YOUNGER........Vol 46: 28, 156—Vol 71: 1108
YOUNGS....Vol 48: 58—Vol 49: 40—Vol 64:
758
YOUNGSBAND........Vol 41: 214—Vol 42: 14
YOUNT....Vol 74: (7-52), (8-52)—Vol 75:
(4-55)—Vol 77: 481—Vol 78: 457—Vol 79:
113
YOUSE................................Vol 39: 225

Z

ZAIN................................Vol 42: 268

ZANE....Vol 17: 480, 568—Vol 18: 57—Vol
30: 65—Vol 81: 630—Vol 82: 140, 397
ZEIBER................................Vol 61: 784
ZELL................................Vol 71: 87
ZERFOSS................................Vol 60: 50
ZEVERLY................................Vol 46: 337
ZICKAFOOSE................................Vol 84: 68
ZIEGLE................................Vol 53: 571
ZIEGLER....Vol 43: 489—Vol 52: 323—Vol
60: 572—Vol 67: 148—Vol 80: 511
ZIMMERMAN........Vol 43: 486, 489, 598
ZINE................................Vol 46: 393
ZITTLER................................Vol 84: 324
ZOOK....Vol 58: 587—Vol 67: 646—Vol 74:
(11-58)
ZUCK................................Vol 56: 625
ZUMWALT................................Vol 48: 123
ZUVER................................Vol 77: 240, 332

BIBLE AND FAMILY RECORDS

FEDERAL AND STATE RECORDS

UNITED STATES—Presidents of:
Revolutionary Ancestry (through President Wilson)....Vol 55: 134
Ancestry of Wives (through President Coolidge) Vol 58: 228, 297
Where Buried (through President Wilson) Vol 64: 230

UNITED STATES COURT REPORTS—Estates, Boundaries, Miscellaneous, Various Localities....Vol 66: 45, 153, 675

UNITED STATES—FEDERAL APPOINTMENTS, Adams' and Jefferson's Administrations....Vol 83: 87, 431

ALABAMA—
Wills...Vol 74: (5-36)
Clairborne, Cemetery Records....Vol 77: 722
Clark County, Census 1816.......Vol 83: 433
Lawrence County, Marriage Bonds.......Vol 79: 609
Madison County, Deeds..............Vol 77: 723
Monroe County, Census 1816......Vol 83: 327
Morgan County, Cemetery Records....Vol 83: 88
Wilcox County, Cemetery Records....Vol 77: 721

CAROLINA—
Swiss Colonists.....................Vol 75: (2-50)

COLORADO—
Marriage Records.................Vol 42: 195, 271

CONNECTICUT—
Signers Oath of Fidelity............Vol 56: 113
Berlin, Cemetery Records...........Vol 37: 99
Brooklyn, Cemetery Records......Vol 48: 50
Brooklyn, Marriage Records....Vol 47: 261, 338
Greenwich, Marriage Records....Vol 44: 322
Killingly, Cemetery Records.....Vol 47: 339
Litchfield County, Early Settlers....Vol 8: 163
Poquonock, Cemetery Records....Vol 47: 260
Putnam, Cemetery Records..........Vol 38: 14
Salisbury, Cemetery Records......Vol 48: 51
Southfort, Pequot Massacre.......Vol 23: 203
Stratford, Early Settlers..............Vol 14: 180
Wethersfield, Donors to "Relief of Boston" Vol 79: 109, 277

DELAWARE—
Signers Oath of Fidelity............Vol 76: 1, 67
Kent County, Probate Records....Vol 79: 324

DISTRICT OF COLUMBIA—
Alexandria County, Marriage Records....Vol 49: 121

FLORIDA—
St Augustine Exiles.................Vol 80: 39

GEORGIA—
Early Settlers..........................Vol 68: 217
In the Revolution....................Vol 23: 257
Presidential Electors...............Vol 45: 7
Wills..Vol 74: 5, 36
Augusta, Early Newspaper Items....Vol 69: 370

Camden County, Wills...............Vol 60: 251
Greene County, Wills...............Vol 66: 310
Greene County, Marriage Licenses....Vol 66: 310
Savannah, Early Newspaper Items......Vol 56: 725
Terrell County, Early Records....Vol 80: 151

ILLINOIS—
Clark County, Vital Records.......Vol 80: 39
Lawrence County, Cemetery Records....Vol 68: 500
Lawrence County, Marriage Records....Vol 68: 500
Palestine, Early Records............Vol 78: 244
Stephenson County, Marriage Records..Vol 44: 33, 90, 167, 257
Union County, Marriage Records....Vol 79: 156

INDIANA—
Agency Rolls....Vol 83: 609, 701, 776, 855, 928, 996
Gibson County, Marriage Records....Vol 77: 333
Jefferson County, Wills...............Vol 79: 108
New Harmony, Early Records.......Vol 38: 60
Parke County, Early Records....Vol 77: 536
Richmond County, Cemetery Records....Vol 80: 546

IOWA—
Old Zion Church Records.............Vol 39: 9

KENTUCKY—
Boonesborough in the Revolution....Vol 28: 193
Bourbon County, Cemetery Records....Vol 46: 36
Bourbon County, Marriage Records....Vol 66: 463, 538
Bourbon County, Vital Records....Vol 47: 88
Fayette County, Marriage Bonds....Vol 82: 53, 128, 209, 301, 382, 388, 487, 492, 497
Fincastle County, Early Settlers..Vol 13: 13
Kentucky County, Early Settlers....Vol 13: 13
Knox County, Marriage Records....Vol 69: 122, 248
Mason County, Marriage Bonds....Vol 79: 32, 189, 326, 365, 465, 557, 611, 655—Vol 80: 42, 83, 273, 333, 381, 429, 555, 586—Vol 81: 69—Vol 83: 615, 707, 783, 865, 936, 1005—Vol 84: 59, 153, 237, 310, 437, 510, 618
Mason County, Court Records....Vol 78: 552
Ohio County, Early Settlers.......Vol 61: 709
Shelby County, Cemetery Records....Vol 63: 740
Simpson County, Vital Records....Vol 68: 623
Woodford County, Marriage Records...Vol 66: 538

LOUISIANA—
New Orleans, City Records..Vol 82: 379, 380
Parish Archives.........................Vol 79: 185

MAINE—
Berwick, Marriage Records—Vol 59: 243
—Vol 69: 367
New Sweden, Early Days—Vol 73: (8-77)

MARYLAND—
Marriage Records—Vol 84: 699
Anne Arundel County, Marriage Bonds—
Vol 43: 612—Vol 46: 132
Anne Arundel County, Signers Oath of Fidelity—Vol 51: 49, 84
Baltimore County, Marriage Bonds—Vol 43: 559
Cecil County, Signers Oath of Allegiance—Vol 62: 561
Charles County, Marriage Records—Vol 61: 233, 453
Harford County, Declaration Signers—Vol 31: 605
Montgomery County, Marriage Records—Vol 46: 34
Prince George's County, Marriage Records—Vol 42: 332—Vol 43: 403
St. Mary's County, Signers of an Early Petition—Vol 46: 35
Worcester County, Marriage Records—Vol 45: 249

MASSACHUSETTS—
Maritime Records—Vol 81: 463, 510, 561, 621
Boston, Vital Records—Vol 23: 439
Fall River, Marriage Records—Vol 43: 666, 743
Huntington, Marriage Records—Vol 61: 588
Medford, Town Records—Vol 19: 19
Northbridge, Marriage Records—Vol 49: 194
Sheffield, Cemetery Records—Vol 48: 51
Troy, Marriage Records—Vol 43: 666, 743

MICHIGAN—
Ionia, Dexter Colony—Vol 39: 211

MISSISSIPPI—
Early Records—Vol 79: 29
Green County, Census 1816—Vol 83: 254

MISSOURI—
Agency Rolls—Vol 82: 563, 641, 716, 783
Clay County, Marriage Records—Vol 44: 393
Randolph County, Marriage Records—Vol 76: 711—Vol 77: 334, 477—Vol 78: 103, 455
Randolph County, Wills—Vol 78: 425

NEW ENGLAND—
Women of the Revolution—Vol 42: 303

NEW HAMPSHIRE—
Early Days—Vol 12: 254
Early Settlers—Vol 10: 1034
Antrim, Cemetery Records—Vol 46: 341
Canterbury, Marriage Records—Vol 46: 266, 348—Vol 47: 80
Chichester, Old Records—Vol 44: 224
Claremont, Marriage Records—Vol 45: 31
Derry, Old Records—Vol 8: 169
New Castle, Early History—Vol 50: 309

NEW JERSEY—
Signers of Oath—Vol 82: 643
Burlington County, Revolutionary History Vol 43: 591
Cumberland County, Signers "Oath of Government"—Vol 80: 272
Fort Mercer Defenders—Vol 7: 20
Freehold, Vital Records—Vol 40: 9
Marlboro, Cemetery Records—Vol 10: 1047
Monmouth County, Church Records—Vol 39: 240
Morris County, Marriage Records—Vol 56: 535

NEW YORK—
Charleston, Marriage Records—Vol 49: 37
Chautauqua County, Early Records—Vol 39: 291
Dutchess County, Early Records—Vol 54: 160
Dutchess County, Wills—Vol 69: 500
Fishkill, Cemetery Records—Vol 46: 333
Fonda, Marriage Records—Vol 50: 338
Herkimer County, Marriage Records—Vol 60: 560
Kinderhook, Church Records—Vol 59: 246
Kinderhook, Marriage Records—Vol 58: 95—Vol 69: 436
Long Island, Church Records—Vol 84: 964
New York City, Church Records—Vol 68: 692
Olean, Marriage Records—Vol 48: 362
Orange County, Marriage Records—Vol 68: 248
Orange County, Wills—Vol 83: 699, 780, 862, 934, 999
Tryon County, Early Settlers—Vol 14: 357
Ulster County, Wills—Vol 83: 514
Washington County, Argyle Patent—Vol 82: 299—Vol 83: 166

NORTH CAROLINA—
Land Warrants—Vol 60: 37
Marriage Notices—Vol 84: 832, 889
Women of the Revolution—Vol 45: 145
Cabarrus County, Cemetery Records—Vol 69: 365
Cape Fear, Early Settlers—Vol 11: 371, 457
Edenton Records—Vol 31: 355—Vol 56: 327
Mecklenburg County, Cemetery Records—Vol 44: 239
Mecklenburg County, Early Records—Vol 31: 626
Mecklenburg County, Signers of Declaration—Vol 53: 558
Rowan County, Marriage Bonds—Vol 43: 547, 654—Vol 45: 129—Vol 46: 33, 105
Rowan County, Signers Oath of Allegiance—Vol 82: 208
Tyrrell County, Marriages—Vol 80: 380

OHIO—
Gallipolis, Records—Vol 74: (7-16), (8-16)
Georgetown, Cemetery Records—Vol 46: 36
Holmes County, Census 1830—Vol 68: 250, 504
Huron County, Marriage Bonds—Vol 82: 566, 645, 718, 785, 850, 921

VERMONT—

Barton, Vital Records............Vol 66: 529
Bennington, Signers of Declaration—Vol
61: 277
Franklin County, Births....Vol 84: 54, 140,
228, 309, 428, 505
Middlebury, Marriage Records....Vol 48:
362
Rutland, Marriage Records.........Vol 46: 165
Shaftsbury, Marriage Records....Vol 49: 344
Wells, Marriage Records....Vol 48: 431—
Vol 49: 34
Wells, Vital Records...............Vol 39: 120

VIRGINIA—

Huguenots...........................Vol 31: 788
Parish Records....Vol 75: (12-61), (12-62)
Alexandria, Marriage Records.........Vol 49:
277—Vol 50: 55, 195, 240, 241—Vol 54:
454, 586
Amelia County, Marriage Bonds....Vol 66:
513, 582, 665
Amelia County, Wills.............Vol 75: (2-52)
Bedford County, Court Records.........Vol 76:
59, 141, 216
Bedford County, Early Records....Vol 30:
104
Botetourt County, Claims.........Vol 69: 471
Brunswick County, Patriots......Vol 68: 244
Brunswick County, Wills.........Vol 69: 438
Buckingham County, Marriage Bonds....Vol
83: 782
Campbell County, Marriage Records....Vol
64: 295, 363, 505, 512, 703, 741
Chesterfield County, Wills....Vol 75: (2-52)
Cumberland County, Marriage Bonds....Vol
65: 40, 110, 301, 432, 627, 737
Fairfax County, Committee of Safety....Vol
49: 239
Fauquier County, Signers Oath of Alleg-
iance....Vol 62: 776
Frederick County, Early Settlers....Vol 79:
110, 215
Goochland County, Records.......Vol 82: 848
Greensville County, Early Records.........Vol
45: 250
Greensville County, Marriage Bonds....Vol
43: 509
Hardy County, Wills.........Vol 74: (6-32),
(9-47)
Harrison County, Marriage Records....Vol
48: 190
Isle of Wight, Marriage Bonds....Vol 64:
260, 523, 584
Jamestown, Early Records......Vol 10: 1044

Kings Mountain Volunteers........Vol 45: 154
Loudoun County, Marriage Records....Vol
45: 152
Loudoun County, Wills....Vol 82: 556, 635,
708, 779, 844, 917—Vol 83: 167
Mecklenburg County, Marriage Records....
Vol 75: (12-62)
Monongalia County, Marriage Bonds....Vol
62: 310, 418, 565—Vol 63: 22, 88, 240,
557, 612—Vol 64: 295, 363, 505, 512, 703,
741—Vol 66: 50, 150, 314, 679
Nottoway County, Wills....Vol 75: (2-52),
(4-52)
Pittsylvania County, Marriage Bonds....Vol
70: 722
Pittsylvania County, Early Records....Vol
40: 254
Prince Edward County, Wills....Vol 75:
(1-50), (2-52)
Richmond County, Marriage Records....Vol
57: 675—Vol 58: 620—Vol 66: 462
Spotsylvania, Marriage Licenses....Vol 80:
187
Staunton, Records..................Vol 8: 339
Sycamore Shoals, Records........Vol 33: 883
Washington County, Marriage Records....
Vol 57: 159
West Augusta, Early Settlers....Vol 10: 25
Westmoreland County, Marriage Records....
Vol 66: 462
Winchester, Records..............Vol 8: 335

WASHINGTON—

Clark County, Early Days....Vol 73: (9-52)

WEST VIRGINIA—

Hardy County, Wills...........Vol 74: (6-32),
(9-47)
Monongalia County, Marriage Bonds....Vol
62: 310, 418, 565—Vol 63: 22, 88, 240,
557, 612—Vol 64: 295, 363, 505, 512, 703,
741—Vol 66: 50, 150, 314, 679
Monongalia County, Wills.........Vol 80: 548
Morgan County, Wills....Vol 81: 467, 512,
563, 622
Shepherdstown, Baptismal Records....Vol
61: 371
Shepherdstown, Church Records....Vol 69:
369
Shepherdstown, Marriage Records.......Vol
61: 589

WISCONSIN—

Early Settlers.....................Vol 17: 438
Janesville, Early Days.........Vol 73: (10-46)

Supplement
to
Genealogical Guide

✦

MASTER INDEX
OF
GENEALOGY
IN THE
Daughters of the American
Revolution Magazine

VOLUMES 85–89
1950–1955

✦

Compiled by
ELIZABETH BENTON CHAPTER, N.S.D.A.R.
Kansas City, Missouri
MRS. HUGH P. HARTLEY, *Regent*
MRS. OMIE P. MACFARLANE, *General Chairman*

✦

Published by
DAUGHTERS OF THE AMERICAN REVOLUTION MAGAZINE
Gertrude S. Carraway, *President General*
1776 D Street, N. W.
Washington 6, D. C.

1956

DEDICATED
To
Our Pioneer Ancestors
Whose
Foresight and Indomitable Courage
Gave Us
OUR AMERICA

—MURIEL LOVELAND (Mrs. Omie P.) MACFARLANE
General Chairman

SECTION I

Queries and Answers

SECTION II

Bible and Family Records

Federal and State Records

SECTION I

Queries and Answers

BARROWS..............Vol 89: 1168
BARTHOLEMEW..............Vol 89: 865
BARTLETT....Vol 85: 816—Vol 87: 1289—
 Vol 88: 968, 1260—Vol 89: 600
BARTON..............Vol 88: 141, 272, 967
BARRY..............Vol 88: 895
BARTRAM..............Vol 86: 763
BASFORD..............Vol 87: 1180
BASS..............Vol 88: 1066—Vol 89: 941
BASSETT....Vol 85: 741—Vol 87: 802—Vol
 88: 270
BATES..............Vol 85: 160—Vol 87: 1029
BAY..............Vol 86: 1060—Vol 88: 790
BAYHA..............Vol 89: 600
BEACH..............Vol 87: 802
BEACHMAN..............Vol 87: 1028
BEALL....Vol 86: 488—Vol 89: 436, 600
BEAN..............Vol 85: 606—Vol 86: 984
BEARD..............Vol 87: 1250
BEARDEN..............Vol 88: 52, 1262
BEATTY..............Vol 86: 986—Vol 88: 1262
BEAUCHAMP..............Vol 89: 435
BEAVER..............Vol 85: 955—Vol 86: 1061
BEAVERS..............Vol 89: 599
BECK....Vol 85: 242, 816—Vol 89: 598
BECKERDITE..............Vol 88: 1199
BECKWITH..............Vol 87: 1076
BEDFORD....Vol 86: 1325—Vol 87: 576
BEECHER..............Vol 89: 1012
BEEKMAN..............Vol 86: 62
BEEM..............Vol 86: 984
BEESON....Vol 85: 497—Vol 87: 1078
BEGUN..............Vol 89: 601
BELANGEE..............Vol 88: 1262
BELL....Vol 85: 160—Vol 86: 640—Vol 87:
 1076—Vol 88: 54—Vol 89: 299, 720
BENEDICT..............Vol 87: 1028
BENHAM..............Vol 89: 719
BENJAMIN..............Vol 87: 1180
BENN..............Vol 89: 1168
BENNEDICT..............Vol 88: 226
BENNET..............Vol 89: 720
BENNETT....Vol 85: 677—Vol 86: 640, 914
 —Vol 88: 1197, 1198, 1261—Vol 89: 299
BENNINGHOFF..............Vol 86: 914
BENSON..............Vol 88: 142
BENSYL..............Vol 86: 984
BENTLEY..............Vol 87: 1077—Vol 89: 1072
BENTON..............Vol 89: 46
BERKLEY..............Vol 87: 1289
BERNARD..............Vol 89: 599
BERRY....Vol 85: 326, 677, 1045—Vol 87:
 1251—Vol 88: 141, 575, 897—Vol 89: 1070
BEST..............Vol 87: 801—Vol 88: 1065
BEVERLY..............Vol 88: 897
BEVINGTON..............Vol 87: 1182
BICKERSTAFF..............Vol 85: 1046
BIDDLE..............Vol 86: 167
BIGELOW..............Vol 87: 673
BIGGS..............Vol 88: 271, 272
BILLINGS..............Vol 88: 1064
BINFORD..............Vol 88: 966
BINGHAM..............Vol 88: 53
BINYON..............Vol 89: 939
BIRD..............Vol 88: 272—Vol 89: 45
BISHOP....Vol 86: 985—Vol 87: 1077, 1182
 —Vol 89: 435
BLACK....Vol 86: 763, 1327—Vol 87: 935—
 Vol 88: 271—Vol 89: 598, 867
BLACKBURN....Vol 85: 606—Vol 86: 1260
 —Vol 88: 141

BLACKLEDGE..............Vol 88: 896
BLACKMAN..............Vol 89: 434
BLACKMON..............Vol 85: 497
BLACKSHEAR..............Vol 87: 1252
BLACKWELL....Vol 86: 912, 1115—Vol 87:
 674
BLAINE..............Vol 86: 640
BLAIR....Vol 85: 160—Vol 89: 44, 300, 435
BLAKE....Vol 86: 914—Vol 89: 601, 1012
BLAKENEY..............Vol 88: 1262
BLANKENBAKER..............Vol 89: 719
BLANKENSHIP....Vol 85: 243—Vol 86:
 1260—Vol 89: 1072
BLANKS..............Vol 86: 1178
BLANTON..............Vol 87: 1181—Vol 89: 864
BLEDSOE..............Vol 86: 985
BLEVINS..............Vol 87: 414
BLOUNT..............Vol 88: 968
BLYDENBURGH..............Vol 89: 169
BLYTHE....Vol 86: 853—Vol 87: 936
BOAZ..............Vol 89: 299
BODEN..............Vol 86: 1326
BODINE..............Vol 88: 420
BOGARD....Vol 86: 1178—Vol 89: 719
BOGET..............Vol 89: 599
BOHANNON..............Vol 85: 608
BOHON..............Vol 86: 987
BOHUN..............Vol 86: 987
BOISE..............Vol 88: 142
BOLER..............Vol 89: 1012
BOLLING..............Vol 89: 298, 300
BOND....Vol 85: 1044—Vol 86: 761, 986
BONHAM....Vol 85: 160—Vol 89: 868
BONNELL..............Vol 88: 789
BONNER..............Vol 89: 864
BONNETT..............Vol 87: 934
BOOEN..............Vol 88: 564
BOOKER..............Vol 86: 853
BOONE..............Vol 89: 170, 868
BOSTON..............Vol 85: 817
BOSWELL..............Vol 88: 1065
BOTHWELL..............Vol 89: 300
BOTTOM..............Vol 87: 414
BOUCHER..............Vol 89: 434
BOULWARE..............Vol 88: 421
BOUTON..............Vol 89: 1072
BOWDEN..............Vol 88: 894
BOWEN....Vol 87: 803—Vol 89: 869, 1167
BOWERS..............Vol 88: 1197—Vol 89: 171
BOWIE..............Vol 88: 421
BOWLES..............Vol 89: 599, 940
BOWMAN....Vol 85: 675—Vol 86: 488, 913
 —Vol 87: 576
BOWSER..............Vol 87: 1181
BOX..............Vol 87: 223
BOYD....Vol 85: 677—Vol 88: 566—Vol 89:
 939
BOYER..............Vol 89: 512
BOYLSTON..............Vol 86: 638
BOYS..............Vol 87: 803
BRACEY..............Vol 89: 1010
BRACKEN....Vol 86: 168, 1061—Vol 87:
 1250—Vol 88: 687—Vol 89: 44
BRACKIN..............Vol 88: 687
BRADBURY..............Vol 86: 913
BRADFORD....Vol 85: 497—Vol 88: 54, 967,
 1261
BRADLEY....Vol 87: 803—Vol 89: 601, 867
BRADSHAW..............Vol 89: 719
BRADSTREET..............Vol 86: 169
BRADY..............Vol 88: 686

BRAGDON...........................Vol 88: 272
BRAKE.................................Vol 89: 512
BRAMAN...........................Vol 87: 595
BRANCH...........Vol 85: 160—Vol 86: 1179
BRANN...............................Vol 88: 1066
BRASHEAR.......................Vol 89: 721
BRAY.................................Vol 85: 678
BRECKENRIDGE.................Vol 85: 67
BRECKETT.......................Vol 88: 896
BRENTS.............................Vol 89: 942
BRESSIE............................Vol 89: 1010
BREWER..........Vol 85: 268—Vol 89: 863
BREWSTER.......................Vol 88: 420, 1198
BRIAN...............................Vol 89: 726
BRIANT.............................Vol 89: 43
BRICKHOUSE....................Vol 87: 1180
BRIDGES...........................Vol 89: 869
BRIDGHAM.......................Vol 86: 1327
BRIGGS.............................Vol 86: 639, 1061
BRIDGEWATER.................Vol 88: 686
BRINDLE...........................Vol 86: 487
BRITTS..............................Vol 85: 677
BROACH............................Vol 86: 167
BROADSWORD..................Vol 87: 1076
BROADWAY......................Vol 88: 968
BROCKWAY......................Vol 89: 864
BROKENBROUGH.............Vol 88: 1199
BRONSON..........................Vol 88: 789
BROOKE............................Vol 85: 1046
BROOKING........................Vol 86: 61
BROOKS............................Vol 88: 566, 1261
BROOME...........................Vol 89: 43
BROTHERS........................Vol 86: 168
BROUGHTON....................Vol 88: 141
BROWER...........................Vol 87: 1028
BROWN....Vol 85: 326, 608, 818, 1044, 1046
—Vol 86: 61, 62, 167, 317, 487, 760, 761,
984—Vol 87: 674, 675, 1028—Vol 88: 51,
54, 575, 896, 1064, 1197—Vol 89: 170, 297,
432, 864, 1010, 1071
BROWNFIELD.....................Vol 88: 272
BROWNLOW.......................Vol 89: 1070
BRUCE...............Vol 88: 421—Vol 89: 939
BRUNNER........................Vol 89: 432
BRUNSON.........................Vol 88: 968
BRUSTER..........................Vol 88: 420
BRYAM...............Vol 88: 894—Vol 89: 1010
BRYAN....Vol 86: 487—Vol 87: 1289—Vol
88: 686—Vol 89: 298, 300
BRYANT....Vol 85: 676—Vol 87: 414, 1028
—Vol 88: 1066—Vol 89: 43
BRYSON.............................Vol 89: 435
BUCHANAN....Vol 87: 413, 937—Vol 88:
1965
BUCK.................................Vol 89: 300
BUCKINGHAM...................Vol 88: 789
BUCKMASTER...................Vol 87: 1182
BUCKNER..........................Vol 89: 169
BUELL...............................Vol 86: 987
BUER.................................Vol 86: 853
BUFFINGTON...................Vol 89: 1011
BUFORD............................Vol 87: 803
BULLISS............................Vol 87: 1288
BULLOCK...........Vol 86: 487—Vol 88: 272
BULLS...............................Vol 87: 1289
BUNTAIN..........................Vol 86: 761
BUNYON............................Vol 86: 488
BURBRIDGE......................Vol 87: 934
BURCH...............Vol 88: 224—Vol 89: 432
BURD.................................Vol 88: 1199
BURGESS...........................Vol 87: 1181

BURKHART........................Vol 86: 1115
BURKS................................Vol 87: 804
BURLEIGH.........................Vol 85: 159
BURLINGAME....................Vol 86: 639
BURNES.............................Vol 85: 677
BURNETT...........................Vol 87: 1288
BURNHAM.........................Vol 85: 740
BURNSIDE.........................Vol 89: 868
BURRIL..............................Vol 89: 721
BURROWS.........................Vol 86: 488
BURSON.............................Vol 87: 675
BURT.................................Vol 85: 676
BURTON....Vol 85: 74—Vol 87: 224—Vol
89: 433
BUSBY................................Vol 88: 272
BUSH..................Vol 87: 55—Vol 89: 719
BUSHONG..........................Vol 86: 640
BUTLER....Vol 86: 1325—Vol 87: 156, 1026,
1078—Vol 88: 686
BUTT.................................Vol 86: 61
BUTTERFIELD...................Vol 87: 675
BUTTERWORTH..................Vol 86: 61
BUTTS...............................Vol 86: 61
BYERS...............................Vol 86: 168
BYRAM.............................Vol 86: 984
BYRAN..............................Vol 86: 985
BYRD..................Vol 86: 1325—Vol 87: 576
BYRNS...............................Vol 86: 316
BYRON...............................Vol 86: 985
BYRUM.............................Vol 86: 985

C

CABLER.............................Vol 89: 435
CADY.................................Vol 89: 1072
CAGE.................................Vol 85: 816
CAIN..................................Vol 87: 1078
CALDWELL....Vol 87: 1251—Vol 88: 686—
Vol 89: 600
CALHOUN.........................Vol 88: 565
CALL..................Vol 85: 955—Vol 86: 60
CALLAWAY........................Vol 89: 1072
CALTON.............................Vol 85: 677
CALVERT....Vol 87: 672—Vol 88: 141, 685
CALWALLADER.................Vol 89: 863
CAMERON.........................Vol 89: 601
CAMP.................................Vol 88: 790
CAMPBELL....Vol 85: 816—Vol 86: 168,
762, 852, 1052—Vol 87: 414, 936—Vol 88:
141—Vol 89: 862, 866, 867, 1166
CAMPHOR.........................Vol 88: 271
CANIFF..............................Vol 88: 271
CANTRELL........................Vol 86: 168
CAPEN...............................Vol 88: 789
CAREY...............Vol 85: 427—Vol 89: 1110
CARGILE...........................Vol 89: 1110
CARHART..........................Vol 85: 818
CARL.................................Vol 88: 897
CARLISLE..........................Vol 89: 868
CARLTON...........................Vol 85: 677
CARMICHAEL....Vol 86: 1325—Vol 89: 434
CARPENTER....Vol 86: 639—Vol 88: 140,
1065
CARR....Vol 87: 1289—Vol 88: 897—Vol 89:
171, 1071
CARRAWAY........................Vol 88: 686
CARRIER............................Vol 89: 869
CARROLL.......Vol 85: 497—Vol 86: 1179
CARSON....Vol 86: 1062—Vol 87: 1288—
Vol 89: 721
CARTER....Vol 85: 606, 1045—Vol 86: 61,
1327—Vol 87: 803, 1027, 1181, 1289—Vol

88: 140, 271, 1262—Vol 89: 300, 598, 866
CARTWRIGHT......Vol 85: 326—Vol 88: 421
CARVER......................................Vol 85: 606
CARY..Vol 89: 1110
CASE..Vol 89: 432
CASS....Vol 85: 956—Vol 86: 167—Vol 87:
225—Vol 88: 224—Vol 89: 601
CAST..Vol 85: 956
CASTLEBERRY............Vol 87: 803
CASWELL..............................Vol 89: 170
CATES......................................Vol 88: 968
CATHERS..............................Vol 89: 720
CATLIN......................Vol 89: 300, 432
CAUSEY....................................Vol 87: 801
CAUTHON..............................Vol 85: 68
CHAFIN....................................Vol 89: 939
CHAMBERLAIN....Vol 86: 169, 762—Vol
87: 595, 1287—Vol 89: 432
CHAMBERLIN........................Vol 87: 934
CHAMBERS............................Vol 88: 788
CHAMPLIN....................Vol 88: 686, 967
CHANDLER....Vol 85: 677—Vol 88: 53—
Vol 89: 436, 867, 868
CHAPEL..................................Vol 86: 316
CHAPIN..................................Vol 88: 687
CHAPMAN....Vol 85: 243—Vol 86: 640,
1061—Vol 88: 565, 789—Vol 89: 435
CHARLES....Vol 87: 413—Vol 89: 867, 1168
CHARLESWORTH....................Vol 87: 934
CHARLTON............................Vol 88: 564
CHASE......................................Vol 86: 762
CHASTAIN............................Vol 89: 1168
CHEAIRS..................................Vol 89: 43
CHEEZEM..................................Vol 89: 44
CHEEZUM..................................Vol 89: 44
CHENEY..................................Vol 86: 761
CHEZEM....................................Vol 89: 44
CHILDERS............................Vol 86: 913
CHILDS..................................Vol 89: 298
CHILES......................................Vol 85: 606
CHILSON........Vol 88: 1260—Vol 89: 600
CHINA....................................Vol 88: 968
CHINN......................................Vol 88: 421
CHIPMAN..............................Vol 89: 434
CHIZEM......................................Vol 89: 44
CHOICE..................................Vol 89: 300
CHRISTIAN....Vol 85: 427—Vol 86: 987—
Vol 88: 788
CHRISTOPHER......................Vol 86: 488
CHURCH............Vol 87: 674—Vol 88: 687
CHYNNE................................Vol 88: 421
CLAPP......................................Vol 89: 435
CLARK....Vol 85: 160, 243, 327, 607, 740,
954, 955—Vol 86: 639, 1326—Vol 87: 595,
1078, 1181—Vol 88: 685—Vol 89: 297,
300, 436, 600, 719, 722, 940, 1010, 1167
CLARKE....Vol 86: 638, 914—Vol 87: 935—
Vol 88: 1199
CLARY......................................Vol 87: 575
CLAWSON................................Vol 87: 431
CLAY..Vol 86: 763
CLAYTON....Vol 87: 225—Vol 88: 271, 969,
1262—Vol 89: 512, 598
CLEAVER................................Vol 86: 489
CLEM..Vol 89: 597
CLEMENT............Vol 88: 270—Vol 89: 597
CLEMENTS........Vol 88: 897—Vol 89: 597
CLEMON..................................Vol 89: 597
CLEMONS..............................Vol 89: 600
CLEVELAND..........................Vol 89: 864
CLEVER..................................Vol 86: 489

CLICE......................................Vol 86: 317
CLIFFORD............................Vol 85: 1045
CLIFFORD............................Vol 86: 915
CLINE......................................Vol 88: 53
CLINKSCALES........................Vol 86: 60
CLOUGH................................Vol 88: 967
CLOVE......................................Vol 86: 760
CLUTTON..............................Vol 88: 421
COATS................Vol 85: 159—Vol 86: 488
COBB........Vol 85: 67, 69—Vol 87: 55, 1252
COBURN................................Vol 86: 168
COCK......................................Vol 87: 1029
COCKBURN............................Vol 86: 168
COCKERHAM........................Vol 88: 141
CODDINGTON....................Vol 86: 1326
COE....................Vol 87: 576—Vol 89: 719
COFFEE..................................Vol 89: 866
COFFMAN..............................Vol 86: 488
COHEEA..............................Vol 87: 1027
COLE....Vol 87: 804—Vol 88: 564, 1261—
Vol 89: 45, 297, 597, 1010
COLEMAN.....Vol 85: 68, 243, 818—Vol 86:
912—Vol 87: 55—Vol 88: 52
COLES......................................Vol 88: 687
COLLAR..................................Vol 87: 574
COLLARD................................Vol 87: 574
COLLAR'D..............................Vol 87: 574
COLLIER................................Vol 87: 673
COLLINS....Vol 85: 159—Vol 86: 986—Vol
88: 421, 790, 1008—Vol 89: 721, 867
COLLINSWORTH..................Vol 89: 939
COMPTON............................Vol 87: 1027
CONKLIN............................Vol 87: 1180
CONN..Vol 85: 676
CONNELLY............................Vol 87: 674
CONNER............Vol 86: 914—Vol 89: 1070
CONRAD............Vol 86: 61—Vol 87: 1026
CONWAY................................Vol 89: 720
COOK....Vol 85: 68, 607—Vol 86: 60, 317,
638—Vol 87: 1181—Vol 88: 422, 565—
Vol 89: 1166, 1167
COOKE....................Vol 86: 322—Vol 88: 54
COOKSTON............................Vol 89: 939
COOLEY............Vol 86: 852—Vol 89: 601
COOPER............Vol 86: 62—Vol 87: 56, 802
COPELAND............................Vol 86: 168
CORBIN............Vol 88: 967—Vol 89: 1010
CORD......................................Vol 89: 1168
CORDELL................................Vol 86: 760
CORN................Vol 88: 894—Vol 89: 1071
CORNELIUS............................Vol 85: 607
CORNELL..............................Vol 89: 298
CORRIGAN..........................Vol 87: 1026
CORWIN..................................Vol 85: 327
CORY......................................Vol 86: 1326
COSBY..................................Vol 88: 1261
COUCH....................................Vol 88: 687
COUILLIARD........................Vol 87: 574
COURSON............................Vol 87: 413
COURTNEY..........................Vol 89: 1169
COURTRIGHT......................Vol 89: 1010
COVINGTON........................Vol 85: 606
COWAN............Vol 85: 677—Vol 89: 433
COWLES................................Vol 89: 436
COWLEY................................Vol 86: 852
COX....Vol 85: 955—Vol 87: 1028, 1029, 1289
—Vol 88: 575, 1198
CRABBIN..............................Vol 88: 789
CRAGO....................................Vol 89: 45
CRAIG............Vol 86: 62, 852—Vol 89: 45
CRAMER..............................Vol 87: 355

CRAMPTON............Vol 86: 640
CRAWFORD.....Vol 85: 327—Vol 87: 673,
934, 1182—Vol 89: 300, 938
CREAMER.................Vol 87: 355
CREEL.....................Vol 85: 955
CREW............Vol 87: 224, 1078, 1251
CREWS.....................Vol 88: 896
CRIDER....................Vol 87: 804
CRISLER...................Vol 86: 639
CRIST......................Vol 87: 934
CRISWELL................Vol 87: 804
CRITCHFIELD..............Vol 86: 62
CROCKETT....Vol 86: 852—Vol 87: 1288—
Vol 88: 1261
CRONKHITE...............Vol 88: 270
CROSBY......Vol 87: 414—Vol 88: 142, 1066
CROSS......................Vol 89: 866
CROW.............Vol 85: 243—Vol 87: 674
CROWELL................Vol 87: 1180
CRUM......................Vol 89: 719
CRUMB.....................Vol 89: 597
CRUMP.....................Vol 86: 853
CRUMPLER................Vol 89: 722
CRUMPTON................Vol 88: 686
CULLERS...................Vol 89: 599
CULLOM...................Vol 89: 721
CULLY.....................Vol 85: 678
CUNION...................Vol 89: 1010
CUNNINGHAM....Vol 85: 818, 1045—Vol
87: 1287—Vol 88: 686—Vol 89: 939
CULVER...................Vol 85: 327
CUMMINGS...............Vol 87: 1287
CURRAN..................Vol 89: 1072
CURRANT..................Vol 89: 863
CURRENT..................Vol 89: 863
CURTIS....Vol 85: 242, 426—Vol 86: 1260—
Vol 89: 721
CURTRIGHT...............Vol 87: 223
CUSTER...................Vol 87: 1181
CUTHBERT................Vol 89: 299
CUTSHAW.................Vol 88: 1262
CUTTER...................Vol 85: 327

D

DABNEY............Vol 89: 597, 598
DADE......................Vol 89: 43
DANIEL....................Vol 89: 46
DAKIN...........Vol 86: 489—Vol 87: 56
DALTON......Vol 86: 168—Vol 87: 1181
DANIEL....................Vol 88: 790
DANIELS..................Vol 86: 1178
DARBMORE...............Vol 86: 1115
DARBY.....................Vol 85: 69
DARNABY..................Vol 88: 421
DARROW...................Vol 87: 935
DARTMORE...............Vol 86: 1115
DAUCHY...................Vol 85: 327
DAUGHERTY..............Vol 87: 1182
DAVENPORT....Vol 86: 169—Vol 89: 721
DAVIDSON....Vol 85: 158—Vol 87: 224, 675
DAVIS.....Vol 85: 67, 428, 955, 1046—Vol 86:
169, 317, 985—Vol 87: 803, 1287—Vol 88:
272, 897, 968, 1065—Vol 89: 171, 599, 601,
863, 864, 865, 1169
DAVISON...................Vol 86: 137
DAWES.....................Vol 86: 761
DAWKINS.................Vol 88: 1199
DAWSON....Vol 85: 243—Vol 86: 640—Vol
88: 54—Vol 89: 435
DAY............Vol 86: 1326—Vol 87: 1027
DEAN...Vol 85: 496, 676—Vol 86: 316—

Vol 88: 1066—Vol 89: 433
DEANE................Vol 85: 326—Vol 86: 316
DEARING..................Vol 85: 327
DEARTH...................Vol 87: 1026
DEATH........Vol 87: 1026—Vol 88: 969
DEAVER....................Vol 86: 985
DE BERRY.................Vol 89: 601
DE BOW....................Vol 85: 956
DECKER....................Vol 88: 685
DECKSON..................Vol 85: 327
DEEN............Vol 85: 325—Vol 86: 316
DEENE.....................Vol 86: 316
DEETZ.....................Vol 87: 1026
DE FORREST.............Vol 87: 1288
DE GRAFF.................Vol 87: 1288
DE GRAFFENRIED.........Vol 88: 1261
DEGRAFFENREID.........Vol 89: 721
DE GRAFFEURIED........Vol 86: 1060
DE HART...................Vol 85: 159
DE LA MONTAGNE.......Vol 87: 1288
DEITER....................Vol 88: 142
DE JARNETT................Vol 86: 60
DE LIESSELINE...........Vol 87: 937
DE LOZIER................Vol 88: 566
DEMBY....................Vol 89: 865
DENITH...................Vol 89: 298
DENNIS......Vol 87: 225, 1181—Vol 88: 967
DENSON............Vol 88: 420, 788
DENT....Vol 85: 1046—Vol 89: 299, 600
DERING...................Vol 86: 1178
DE RUSSY.................Vol 85: 677
DE ST. JULIEN.....Vol 88: 142, 788
DEWEY....................Vol 88: 564
DEWITH...................Vol 89: 298
DEWITT...................Vol 89: 298
DEXTER.......Vol 86: 167—Vol 89: 432
DICE......................Vol 86: 487
DICKINSON......Vol 86: 912, 1325
DICKSON......Vol 86: 1325—Vol 89: 1011
DIETER....................Vol 88: 142
DIETERICH................Vol 88: 142
DIETRICH..................Vol 87: 55
DILLARD....Vol 85: 160, 816—Vol 89: 434
DILLS......................Vol 88: 53
DILS.......................Vol 88: 53
DINWIDDIE......Vol 85: 242, 1045
DISHMAN..................Vol 87: 673
DISSTON...................Vol 89: 601
DIX........................Vol 88: 53
DIXON........Vol 89: 168, 863, 1011
DOAK.....................Vol 85: 160
DOBSON......Vol 86: 488—Vol 88: 969
DODGE....Vol 85: 242—Vol 86: 1060—Vol
87: 412, 1181—Vol 89: 44, 720, 1169
DOMER....................Vol 87: 1026
DONALDSON...............Vol 88: 140
DONECA...................Vol 89: 300
DOOLITTLE................Vol 85: 326
DORRIS....................Vol 87: 414
DORTCH...................Vol 85: 1046
DOTSON...................Vol 89: 1110
DOTY......................Vol 88: 1261
DOUGHTY..................Vol 88: 272
DOUGLAS....Vol 87: 1076—Vol 89: 299
DOUTHET..................Vol 88: 969
DOUTHITT.................Vol 88: 969
DOVE......................Vol 89: 298
DOWDEN....Vol 86: 1178—Vol 87: 55—Vol
89: 719
DOZIER....................Vol 86: 984
DRAKE........Vol 85: 496—Vol 87: 1026

FOARD...................................Vol 89: 170
FOCKE...................................Vol 87: 935
FONTAINE...........................Vol 88: 1065
FOOSE...................................Vol 86: 640
FORBES.................................Vol 87: 1251
FORAKER.............................Vol 88: 896
FORBIS.................................Vol 89: 868
FORD.....Vol 86: 639, 853, 1060—Vol 87: 673
    Vol 88: 52, 1065, 1066
FOREAKER...........................Vol 88: 896
FORKNER.............................Vol 89: 1012
FORSYTH..............................Vol 87: 1026
FOSTER.....Vol 85: 67, 69—Vol 86: 1326—
    Vol 87: 56, 1180—Vol 88: 966—Vol 89:
    43, 866, 1010
FOURACRE..........................Vol 88: 896
FOURMAN............................Vol 88: 895
FOUTS...................................Vol 85: 68
FOWLER.....Vol 86: 914—Vol 88: 789, 966
FOWLKES............................Vol 89: 1168
FOX.......................................Vol 88: 272
FRAME..................................Vol 89: 435
FRANCIS.....Vol 85: 740—Vol 87: 1030—
    Vol 88: 420, 968—Vol 89: 435, 865
FRANKLIN.....Vol 87: 803—Vol 88: 684,
    1261
FRAZER................................Vol 89: 298
FRAZIER.............Vol 87: 1287—Vol 89: 168
FREEHOUR..........................Vol 88: 967
FREEMAN.....Vol 86: 317, 1062—Vol 87:
    576—Vol 89: 868
FRENCH.................................Vol 88: 575
FREY.....................................Vol 86: 914
FRITTS...............Vol 88: 967—Vol 89: 598
FROST...................................Vol 86: 487
FRY..................Vol 87: 55—Vol 88: 686
FRYE.....................................Vol 87: 413
FUEL.....................................Vol 85: 955
FULBRIGHT........................Vol 86: 1060
FULENWIDER.....Vol 85: 817—Vol 89: 940
FULLER.....Vol 85: 740—Vol 86: 915, 985—
    Vol 87: 803
FULLINWIDER....................Vol 87: 1287
FURRY..................................Vol 88: 896
FUTRELLE..........................Vol 89: 1071
FYFFE..................................Vol 86: 640

G

GAAR....................................Vol 89: 719
GABBARD.............................Vol 85: 676
GADSDEN.............................Vol 89: 863
GAGNIER.............................Vol 88: 1198
GAINES.............Vol 86: 168—Vol 87: 674
GALBRAITH.........................Vol 89: 434
GALBREATH........................Vol 87: 1180
GALLAHER..........................Vol 86: 168
GALLASPIE..........................Vol 88: 967
GALLISHAM.........................Vol 89: 864
GALLOWAY.........................Vol 87: 413
GAMBER...............................Vol 87: 1029
GAMBILL..............................Vol 87: 1026
GAMBLE...............................Vol 89: 864
GANDY..................................Vol 89: 1166
GANO....................................Vol 89: 939
GANSHORN.........................Vol 88: 894
GARD.................Vol 87: 804—Vol 88: 1197
GARDE..................................Vol 87: 804
GARDEN...............................Vol 88: 1262
GARDENHIRE......................Vol 88: 1262
GARDINER..........................Vol 89: 722

GARHAM..............................Vol 87: 1181
GARLAND.............................Vol 86: 985
GARNETT.............................Vol 86: 761
GARR....................................Vol 89: 719
GARRARD.............................Vol 87: 675
GARRISON............................Vol 89: 168
GARSE..................................Vol 86: 851
GASTINEAU.........................Vol 87: 1077
GASTON................................Vol 87: 1029
GATES..............Vol 86: 1179—Vol 87: 936
GATEWOOD.........................Vol 86: 169
GAUNT.................................Vol 86: 488
GAUT....................................Vol 87: 1250
GAUTIER..............................Vol 89: 866
GAY.....Vol 86: 912—Vol 89: 298, 435, 488,
    1168
GEAR....................................Vol 89: 658
GEERS...................................Vol 88: 968
GENTRY.............Vol 85: 74—Vol 89: 720
GEORGE.....Vol 85: 817, 818—Vol 86: 638—
    Vol 88: 1261—Vol 89: 939
GERARD................................Vol 87: 675
GERLACH.............................Vol 89: 434
GERRELL..............................Vol 88: 789
GETTYS..............Vol 87: 1027—Vol 89: 868
GHOLSON...........Vol 88: 1008—Vol 89: 867
GIBBINS...............................Vol 89: 865
GIBBS.....Vol 85: 243—Vol 86: 912—Vol 87:
    1029—Vol 88: 968, 1066
GIBSON.....Vol 85: 160—Vol 88: 198—Vol
    89: 299
GIDDENS.............................Vol 87: 1076
GIDEON................................Vol 87: 1076
GIFFORD.............Vol 85: 740—Vol 87: 803
GILBERT.....Vol 85: 427, 676, 817—Vol 86:
    168, 316, 488
GILBREATH.........................Vol 89: 1167
GILL......................................Vol 87: 1029
GILLESPIE.......Vol 88: 967—Vol 89: 868
GILLETT...............................Vol 87: 675
GILLIAM...............................Vol 89: 168
GILLIAND.............................Vol 88: 272
GILLILAND...........................Vol 85: 742
GILMAN................................Vol 89: 868
GILMORE.........................Vol 89: 44. 1071
GILMOUR.............................Vol 89: 599
GILPIN.................................Vol 86: 913
GIVENS...............Vol 87: 355, 803—Vol 88: 141
GLASCOCK...........................Vol 88: 566
GLASS...................................Vol 85: 242
GLOVER.....Vol 85: 68—Vol 87: 802, 1250—
    Vol 89: 44
GODDARD.............................Vol 86: 985
GOE......................................Vol 85: 956
GOFORTH.............................Vol 89: 600
GOLSON................................Vol 88: 1008
GOOCH.................................Vol 89: 297
GOODELL..............................Vol 88: 1261
GOODENOW..........................Vol 89: 601
GOODMAN............................Vol 89: 1012
GOODNOUGH........................Vol 89: 1012
GOODRICH............................Vol 89: 865
GOODWELL..........................Vol 86: 61
GOODWIN.............................Vol 85: 606
GOOLD..................................Vol 89: 1167
GOOSHORN...........................Vol 88: 894
GORDEN................................Vol 87: 934
GORDON.............Vol 88: 897—Vol 89: 1071
GORDOR................................Vol 88: 897
GORSUCH.............................Vol 87: 1077
GOSHORN............................Vol 88: 894

GOSS......Vol 86: 851—Vol 87: 223—Vol 88: 1198
GOSSE..Vol 86: 851
GOULD.................Vol 85: 243—Vol 89: 1167
GRADY...Vol 89: 941
GRAEF...............................Vol 88: 52, 54
GRAF.................................Vol 88: 52, 54
GRAFF..............................Vol 88: 52, 54
GRAHAM....Vol 85: 607—Vol 86: 168—Vol 88: 140, 789—Vol 89: 299, 940
GRAINGER...............................Vol 85: 816
GRANBY...........Vol 88: 789—Vol 89: 940
GRANT.....................................Vol 88: 967
GRAVES.........Vol 88: 270—Vol 89: 488, 1167
GRAY....Vol 85: 1046—Vol 86: 169, 985—Vol 87: 224, 936—Vol 88: 142, 895, 1199
GREATHOUSE......Vol 86: 913—Vol 89: 1010
GREEN....Vol 85: 160—Vol 86: 851, 852, 914, 1060—Vol 87: 56, 575—Vol 88: 53, 966—Vol 89: 435, 863, 1011, 1070, 1169
GREENE.........Vol 86: 1060—Vol 88: 54, 272
GREEN(E)...............................Vol 88: 141, 1198
GREENHALGH..................................Vol 89: 512
GREENLAW..................................Vol 89: 171
GREENING.................................Vol 87: 935
GREENWOOD........Vol 87: 56—Vol 88: 421
GREER............Vol 88: 686—Vol 89: 1071
GREGG..........Vol 86: 487, 914—Vol 87: 575
GREGORY.......Vol 85: 740—Vol 88: 687
GREY.......................................Vol 88: 895
GRIDER.....................................Vol 86: 487
GRIFFIN....Vol 85: 67—Vol 86: 853, 986—Vol 87: 1289—Vol 88: 51, 271, 1008, 1261
GRIFFITH....Vol 86: 167, 763—Vol 87: 1290 —Vol 89: 867, 1011
GRIGSBY...................................Vol 89: 1070
GRIM...Vol 85: 816
GRIME..Vol 89: 940
GRIMES...........Vol 86: 852—Vol 88: 1199
GRIMM.......................................Vol 85: 816
GRIMMET..................................Vol 89: 940
GRINDER..................................Vol 87: 936
GRINER.....................................Vol 87: 936
GRISHAM.................................Vol 87: 1290
GRISWOLD...............................Vol 89: 721
GROAFFE................................Vol 88: 565
GROESBECK.............................Vol 85: 173
GROF........................Vol 88: 51, 52, 54
GROFF.............................Vol 88: 52, 54
GROSSCUP...............................Vol 85: 607
GROSVENOR...........................Vol 89: 1011
GROVE........Vol 85: 676—Vol 88: 51. 52, 54
GROVES....................................Vol 89: 169
GRUBB......................................Vol 88: 894
GUARD......................................Vol 87: 804
GUILD.......................................Vol 88: 422
GUION.......................................Vol 85: 676
GUITON....................................Vol 87: 1076
GUM...Vol 89: 46
GUNBY.......................................Vol 89: 866
GUNIER....................................Vol 88: 1198
GUNN...............Vol 89: 720, 867, 1168
GUTHRIE..........................Vol 89: 433, 867
GUY..Vol 89: 1168
GWIN...Vol 89: 1071
GWYN..Vol 89: 1071

H

HADDEN...................................Vol 89: 865
HAGER......................................Vol 86: 317

HAILE.......................Vol 87: 413—Vol 89: 941
HAINES....................................Vol 89: 942
HAKES.......................................Vol 87: 414
HALADAY..................................Vol 86: 316
HALDERMAN...........................Vol 86: 852
HALE........Vol 86: 62—Vol 88: 52, 271, 1199
HALEY......................................Vol 85: 159
HALL....Vol 85: 326—Vol 87: 412—Vol 88: 140, 788, 897, 967—Vol 89: 432, 865, 1166
HALLECK.................................Vol 87: 1076
HALSEY....................................Vol 87: 802
HAMBLEN................................Vol 89: 43
HAMBLETON............................Vol 87: 804
HAMBRIGHT............................Vol 86: 986
HAMILTON....Vol 87: 1287—Vol 89: 299, 865, 866
HAMLIN.........Vol 86: 317—Vol 87: 1029
HAMM.......................................Vol 88: 1262
HAMMER..................................Vol 85: 955
HAMMOND...............................Vol 85: 817
HAMPTON....Vol 87: 412—Vol 89: 601, 720
HANCOCK....Vol 86: 761, 852—Vol 89: 44, 298, 939
HANIS.......................................Vol 89: 435
HANKS......................................Vol 87: 935
HANN..Vol 89: 1010
HANNAH....Vol 87: 1288—Vol 89: 434
HANSARD................................Vol 85: 427
HANSCOMB.............................Vol 88: 272
HARDIC.....................................Vol 85: 68
HARDICK..................................Vol 85: 68
HARDING......Vol 88: 564—Vol 89: 434, 868
HARDY.........Vol 85: 606—Vol 87: 56
HARE...Vol 86: 1060
HARER......................................Vol 87: 935
HARGIS.....................................Vol 87: 1077
HARGON...................................Vol 85: 428
HARGROVE..............................Vol 87: 224
HARKLESS.........Vol 86: 985—Vol 89: 867
HARLOW...................................Vol 89: 434
HARMAN..................................Vol 88: 1199
HARMON...................................Vol 89: 299
HARPER.....................................Vol 89: 940
HARRELL..................................Vol 87: 672
HARRER....................................Vol 87: 935
HARRINGTON....Vol 86: 640—Vol 89: 433, 719
HARRIOD..................................Vol 89: 601
HARRIS....Vol 86: 1178—Vol 87: 224, 1078 —Vol 88: 894, 967—Vol 89: 44, 170, 435, 720. 867, 1168
HARRISON....Vol 85: 243—Vol 86: 61—Vol 88: 968, 1262—Vol 89: 494
HARROD...................................Vol 88: 895
HARROLD.........Vol 85: 243—Vol 89: 169
HARSHA....................................Vol 89: 432
HARSHMAN............................Vol 88: 422
HART....Vol 85: 327—Vol 86: 317—Vol 88: 896. 966—Vol 89: 864
HARTGROVE...........................Vol 87: 224
HARTLESS................................Vol 89: 867
HARVEY........Vol 86: 987—Vol 88: 53, 789
HARVIE....................................Vol 88: 967
HARWOOD...............................Vol 89: 168
HASEY.................Vol 88: 272. 1261
HASLETT..................................Vol 87: 935
HATCHER.................................Vol 85: 160
HATFIELD....Vol 87: 935, 1026—Vol 88: 1260
HATTON...................................Vol 89: 868
HAUGHEY................................Vol 88: 52

HAUKENBERRY..................Vol 87: 225
HAUPT.................................Vol 85: 818
HAVES.................................Vol 88: 52
HAWES................................Vol 88: 52
HAWKINS.............Vol 88: 896, 966, 1262
HAWTHORN.........................Vol 85: 68
HAWVER.............................Vol 87: 934
HAYDEN.............................Vol 89: 601
HAYDON.............................Vol 88: 141
HAYES.....Vol 85: 74, 160, 677—Vol 87: 804,
934, 936—Vol 88: 272, 686—Vol 89: 722
HAYGOOD.........................Vol 87: 223
HAYLEMAN........................Vol 88: 789
HAYNIE.............Vol 85: 742—Vol 89: 600
HAYNSWORTH.................Vol 87: 935
HAYS...Vol 85: 160, 677—Vol 87: 804—Vol
88: 272, 686—Vol 89: 1011
HAYWARD.........................Vol 85: 496
HAZELETT.........................Vol 89: 720
HAZELTIME......................Vol 89: 601
HEACOX.............................Vol 85: 677
HEAD.................................Vol 85: 1046
HEADY................................Vol 86: 761
HEARD...............................Vol 89: 170
HEATH...Vol 85: 496—Vol 86: 315—Vol
88: 969
HEAPS................................Vol 86: 1179
HEDGER.............................Vol 88: 420
HEDRICK............................Vol 88: 894
HELLER..............................Vol 88: 566
HELPS.................................Vol 86: 1179
HENDERSON.....Vol 85: 160, 740—Vol 86:
1260—Vol 88: 141, 895, 1199, 1261—Vol
89: 599
HENDRICKS.....Vol 85: 243—Vol 87: 575—
Vol 89: 598
HENKEL..............................Vol 86: 62
HENRY...............Vol 86: 167—Vol 88: 142
HENSLEY.............................Vol 86: 316
HERCULES.........Vol 86: 985—Vol 89: 867
HERNDON...........................Vol 89: 1070
HERRING....Vol 85: 816—Vol 87: 1026—
Vol 89: 1168
HERRINGTON.....................Vol 87: 414
HEYMAN............................Vol 88: 565
HIATT.................................Vol 87: 575
HICKEY............Vol 87: 675—Vol 88: 968
HICKS..............Vol 86: 167—Vol 88: 966
HIDE.................Vol 87: 224, 1288
HIGHFILL..........................Vol 88: 967
HIGHSMITH.......................Vol 86: 1178
IILEY.................................Vol 86: 761
HILL...Vol 85: 739—Vol 86: 640—Vol 87:
1078, 1180—Vol 88: 1197—Vol 89: 720,
939, 1167
HILLIS...............................Vol 88: 895
HINDS................................Vol 87: 1026
HINEMAN...........................Vol 86: 851
HINMAN.............................Vol 87: 156
HINSHAW...........................Vol 85: 159
HISRODT............................Vol 88: 270
HIX....................................Vol 86: 167
HIXON................................Vol 88: 896
HOBSON.............................Vol 89: 721
HOCKENBERRY.................Vol 86: 1178
HODGE...............................Vol 88: 968
HODGKIN...........................Vol 86: 168
HOES.................................Vol 88: 52
HOEY................................Vol 88: 52
HOFFER...........Vol 86: 62, 761—Vol 89: 1072
HOFFMAN..........................Vol 88: 422

HOGAN...............................Vol 88: 141
HOGEBOOM.......................Vol 89: 601
HOGG.................................Vol 88: 968
HOGGSHEAD.....................Vol 87: 56
HOLBROOK....Vol 87: 802—Vol 88: 421,
1262
HOLBROOKS.....................Vol 88: 421
HOLCOMB.........................Vol 89: 1166
HOLEYFIELD.....................Vol 88: 53
HOLLAND.........Vol 89: 863, 1110
HOLLENBECK....................Vol 86: 488
HOLLEY.............................Vol 88: 1199
HOLLINGSWORTH............Vol 88: 1065
HOLLON..............................Vol 89: 1110
HOLLOWELL......................Vol 86: 852
HOLMAN.......Vol 86: 316, 912—Vol 89: 435
HOLMES....Vol 87: 595, 802—Vol 88: 685—
Vol 89: 1011
HOLSAPLE.........................Vol 88: 421
HOLT....Vol 86: 322, 1178—Vol 88: 142,
790, 966, 968
HOLTSAPPLE.....................Vol 88: 421
HOLTZAPFEL....................Vol 88: 421
HOOD.................................Vol 89: 868
HOOK.................................Vol 87: 1077
HOPE.................................Vol 88: 1197
HOPKINS....Vol 85: 955—Vol 86: 166—Vol
88: 564—Vol 89: 300, 435
HORAN..............................Vol 88: 968
HORD.................................Vol 87: 1028
HORNEY.............................Vol 88: 894
HORNING...........................Vol 87: 413
HORRALL...........................Vol 88: 52
HORTON.............................Vol 89: 168
HOUSE...........Vol 85: 427, 956—Vol 86: 985
HOUSTON....Vol 85: 1046—Vol 87: 56—Vol
88: 1262—Vol 89: 434, 1168
HOWARD...Vol 85: 534—Vol 86: 61—Vol
87: 674—Vol 88: 967
HOWE.................................Vol 89: 169
HOWELL....Vol 87: 223—Vol 88: 1008—Vol
89: 600, 867, 868, 1167
HOWES................................Vol 89: 45
HOWLAND.........Vol 87: 413—Vol 88: 422
HUBBARD....Vol 85: 607—Vol 87: 1076—
Vol 89: 867
HUCKAHEE........................Vol 89: 867
HUCKELBERRY.................Vol 86: 1178
HUCKLEBERRY.................Vol 86: 1178
HUDDLESTON...................Vol 86: 169
HUDGINS............................Vol 88: 421
HUDSON.....Vol 85: 1044—Vol 89: 601, 1166
HUEY................Vol 88: 1008—Vol 89: 867
HUFFER......Vol 86: 62, 761—Vol 89: 1072
HUGGINS...........................Vol 89: 1168
HUGHES....Vol 85: 741—Vol 86: 60—Vol
89: 939, 1011
HUGHEY...Vol 88: 1008—Vol 89: 862, 867
HULL.................Vol 89: 1010, 1011
HUMAN............Vol 87: 1287—Vol 89: 168
HUME................Vol 86: 640—Vol 88: 1065
HUMES...............................Vol 89: 939
HUMPHREY....Vol 87: 934, 1252—Vol 88:
968
HUNE.................................Vol 86: 640
HUNT................Vol 86: 915—Vol 89: 432
HUNTER....Vol 85: 740—Vol 86: 317—Vol
87: 1252
HUNTINGTON....................Vol 89: 300
HUNTSINGER....................Vol 87: 575
HURLEY.............................Vol 86: 639

LYTELL..Vol 86: 317

Mc

McAFEE.......................................Vol 89: 1010
McBEE...Vol 87: 1076
McBRIDE....Vol 88: 565—Vol 89: 297, 863, 868
McBRIDES..................................Vol 87: 1181
McCADDEN..............................Vol 89: 600
McCALL...Vol 88: 687
McCARDELL..............................Vol 88: 897
McCARTNEY.....Vol 85: 67—Vol 88: 142—Vol 89: 298
McCLANAHAN...............................Vol 86: 60
McCLELLAN.....Vol 85: 742—Vol 86: 1326—Vol 87: 1076—Vol 88: 54—Vol 89: 1012
McCLELLAND................................Vol 89: 434
McCLEMENT.................................Vol 89: 866
McCLERRY....................................Vol 89: 599
McCLURE.......................................Vol 86: 488
McCOMB............................Vol 88: 53, 790
McCOOL...Vol 89: 720
McCORKLE..........Vol 87: 936—Vol 89: 1011
McCORMICK........Vol 87: 412, 576—Vol 89: 43, 597
McCOUN.......................................Vol 89: 1010
McCOY..Vol 88: 1199
McCRARY......................................Vol 89: 435
McCREARY....................................Vol 89: 435
McCREERY....................................Vol 88: 968
McCRERY.......................................Vol 89: 435
McCRIDDY....................................Vol 88: 790
McCRORY......................................Vol 88: 968
McCULLOUGH.............................Vol 89: 862
McCULLY.......................................Vol 88: 1262
McCURRY......................................Vol 88: 968
McDADE...Vol 87: 673
McDANIELS..................................Vol 89: 598
MacDONALD.................................Vol 85: 607
McDONALD.....Vol 88: 197—Vol 89: 863, 1010
McDOWELL..........Vol 86: 987—Vol 89: 719
McELHANEY...............................Vol 85: 606
McELROY.....Vol 86: 639—Vol 87: 223—Vol 89: 169
McELWAIN...................................Vol 88: 968
McEWEN..Vol 86: 914
McFALL..Vol 85: 243
McGEATH......................................Vol 87: 675
McGEE...........Vol 86: 1327—Vol 89: 1010
McGINNIS.....................................Vol 89: 1010
McGUFFEY...................................Vol 85: 160
McGUIRE.............Vol 87: 574—Vol 89: 598
McHENRY......................................Vol 86: 851
McILRATH....................................Vol 85: 242
McINTEER....................................Vol 89: 868
McKAY...Vol 89: 169
McKEAN...........Vol 88: 565—Vol 89: 599
McKENDREE...............................Vol 88: 421
McKINLEY....................................Vol 87: 804
McKINNEY.....Vol 88: 968, 969, 1008—Vol 89: 867
McKINSTRY................................Vol 87: 1252
McKITRICK.................................Vol 88: 1262
McKNOWN...................................Vol 86: 762
McLELLAND................................Vol 89: 1012
McLEROY.......................................Vol 87: 223
McMAHON...................................Vol 88: 686, 967
McMICHAEL................................Vol 87: 675
McNEAL...Vol 87: 595
McNEIL..........Vol 87: 1287—Vol 88: 270

McNIGHT.....................................Vol 87: 1026
McWHORTER..............................Vol 88: 687

M

MABRY..Vol 85: 741
MACE...Vol 89: 869
MackGEHEE................................Vol 86: 1325
MacKAY...Vol 89: 169
MACKAY..Vol 89: 169
MACKEY..Vol 89: 170
MACKINTOSH............................Vol 88: 421
MACON..Vol 88: 421
MADDEN.......................................Vol 88: 1065
MADDOX.............Vol 88: 789—Vol 89: 298
MADISON............Vol 87: 1287—Vol 89: 863
MAGEE..Vol 89: 721
MAGIE..Vol 88: 1261
MAGILL.............Vol 87: 1028—Vol 88: 54
MAGRUDER.....Vol 85: 325, 428—Vol 87: 1290—Vol 88: 790—Vol 89: 598
MAIN...Vol 88: 270
MAJOR..Vol 88: 52
MALBON...Vol 85: 607
MALONE...Vol 89: 720
MANCHESTER.............................Vol 89: 299
MANN..Vol 88: 790
MANNING............Vol 85: 160—Vol 89: 597
MANSFIELD..................................Vol 85: 428
MANSON..Vol 86: 913
MARCH...Vol 87: 1290
MARCUM.......................................Vol 88: 566
MARK..Vol 89: 601
MARKLAND.................................Vol 89: 1012
MARSH.....Vol 86: 912—Vol 87: 1287—Vol 89: 45
MARSHALL.....Vol 85: 243, 496, 818, 1046—Vol 86: 62, 912—Vol 88: 564, 789, 1198, 1262
MARTIN—Vol 86; 168, 317, 762, 853—Vol 87: 1076—Vol 88: 54, 224, 421, 575, 686—Vol 89: 598
MARTINDALE..............................Vol 87: 1182
MARVIN...Vol 89: 598
MASON....Vol 86: 489, 762—Vol 87: 1182, 1287—Vol 88: 564—Vol 89: 436
MASSENGALE...............................Vol 85: 69
MASSEY.....Vol 85: 497—Vol 86: 984, 987—Vol 87: 935
MASTELLER................................Vol 85: 325
MASTIN..Vol 89: 941
MATHEWS.....Vol 86: 1179—Vol 87: 412, 595
MATHEWSON.....Vol 86: 1326—Vol 89: 941
MATLOCK......................................Vol 87: 934
MATTHEWS.....Vol 86: 62—Vol 87: 1182—Vol 89: 512, 721
MATTHEWSON..........................Vol 88: 141
MATTOON....................................Vol 87: 673
MATTOX.......................................Vol 88: 789
MAUPIN...........Vol 87: 1078—Vol 88: 224
MAURCE.......................................Vol 89: 940
MAURICE......................................Vol 89: 940
MAURY..Vol 88: 1065
MAXSON.......................................Vol 86: 315
MAXWELL......Vol 85: 677—Vol 87: 675
MAY.....Vol 86: 1062—Vol 88: 566—Vol 89: 435
MAYES...Vol 89: 434
MAYFIELD........Vol 86: 60—Vol 88: 967
MAYO...Vol 87: 1252
MEACHAM...................................Vol 88: 893

MEADE..............Vol 86: 639—Vol 89: 300
MEAIS..............Vol 86: 488
MEARS..............Vol 88: 685
MEDARIS..........Vol 85: 1045—Vol 88: 789
MEDAUGH..........Vol 89: 1010
MEISENHEIMER..........Vol 89: 869
MELSHEIMER..............Vol 89: 939
MENDELL..............Vol 88: 1198
MENDENHALL..............Vol 89: 1071
MERCER.....Vol 87: 935—Vol 88: 565—Vol 89: 1071
MERIWETHER..............Vol 85: 160
MERRILL..............Vol 89: 869
MEYERS..............Vol 88: 270
MICHAEL.....Vol 87: 1287—Vol 88: 52—Vol 89: 432
MICHELS..............Vol 89: 170
MIDDEKAUF..............Vol 89: 432
MIDDLETON.....Vol 86: 986—Vol 88: 420, 790
MILES—Vol 86: 761—Vol 88: 1197
MILLER.....Vol 85; 327, 607, 818—Vol 86: 169, 317, 639, 761, 851—Vol 87: 355, 1289, 1290—Vol 88: 271, 967—Vol 89: 169, 171, 599
MILLET..............Vol 89: 44
MILLIGAN..............Vol 89: 719
MILLINGTON..............Vol 85: 955
MILLS.....Vol 86: 852—Vol 87: 576—Vol 89: 297, 434
MILTON—Vol 87: 1028—Vol 88: 1065—Vol 89: 864
MINER..............Vol 87: 1027
MINICH..............Vol 85: 427
MINNICH..............Vol 88: 789
MINNIER..............Vol 88: 1199
MINNIS..............Vol 89: 1071
MINOR..............Vol 85: 816—Vol 87: 1027
MINTER..............Vol 86: 1061
MISKELL..............Vol 88: 1199
MITCHELL.....Vol 85: 606—Vol 86: 914, 1115, 1326—Vol 88: 686, 896—Vol 89: 44, 1072
MIXER..............Vol 87: 55
MIZELL..............Vol 88: 51
MOFFAT..............Vol 88: 1198
MOFFETT..............Vol 86: 987
MON..............Vol 89: 598
MONTAGUE.....Vol 86: 317—Vol 87: 1250 —Vol 89: 46
MONTGOMERY.....Vol 87: 936, 1288—Vol 89: 170
MOOK..............Vol 89: 865
MOORE.....Vol 85: 67, 428—Vol 87: 413, 1026, 1029—Vol 88: 53, 141, 686, 895, 967, 1066—Vol 89: 600, 601, 866, 939, 1011
MOREHEAD..............Vol 88: 140
MOREHOUSE..............Vol 87: 355—Vol 89: 939
MORELAND.....Vol 85: 67—Vol 89: 865, 939
MORGAN.....Vol 85: 534—Vol 86: 486—Vol 87: 1026—Vol 88: 565—Vol 89: 1166
MORRIS.....Vol 85: 496, 1045—Vol 86: 62— Vol 88: 142—Vol 89: 862, 940
MORRISON..............Vol 87: 1289
MORROW.....Vol 87: 414, 1026—Vol 89: 297
MORTON..............Vol 88: 271—Vol 89: 1072
MOSELEY..............Vol 88: 966
MOSER..............Vol 86: 317
MOSS..............Vol 85: 68—Vol 87: 413
MOTLEY..............Vol 88: 421
MOTT..............Vol 87: 673, 802

MOUDY..............Vol 86: 1178
MOURCE..............Vol 89: 940
MOWRY..............Vol 89: 941
MOYER..............Vol 85: 160
MUCHMORE.....Vol 87: 223, 1252—Vol 88: 566
MUCKELROY..............Vol 86: 639
MULFORD..............Vol 88: 790
MULLINS.....Vol 86: 914—Vol 89: 720, 1168
MUNCH..............Vol 88: 789
MUNCY..............Vol 89: 940
MURPHY..............Vol 85: 243
MURRAIN..............Vol 85: 243
MURRAY.....Vol 87: 1182—Vol 88: 1065—Vol 89: 862
MUSSER..............Vol 86: 1178
MUSSELMAN..............Vol 88: 966
MYERS.....Vol 85: 954—Vol 87: 1250—Vol 88: 1066—Vol 89: 1012
MYRTLE..............Vol 88: 1065

N

NALLE..............Vol 87: 575
NALLEY..............Vol 87: 575
NALLY..............Vol 87: 575
NAPIER..............Vol 86: 316, 985
NASH..............Vol 87: 674—Vol 89: 864
NAUMAN..............Vol 89: 599
NEAL.....Vol 87: 55, 936—Vol 89: 1010
NEALY..............Vol 89: 1011
NEELEY..............Vol 89: 1011
NEELY..............Vol 86: 984
NEFF..............Vol 86: 984—Vol 89: 864
NELL..............Vol 86: 1178
NELSON.....Vol 85: 496—Vol 86: 851, 915— Vol 87: 56, 1182, 1250—Vol 88: 1197— Vol 89: 432, 722, 1011, 1072
NESBIT..............Vol 85: 268
NETTLES..............Vol 88: 968
NEW..............Vol 89: 866
NEWBERRY..............Vol 87: 225
NEWLAND..............Vol 85: 955
NEWMAN.....Vol 87: 1028, 1182—Vol 88: 1065
NEWTON.....Vol 85: 326, 816—Vol 87: 675 —Vol 88: 687, 1066
NICHOLS.....Vol 86: 984—Vol 87: 575—Vol 88: 968—Vol 89: 170, 864
NICHOLSON..............Vol 88: 422
NIKIRK..............Vol 89: 432
NILES..............Vol 89: 868
NISWANGER..............Vol 89: 1071
NIXON..............Vol 89: 168
NOBLE..............Vol 86: 61
NOELL..............Vol 88: 421
NOLAN..............Vol 88: 564
NOLAND..............Vol 87: 937
NOLES..............Vol 89: 45
NORRIS..............Vol 87: 1028
NORTHCUTT..............Vol 86: 914
NORTHEND..............Vol 87: 1181
NORTON..............Vol 87: 414—Vol 88: 968
NORWOOD.....Vol 85: 68—Vol 87: 1250—Vol 89: 44, 867
NUNN..............Vol 89: 719
NUTTER..............Vol 88: 685

O

OATMAN..............Vol 88: 271
O'BANNON.....Vol 86: 489—Vol 87: 1077—Vol 88: 1197

O'BRIAN..............Vol 89: 726
ODEL..............Vol 88: 422
ODELL.....Vol 87: 1182—Vol 88: 422—Vol 89: 1071
ODLE..............Vol 88: 422
OFFUTT..............Vol 89: 940
OGDEN..............Vol 89: 939
OGLE..............Vol 87: 674
O'HAVER..............Vol 85: 427
OILES..............Vol 85: 818
OLDHAM..............Vol 87: 1289
OLDS..............Vol 86: 639
OLIVER..............Vol 88: 895—Vol 89: 721
ONEAL..............Vol 87: 1028
O'NEIL..............Vol 87: 1028
ORFORD..............Vol 87: 1251
ORMAND..............Vol 87: 1076
ORR.....Vol 87: 1027—Vol 88: 897—Vol 89: 939
ORRELL..............Vol 89: 1012
ORSBORNE.......Vol 87: 1076—Vol 88: 790
OSBORN.....Vol 85: 496—Vol 87: 1076—Vol 88: 272
OSBURN.....Vol 87: 1078—Vol 88: 1262
OSMER..............Vol 89: 940
OSMUN..............Vol 89: 45
OSTEEN..............Vol 88: 968
OSTERHOUT..............Vol 89: 1072
OUTMAN..............Vol 88: 271
OVIATT..............Vol 89: 940
OWEN.....Vol 85: 817—Vol 87: 1030—Vol 88: 270, 271—Vol 89: 941
OWENS—Vol 87: 1077—Vol 89: 941, 1010
OWINGS..............Vol 87: 1290—Vol 89: 867
OWSLEY..............Vol 88: 420

P

PACE..............Vol 89: 719
PACKARD..............Vol 89: 298
PAGE.....Vol 85: 69, 326, 741—Vol 86: 60—Vol 89: 1011
PAINE..............Vol 85: 74
PARCELL..............Vol 89: 1072
PARDEE..............Vol 86: 984
PARDY..............Vol 89: 434
PARK..............Vol 86: 852—Vol 87: 1289
PARKE..............Vol 87: 1289—Vol 89: 46
PARKER.....Vol 85: 158—Vol 86: 488, 913—Vol 87: 804, 1252—Vol 88: 224, 272, 1066, 1261—Vol 89: 597, 601
PARKHURST..............Vol 85: 427
PARKINSON..............Vol 86: 639
PARKS.....Vol 85: 74—Vol 87: 576—Vol 88: 198—Vol 89: 719
PARR..............Vol 85: 68
PARRISH..............Vol 87: 1290
PARRIOTT..............Vol 88: 575
PARROTT..............Vol 88: 575
PARRY..............Vol 87: 674
PARSONS..............Vol 88: 422
PARTRIDGE..............Vol 86: 62, 915
PASSWATER..............Vol 87: 56
PATRICK.....Vol 85: 741—Vol 87: 1182
PATTERSON.....Vol 85: 242, 817, 955—Vol 88: 421—Vol 89: 299, 864, 868
PATTILLO..............Vol 87: 412
PATTISON..............Vol 86: 915
PATTON..............Vol 88: 687, 895, 966
PAUL..............Vol 85: 243—Vol 87: 1290
PAXTON..............Vol 87: 674
PAYNE.....Vol 85: 159—Vol 86: 486, 853, 985

—Vol 87: 935—Vol 88: 895
PEARCE..............Vol 86: 914
PEARSON.....Vol 85: 159, 955—Vol 86: 488—Vol 89: 171
PEASE..............Vol 87: 1180—Vol 88: 789
PEAVY..............Vol 87: 223
PECK..............Vol 86: 1178
PECKENPAUGH..............Vol 87: 575
PECKINPAUGH.....Vol 87: 1287—Vol 88: 140
PEDDICORD..............Vol 86: 912
PEET..............Vol 86: 762—Vol 88: 271
PEIRSON..............Vol. 85: 159—Vol. 86: 169
PENDLETON.....Vol 85: 955—Vol 87: 224—Vol 88: 789
PENNINGTON.....Vol 86: 914—Vol 87: 595, 802
PENNY..............Vol 89: 297
PERCIVAL..............Vol 87: 576
PERINE..............Vol 89: 1010
PERKINS.....Vol 86: 317—Vol 87: 1251—Vol 89: 43, 494
PERRINE..............Vol 89: 1010
PERROTT..............Vol 88: 575
PERRY.....Vol 85: 955—Vol 87: 1289—Vol 88: 422, 687, 969
PERSON..............Vol 85: 326
PETERS..............Vol 86: 761—Vol 89: 1072
PETERSON..............Vol 86: 914—Vol 89: 169
PETTIGREW..............Vol 85: 608
PETTIS..............Vol 88: 1262
PETTUS..............Vol 86: 488
PETTY..............Vol 88: 1199
PETTYPOOL..............Vol 85: 818
PEW..............Vol 89: 1072
PFAFFENBERGER..............Vol 89: 432
PHARIS..............Vol 86: 763
PHAYLER..............Vol 89: 939
PHELPS.....Vol 88: 272—Vol 89: 1010
PHILLIPI..............Vol 85: 427
PHILLIPS.....Vol 86: 168—Vol 87: 936—Vol 88: 1260, 1261—Vol 89: 597, 868
PICKARD..............Vol 89: 940
PICKENBAUGH..............Vol 89: 865
PICKENS.....Vol 85: 1045—Vol 89: 941
PIERCE..............Vol 87: 1078—Vol 89: 434
PIERSON..............Vol 85: 159—Vol 86: 169
PIKE..............Vol 89: 297
PILCHER..............Vol 86: 169
PILLSTROM..............Vol 85: 816
PINER..............Vol 86: 760
PINNELL..............Vol 87: 934
PIPES..............Vol 89: 601
PITCOCK..............Vol 87: 1027
PITKIN..............Vol 89: 601
PITMAN..............Vol 85: 1046
PIXLEY..............Vol 88: 272
PLASTER..............Vol 85: 816
PLATT.....Vol 85: 158—Vol 89: 866
PLATTS..............Vol 87: 675
PLUMB..............Vol 89: 721
PLUMBERS..............Vol 89: 598
PLUMMER.....Vol 86: 985—Vol 89: 864
POAGE..............Vol 89: 435
POFFENBERGER.....Vol 87: 1287—Vol 89: 432
POLING..............Vol 89: 298
POLLARD.....Vol 87: 673—Vol 88: 685, 967
POLLIARD..............Vol 87: 576
POLYARD..............Vol 87: 576
POND..............Vol 86: 986—Vol 87: 1077

POOL..Vol 85: 428
POOR..Vol 89: 45
POPE............Vol 86: 167—Vol 88: 1066
PORTER....Vol 85: 426, 676—Vol 86: 640,
1062—Vol 87: 1077—Vol 88: 684, 1065,
1066—Vol 89; 601
PORTMAN..Vol 86: 852
POST...Vol 87: 575
POTTER............Vol 85: 676—Vol 88: 141, 894
POTTERS.......................................Vol 85: 677
POTTORFF....................................Vol 89: 597
POTTS..Vol 86: 1179
POWELL....Vol 86: 760, 762, 1115, 1179—
Vol 87: 1030—Vol 88: 271, 687, 1066—
Vol 89: 46, 300, 863, 941, 1070
POWERS....Vol 86: 487, 985—Vol 87: 224—
Vol 88: 969
POYAS..Vol 87: 937
PRAGER................Vol 87: 935—Vol 89: 600
PRATER..Vol 87: 803
PRATT..Vol 85: 159
PRAY..Vol 86: 487
PRAYTOR......................................Vol 87: 803
PRESSEAU....................................Vol 85: 427
PRESTON............Vol 85: 427—Vol 87: 1288
PREWET................Vol 86: 1062, 1325
PREWITT....Vol 86: 1062, 1325—Vol 87:
1076
PRICE....Vol 86: 852—Vol 87: 595—Vol 88:
894—Vol 89: 43, 722, 1010, 1167
PRICHARD....................................Vol 89: 1011
PRITCHARD....Vol 87: 803—Vol 89: 168,
1011
PRITCHETT....................................Vol 89: 1011
PROFFITT......................................Vol 89: 170
PROTZMAN....................................Vol 88: 422
PRUITT....Vol 85: 268—Vol 86: 1062, 1325
—Vol 87: 1076
PUGH............Vol 88: 142, 788—Vol 89: 170
PUSEY..Vol 89: 297
PUTNAM..Vol 89: 298
PYLE..Vol 85: 497

Q

QUAINTANCE................................Vol 89: 863
QUICK..Vol 85: 428
QUIGLEY......................................Vol 86: 316
QUIMBY..Vol 88: 967
QUINN..Vol 85: 741

R

RAGLAND......................................Vol 88: 271
RAGSDALE............Vol 85: 243—Vol 86: 852
RAIFORD......................................Vol 89: 300
RAILSBACK........Vol 85: 742—Vol 87: 1289
RAINO................................Vol 88: 271, 722
RAMEY..Vol 87: 574
RAMSEY..Vol 86: 317
RAMSEY............Vol 87: 675—Vol 89: 1072
RAN..Vol 86: 915
RANDALL......................................Vol 87: 802
RANDLETT............Vol 86: 913—Vol 87: 413
RANDOLPH....Vol 86: 1061—Vol 87: 1027
—Vol 89: 300, 658, 1072
RANEY..Vol 89: 864
RANKIN............Vol 85: 955—Vol 88: 967
RANN..................................Vol 88: 271, 722
RANO..................................Vol 88: 271, 722
RANSOM............Vol 87: 1028—Vol 88: 52, 789
RASE..Vol 88: 1199
RASER..Vol 88: 1199

RATCHFORD..................................Vol 88: 1261
RAWLINGS....................................Vol 89: 864
RAWLINS............Vol 85: 955—Vol 88: 54
RAYBURN......................................Vol 87: 1078
RAYMOND....Vol 85: 428—Vol 87: 595—
Vol 89: 1071
RAYNES..............................Vol 88: 271, 722
REA................Vol 88: 895—Vol 89: 941
READ....Vol 85: 741—Vol 87: 934—Vol 89:
1071
REAGOR..Vol 85: 955
REDMAN............Vol 86: 639—Vol 88: 51
REED....Vol 86: 1326—Vol 87: 414—Vol
89: 45, 597
REEDER..Vol 86: 984
REES..Vol 87: 1250
REESER..Vol 88: 1199
REEVES..Vol 85: 955
REGAN..Vol 86: 762
REID..Vol 87: 414
REINHART....................................Vol 89: 866
REMSEN..Vol 89: 866
REMSON..Vol 89: 866
REMY..Vol 88: 53
RENFREW......................................Vol 87: 1028
RENFRO................Vol 87: 1028, 1287
RENICK............Vol 87: 595—Vol 88: 141
RENNIX..Vol 88: 141
RENTFRO................Vol 87: 1028, 1287
RENTFROE....................................Vol 87: 1028
RENTFROW....................................Vol 87: 1028
REYNOLDS....Vol 86: 763—Vol 88: 575,
969—Vol 89: 866
REXFORD......................................Vol 89: 435
RHOADE..Vol 85: 742
RHOADS..Vol 87: 1076
RHODE..Vol 85: 742
RHODES............Vol 86: 488—Vol 87: 802
RHOODS..Vol 88: 566
RICE............Vol 86: 913, 1061—Vol 87: 412
RICH............Vol 87: 1287—Vol 89: 169
RICHARDS............Vol 87: 936—Vol 89: 941
RICHARDSON....Vol 85: 69—Vol 86: 316—
Vol 87: 156—Vol 88: 422, 967
RIDDLE................Vol 88: 789, 1064
RIDENOUR....................................Vol 87: 575
RIDER..Vol 86: 762
RIDGEWAY....................................Vol 88: 272
RIDLEY................Vol 89: 168, 722
RIGDON............Vol 89: 863, 1070, 1072
RIGGINS......................................Vol 88: 141
RIGGS..Vol 88: 271
RING............Vol 86: 1060—Vol 89: 44
RINGER..Vol 87: 1026
RINKER..Vol 88: 1199
RITCHEY......................................Vol 89: 434
RITTENBERG..................................Vol 85: 426
RITTER..Vol 88: 422
RIVERS..Vol 87: 934
RIVES..Vol 85: 741
ROAN..Vol 89: 721
ROANE..Vol 89: 721
ROBBINS....Vol 85: 159, 426—Vol 86: 914—
Vol 88: 968—Vol 89: 722
ROBERSON............Vol 86: 1061—Vol 88: 790
ROBERT..Vol 89: 436
ROBERTS....Vol 87: 575, 1030—Vol 88:
1065, 1066—Vol 89: 597, 863, 942, 1070
ROBERTSON....Vol 86: 315, 639—Vol 88:
421, 790—Vol 89: 598
ROBESON......................................Vol 88: 1198

ROBEY..Vol 86: 316
ROBINS..Vol 88: 968
ROBINSON....Vol 85: 159, 327, 427, 607—
  Vol 87: 934, 1287—Vol 88: 270, 894,
  1008, 1261—Vol 89: 432, 863, 867, 868,
  869, 1010, 1072
ROBISON...Vol 89: 1010
ROCKWELL..................................Vol 85: 327
RODGERS.............Vol 85: 69—Vol 86: 1060
RODMAN..Vol 87: 1182
ROE...................Vol 85: 68—Vol 89: 1012
ROEBUCK......................................Vol 87: 1026
ROELOFSEN..................................Vol 89: 1011
ROGERS.....Vol 85: 68—Vol 87: 576, 672,
  1180, 1252—Vol 88: 422, 789—Vol 89:
  169, 658, 720, 1167
ROHR...Vol 89: 721
ROHRER...Vol 89: 721
ROLAND.........................Vol 86: 640—Vol 89: 941
ROLLING...Vol 86: 640
ROLLINS...Vol 85: 740
ROLLISON..Vol 89: 1011
RONEMAS..Vol 87: 1076
ROOT.........................Vol 85: 327—Vol 89: 170
ROSE....Vol 87: 803—Vol 89: 170, 866,
  1071
ROSECRANS..................................Vol 85: 427
ROSER..Vol 88: 1199
ROSS...........Vol 85: 426—Vol 87: 803, 934
ROSSER...Vol 85: 817
RORIE..Vol 89: 863
ROUMTREE....................................Vol 85: 325
ROUNDS..Vol 85: 817
ROUTH..Vol 88: 140
ROWDEN...Vol 85: 268
ROWE..Vol 86: 763
ROWELL...Vol 88: 422
ROWLAND.......................................Vol 86: 640
ROWLINSON...................................Vol 89: 1011
RUBY...Vol 86: 316
RUCKER..Vol 89: 598
RUDD...Vol 87: 1290
RUNNELS..Vol 88: 969
RUSH..Vol 88: 1199
RUSHING...Vol 89: 939
RUSSEL..Vol 88: 420
RUSSELL—Vol 85: 496, 606—Vol 86: 852
  —Vol 88: 966—Vol 89: 433, 865, 869
RUSSEY..Vol 85: 677
RUST..Vol 86: 985
RUTHERFORD...............................Vol 86: 1327
RUTLEDGE.............Vol 86: 168—Vol 89: 436
RYAL..Vol 88: 1261
RYAN.................Vol 88: 1199—Vol 89: 598

S

SAFFORD...Vol 89: 658
SALISBURY........Vol 85: 495—Vol 88: 270
SALMON..Vol 88: 141
SAMMONS......................................Vol 88: 52, 141
SAMPLE..Vol 88: 897
SAMPSEL..Vol 88: 897
SAMPSON..Vol 85: 497
SAMSEL................Vol 88: 897—Vol 89: 600
ST. CLAIR......................................Vol 85: 676
SANDERS...Vol 89: 939
SANDLIN...Vol 89: 44
SANDIDGE......................................Vol 86: 1178
SANDLIN...............Vol 86: 62—Vol 87: 1288
SANDY...Vol 88: 896
SANFORD...Vol 88: 53

SATTERWHITE.............................Vol 89: 939
SAUNDERS....Vol 85: 497—Vol 89: 1010,
  1166
SAVAGE..Vol 89: 297
SAXON.......................Vol 86: 761—Vol 89: 1071
SAXTON...Vol 89: 169
SCALES...Vol 88: 421
SCARCE..Vol 86: 1326
SCHAPMAN.....................................Vol 88: 789
SCHERMER.....................................Vol 85: 607
SCHLOSSER....................................Vol 89: 432
SCHOFIELD.....................................Vol 89: 601
SCHOONMAKER...........................Vol 86: 852
SCHUYLER......................................Vol 89: 940
SCITES...Vol 89: 597
SCOTT....Vol 85: 158—Vol 86: 316, 986,
  1178—Vol 87: 56, 224, 225, 674, 1027,
  1182—Vol 88: 84, 421, 565, 1197—Vol 89:
  43, 170, 436, 863
SCUDDER...Vol 89: 720
SEA..Vol 86: 638
SEAL..Vol 86: 169
SEALE.........................Vol 86: 852—Vol 89: 719
SEAMANS...Vol 87: 414
SEARS....................Vol 85: 678—Vol 88: 422
SECOR...Vol 87: 595
SEE...Vol 85: 741
SEELEY...Vol 89: 435
SEITS...Vol 89: 597
SEITZ...Vol 89: 597
SEITZLER..Vol 86: 639
SELBY..Vol 85: 325
SELF...Vol 85: 243
SELLERS...Vol 85: 740
SELLS...Vol 85: 607
SELMAN..Vol 89: 436
SETTLE................Vol 85: 67—Vol 86: 60, 985
SEVER...Vol 88: 1198
SEWARD..................Vol 88: 270—Vol 89: 432
SEXTON................Vol 87: 224, 225, 935, 1181
SEYBERT..Vol 85: 160
SEYMOUR..Vol 89: 1169
SHACKELFORD.............................Vol 88: 422
SHAFER...Vol 89: 1011
SHAFFEY..Vol 89: 600
SHANK..Vol 89: 598
SHANKLE..Vol 88: 270
SHANKLIN..Vol 88: 54
SHANNON.............Vol 86: 762—Vol 88: 685
SHARLAH..Vol 86: 167
SHARP....Vol 86: 168—Vol 88: 897—Vol
  89: 940
SHARPE...Vol 88: 54
SHARRITT..Vol 88: 142
SHAVER..................Vol 86: 640—Vol 89: 1072
SHAW....................Vol 87: 414—Vol 89: 869
SHEARER..Vol 85: 1044
SHEETS...Vol 86: 761
SHEFFIELD......................................Vol 89: 864
SHELTON.............Vol 86: 168—Vol 87: 575
SHEPARDSON...............................Vol 88: 687
SHEPHERD.......................................Vol 87: 575
SHEPPARDS.....................................Vol 87: 412
SHERER...Vol 85: 427
SHERIFF..Vol 88: 420
SHERMAN...Vol 85: 956
SHERROD...Vol 89: 45
SHERRIT...Vol 88: 142
SHERWOOD....................................Vol 88: 272
SHIRK..Vol 89: 865
SHIRLEY...Vol 88: 420

STODDARD..Vol 85: 426
STONE..Vol 86: 638
STONEMAN..Vol 87: 1027
STORY..................................Vol 85: 160—Vol 88: 54
STOUFFER..Vol 85: 955
STOUT..Vol 85: 68
STOUTT..Vol 88: 142
STOWMAN..Vol 87: 1027
STRATTON..............................Vol 89: 1012(2x)
STREET..Vol 86: 1062
STRICKLAND..Vol 85: 242
STROBHAR..Vol 89: 940
STROTHER..........Vol 87: 412—Vol 89: 866
STUART................Vol 88: 1008—Vol 89: 1071
STUBBLEFIELD......................................Vol 89: 434
STUBBS..Vol 89: 435
STUMP..................Vol 86: 1327—Vol 89: 867
STUTTARD..Vol 85: 426
SUBLET..Vol 85: 428
SULLIVAN..Vol 89: 300
SUMAKER..Vol 89: 942
SUMMERSIDE..Vol 88: 967
SUMPSTER..Vol 87: 1028
SUMPTER..Vol 87: 1028
SUMTER..Vol 87: 1028
SUTHERLAND........Vol 87: 673—Vol 88:
1262
SUTTON................Vol 87: 802—Vol 89: 45
SWAIM..Vol 85: 69
SWAIN................Vol 87: 576—Vol 89: 435
SWAN..................Vol 88: 270—Vol 89: 599
SWANGAR..Vol 87: 935
SWANGO..Vol 87: 935
SWANSON..Vol 89: 298
SWEARINGEN..Vol 88: 270
SWIFE..............................Vol 87: 576, 1029
SWIFT....................Vol 88: 54—Vol 89: 435
SYLVESTER..Vol 85: 741
SYTES..Vol 89: 597

T

TABER......................Vol 86; 762—Vol 89: 942
TABOR..................Vol 88: 1197—Vol 89: 942
TAFT..Vol 85: 1046
TAGART..Vol 89: 435
TAGERT..Vol 89: 435
TAGGART................Vol 85: 67—Vol 89: 435
TAGGERT..Vol 85: 67
TALLMAN..........Vol 85: 954—Vol 86: 915
TALMADGE..Vol 87: 802
TANKERSLEY..Vol 86: 638
TANNEHILL..Vol 86: 1179
TARBOX..Vol 85: 606
TARBUSH..Vol 89: 432
TARLETON..Vol 86: 852
TARR..Vol 87: 1028
TATE..Vol 88: 788
TATMAN..Vol 89: 1167
TATTERSOLE..Vol 88: 789
TATUM..............Vol 85: 497—Vol 89: 436, 720
TAWANT..Vol 86: 985
TAYLOR..Vol 85: 242, 325, 327, 740, 1045
—Vol 86: 487, 488, 761, 914, 1326—Vol
87: 574, 576, 937, 1181—Vol 88: 789, 895,
968, 1198—Vol 89: 169, 598, 600, 722, 940
TEACKLE..Vol 87: 804
TEEL..Vol 89: 1011
TEMPLETON......Vol 88: 421—Vol 89: 170,
171
TERRELL......Vol 85: 327, 740—Vol 88: 141,
967—Vol 89: 43, 721

TERRILL..Vol 89: 720
TERRY......................Vol 85: 497—Vol 89: 299
TERWILLIGER..Vol 87: 1289—Vol 89: 601
TETER..Vol 87: 55
THATCHER......Vol 87: 1029—Vol 89: 1012
THISTLEWOOD....................................Vol 89: 866
THOMAS....Vol 85: 242, 1046—Vol 86: 61,
639, 761—Vol 87: 802—Vol 88: 967—Vol
89: 299, 601
THOMPSON......Vol 86: 638, 1178—Vol 87:
595, 1252—Vol 88: 53, 270, 421, 968, 1065
—Vol 89: 719, 866, 868, 1010
THOMSON..Vol 87: 413
THORNBURG..Vol 89: 1166
THORP..Vol 86: 1177
THORPE..Vol 86: 640
THRAGMORTON....................................Vol 86: 61
THRAILKILL..Vol 85: 242
TILFORD..Vol 88: 1066
TILMAN..Vol 85: 676
TIMBERLAKE..Vol 85: 74
TIMMONS..Vol 88: 968
TINDALL..Vol 88: 687
TINDLE..Vol 88: 687
TINKHAM..Vol 86: 1326
TINKLE..Vol 88: 687
TINSLEY............Vol 86: 985—Vol 89: 597
TOBIN..Vol 89: 436
TOD..Vol 88: 421
TODD....Vol 85: 74, 158—Vol 86: 639—Vol
87: 1028—Vol 88: 421
TOLAND..Vol 89: 168
TOOKER..Vol 88: 969
TOOLEY..Vol 89: 1012
TORBET..Vol 89: 600
TORBETT..........................Vol 89: 598, 600
TORREY..Vol 86: 1060
TOWNSEND—Vol 85: 496, 741—Vol 86:
62—Vol 87: 156, 1076
TOWNSLEY..Vol 88: 1261
TOZER..Vol 89: 867
TRACY..Vol 88: 896
TRAFTON..Vol 88: 687
TRANUM..Vol 88: 272
TRAVERS..Vol 88: 421
TRAVIS................Vol 87: 412—Vol 89: 599
TRENT..................Vol 87: 412—Vol 89: 865
TRIMBLE..............Vol 88: 272—Vol 89: 43
TRIPLETT..Vol 89: 868
TROUT..Vol 85: 69
TRUAX..Vol 88: 896
TRUE....................Vol 85: 606—Vol 88: 687
TRUITT..Vol 88: 141
TRUSSELL..Vol 88: 421
TRUST..Vol 89: 1167
TRYON......Vol 86: 640, 1060—Vol 89: 600
TUBB..Vol 89: 719
TUCKER....Vol 85: 327, 816—Vol 86: 762
—Vol 87: 675, 1180—Vol 88: 271, 969,
1065—Vol 89: 436, 869, 941
TUFTS..Vol 85: 327
TULLER..Vol 85: 496
TUMLIN..Vol 87: 1252
TUPPER..Vol 87: 1029
TURBETT..Vol 89: 598
TURK....................Vol 86: 1179—Vol 89: 1167
TURKHAM..Vol 88: 142
TURLEY..Vol 89: 43
TURNER....Vol 85: 326—Vol 86: 103, 486
—Vol 87: 1287—Vol 88: 565, 790—Vol
89: 722, 940

WIATT..Vol 86: 853
WIBRIGHT...Vol 88: 894
WICKHAM..Vol 87: 934
WIDEMAN..Vol 86: 1326
WIGHTMAN...Vol 88: 564
WIKOFF..Vol 85: 160
WILBORN...Vol 89: 1011
WILBURN..Vol 85: 69
WILCOX.....Vol 87: 935, 1287, 1288—Vol 89: 868
WILCOXEN...Vol 89: 868
WILDE...Vol 88: 421
WILEY................Vol 88: 968—Vol 89: 44
WILHITE...Vol 89: 719
WILHOIT...Vol 88: 1064
WILKERSON.....Vol 85: 607, 675—Vol 86: 488
WILKINS.....Vol 85: 676—Vol 88: 1064—Vol 89: 600, 862
WILKINSON..............Vol 85: 68—Vol 88: 422
WILLAIER...Vol 89: 865
WILLCOX..Vol 89: 434
WILLHOWARD..Vol 89: 865
WILLHOWER...Vol 89: 865
WILLIAMS.....Vol 85: 69, 242, 243, 325, 365—Vol 86: 103, 914, 915—Vol 87: 55, 225, 575, 802, 1252—Vol 88: 141, 893—Vol 89: 297, 433, 434, 436, 598, 720, 863, 867, 1167, 1168
WILLIAMSON.....Vol 87: 803—Vol 88: 790
WILLIS.................Vol 88: 1066—Vol 89: 865
WILLKINGS...Vol 89: 171
WILLOR...Vol 89: 435
WILLOW...Vol 89: 435
WILLS...Vol 85: 606, 818
WILSON.....Vol 85: 68, 69, 740, 955, 1045—Vol 86: 61, 62, 488, 639, 760—Vol 87: 575, 936, 1287—Vol 88: 53, 54, 687, 894, 895—Vol 89: 171, 300, 599, 721, 865, 866, 868
WINBURN...Vol 86: 168
WINDEL...Vol 87: 935
WINDSOR...Vol 89: 866
WINEBURG...Vol 85: 428
WING............Vol 85: 495, 817—Vol 86: 486
WINKLER.....Vol 88: 271, 1199—Vol 89: 434
WINKS...Vol 89: 45
WINN...............Vol 86: 1325—Vol 87: 576
WINNEBERG...Vol 89: 1071
WINSLOW.....Vol 88: 422—Vol 89: 171, 299
WIRE...Vol 85: 428
WISE...................Vol 85: 741—Vol 88: 54
WISNER...Vol 88: 1198
WITHERS...Vol 89: 1011
WITHINGTON......................................Vol 85: 676

WITT...Vol 86: 985
WOFFORD...Vol 87: 801
WOLF.....Vol 86: 60, 984—Vol 87: 414, 934—Vol 88: 896
WOLFE...Vol 88: 896
WOMACK...Vol 85: 268
WOOD.....Vol 85: 159—Vol 87: 224, 935, 1290—Vol 88: 420, 687—Vol 89: 432, 436, 597
WOODBURN...Vol 88: 1065
WOODFORD.....Vol 86: 1179—Vol 87: 1287
WOODROOFE...Vol 88: 1065
WOODS.....Vol 85: 1045—Vol 86: 316, 851, 853—Vol 87: 1026, 1076—Vol 88: 1066—Vol 89: 1010
WOODSON...Vol 86: 762
WOODWARD.....Vol 87: 1027—Vol 88: 421—Vol 89: 46
WOOLEY...Vol 86: 169
WOOLFOLK...Vol 88: 421
WOOTEN...Vol 86: 1178
WORD...Vol 85: 68
WORDEN...Vol 86: 1177
WORLEY...Vol 87: 935
WORTHINGTON...................................Vol 86: 103
WRIGHT.....Vol 85: 327—Vol 86: 915—Vol 87: 1078—Vol 88: 421, 1262—Vol 89: 171, 1012
WUNNENBURGH.................................Vol 85: 428
WYATT...........Vol 86: 853—Vol 89: 940, 1166
WYNNE...............Vol 88: 51—Vol 89: 940

Y

YANDAS...Vol 85: 365
YANTIS...Vol 85: 365
YARBOROUGH.....................................Vol 86: 852
YARBROUGH...Vol 88: 687
YARD...Vol 87: 576
YATES...Vol 85: 243, 817
YEATMAN...Vol 87: 1289
YENDES...Vol 85: 365
YERIAN...Vol 88: 565
YOE...Vol 89: 719
YONGS...Vol 89: 1167
YORKS...Vol 88: 788
YOST...Vol 89: 938
YOUNG.....Vol 86: 761, 1178—Vol 87: 1027—Vol 88: 141—Vol 89: 1167
YOUTSEY...Vol 88: 968
YURRIEN...Vol 88: 565

Z

ZADOK...Vol 89: 864
ZARTMAN...Vol 89: 170
ZOLLINGER...Vol 89: 434

Bible and Family Records

Federal and State Records

Bible and Family Records

Federal and State Records

DECLARATION OF INDEPENDENCE: SIGNERS..............................Vol 89: 757

REVOLUTIONARY ANCESTORS............Vol 87: 1177

REVOLUTIONARY— PENSION CLAIMS..............Vol 87: 561

ALABAMA—
Census, 1820................................Vol 89: 718
Barbour County, Cemetery Records.....Vol 86: 1320
North Houston County, Cemetery Records..Vol 86: 1323

CONNECTICUT—
Fairfield, Revolutionary Records............Vol 87: 1177
Marlborough, Baptisms.........Vol 86: 57, 163
New London, Probate Records.....Vol 87: 925, 1017

DELAWARE—
Newark, Cemetery Records.....Vol 88: 787

INDIANA—
Franklin County, Tax List..........Vol 87: 667

KENTUCKY—
Logan County, Pension List.....Vol 85: 739
Russellville, Cemetery Records.........Vol 88: 787

MARYLAND—
Revolutionary Records.............Vol 89: 1008
Baltimore Marriages.....Vol 88: 963, 1193, 1257—Vol 89: 39, 165, 294, 593, 713, 860, 1065, 1159
Cecil County, Wills.....Vol 86: 481, 979, 1053, 1171—Vol 87: 1070
Frederick County, Marriages.....Vol 85: 61, 151, 235, 318

MASSACHUSETTS—
Colrain, Early Settlers...................Vol 89: 9

MISSISSIPPI—
Court Records.....Vol 85: 675—Vol 86: 59
Early Settlers...........................Vol 87: 218

NEW JERSEY—
Revolutionary Records.............Vol 89: 1008

NEW YORK—
Revolutionary Records.............Vol 89: 1008
Hempstead, Church Records.....Vol 87: 670

Southampton, Vital Records.....Vol 87: 409, 1247
Washington County, Salem, Cemetery Records....................................Vol 89: 685

NORTH CAROLINA—
Governor's Council.......................Vol 88: 50
Revolutionary Records.............Vol 89: 1008

OHIO—
Delaware County, Church Records.....Vol 88: 137
Highland County, Cemetery Records.....Vol 88: 891, 1260
Miami County, Cemetery Records.....Vol 88: 266, 415, 559
Miami County, Pensioners.......Vol 88: 563
Miami County, Revolutionary Soldiers Vol 88: 564

PENNSYLVANIA—
Revolutionary Records.............Vol 89: 1007
Berks County, Miscellaneous.....Vol 88: 46
Fayette County, Cemetery Records.....Vol 85: 1040, 1044—Vol 86: 1059
Merriststown, Cemetery Records.....Vol 85: 1044

RHODE ISLAND—
Revolutionary Records.............Vol 89: 1009

TENNESSEE—
Petitioners...............................Vol 86: 850
Weakley County, Cemetery Records.....Vol 88: 784

TEXAS—
Corpus Christi, Cemetery Records.....Vol 86: 1057

VERMONT—
Bennington, Marriages.....Vol 85: 422, 491, 602, 671, 735, 811
Fairfield, Revolutionary Soldiers.....Vol 87: 798

VIRGINIA—
Prince Edward County, Marriages.....Vol 85: 605
Shenandoah County, Marriage Bonds Vol 87: 47

WASHINGTON, D. C.—
Diocesan Archives.....................Vol 89: 688

WEST VIRGINIA—
Greenbrier County, Military Records.....Vol 85: 952